GUIDE FOR
THE CHRISTIAN ASSEMBLY

THIERRY MAERTENS – JEAN FRISQUE

GUIDE FOR THE
CHRISTIAN ASSEMBLY

REVISED EDITION

1st to 8th WEEKS—
2nd to 8th SUNDAYS

Notre Dame, Indiana 46556

TRANSLATED FROM THE FRENCH BY MOLAISE MEEHAN, O.S.B.

Nihil Obstat: V. Descamps
can. libr. cens.

Imprimatur: J. Thomas, *vic. gen.*
Tournai, October 3, 1969

© Copyright, 1972, Fides Publishers, Inc.
Notre Dame, Indiana

LCCCN: 72-114245

ISBN: 0-8190-0002-7

2773

Translated from the original French edition,
Guide de l'assemblée chrétienne, Casterman, 1969.
An edition of St. Andrews Abbey, Bruges.

CONTENTS

FIRST WEEK

I. Hebrews 1:1-6
1st reading
1st cycle
Monday
In these opening verses of the letter to the Hebrews we have a description of the celestial enthronement of the Lord in terms reminiscent of the prologue to the fourth gospel. The author especially stresses two consequences of this enthronement: Jesus, now become Lord, is superior to the prophets (vv. 1-3), and he is above the angels (vv. 4-13).

The whole is designed to persuade Christians of Jewish origin to relinquish certain outmoded concepts, such as the ultimate restoration of the temple sacrifices, or a return to the law of Moses. The Law was good, but it had been brought by prophets and angels, above whom we have now Jesus as Lord.

a) The earlier portion of our reading, which is devoted to Christ's *primacy over the prophets*, gives us a rapid review of salvation history. During this God has not ceased to speak to men, until the day when his word was totally revealed by the Son. There are two great stages ("times past—these which are the final days"; "to our fathers—to us"; "by the prophets—by the Son") (vv. 1-2) of this history, which is now accomplished. Christ has made his appearance as the beginning and end of the universe (v. 2). The prophets contributed to the evolution of history, but they constitute neither its purpose nor its end. Christ on the other hand, as man-God is heir to all that he has created as Word.

Furthermore, he radiates the glory of God (v. 3) which the temple had purported to enshrine (Ex 40:34-35; 1 K 8:10-11). And, finally, he offers the decisive sacrifice which purifies from sin (v. 3; cf. He 8-10), and enables him once for all to enter the Holy of Holies and sit at the right hand of the Father. This means that everything connected with the prophecies and the ancient sacrifices has been made obsolete.

b) First century angelology gave an important place to these

1

intermediary beings between God and man (cf. Ph 2:11; Rev 4:5). The enthronement of the Son of God on the right hand of the Father ensures his *primacy over the angels,* specifically in the governing of the universe. He has received the name of "Son" (Ps 2:7; v. 5). By this royal title doubtless the author means to indicate elevation to the universal primacy by the resurrection (cf. Rm 1:4; Ac 13:33); but it would not have been possible were he not the very Word of God. In any case his being Son, by nature and by reason of his Lordship, surpasses the highest names that have been achieved by the angels and makes any recourse to their cult futile.

In contradistinction to the primacy given the prophets by Judaism, and the preponderance accorded the angels by gnosticism, in the evolution of the universe, our author here is insisting on the birth of a new world. It is based on a foundation much more stable and universal than the previous one: the Lordship of the man-God.

Today we no longer place the same emphasis on prophets and angels as in the past. In the quest of salvation other mediations preoccupy us: man, progress, technology. To acknowledge Christ's supremacy over prophets and angels means that we must exalt it over all other mediations too. However important ideals of human progress be, we must never forget that man will only find salvation by being divinized through the Incarnation, and by filial attachment to the Father. Yet both divinization and filiation require involvement in the human predicament.

It is the Eucharist that gradually initiates us to these insights. We move towards divine life and towards genuine human progress. In total attachment to the Father, we take up our responsibilities at once as creatures, and as masters of the universe.

II. 1 Samuel
1:1-8
1st reading
2nd cycle
Monday

In the books of Samuel we have traditions combined from different periods and environments. We cannot be certain for instance that the story of the birth of Samuel is very old. Today's reading describes the household into which Samuel was born, and the prominence of feminine influence at this epoch is noteworthy.

a) Sterility for the Jewish *woman* (v. 5) spelled failure and consequent bitterness (vv. 7, 10). No conjugal tenderness on the part of her husband could overcome this (v. 8), because sterility meant that conjugal love itself had failed, not reaching its fruition.

Polygamy of course was an aggravating circumstance. If another could consummate the love that she herself could not realize, the barren woman naturally would feel misgivings concerning a husband who shared her with the one who mothered his children. Hence her anguish and depression (v. 6).

b) It was such a condition of extreme spiritual poverty that Anna discovered the power of *God's paternity.* Childbirth, for the Jews, was a sign of God's intervention. Anna understands that in order to become fruitful one must be pleasing to God.

It is difficult for a modern mentality to appreciate the full import of these biblical pieces about virginity and fruitfulness. Samuel's conception is the result of a physiological act, true; but we must remember that conjugal love itself, and parental love, were attitudes that required communion with God himself.

III. Mark 1:14-20
Gospel
Monday

Commentary on this gospel will be found in the second cycle of the Third Sunday, p. 83.

**IV. Hebrews
2:5-12**
1st reading
1st cycle
Tuesday

Earlier, in Hebrews 1:5-12, the author had demonstrated Christ's superiority over the angels, to whom such a prominent role was attributed by the Jews in the conduct of the universe. Yet the angels' role in the books of Tobit and Daniel, and the two first chapters of Luke, is minimal by comparison with that accorded them by the gnostics. For this sort of mediation the author substitutes the exclusive mediation of Christ.

a) To his previous arguments he now adds a new theme, Christ's *abasement* beneath the angels during his earthly life (v. 9: Ps 8: 5-7, cited in vv. 6-8 acording to the Septuagint version). We do not have here the obedience contemplated in Philippians 2:5-10. It is rather Christ's submission to the laws of existence, death included, something that contemporaries considered to be precisely the angels' province (Col 2:15; Rm 8:38-39; Ga 4:3-9).

Because Christ is no longer subject to these natural laws dictated by the angels, men too in turn will be liberated from them. There will no longer be cosmic laws other than those radiated through the universe by the glorified Jesus.

b) The author goes on to stress the *solidarity* (vv. 11-13) between Christ and humanity; solidarity in submission to natural laws, and in deliverance from them by the victory over evil. He is thinking of the bond between a people and the priest who issues from their blood. A priest is not a priest unless he comes from the blood of those he represents before God (He 2:14-18). There could never be such brotherhood between angels and men; angels could never exercise a priesthood for men. By citing Psalm 21/22: 23 (v. 12), he reminds us that such a bond between Christ and Christians only became possible after the offering of his life as a poor man of Yahweh.

We do have cosmic and physiological laws to be sure, but today we are not so much concerned to determine whether they are directed by God or the angels. We know that the future reign of Christ means, not the destruction of the cosmos, but its spiritualization in some mysterious manner by his lordship. That is the hope towards which we are summoned by the author of Hebrews, and perhaps it is beginning to be realized in man's growing control and mastery over natural laws. Could not a world shaped by technology be a better reflection of God than one contorted by laws that we call natural? May we not regard it as the best sign that Christ's mediation is being extended over humanity and creation?

V. 1 Samuel **1:9-20** *1st reading* *2nd cycle* *Tuesday*	Samuel, an honored man (cf. 1 S 9:6) was led through circumstances to anoint King Saul (1 S 9:1-10, 16). This memory was preserved originally at Silo among antiroyalist prophets above all, particularly by a certain Ahiyya of Silo (1 K 11:29-39). Subsequently, in the time

of Achab, when the prophets' struggle against royalty reached its peak (9th century), tradition little by little began to discern in Samuel the father of prophets, the anointer of kings. He seemed the hero of liberation from foreign influence. The true leader of the people, the man chosen before his conception by God to accomplish a mission of delivery. Glorification of Samuel in this fashion tended to increase the prestige of the prophetic profession among the chosen people.

a) Today's reading describes the circumstances of Samuel's conception. Anna will be barren (v. 6; cf. Gn 11:30; 25:21; 29:31; Wi 13:3) until the day she discovers God's part in the beginning of life. Man can do nothing of himself. Prayer opens to God's action (vv. 10, 12), and in return for fruitfulness man offers God a fidelity that will not be rejected (v. 11). We remember the prayer of Tobit and Sarah before their wedding night (Tb 8:1-9).

b) To indicate the place of the prophet in God's design, Scripture tends to use this image of divine intervention at the moment of conception. It is a literary device for emphasis that, in man's *call* by God, all comes from God, all is gratuitous. If God intervenes even before the prophet can act, this becomes very clear (Jr 1:5, Lk 1:11-22).

Ought we perhaps to see divine vocation always in terms of human barrenness? Should we regard calls from God as something destined? Is this account no more than a certain literary device?

The true vocation is seen primarily in the texture of experience. It means being true to oneself, to one's ideal, one's possibilities, some sort of integration with events and persons. These have to be discerned throughout the whole tenor of life, often after many wrong turnings. Each turning we confront challenges us to go further, to encounter the Totally-Other God, and the other person. It summons us to renewal, to service in a deeper sense, to more genuine self-renunciation. We are always discovering our vocation by the daily discovery of ourselves, and by the glance we direct towards that mysterious source from which all we have comes.

Our passage supposes the accomplished vocation; it only sees the omega point.

VI. Mark 1:21-28   Commentary on this Gospel will be found in
   Gospel   the second cycle of the fourth Sunday, p. 140.
   Tuesday

VII. Hebrews   Here we have a continuation of the discussion
   2:14-18   about Christ's exclusive mediation. In the pre-
   1st reading   ceding verses the author had pointed out that
   1st cycle   Christ was exercising on behalf of humanity
   Wednesday   a mediation much more efficacious than that
   of the angels, and that he had removed men
from their tutelage. Now he describes the manner in which Christ acts.

a) The *relationship of blood* is seen by the author of Hebrews as essential in the order of salvation (vv. 14, 18). Christ did not wish to save man without his cooperation from above, as it were. He wanted to save him from below, by taking on his flesh and blood. It was as man-God that he rescued man from the angels' tutelage (cosmic laws), specifically the control of death (vv. 14-15). Of such deliverance angels are incapable, because they do not share the human condition.

b) Christ's *priestly* role, in the same way, derives its value from the fact that he is able to have compassion (vv. 17-18; cf. He 4: 14-20; 5:7-8).

The view then of Christ's priesthood and his work that we have here is diametrically opposed to Jewish ideas, but above all to pagan ones. These saw salvation as something that emanated from God certainly, but as something altogether exterior. Priesthood was essentially a matter of seclusion and segregation.

The kind of secularization that is going on now in ecclesial institutions and priesthood is thus not *a priori* opposed to the order of salvation. It is only by himself becoming a worker like others that the priest will save the working world. It is only by becoming African that the Church will save Africa.

VIII. 1 Samuel 3:1-10, 19-20
1st reading
2nd cycle
Wednesday

This reading will be found, differently arranged, in the second cycle of the second Sunday, with commentary, p. 22.

IX. Mark 1:29-39
Gospel
Wednesday

This Gospel is commented on in the second cycle of the fifth Sunday, p. 186.

X. Hebrews
3:7-14
1st reading
1st cycle
Thursday

The author has just shown the superiority of Christ to Moses. The Lord is the architect of the building, whereas the patriarch was but the executor. The edifice of Moses was material only; that of Christ is spiritual.

Christ however is not alone as he constructs his spiritual edifice; the faith and loyalty of his disciples provides cooperation (cf. v. 6).

Like Paul in 2 Corinthians 10, the author of Hebrews refers to Israel's *murmuring* in the desert (Ps 94/95:7-11; Ex 15:23-24; Nb 20:5), which hindered the work of Moses and might also that of Christ. For the Jewish Christians who were the recipients of the letter, the temptation to murmur was very actual. Their situation was not dissimilar to that of their ancestors in the desert. They had fled Jerusalem at the time of Stephen's martyrdom (Ac 11:19-20), and were now dispersed among the nations. Jewish as they were, they could not easily accept a state of affairs that made them nomads and pilgrims, just at the moment when they believed Jerusalem was about to become the eschatological city of reassembly and "rest."

Murmuring in their case meant refusal to enter the Promised Land, just as the Jews had refused to enter Canaan. It meant attachment to the past (Jerusalem in this case, previously Egypt), as if this could provide the answer in the search for God. It meant failure to discern God's presence in the texture of actual events, because of some imagined dream of a different sort of presence.

Probably some among them, who were particularly discouraged, proved to be "bad heads" (v. 12) for the scattered groups. They did not try to see the finger of God in the actual situation, but tried to induce the brethren to revert to a Judaism that was reassuring and "restful."

What was really required was that they should preserve *faith* and look towards the real blessings that were destined for men ("the end": v. 14; cf. He 11:1). Christians had to be convinced that their diaspora and their desert of the moment was but the prelude to eschatology. The condition was that they must live the actuality instead of attempting to evade it, or pretending it was not there.

Faith was to prove the secret for these Jewish Christians, in discerning the total transformation of institutions. They had to learn that there was no need to return to Jerusalem now that Jesus had died outside the city (He 13-12); that there was no longer need to offer sacrifice (He 10:6-8) because Jesus had offered it once for all, and sacrifice now consisted, not in immolation, but in obedience (He 10:8) and love (He 13:16); that there was no longer need for the temple priesthood because Jesus was no more than a "layman" (He 8:4; 7:13-14). Henceforward it is the profane life of the lay person that will be directly laid before God.

A similar faith is required from Christians now whose situation sometimes is not dissimilar to that of these Jewish Christians. Their life has become "secularized," all sacral reference being blurred, and they find themselves dispersed in a profane world. They are challenged and forever searching, though they yearn for "rest" in the secure possession of truth and efficacious rites. Corresponding to the Hebrew murmuring, we have that sort of integrism which wants rest, and institutions of the Jerusalem kind. The truth is that events are leading the Church towards change and dispersion, towards the precariousness and vicissitudes of nomadism again.

We should then make this letter to the Hebrews one of our most important sources of inspiration, as we endeavor to detach ourselves from cherished institutions, and learn to see the presence of Christ in all the new situations we must confront. We continue to be members of the people of God in the midst of it all.

XI. 1 Samuel   This piece, which belongs to the same stratum
   4:1c-11   as I Samuel 2:27-36, received its definitive
   1st reading   redaction at a stage later than the reform of
   2nd cycle   Josias (7th century). The tradition explains
   Thursday   the substitution of the priestly caste of Sadog
    for the more ancient one of Eli (1 S 2:35; cf.
1 K 1:38); the massacre of Eli's descendants (1 S 2:31; cf. 1 S 22:
18-19), with the exception of one who will not disappear until
Solomon's time (1 S 2:33; cf. 1 K 2:27); and finally the depressed
condition of the rural priesthood by contrast with the powerful
clergy of Sion (1 S 2:36; cf. 2 K 23:9). The death of the two sons
of Eli (v. 11) is regarded as a premonition (1 S 2:34) of the down-
fall of a priestly caste which chose attachment to the rural sanctuaries rather than alliance with the temple of Jerusalem. The rural
culture is outmoded, since it was not able to preserve the ark of
the covenant, removed amid the general indifference by the
Philistines to Israel.

It is possible that there was a reproduction of the "face of God"
on one of the sides of the *ark,* a design borrowed by the Hebrews
from the surrounding culture. The casket was surmounted by a
cover ("propitiatory") on which the blood of sacrifices was poured.
Originally the ark suggested the God of battles, the God of hosts
(v. 4). It had presided over the people's journey through the
desert and the conquest of Canaan (Nb 10:33), while the war
song resounded round about it (v. 5; cf. Nb 10:35). It was looked
upon as a sign of God's presence, accompanying the still nomad
people in all their journeyings; but God was not associated with
it in any automatic fashion. The episode of its removal to foreign
soil demonstrates this (v. 11); God could not be annexed in this
fashion.

The seizure of the ark by the Philistines is furthermore indica-
tive of some disinterest in it during this period. It was not automatically thought of before engaging in battle, and it was left in
Philistine hands for a considerable time before measures were

taken to recover it. The people was gradually changing its nomad, warlike character in favor of stability. Quite soon the temple of Sion would be substituted for the ark, and become the repository of its prerogatives.

The presence of God among his people, which was symbolized by the ark, was destined subsequently to be associated with the holy city and its temple (Jr 3:16-17), and after that again with the heart of the just man, the servant of God (Jr 21:31-34). A re-appearance of the ark at the end of time was anticipated in Judaism (2 M 2:1-8; cf. Rev 11:19); but the new place of encounter between God and man was destined to be not this, but the humanity of Jesus, the new "propitiatory" (Rm 3:25; Col 1:19-20).

By fixing on the ark as the center of their religion, the Israelites were making a considerable step towards desacralization. They were affirming the mobility of God. Unlike the contemporary Baals, Yahweh cannot be tied to a place or linked to a culture; he does not lend himself to the sacralization of any idea or country. The seizure of the ark actually brings him nearer to his enemies. Its capture warns of the utlimate destruction of the temple and the disappearance of a particular cultural environment.

This "despatialization" of Yahweh carries a special message for our time, a time when social and geographical mobility is the order of the day. The people of our day are too prone to change to rest content with fixed Baals, with one system of thought, one absolute truth, one immovable social structure. They are open to movement and newness; it is there that the true God is to be encountered.

XII. Mark   Commentary on this Gospel will be found in
    1:40-45   the second cycle of the sixth Sunday, p. 246.
    Gospel
    Thursday

XIII. Hebrews   This passage is closely linked to the preceding
      4:1-5, 11   argumentation. The author is trying to con-
      1st reading   vince Christians of recent Jewish origin, and
      1st cycle   now dispersed among the nations, that they
      Friday   should not be concerned with a return to
      Jerusalem, as if this city were still the ideal
of eschatological rest. For this purpose he uses Psalm 94/95. The
theme of Meriba however is softened, in order to stress the entry
to Canaan.

The main topic of today's reading is the nature of this *rest* in
the promised land which the Jews in the desert did not experience
(v. 3 Ps 94/95:11). In like manner his Christian listeners may fail
to achieve it, if they continue to murmur and show themselves
without faith just now, when the "rest" of Jerusalem seems to be
withdrawn from them (v. 1).

It was lack of faith that deprived their ancestors of entry into
rest (v. 3). They are called to a higher sort of rest in life with
God (vv. 4-5), a rest that was begun on the eighth day of creation
as its accomplishment. This means that they are summoned to
that calibre of faith which can see God's finger in all events,
however disconcerting.

It is perhaps somewhat surprising to have life with God presented in terms of rest, as if work were always associated with
some form of alienation, that could only be canceled by rest. As
if the ideal of eternal happiness were some sort of secure retire-
ment. As against this there was a biblical tradition which we find
in John 5:17, and which affirms that God does not cease to work,
that happiness will consist in increased responsibilities (Mt 24:
47; 25:21). The word rest then must be taken in a wider sense.
Jewish mentality found it a symbol of peace, harmony and joy.

Modern concepts of leisure as a vehicle of culture are not un-
related to this, and give prominence to a value that was obscured
by nineteenth century industrialization. In the 16th century his

work provided the artisan with a focus at once of cult and culture. Religion, creativity, art, folklore all flourished in that context. In the 20th, the worker is part of a dehumanized chain, where personal fulfillment and culture are excluded. Consequently he has every right to look for leisure, for physical rest of course, but also to satisfy a cultural want unprovided for in industrial toil. In Western civilization actually culture has been the preserve of those social classes, who could devote themselves to creative pursuits, the intellectual classes exclusively, that is. Popular democracies now, even in the West, have fortunately embarked upon a return to culture of the masses.

In this domain we still have a long way to go. If leisure becomes merely inactivity, if it be devoted simply to a different professional activity that is equally alienating, if it is merely time for passive viewing of sports or movies, its purpose will not be fulfilled. It should prove the opportunity for political or social involvement, for finding new patterns of social intercourse, for personal investigation of what is fine and beautiful. It is only when leisure acquires the proper dimension of culture that it can be properly integrated with cult.

If we are to enter the "rest" of God, a rest where God continues to work for the advancement of man, we must develop means of kindling enthusiasm. That is something sadly lacking in our industrialized, individualist world.

XIV. **1 Samuel 8:4-7, 10-22a** *1st reading* *2nd cycle* *Friday* Here Jewish political development takes one of its most important turns. Hitherto the twelve tribes have lived without any central organization. They continued to be faithful to their nomad traditions, and would only resort to federation in a provisional fashion, under the pressure of a better organized invasion by neighboring peoples, or because of the political and economic demands of the moment.

It is indeed astonishing that Israel, with such archaic political ideas, was able to resist foreign pressure, and even inflict defeats. Success in this domain they saw as a sign of God's election. The military leader or victorious "judge" would be thought to have a divine charism. As expression of this belief we have those ancient traditions which recount *investitures* that were more or less marvelous, miraculous birth for instance.

Thus Saul, a judge and liberator, derives the efficacy of his role from a prophetic investiture (1 S 9-10). This would have been, at least, the old monarchist view.

Later traditions however tended to desacralize. Saul did not receive investiture exclusively at the hands of a "seer," but by the people's will (v. 19) in pursuance of a plan to rival the strength of neighboring peoples politically and militarily (v. 5). In the idiom of our time, it was a sage political and sociological measure, developing new structures to meet new needs.

One gets a feeling however that the redactor of the passage does not approve of this. He stresses the fact that the people, which was a "people apart," wanted to become "as other nations" (v. 5). He indicates Saul's evasions (vv. 9 and 21), and speaks of God's weariness as he complains of this people which forgets its only true king (vv. 8 and 21). He indicates all the faults inherent to monarchy (vv. 9-18; cf. 1 K 4:2-19; 5:2-8; 10:14-29) while closing his eyes perhaps to those of the previous regime. He finds in the desacralization (which is only partial, because the king always continued to be anointed as a man of God) the reason for the later faults and failures of this monarchy. He is too nostalgic for the freedom acquired by the old regime to acquiesce easily in the general acceptance of the monarchist principle.

The profound differences between these two traditions (1 S 8 and 1 S 9-10) are frequently to be seen also in the history of Christianity. Does belief that God is present in his people, and in each of its members, imply that he intervenes directly in a more or less marvelous fashion? Is it not rather a conviction that, when man undertakes his proper human, social or political responsibilities, God is present too. Often in Jewish history God chose the marvelous way; but, after the Incarnation of his Son, the divine purpose was accomplished rather by means of man and by human methods.

The challenge to authority in the Church now brings the problem into sharp focus. A great many people think like Samuel, that any questioning of the actual status of the hierarchy jeopardizes the very presence of God in the Church and represents undue concession to modern trends and humanist ideas. Let us hope that like Samuel they will come to realize that this challenge is directed, not against apostolic authority, but rather against anachronism in its exercise. One day perhaps they will follow him in supporting a new concept of authority, one closer to the service concept of Jesus, one less loaded with the autocratic relics of a medieval society, through which the Church passed and with which she became too much identified.

XV. **Mark 2:1-12**   Commentary on this Gospel will be found in
    Gospel   the second cycle of the seventh Sunday, p.
    Friday   298.

XVI. **Hebrews**   The first Christian converts from Judaism con-
    4:12-16   tinued to be zealous observers of the Law (cf.
    1st reading   Ac 21:20) even while professing faith in Jesus.
    1st cycle   They did not see that profession entailed such
    Saturday   a break with Judaism as would require aban-
                      donment of their habits. Thus they continued
to attend the temple (Ac 3:1-4; 2:46; 21:26), and priests even became disciples without relinquishing their profession (Ac 6: 6-7). Ideas about priesthood and sacrifice that seem basic to us were not yet precisely grasped. Indeed it is not certain that the Eucharist celebrated in such environs was understood in the same priestly and sacrificial terms as it was to be in later theology.

Jewish persecution however (Ac 6:11, 19) forced these first Christians to leave Jerusalem and its temple. Being "Jews" they found this deprivation of the lawful priesthood, and the opportunity to offer sacrifice, a considerable hardship. Our author reassures them that they have not lost contact with God's Word, the priesthood, or sacrifice. The Word is always available. The true high-priest is no longer the one who celebrates in the Holy of Holies, but Jesus who has celebrated once for all. The true sacrifice no longer consists of the immolation of bulls and goats but in the constant offering of the community of believers.

a) The Jews were wont to measure the efficacity of God's Word (cf. Is 55:11). This was evident above all in those who proclaimed it, sometimes at the price of a violent struggle (Jr 20:7; Ez 3: 26-27). It made of the prophet an authentic witness, perhaps even an active parable of the Word (Is 8:1-17; Ho 1-3; Ps 68/69: 12). In Jesus this power of the Word in its proclaimer was to be intensified still further. He was so possessed by the Word that it is to be identified with his activity, which was the sign of salvation for all men (He 1:1-2).

The function performed by the Word in the case of the prophets and Jesus extends in like fashion to every Christian. It clarifies his deepest motives, and leads him to decisions. In that sense it is judgment, not only because it judges man's conduct exteriorly as a legislative norm; but, at a deeper level still, because it forces a man to choose between it and his own natural urges. It is a sword (Lk 2:35), which imposes the most radical abregations on the Christian.

b) According to the standards of the Word then, the Christian is in no further need of the temple priesthood. Jesus is his one and only mediator, the only object of his faith.

At verse 14 the author recalls the content of the Christian profession of faith. Christ is the "heir of all things," and is united with the Father ("seated at his right hand": He 1:2-3). He goes on to show that Christ is priest and mediator (He 4:15-5:10).

His argument is double. On the one hand Christ, because he became man, represents humanity (vv. 15-16). On the other hand because he is Son of God, seated the right hand of the Father, he represents the divine world too (v. 1). He is the perfect *mediator*.

Christ represents humanity because he has taken on its state, known its failures, endured its limitations, and undergone its temptations. All this weakness has been transformed into the accomplishment of his priesthood. Why should not the faithful too enjoy this privilege?

The conclusion follows. We should advance with confidence towards the "throne of grace" (v. 16; cf. He 1:22), towards the king of goodness, that is, who bestows grace even on the guilty and is generous towards those who seek (cf. Est 4:11; 5:1-2).

However, it is not sufficient that Christ be welcoming and good. He must reconcile humanity to God, and thus fulfill a typically priestly and sacrificial ministry (v. 1). The sign of communion between God and men is sacrifice and this can only be carried out by someone fully accredited on both sides. It will be perfect insofar as the victim belongs fully to both worlds. Here the victim is Christ in all his humanity, offering himself under the impulse of God's Spirit. So his sacrifice and his priesthood become decisive and unique, something into which Christian life and the Eucharist absorb all believers (Rm 12:1; He 13:10-15; 1 P 2:5).

XVII. 1 Samuel This passage was commented on with the
9:1-4, 17-19; preceding passage (no. XIV), p. 13.
10:1
1st reading   God then chooses to follow the tenor of
2nd cycle   human decision; he will be present with his
Saturday   people by sharing their involvements. Inevitably one day the Israelites would have to undergo the experience of monarchy. However, in consecrating the king, God does not make him any sort of absolute; he shows that he, God, is anterior to monarchy. The Israelite monarchy will

have to confess itself provisional. Dynasties will disappear as rapidly as they arise, and history will find the Israelites finally a longer period without a King than with one. Israel of course could never have an absolute monarchy; her destiny was not just to be a state. One day she would become a simple community of faith transcending nationalism.

Yahweh endorsed the Jewish kingship because it led towards the Kingdom of God that would be proclaimed. This Kingdom might need the service of kings, but would never be subject to their earthly sway. No Jewish king ever resembled the absolute monarchs of other countries.

XVIII. Mark 2:13-17
Gospel
Saturday

The juxtaposition of Levi's call with the banquet of the publicans may not be primitive. The synoptics doubtless resorted to it because of the "paradigm" principle, whereby an event (Levi's call) is always made to follow a teaching (v. 17).

The incidents mentioned in today's Gospel are differently stressed according to the different redactions. In Matthew, the banquet takes place in "the" house of Jesus (Mt 9:10), whereas in Mark it is in Levi's house (v. 15); and Luke 5:29 conjoins the two incidents even more firmly. It is not the idea of vocation though, really which forms the link between the accounts. We have Jesus summoning an apostle to follow him on the one hand, and, on the other, calling sinners to the Kingdom. The unifying element is rather the publicans. Jesus recruits his disciples among them (v. 14), and shares their meal (vv. 15-16). Mark emphasizes this by pointing out that many sinners, guests with Jesus, would be among his followers (v. 15). The sinful state, with the gratuitous grace of God, would be sufficient for entry to the Kingdom.

a) Our passage then fits into the general context of Christ's attitude to sinners. He bears witness to *divine mercy*. There is

no further call that can be given to the "just," to the observers of
the Law that is. They have already received God's call in the
Law and it ought to lead them to the gospel. Apart from these,
there are those multitudes who have not heard the call, or yet
discovered in the Law a call from God. It is to such people that
Jesus addresses himself; he wants to succeed where the Law and
the prophets have failed. That seems to be the meaning of the
first part of his discourse (v. 17a). At this point in the passage
indeed we get the impression that this call can be ignored by the
just; it is only for sinners.

b) The synoptics however reinterpreted the words of Jesus to
stress the contrast between Pharisees and Publicans (v. 16). This
constant contrast reflects the mentality of the primitive communities. They would contrast that Judaism which refused to be
converted with the masses of the poor and sinners. These latter
were more or less practicing observers of the Law; but they were
open to the gospel message of hope and happiness. As in the case
of Matthew 22:1-4, or Luke 14:16-20, the redactor reflects the
polemics between Judaism as represented by the Pharisees and
the "just," and Christianity as represented by Publicans and
"sinners." The word just begins to be ironical, designating those
who believe themselves perfect, and refuse to participate in God's
mercy towards the poor and sinners. Thus an account, which
originally stressed Christ's pastoral mercy, in its final redaction
is made to illustrate Jewish opposition and contempt for Christians. Sinners, the class traditionally opposed by the Bible to the
just, and condemned, here become the exponents of an essential
religious quality. Humility that is, which is open to God's call,
and opposed to the pride of the self-righteous.

The call of Levi and of sinners has its message for Christians
today. We are asked to extend the mercy we have received from
God to them. We, like all men, are sinners; but what a joy to
realize that God's love extends to our sinfulness. It is not a matter
of turning to God to ease our conscience. We are not dispensed
from our responsibilities; that would be alienation. The sinner

will not really have encountered God's mercy, unless he feels the urge to be converted and to change his life (a precise detail that is inserted in Luke's version: 5:32), and furthermore to apostolic mission. He must bear witness, in the world, to mercy and pardon. How well this was realized by Levi, who, under the name of Matthew, builds his Gospel around the central theme of pardon!

Only Jesus of Nazareth was capable of showing perfect divine mercy towards men, and this led him to the cross. Through the Eucharist we get the opportunity of following him in this path. It is not a way of evasion or a facile solution.

SECOND SUNDAY

A. THE WORD

I. Isaiah 49:3, 5-6
1st reading
1st cycle

In this extract from the third Servant Song exegetes have distinguished two traditions. The first (vv. 1-3 and 5b-6) manifests a universalist spirit. The second (vv. 4-5a) is an account of prophetic investiture. Having originally seen Cyrus as God's envoy, Second Isaiah is expressing his disillusion. Simultaneously with his concessions for the reconstitution of Israel comes a reestablishment of the temples of Mardouk and the pagan festivals of the New Year. Cyrus is reproved. Soon God will send his people another messenger.

Having voiced the sentiment that Cyrus' mission has failed, Second Isaiah begins to consider himself as the envoy of God that Cyrus ought to have been. He praises his own *prophetic function* in terms that he had hitherto reserved for Cyrus' mandate. His mission will even have a universal dimension and his name will be pronounced by God (v. 1; cf. Is 41:25). The sword of Cyrus that was to have dispatched the kings is entrusted to him (v. 2; cf. Is 41:2). He becomes the light of the nations that Cyrus might have been (v. 6; cf. Is 42:16).

He finds that he was called by God from his conception, like Jeremiah (vv. 1 and 5; cf. Jr 1:5). Like Ezechiel, his mission is to turn aside the sword (v. 2; cf. Ez 21:14-22). Like a new Jacob, he must struggle throughout the night without failing (v. 3; cf. Gn 32:23-33). Discouraged though he is, he wants to feel himself one with his predecessors, the prophets of Israel (v. 4; cf. Jr 15:10; 20:9 and Is 49:4).*

In this portrait of a prophet the primitive Church will discover

* See the doctrinal theme: *vocation*, p. 41.

21

the characteristics of Christ (compare v. 3 with Mt 3:17; verse 6b with Lk 2:32). Yet the prophetic office which reached fulfillment in Jesus did not end with him.

The prophet in this reading was able to see in the present event (Cyrus' intervention, that is, in Israel's history) the possibilities for alliance and communion between God and men. Christ rightly bore the title of prophet because he too revealed God's salvation in events and in his own person.

The Church is prophetic in that she related secular events to the Kingdom that is coming. She preserves her right to criticize any and every social system, radical or conservative. The norm she uses in judging everything is the goal of unity for all humanity in Jesus Christ.

She does not know what the real link is between this world and the Kingdom. She does know, and she does proclaim, that this world whatever we make of it, a hell of hate and suffering or a habitable place, is the material out of which Christ will mold his Kingdom.

In this context the individual Christian too has his prophetic role. He must learn to discern in the world what leads towards the Kingdom and what blocks its coming. He must learn to oppose, in the Church, all those structures and styles which obscure its prophetic mission.

Because the Eucharist is, in the Church, the institution *par excellence,* it should have present at the celebration even the sharpest critics of some ecclesial structures. Everyone should go away convinced of his prophetic mission in the world.

II. 1 Samuel
3:3b-10, 19
1st reading
2nd cycle

This passage belongs to the prophetic tradition of the 9th or 8th century which made Samuel a significant figure in stressing the grandeur of the prophetic mission.

The account of Samuel's vocation has many elements that are already highly spiritual. It is not in a dream that he discerns

God's will; he does not have a vision. He merely hears a Word. His vocation, in this spiritualized sense, consists in the certitude that his interpretation of events corresponds to God's thought (vv. 11-14). In the Old Testament the "Word" could describe an event just as much as a voice. The prophet however cannot assume his privilege if he does not bind himself to listen to God in personal obedience to his will (v. 10). His dialogue with God becomes an insight of conscience. The brief episode shows us Yahweh three times acting to inspire this insight.

This sort of binding oneself to listen to God, in order to discern his presence in the free exercise of our wills, can be extremely agonizing. Samuel discovers the sacrificial element in his obedience when he finds himself torn between the monarchist side and the antimonarchist, between the old nomad way of life represented by Eli and a settled rural-urban culture, between his mother's desires and his prophetic call. Mysticism and politics are not always in harmony. It was Samuel's achievement that he refused to tear them apart, despite the cost in confusion and ambiguity.

III. Isaiah 62:1-5   Cyrus had just issued an edict (538) author-
   1st reading   izing the rebuilding of the temple. Doubtless
   3rd cycle   a first caravan of exiles had already left Babylon for Jerusalem. A disciple of Second Isaiah
celebrates their hopes.

By this time Jerusalem had already recovered some of his pristine vigor, and was now the capital of a province of Cyrus' empire by the time the exiles reentered. What meaning however could this sort of restoration have, something favoring a native population that had in the interval become indifferent to Yahweh? The prophet sustains the exiles' courage by sketching the religious future of the city.

Sion will receive a new name (vv. 2 and 4) to signify the change. She will no longer be called "abandoned," but the "spouse." She shall be as a young bride arrayed for her husband (v. 5).

The source of blessing for this future city will be Yahweh's presence. The prophet imagines him seated on Sion, his brow girdled with the city's ramparts like a crown (v. 3).

The author is actually using a highly important biblical image that was to become à prominent Christian symbol: the espousals of Yahweh and Jerusalem. God's love for the city is described in these terms because this form of love indicates best sharing and mutual giving. The incarnation whereby Christ shared his divinity with our humanity, and the Eucharist which was the consequence of this, become the highest moments of this exchange in love.

IV. 1 Corinthians The first letter to the Corinthians, which is
    1:1-3   read on the early Sundays of the year, was
    2nd reading compiled about 57. It deals with the major
    1st cycle   problems confronting Christians in the pagan
world, above all in a decadent society such as
the Corinthian.

a) The fundamental themes of the letter are already adumbrated in the address. Paul begins by stressing his role as *apostle* (v. 1). The authority by which he disciplines Christians in Corinth does not depend on his being the founder of a religious sect or philosophic school, but on God's call. The words that he is going to speak are not his but the Words of God loyally transmitted.

b) Whatever their faults, the Corinthian Christians too have their noble qualities; and Paul indicates that this should be remembered in the attempt to solve their problems. The first of these is *holiness* (v. 2). In this they are the successors of ancient Israel, which was separated from pagan ways to become a holy assembly before God (Ex 19:6-15; cf. 1 Co 6:2-4, 11). Likewise the Corinthians are obliged by holiness to reject the amoralism of their society and be witnesses of divine transcendence in a pagan world.

c) The second quality to be remembered in solution of their problems is their *solidarity* with all those throughout the world who invoke the name of the Lord (v. 2). This cult of the name of Yahweh had been previously Israel's privilege among the nations (Jr 10:25; cf. Is 43:7). It was the mediation that she exercized for the world. Christians now, by invoking the name of Jesus, take on this responsibility of the world's salvation. They can assure it by their prayer and their comportment.

V. 1 Corinthians
6:13-15, 17-20
2nd reading
2nd cycle

It seems that the Corinthian Christians were taking a wrong interpretation of one of Paul's favorite sayings: "everything is permissible for me" (v. 12; cf. 1 Co 10:23; Rm 6:15). Some people were using it as an excuse for fornication, arguing that it was a simple physical need like eating and drinking (v. 13). Accordingly Paul states the fundamental principles of the Christian ethic here.

a) The first principle is that man is the *temple of the Spirit.* This does not mean that the Spirit "dwells" in him as God dwelt in the temple of Jerusalem. God's Spirit cannot be localized in this fashion; rather does he invest and inspire man's faculties. The manner in which the Christian's body is consecrated is not an exterior one, making him tabu, as it were, like the walls of a temple. His consecration consists in the fact that his free will cooperates with the Spirit. Thus, just as the Jews "purified" themselves before entering the temple, the Christian too must seek purity. He must "fear" (in the biblical sense of the term) God's presence. Yet he realizes that this presence is something that invests his faculties and his activity. Unlike the Jew, for whom the temple was another world, to enter which he must become alienated from himself, the Christian by his own freedom and the concourse of the Spirit can build his own temple. There is no more alienation; man's whole being is drawn to heights beyond himself.

b) His second consideration is the fact that we are *ransomed* by Christ; the Christian no longer belongs to himself (vv. 13, 20). Does not this mean alienation in the sense that he comes under the power of the one who ransoms him (cf. Rm 6:12-18)? We must understand the affirmation correctly. For Paul man dependent on his own resources is a slave, the slave of the "flesh" (in the Pauline sense, a state where salvation is made to depend on human resources exclusively, cf. Rm 8:1-13). Christ was the first man to provide a new means of salvation, the Spirit of God within him. He was thus made free of the "flesh," which, left to itself, can only fail. Furthermore he was made free of the law, because the Spirit's presence guided his faculties towards true salvation. This liberation and lordship was endorsed in the resurrection.

His achievement points the way for all humanity who seek salvation. The freedom he won involves us, not merely exteriorly as an achievement, but deep-down because we share it at his offer. His mediation in this sense, offered to every member of the new humanity, is constantly proclaimed by Paul in his letters to Corinth (1 Co 6:19-20; 11:3; 2 Co 10:7; cf. Rm 6:11; 6:15; 8:9, etc.).

Because he frees us from the "flesh" and the law, Christ can be compared to someone who ransoms a slave (1 Co 7:23). Once liberated however, the slave can never depart from the Spirit that has given back his life. That is why we no longer "belong to ourselves." We rely on the gift of God . . . something that enlarges our liberty instead of crushing it.

Seen thus, against the background of the Pauline concept of the slavery of the flesh and the freedom of the Spirit we acquire in Jesus Christ, the phraseology of ransom and belonging becomes understandable.

c) Paul's third consideration is concerned with the resurrection (v. 14) and *glorification* (v. 20) promised to mankind.

This point is related to the first, but we need the second in order to clarify its full implications. Traditionally, the temple was looked upon as the focus of God's "presence" with his people and in the world. The presence had often been described by the term "glory" (*shekina-doxa*). In the old cult God was glorified by celebrating the glory present within the temple walls. Now that the temple is no more, and its worship superseded, there is a change. The glorification of God is not merely praising his glory. It is making him present in our actions, bearing wtiness that he is present in us until the day when he will be so totally, in the resurrection of the body. The measure of his presence now will be governed by the openness to him our faculties, now adult and enlarged, can display in imitation of the new Adam.

Two convictions lie behind Paul's argumentation. First: sexuality is not just a physical "need." It expresses our whole being in a personal relationship and can never be exclusively physical. Second: our whole being is taken over by the Lord. Relationship in sex then becomes a bond between two people who have been "Christified" until the day when, transparent to ourselves, we become transparent also to the Lord in glory.

VI. 1 Corinthians 12:4-11 *2nd reading* *3rd cycle*   In the Corinth community there was a temptation to syncretism. The surrounding pagan world claimed to acquire a "knowledge" of God by means of trances and ecstasies. Paul tells his correspondents of another type of knowledge based on faith. Sometimes this was accompanied by signs and charisms which were not distinguished very well from pagan phenomena. Throughout chapters 12 to 15 the apostle is providing criteria by which the charisms of the Spirit can be distinguished.

In 1 Corinthians 12:1-3 a first criterion had been stated; char-isms must inevitably be based on a Christian profession of faith. In today's passage Paul passes to other criteria.

He points out, to begin with (vv. 4-6), that if ancient polythe-ism had *charisms* of all kinds, these came from various murky sources. In the Church on the other hand, whether we are deal-ing with community functions or extraordinary phenomena, all is unified by trinitarian life. Charisms are accorded for the com-mon good. By this criterion all pagan intoxication and individual trance is excluded. Since one and the same Spirit is the source of all gifts, these cannot be opposed one to the other. Nor indeed can those who benefit by them. If charismatics be in opposition, the reason is that they are not inspired by the Spirit. Their gifts do not come from Christ (v. 7).

Paul gives a rather exhaustive list of the principal gifts of the Spirit. He classifies them according to well-established principles and exhorts the Corinthians to seek the higher charisms, unknown to paganism.

In the first place we have two charisms of the intelligence: wisdom, the knowledge of God's designs (1 Co 2:7), and science, the capacity to present the truths of faith in an articulate system. Then come faith, which does not here designate the theological virtue, but rather the possibility of bringing about miracles (1 Co 13:2; cf. Mk 11:19-26); the gift of healing, and of miracles. These three, all considered, seem fairly identical. Lastly we have those charisms that were common to paganism too: prophecy, discern-ment, and the gift of tongues. The function of the first is to pro-claim God's word, of the second to understand and interpret the third, which consists in some sort of mysterious communication, not comprehensible without the key.

Today we no longer live in an atmosphere of Corinthian syn-cretism. Yet the subject of today's reading is by no means an anachronism. The Spirit continues to direct the Church by means of the hierarchy, but for purposes of mission or reform he will inspire individual initiatives. In this domain our criteria must continue to be those of Saint Paul. Any valid charismatic initiative must first and foremost spring from a fundamental faith in the Lord. It must be directed towards the common good, and indicate willingness to subordinate private advantage to the unity of the whole. It must not cause scandal or sow discord. Everything comes originally from the spirit of love and unity.

VII. John 1:29-34 John the Baptist has turned attention from
Gospel   his own person to that of Christ, who is al-
1st cycle   ready present, but not "known" (Jn 1:26).

The text of the passage originally ran probably thus:

(31) I too, I did not know him; but it was in order that he be manifested to Israel that I came to baptize (35 b, c, d). And he who sent me to baptize said to me "He on whom you see the Spirit descending and remaining, this is the one . . ." (34). Yes, I have seen and give testimony that this is the one, the Elu (Son) of God. (29 and 35) The following day John was again there with two of his disciples. Seeing Jesus coming to him he said "Behold the Lamb of God who takes away the sin of the world."

To this primitive account certain details were added by the synoptic tradition, the reference is a baptism by water contrasted with the baptism of the Spirit (vv. 31-33). Another hand still ensured the connection with the context by dating the episode ("the following day"; vv. 29 and 35). This places it in the primordial week and the prophecy invoked in verse 27 is recalled again in verse 30.

The primitive account then is centered on *knowledge* of the personality of Christ. He is in the world; but no one is capable of knowing him (Jn 1:26), not even John the Baptist (Jn 1:31-33), who is for this reason the least in the Kingdom (Mt 11:8-10; Lk 7:38 and Jn 5:33-36).

By a flash of insight however the Baptist realizes that Christ is the "Son of God," the royal Messiah that is (v. 34). While baptizing Jesus, he sees the meaning of texts like Isaiah 11:2; 42:1-7; 61:1, and realizes that this baptism has the import of a messianic investiture. Such was the meaning of the descent of the Spirit in the Baptist's affirmation. In the evangelist's rendering however the Spirit is really a divine person, a divinizing force (Jn 15:26), which invests the Risen Lord with primacy over the universe.

The Baptist had concluded his testimony with the statement that he had really discovered the "Elu of God" or the "Servant of God" of Isaiah 42:1 (v. 34). The evangelist turns to advantage the ambiguity of the Aramaic word by transcending the Baptist's meaning and making him affirm; I have seen the "Son" of God. In verses 29 and 35 the Baptist describes Christ in the Aramaic term *talia*. Here he is doubtless thinking of the servant in Isaiah 42:1-2, and affirming that Jesus is the one who will inaugurate the messianic times, spread his Spirit so that man will sin no more, and he can take away "the sin of the world" (v. 29). *Talia* can also be translated by the word lamb. Thus we see the significance of the designation of the Messiah as lamb. This image suggests at once the pascal mystery and the suffering servant. Both concepts were fulfilled in him who bore and took away the sin of the world.

The section John 1:29–2:11 constitutes a sort of treatise of initiation to the faith, a doctrinal reflection about the catechumenate, or the beginnings of vocation.

The word "see" forms a sort of *leit-motif* throughout. We must "see" the events and persons that surround us and come to know them for what they are. They are among us, but we do not see them, or we deceive ourselves about what they are (1:31; 2:9). We can see them but we do not observe them.

The first essential in any turning towards faith is this proper observation of people and things. "You, who are you? What do you say of yourself?" (1, 19, 22). The answer will only be given after there has been a slow conversion to observation.

Such was the progress in the Baptist's faith. At the beginning he did not know Jesus (1:31, 33). He then discovers in him the Messiah, the lamb or the servant (1:29, 32); and finally realizes his divino-human personality. Such too is the experience of his two disciples (1:35-42, Gospel, 2nd cycle). Having seen in Jesus the lamb of God they follow him to see where he lives (1:39), to commune intimately that is, and share his relations with the Father. Nathanael follows the same route. To begin with he sees in Jesus an ordinary human being like others, the son of Joseph (1:45). Then he sees him as Messiah (1:49), until the day that he sees him finally on the cross, at once God and the Son of Man at once exalted and crushed (1:50-51). Mary passed through the same stages. Having discerned in her son a thaumaturge (Jn 2:1-11, Gospel 3rd cycle) capable of assisting friends, she has to travel the distance towards faith in the Son crucified and risen in the hour of his glory.

So it is that the faith of the baptized person, and the call of the disciple or minister, begin with an analysis of events and situations. These must be interpreted; in the personality of the man-God is to be found the key to their proper meaning. One must "follow" this man-God (1:37; 1:43), "bear witness" to him (1:34).

One cannot go this road without holding dialogue with God, being open to his influence. Several times John stresses this by showing how Jesus' way of seeing his disciples transforms their way of seeing too. He changes Simon into Peter (1:42), Nathanael the doctor of the law into a believer (1:47). No progress in faith can be made without accepting events and persons as God's gifts. No vocation is private: it wells up from encounter and acceptance.

VIII. John   The first events of the public life are nar-
       1:35-42   rated by John in the more or less artificial
       Gospel   framework of a single week (cf. "the following
       2nd cycle   day" in vv. 29, 35, 43; the "third day" in Jn
                       2:1). In any case the events here are spread
over two days, and even the hour of some of them is given us
(v. 39b: the "tenth hour"; v. 41: "at daybreak"), though this
particular version is not well supported. Such surprising chronological precision and the use of words with a second meaning
(like "dwell" in v. 38), suggest that, over and above the narration of events, John is conveying a more mysterious message.

a) The surface lesson of the passage is simple. Two friends,
probably Philip and Andrew (who are always together in the
Gospel: Jn 2:40-45; 6:5-9; 12:20-21; Ac 1:13), both disciples of
the Baptist (v. 35), discover the Messiah and follow him. That
is the beginning of their *apostolic vocation*. They tell their brothers and acquaintances (vv. 41 and 45) and bring about the
vocation of Peter and Nathanael.*

Behind this narrative we have a whole theology of vocation.
It can be brought about by human association. In the case of the
four disciples here, the operative factors are friendship, fellow
citizenship, pursuit of a similar ideal in the entourage of the
Baptist, blood brotherhood.

Nevertheless, the call really comes from God and Christ. The
authority by which Jesus changes the name of Simon (v. 42b),
the look that he turns upon Peter (v. 42a), his mysterious knowledge of Nathanael (v. 48), and above all his attitude to the two
disciples of the Baptist (v. 38) all indicate that, rooted though

---

* See the doctrinal theme: *vocation*, p. 41.

it be in the human, vocation depends on God's initiative. A human attitude set up by divine call, in each person "called" the mystery of the man-God is prolonged.

b) John goes on to some important doctrinal affirmations that are valid for every disciple of Christ. He uses two key-words (follow and seek: vv. 37-38) to describe the essential attitude of the disciple, and three others to describe their reward (find, see, and dwell: vv. 39 and 41).

The phrase *to follow Christ* has a more eschatological emphasis for John than for the other evangelists. It indicates that we take the means determined one day to bring us to where Christ "dwells" (cf. Jn 12:26; 10:9-10). The glory that he lives in has been acquired by the cross. Consequently the disciple must in turn carry his own cross in order to follow him (Mt 16:24; Jn 12:26).

The theme of "dwelling" likewise is akin to that of glory (Jn 14:1-3; 14:10), and the sojourn of Andrew and Philip in the mysterious dwelling of Christ as a consequence of their search, suggests the house of the Father where all Christ's disciples will meet him one day in glory.

The theme of *seeking and finding* is also significant (cf. Lk 2:41-51). The reference principally is to Wisdom, which allows herself to be found by those who seek her (Wi 6:12) as Christ was found by Andrew and his friend (v. 37), "at the morning hour" (Wi 6:14), the hour when Peter found Christ (v. 41). Or she will go forth to meet those who seek her (Wi 6:16), as Christ met Philip and Nathanael "on the way" (vv. 43, 47). Thus, with John, this theme gets a particular sapiental emphasis. In Luke 2:31-41, a passage that is set in the context of a eulogy of Jesus' wisdom (Lk 2:40, 52), and also based on the "seeking-finding" theme, and the "dwelling" of God, we have hints of a similar emphasis.

All the vocations, that of the apostle, the disciple and the Christian, follow the same pattern. They require similar dispositions of soul, and the same attitude on the part of God. He invites people to share his life and glory, to live with him. The road however is essentially the road of a wisdom, that presumes the cross, and the death of selfishness.

IX. John 2:1-12
Gospel
3rd cycle

Jesus begins his ministry as rabbi and thaumaturge in his own territory, at Capharnaum, among his family and those of the apostles. John, however, sees in these discreet beginnings the whole great project of divinizing humanity, and the traces of the paschal mystery. We should read this episode with John's own eyes.

a) Mary's telling Jesus that the guests have no more wine is of course the concern of a woman in the practical order for the details of the reception. Symbolically however (cf. Is 55:1-3 and Jl 2:25-27) it indicates that the people, deprived of the wine of happiness and wisdom, await, in the attitude of the poor, God's initiative which will bring happiness. What Jesus is providing is in fact the "good wine" of promised happiness in the last times. It is the sign of plenitude and wisdom that he brings the world.*

b) The gift however depends on the Messiah's final glorification, on that "week," that "now," which, through death, will consummate the mystery of the Lord's glory.

The chronological precisions in the passage John 1:19–2:1 (1:28; 1:35; 1:39; 1:41; 1:43; 2:1) seem to be deliberate. The only subsequent instance in which the evangelist takes the Lord's words and deeds in this fashion is the Passion. The fact that the miracle takes place on "the third day" (v. 1; cf. Jn 11:6-7; 13:33; Lk 24:7; Ho 6:2-5) similarly points to the accomplishment of the Pasch of Christ. It warns the reader that the events at Cana are going to be interpreted in the light of the paschal mystery.

* See the doctrinal theme: *wine*, p. 37.

The hour theme, in this context, is particularly decisive (v. 4; cf. Jn 2:19; 7:30-39; 8:20; 13:1; 17:1). The hour describes concretely the death of the Lord, which glorifies him, and glorifies the Father because it accomplishes the salvation of the world. However, after John 7:30, the references to Jesus' hour indicate that moment in his life, when he becomes powerless, when he can do no more miracles (cf. Jn 9:4; 11:9-10; cf. the theme of "bonds" in Jn 18:12, 24; 19:40).

We can understand then the exchange between mother and son. Mary seeks a miracle that will solve a domestic embarrassment (v. 3; cf. a similar family situation in Jn 7:3-4). Jesus' reply "woman, what is that to me and you?" (v. 4; we have a similar opposition between "me and you" in Jn 7:6-8) is as much as to say: place yourself in the context of my mission instead of taking an earthly view. The explanation comes then: "my hour (the time, that is to say, when I shall be bound, impeded) has not yet come." He can still do miracles (v. 4, a similar answer in Jn 7:8-10). Immediately Mary falls in with this doctrine, and orders the servants to follow the instructions Jesus will give (v. 5).

Christ then is clearly referring to the "sign," to the work *par excellence* he will accomplish in the humiliation of his death. Nevertheless, until this hour strikes, he can do signs and wonders, the full meaning of which will only become clear in the paschal event. They are provisional, a little like the various liberations of the Old Testament.

His reasoning would be thus. Today I can do the miracle by involving thaumaturgic power that does not yet appear to true faith. The hour will come however when true signs will be wrought by my power because it will be that of my resurrection (Jn 13:1). All miracles that are not touched by my death, and do not appeal to the one true faith in my resurrection, are to that extent limited.

c) In his narrative of this episode at Cana then we see an example of John's style of interpreting a miracle of Jesus, even a relatively ordinary one, as a *sign* (v. 11). He places it at the week's end, he introduces the theme of the hour, he deliberately emphasizes the matter of wine. He points out, as in John 7:1-10, the inability of his own family to interpret the miracle properly. All this demonstrates that a miracle is an appeal to faith. It is not merely a matter of believing that Jesus can perform a miracle, as in the synoptics, but of discerning its mysterious meaning. This could only be grasped by one who understood the paschal mystery and was living the love which inspired it.

The faith which can interpret signs means more than belief that water has been changed to wine (like Mary), or for that matter that wine is changed into Christ's blood in the mass (the extent of faith for some Christians). It means discernment of the paschal dimension of the sign accomplished and involving oneself in this paschal mystery.

B. DOCTRINE

1. The Theme of Wine

In all Mediterranean countries wine is a commodity of exceptional importance. It was an essential part of ancient economy, depending at once on the seasonal rhythm and on man's careful, ingenious labor. Because it is at once the gift of the gods, and the fruit of man's toil, it was very natural that it should become something of religious import, material for religious reflection.

At every important stage in Israel's spiritual pilgrimage, and its culmination in the Kingdom inaugurated by Jesus, we find wine and the vine to be prominent. Today wine continues to be an essential element in the eucharistic celebration. If we follow the various stages of development in this wine-vine theme, we shall be able to throw into relief the stages through which a man must pass in the journey from unbelief to faith in Jesus Christ, and the Church which is his body.

Wine and the vine in Israel

For Israel, as for neighboring peoples, wine is the divine blessing *par excellence*. Material prosperity is measured by a land rich in vines and abundant wine. In quest of happiness man naturally seeks security. Anything that brings such security he regards as a sign of divine blessing. Furthermore wine brings joy. Its festive character makes it particularly suitable as a liturgical element. It, rather than anything else, withdraws a man from the profane and introduces him to the sacral.

Come tempests though, or devastation caused by wars and invasions, and abundance yields place to scarcity. It was at such moments that Israel had to react with faith. Where other peoples tried to appease the anger of their gods with ritual sacrifices, Israel saw the sterility of the vines as a consequence of her own infidelity to the requirements of the covenants. Through the tenor of events Yahweh leads his people and chastizes them for infidelity. Because he is the Totally-Other there can be no question of touching him by means of magical procedures of any kind. There is only one way of recovering his blessing, the way of conversion and fidelity.

The people were thus obliged to see Yahweh's hand in their misfortunes, they were stricken because of sin. Yet invariably, too, their gaze would be directed towards the future. They knew that Yahweh is faithful, that he will never cease to tend the vine he has planted. . . . Misfortune will one day be replaced by the definitive prosperity of the Kingdom Yahweh has prepared for his people. The land of promise, which they entered after forty years in the desert, was a land already rich in vines. But it was nothing to the richness and abundance that would be theirs when the day of Yahweh dawned.

This very yearning towards the future led to a deepening of the people's faith, an interiorization of fidelity. The vine became an ambiguous symbol. It rejoiced the heart of man, but it could also lead to the excesses of drunkenness. More important than wine as beverage, was the wine of the wisdom and knowledge of God. As well as being a material blessing, wine came to signify more essential realities.

Jesus, the vine of the new covenant

The fidelity that Yahweh had wanted from the chosen people he received at last from Jesus. Jesus was the true vine. A new covenant was born. His fidelity, carried through in obedience unto the death of the cross, was not developed from human resources. It was the fidelity of the eternal Son, the true fidelity of a partner. In him the human yearning for the absolute was fulfilled beyond the wildest dreams. The "yes" of the man and the "yes" of the Son are one and the same.

The vine of the new covenant produces abundant fruit. Its wine is called love, a love for men which is identical with the Father's love, and demands the same renunciation. In this universal fraternal love, each one is accepted in his otherness, the unique and incommunicable mystery that sets him apart. Such a love only becomes possible through a renunciation that is prepared to lay down life.

Such is the wine of the new, definitive covenant. Jewish man however recoiled before this concept of love; it scandalized him. It might be that this love was capable of fulfilling his most profound yearnings, but it required total renunciation, the relinquishing of false securities, abandonment of privileges. He greeted this offer of universal love by nailing Christ to the cross. Love, however, is stronger than death. Hate was vanquished on its own territory.

It is for this reason that, in the gospel references to new wine, Jesus' passion, his "hour," is always on the horizon. The new wine is his blood, offered for the redemption of all. That is to say that the wine theme will always have in the gospel a highly paschal emphasis. We have it at its peak on Holy Thursday evening when Jesus said, as he gave the cup to the apostles, "This is my blood."

The Church under the sign of the vine

Tradition has frequently used the theme of the vine to give deeper insight into the mystery of the Church. The principal elements of the theme however were already fairly thoroughly elaborated in Scripture. Let us choose two aspects.

"I am the vine; you are the branches." It would be difficult to imagine a stronger affirmation of the fact that members of the Church are dependent on the unique mediation of Christ, that they are indeed one with him. A branch has no life of its own. Cut off from the tree, it is good for nothing except burning. The life which throbs in the branches then being identical with that of the vine, it follows that Christians are called to the same obedience that Christ showed, the same self-renunciation, the same love for God and men.

This identity of life however does not at all imply passivity on the part of Christians. On the contrary. If members of the

Church share the life of Jesus, they are summoned to make an active contribution to the accomplishment of salvation history. They become collaborators with Jesus in building the Kingdom, veritable laborers in the vineyard of the Father. Identity of life and active contribution go hand in hand. Without Christ nothing can be done. But, in him with him and by him, every baptized person is called upon to make up what is wanting in the passion of the unique mediator.

Mission as a service of love

The wine of the new and definitive covenant is love. The life of Jesus has shown us that this is at once love of the Father and universal brotherly love. Mission is simply the exercise of this unique love on the human plane. It is essential to the Church, for without love the Church would be nothing.

It is first of all the service rendered to the Father's love. It is the accomplishment of a plan that springs continuously from the Father's antecedent initiative. It has no other purpose but to summon men to celebrate with a single voice the glory of God.

Secondly, it is the service of universal brotherly love. Both purposes coincide. This wine bursts the old bottles of privilege and particularism. The Good News is addressed to all without exception. Everyone, no matter how diverse in concrete terms, receives the universal call to salvation. The essence of true love is that it advances to meet the other with full recognition of his individual mystery.

What Jesus did once for all for everyone, the Church must go on doing. She must go forth to meet different peoples and different cultures, so that all may join the brotherhood that builds the Kingdom. Because he loved the way he did, Jesus was persecuted. The missionary will be too. The servant is not greater than his master.

It is by planting the seed of this true love among all peoples that the Church will indirectly lead men towards proper responsibility in the human task as well. The new wine of love assuages the thirst for the absolute. It liberates man from sin and challenges him accordingly to honor the demands of his creatural condition.

The Eucharist and the wine of the new covenant

For the Christian today wine is not just a biblical symbol, however rich in allusiveness, however vivid as an expression of faith. In the sacramental banquet of the Eucharist material wine continues to be central.

"Each time you eat this bread and drink this cup, you proclaim the death of the Lord, until he comes" (1 Co 9:26). With that other element of God's material creation, bread, it is wine that initiates us sacramentally into the saving Act *par excellence,* Christ's death on the cross.

In this eucharistic wine the two great lines of salvation history converge, as it were. In the first place, because God has created everything for love and has so loved men that he gave his own Son as victim for their sins, it is in this sacrifice of Christ that wine, like all the rest of material creation, discloses fully its goodness. In the second place we have the thrust of human response. This too is a response of love. It is in Christ's obedience unto the death of the cross that it reaches once for all definitive stature. Wine is one of the finest fruits of human toil, but this toil can only reach fulfillment in Jesus Christ. In him it becomes a true partner's contribution in the building of God's Kingdom.

The day will come when the symbol becomes reality. With all his adoptive brothers Christ will be festive in the accomplished Kingdom. Then joy will be full.

2. The Theme of Vocation

Here we have a highly important theme, which combines essential elements of the Christian profession. Throughout all history the people of God have constantly resorted to it, above all as an explanation of the sacerdotal ministry and the religious state.

In recent years, with so much concern about the laity in the Church, we have been hearing a good deal of the lay vocation. Yet, at the same time, for some years we notice a decline in enthusiasm for the term. Studies about vocation are less frequent than they used to be in the past. We continue to use the term, true, but is this a matter of habit or of genuine conviction?

The situation however does not seem to warrant any negative conclusions about a deterioration of faith among the people of God. What we are witnessing is an evolution in religious sensibility. Formerly we used to see God's call to the priesthood or religious life as something discerned fairly explicitly in the depths of conscience. It was something unforeseen, disturbing, for which there might be no discernible antecedents. Mistakes were certainly possible and our predecessors had carefully elaborated determining criteria. At no time was it called into question that God could confront the individual conscience. During the ecclesial renewal between the two wars however, a number of authorities thought it well to stress, in discussing priestly vocation, the ecclesial call, in concrete terms the call of the bishop. A development was taking place the trend of which we can see more clearly now. While fully acknowledging the absolute priority of God's initiative, many Christians feel a certain hesitancy about traditional formulations of the vocation theme. What is at issue in reality is the manner of understanding God's intervention in the universe. We of today find it more in accordance with the logic of faith to believe that God's initiative is disclosed *pari passu* with the individual's spiritual development. God's will is not something pre-formed, that we have to discover before conforming ourselves exactly to it.

So important is this new religious insight that we should try to evaluate its implications. All development is not necessarily progress. If we review the stages of salvation history against the background of the mystery of Christ and his Church, we shall find some things that will clarify our thinking.

The vocation of the prophets in Israel

The vocation narratives in the Old Testament are one of the most remarkable consequences brought about by the regime of faith. It was a mutation of colossal dimension in the history of human conscience and the prophets are its witnesses. Prophetism in the wide sense is a phenomenon not exclusive to Israel, and the remote origins of Jewish prophetism probably belong to some original reservoir common to humanity. Origins apart however, the distinctive quality of Jewish prophetism is in exact proportion to progress in the adventure of faith. Of this Israel was the principal architect. It is natural then that the personal experience of any particular prophet tends to reflect the contemporary stage of development in the regime of faith.

A first characteristic of prophetic vocation is that its recipient is seized by a personal call from God. This is to be expected when we remember the importance in Jewish thinking of knowledge of Yahweh, the living God, the Totally-Other God, the only one to possess the secret of salvation. For the fulfillment of her destiny Israel is totally dependent on his gratuitous initiative. He chooses freely and sets apart the people of his choice. The deeper the realization of this insight, the greater the interiorization, the fuller the awareness of the moral and spiritual requirements of the covenant. Gradually God's initiative towards Israel began to be seen in personal and individual terms. The divine summons was something that reverberated down deep in the individual believer's conscience, challenging him to master every energy in his fidelity to the requirements. That is why the vocation theme was so very central. But because man was a sinner, because his natural tendency did not lead him to such a unified focus in life, God's call seemed often disconcerting, unexpected, impossible to answer.

A second characteristic of the prophetic vocation is that it is always linked with a mission, a service to fellowmen. The prophet will be called by Yahweh for a precise task among the people. In season and out of season he must challenge the people to do penance and take up again the adventure of faith in the light of events in history. The prophet is God's servant for the accomplishment of his salvation plan and for this reason he is a servant of men too.

Christ the Lord and the vocation of all men

As exegetes have noted, the evangelists tend not to use at all, or very rarely, the traditional vocabulary of vocation where Jesus is concerned. This is just another way of emphasizing that the mystery of Christ transcends all previous categories. He is Lord, and if the man-God has brought the adventure of faith to fulfillment by responding perfectly in his humanity to the divine initiative, this is because his human response is altogether new. It is the response of the Son.

On the other hand there are numerous passages in the evangelists where the call issues from the mouth of Jesus. In the Old Testament it was always Yahweh who called: in the New, God is still the caller, but through the mouth of Jesus. Now the divine call takes definite shape; Jesus asks people to follow him. He is the inaugurator of the Kingdom. In him men achieve the filial state and are delivered from sin. They become God's partners in the accomplishment of the salvation plan. Around him, as the cornerstone, is concentrated the whole thrust of the human enterprise. Vocation now is more than ever linked to mission, but every mission that comes from God is linked to the mission of Jesus and derives its meaning from that.

We should notice how vocation narratives are juxtaposed by the evangelists with apparitions of the Risen Lord. The passion of Jesus clarifies everything, the meaning of his mission and the mystery of his person. The realization comes that the divine initiative really *is* woven into the texture of human history. When the Risen Lord calls, it is God himself who calls. When the mystery of Christ is revealed in its plenitude, we know that every authentic human vocation is Christological in nature.

The paschal mystery too is the moment when Christian universalism becomes established. God's call through Jesus Christ is addressed to all men, and the mission given by this divine call must be a universal one. The calls that emanated from Jesus during his earthly life had a special quality. All the men and women he met he called; he had come for sinners, that is to say for all. His ministry brought him into contact with Gentiles accidentally only however, and it was in the paschal mystery that the full dimension of his call was seen. Israel's refusal to undertake the mission that the Messiah wanted to entrust to her, made it very clear that God's call was to be extended to all without distinction.

The "Ekklesia" and the call of everyone

From the very beginning we find the vocabulary of vocation applied to the people of the New Covenant. *"Ekklesia,"* the term chosen to describe the Christian assembly, has a basic meaning which suggests God's initiative towards men; "The Convoked," "The Chosen," "The Called." The Church is this because she is Christ's Body. Ecclesial theology has very frequently made use of the double term convocation-assembly, when attempting to delineate the real meaning of the people of God, because the great focus of ecclesiological insight has always been the eucharistic celebration.

The disciples in the Pauline communities were very conscious of being called by God in Jesus Christ. Their profession was a response to this call. It was a disconcerting call, but it touched everyone precisely where he found himself, as he was. The calls were different, as diverse as persons are. Each one was summoned to make the service of God the unifying force in his life, and this meant too the service of men, of the common good. God's call began to be seen as a *"diakonia,"* a definite role that must be played in the building of the Kingdom. The chief criterion for assessment of the call came to be recognition by the assembly. Saint Paul, more than anyone else, clarified both the diversity and the unity that characterize all vocations. They are all traced to the same Spirit. All are called to make their contribution in ful-filling God's plan, but all are members of the one body, the Body of Christ.

Vatican II has taken up again this Pauline insight. Active participation and responsibility are not reserved to any single member, or members, of the people of God; because before God all are fundamentally equal. Each member has his calling and he will follow it precisely according to the way in which he musters all energy for the service of the Kingdom, which is to say, too, for human progress. How then, in the past, did the term vocation come to be reserved for priests and religious? For the simple reason that the great body of the baptized faithful began to be regarded as a body of "consumers." Priests and religious became detached as the active, producing class. By right of course the concept of vocation cannot be restricted to any particular group in the Church. We had only to wait for the reintroduction to responsibility of the laity to hear again about the lay vocation.

The missionary vocation now

A missionary vocation, from the beginning, was always re-garded as something special. Extension to the Gentiles, far away, seemed to be a fundamental need of the Church. Christ's death had broken down all the walls of separation between peoples. Such was the fruit of God's salvific initiative, who willed that all men should be brothers. What Christ had accomplished once for all must go on being accomplished by the Church throughout time. Following the footsteps of Saint Paul, we see that at every epoch Christians have felt this urge under the Spirit to go to the Gentiles and bear witness to incarnate Love, building genuine peace among nations. Such men have always known this urge to be connected with God's call. It was something that commanded their personal fidelity.

So that this missionary vocation is something highly personal, that turns all a man's being to the unpredictable way of love with-out limits. Yet it is something highly ecclesial too. Mission is an essential responsibility of the people of God, and everything connected with it is in one way or another the responsibility of the people of God, all of them. Extension to the Gentiles has always been a responsibility of the Church, but the manner of ecclesial intervention has throughout the centuries been modified. During the early centuries each local community felt itself responsible for mission, and it was the course of events which, under the action of the Spirit, determined the manner of evangelization. Mission was not, properly speaking, organized. From the 4th century onwards however, communion between local Churches began to be organized; and, in the Western Church, everything was gradually centralized around Rome. Mission consequently became institutionalized, and tended to be part of ecclesial strategy generally, something that was not always unconnected with the political strategy of the West. At no time did the call to mission cease to be regarded as a work of the Spirit, but individual initiative tended to be subordinated to collective. The missionary enterprise came to be regarded as the business of the ecclesial institution which would broach new territories as it thought fit in the light of other enterprises and the needs that had to be met.

We are witnessing a change just now. Since Vatican II there is a new approach to Church-world relations. Humanity is groping for new solutions to the future and there is no longer any question of being in the Church's tutelage. The Church's business is to serve. Because of this change, it is by no means unlikely that we shall witness a transformation in the very concept of mission and the missionary vocation. More and more Christians are beginning to be concerned by the obstacles that stand in the way of communion between peoples, something that will in the future be altogether imperative. They are ready to give of their best so that all men everywhere can reach fulfillment. That being so, might it not be that these very individuals are going to be the future recipients of a missionary vocation? The very urge they feel to devote themselves to the ideal of universal communion will lead them to the view that this very ideal takes proper shape only when it emanates from the Spirit with some sort of approval from the ecclesial community.

SECOND WEEK

I. Hebrews
5:1-10
1st reading
1st cycle
Monday

Here we have the preface to the long comparison the author makes between the two priesthoods, Jewish and Christian. At this point he contents himself with stating the problem, laying down first of all the essential conditions of true priesthood (vv. 1-4). He then brings forward two weighty arguments to demonstrate the superiority of Christ's priesthood to any other. These are presented in two biblical texts which constantly recur in the subsequent discussion. Christ's priesthood depends on God's oath (Ps 109/110:4), and on his royal sonship (Ps 2:7).

Christ thus is argued to have all the necessary qualities of any priest in addition to his own qualities.

For priestly qualities we are shown that he is "taken from among men" (v. 1; Nb 8:6; He 2:10-18). He too must be "established" (Tt 1:5; Ac 6:3; 7:10, 27, 35; Ex 2:14; He 2:28; 8:3). He must offer sacrifice (Lv 4; 5; 16), and at the same time welcome the weak and the strayed (Lv 5:18; Ez 40:39). The *priest* will be the more welcoming towards the weak in the measure that he shares their weakness (v. 3; Lv 4:3-12; 16:6-11), but from this requirement Jesus is exempt (He 7:27).

Finally the priest must be called by God (v. 4). This is clearly the case with Aaron (Ex 28), and there was the disaster arising in the case of a usurped priesthood (Nb 16). Christ has this quality. He did not take this glory to himself (v. 5), he who never sought his own glory (Jn 5:41; 8:50, 54; Rm 15:3; Ph 2:6).

Thus Christ is shown to have all the priestly titles, but two others, much more important, are added: his title as eternal Son, which ensures the perpetuity of his priesthood (v. 5); and his title as priest according to the order of Melchizedek (v. 6), the meaning of which will be discussed later.

The great double criterion, solidarity with men and choice by God, is fully verified in the man-God. In Church history this delicate balance is always having to be readjusted. In the sacral society of the Middle Ages for instance a style was followed that is not going to be that of tomorrow's priesthood. The current crisis in the priesthood is sufficient proof. It is certain that the social and psychological environment of the priest now will demand some readjustment of balance. He must be more present to the world in which he lives, undertake the duties and enjoy the rights required by this, and adapt his state of life accordingly. He is the chosen one of God, but he must have full solidarity with his fellowmen.

II. 1 Samuel 15:16-23
1st reading
2nd cycle
Monday

King Saul finds himself disturbed and ill at ease in the solitude of royalty. Samuel does not seem to have assisted him considerably. The prophet indeed resorted to a stubborn silence, waiting for the day when he could condemn the king for one of his faults, and neatly demonstrate his impiety.

His chance came at the end of a war against Ameleg. Saul, more successful as judge-liberator than as administrator-king, had celebrated the action with *eclat*. Our account, which emanates from antimonarchist tradition, censures him for breach of the law of *anathema*. Instead of exterminating every living creature in the vanquished camp, Saul allowed the people to retain the choice portions in order to make due ritual sacrifice to Yahweh (v. 15).

There is a distinction however between the extermination of anathema and extermination by sacrifice. One must not trifle with the regulations governing approach to the sacred. Saul may have felt a surge of pity for the enemy, or may not have proved adamant before the demands of his people. He may even have thought that a sacrifice would render greater homage to God than a procedure of anathema. All this was brushed aside; he should have been careful above all to observe the sacral rubrics.

In condemning Saul's "impiety" (so much more spiritual than the "piety" of Samuel as described in vv. 32-33), the prophetic tradition placed on Samuel's lips what is doubtless some lost oracle of Amos or Hosea (cf. Ho 6:6; Am 5:21-25). It is ironical that this, one of the earliest oracles to summon the people toward spiritual sacrifice, toward conformity of rite with life, should have been directed against the alleged unforgiveable impiety of Saul.

Saul's career was really tragic. He was essentially a lonely figure. He had scarcely been anointed by Samuel, when he found himself abandoned, unable to elicit an answer to his requests (1 S 13:1-11). When Samuel presented himself before him as God's witness, it was to condemn him summarily and withdraw his royal mantle (1 S 15:27-28). He was to be alone up to the day of his death, so alone that he had even to procure his own death. The only contact he could ever establish with Samuel henceforward was to be by means of a ridiculous spectre (1 S 28). He was not really made to be a king. We can more easily see him as a judge, and cannot but resent Samuel's performance in preventing him from using his own resources, while at the same time refusing him daily support.

The viewpoint of the final redactors of the books of Samuel is quite shallow. It will have the failure or success of kings depend on the good or evil they accomplish. Because Saul's career was a failure, the attitude was that there had to be wrongdoing. In David's case however (whose wrongdoing certainly far exceeded Saul's), because his reign was a success, there had to be good. It was a superficial doctrine of retribution that was destined one day to encounter the sombre, and very understandable, anger of Job.

III. **Mark 2:18-22** Commentary on this Gospel will be found
    Gospel   in the second cycle of the 8th Sunday, p. 338.
    Monday

IV. **Hebrews**   The author has just issued the severe judg-
    6:10-20   ment that the apostate cannot repent or bene-
    1st reading   fit a second time from Christ's Passion (He
    1st cycle   6:4-9). He does not however wish to leave his
    Tuseday   readers with this bleak impression and imme-
                     diately reaffirms God's goodness towards the
faithful (v. 9).

a) He bases his optimism on God's justice (v. 10), which must always imitate the faith and patience of those who entered into possession of the promised land (Abraham, in particular), and avoid the murmuring of those who failed to do this (the people in the desert: He 3-4). This faith is a zeal, an ardor. It admits no murmuring or hesitancy. It is based on two important guarantees: God's promise on the one hand which was verified in Abraham (vv. 13-15; Cf. Gn 22:16), on the other hand his oath (vv. 16-18) which makes his decision absolute.

b) At this point faith is reinforced by hope (vv. 19-20), the solid "anchor" which gives assurance of entry to the promised land. Hope is even thought of as a sort of liturgy, during which not only the high-priest but all the people enter the *Holy of Holies*.

Thus, all the time, the author is conscious of the refugee status (v. 18) of his audience. They continue to dream of regaining their normal living, and above all religious, environment: the holy land and Jerusalem city. He proposes for their consideration two somewhat similar precedents. The nomads in the desert, who murmured about their lot to the point of denying themselves their heritage. On the other hand the nomad Abraham, who obtained entry to the holy land because his faith and hope were based on God's promise and his oath.

At this point the immediate objection open to his corespondents would run thus. Even if, in faith and hope, we entrust to God our lot and our heritage, yet we continue to be cut off from the temple liturgy and all ritual expression of our faith. Accordingly the author points out that their very expectation of the land is in itself a liturgy. People are not enabled to enter the spiritual Holy of Holies, whereas, had they remained in Jerusalem, they could never have entered a material Holy of Holies that was reserved to the high priest only.

V. 1 Samuel
16:1-13
1st reading
2nd cycle
Tuesday

This account is certainly to be traced to an isolated prophetic tradition. The anointing of David by Samuel is not known elsewhere, and it is challenged actually by two more plausible anointings, that of the Northern tribes (2 S 5:3) and the tribes of Judah (2 S 2:4). People who could have been eye witnesses of David's anointing, such as Eliab his brother, appear not to have known of it (1 S 17:28).

It seems possible that subsequent prophets were anxious to have the davidic kingship, so rich in messianic promise, begin with a prophetic gesture such as Samuel's, in order to increase its prestige. In addition the account can be taken as a way of whitewashing the memory of the old prophet Samuel. By anointing David he would be making good his mistake after the anointing of Saul.

The fact that David, rather than Saul's descendants, succeeded Saul was of course God's will, and the account of the premature anointing is an attempt to demonstrate this. In verse 7 we have the key. God's attitudes are not those of men, as Samuel discovers in being obliged to discard one after another the elder brothers of David.

This is a familiar literary procedure. We have it in the various conflicts between older and younger brothers where God manifests his choice (Esau and Jacob, Ishmael and Isaac, the two sons of Joseph). The purpose is to show God's freedom in the *choice* of men to collaborate in his design.

Primitive as this episode is, it is nevertheless extremely revealing where the biblical attitude to sacralization is concerned. In primitive Israel pagan cults had attempted to develop criteria whereby people could make pretensions to be chosen instruments of God. It became a matter of sacralizing the claimant; the right of the first-born, membership of a royal dynasty, etc. The prophetic tendency was against such fatalism; claims of this order had better be linked to human liberty itself. God's choice is displayed in man's free action, even when this violates tabus or preestablished criteria. In the long run there is no sign of God's choice other than the free dedication of a man's life as God's chosen one and his fidelity to this undertaking. God only gives himself to his partners; his choice presumes reciprocity.

VI. Mark
2:23-28
Gospel
Tuesday

All the synoptics are unanimous in preserving this echo of Christ's struggle against false concepts of the Sabbath. The redactional differences however are sufficiently noteworthy to argue differences of interpretation.

Mark, especially in the addition of verse 27, shows an anxiety to relate the problem and its solution to a non-Jewish environment, indeed one which actively challenges Jewish legislation.

Our commentary on this passage will deal first with elements common to the synoptic tradition, then with the special emphasis in Mark.

a) The apostles had been caught by the Pharisees in flagrant *violation of the Sabbath*. The violation touched an essential detail: the Sabbath rest. What they had violated, however, was not strictly speaking a precept of the Law as such, but of the Mischna (Sabbath 7:2; one of the thirty-nine prohibitions introduced by Judaism). They also had a precedent in Scripture (v. 25; cf. 1 S 21:2-7).

It is then a domestic Jewish controversy. Can pharisaic legalism be regarded as a valid means of observing the law and following the Father's will? When Jesus says, in Matthew 12:6 that he is greater than the temple, and in Mark 2:28 that he is master of the Sabbath, he is claiming the right by his mission to question legal precision. He will do so even at the price of a desacralization comparable to the loaves of proposition episode (v. 26), when such precisions go against the will of the legislator.

b) Mark suppresses these elements of legal controversy. He has nothing corresponding to Matthew 12:5-6, 11-12. But he adds verse 27. We are quitting the realm of juridical diatribe for that of *person* (cf. Ga 3:23-29). Furthermore we note that Mark inserts this Sabbath discussion at the end of a section where Jesus has three times confronted the Pharisees concerning the same problem; concerning pardon (Mk 2:5-12), relations with sinners (Mk 2:13-17), and fasting (Mk 2:18-22). Thus we have come to the end of an ancient argument where a solution can be delayed no longer. Left to himself man will turn toward absolutes in general, the Sabbath and the Law for instance. Here we have the "flesh" of Pauline theology. But when he is open to God man can pronounce his "yes" to the divine initiative. He has the measure of the Sabbath and the Law. He observes them, but no longer as a slave.

VII. Hebrews
7:1-3, 15-17
1st reading
1st cycle
Wednesday

The author has already demonstrated the priesthood of Christ (He 5:1-10; 6:20). Now he has to analyze the nature and duration of this priesthood. He does so, in contemporary rabbinic fashion, by using the image of Melchizedek.

a) The chief interest of the passage is that a model for Christ is being sought in the patriarchal age. Melchizedek, like Abraham in the letter to the Romans, is anterior to the law. The author is taking the view that patriarchal religion was more pure. Legalism and the institution had degraded it, and it was the duty of Christianity to return to the original spirit. The only priestly figure in the patriarchal period was Melchizedek. Thus a parallel between him and Jesus is set up; because the author wants to show how the Christian priesthood transcends the levitic priesthood of the law.

What we have beyond that belongs to a culture that is altogether foreign to our way of thinking: the etymological argument (v. 2), Melchizedek's superiority to Abraham (and thus to Levi, his grandson: v. 2), the mysterious absence of genealogy (v. 3) which shows the exceptional character of Melchizedek's priesthood, its identity with that of Jesus in uniqueness and duration.

b) Because he had no genealogy, Melchizedek's priesthood could not be derived from carnal descent. It was not then transmitted, but depended on his own personality. Similarly the priesthood of Jesus had its source and meaning in the very *person* of the *man-God*.

How then could legal prescriptions determine the priesthood of someone who derived it from his own being (vv. 15-16)? There was a further consideration. Being as it was outside the law, the law could have nothing to do with the initiation of Christ's priesthood nor with its ending. In fact from now on the law could have nothing to do with Christ. He is imperishable in the fullest sense, "for eternity" (v. 17).

VIII. 1 Samuel David's initial interventions in the history
17:32-33, of his people have been recorded by two very
37, 40-51 different traditions. The oldest makes him a
1st reading minstrel or equerry of Saul. In this capacity
2nd cycle he accompanies the king to war, or distin-
Wednesday guishes himself in single combat (1 S 16:14-
23; 17:1-11, 32-53). The other, more recent,
makes him a chosen shepherd of the Lord (1 S 16:1-13) who
visits his brothers during combat (1 S 17:12-30), and is found
there by the king who attaches him to his service (1 S 17:55-
18:2).

The former, older tradition has a better chance of being
accurate. It is dominated by the famous single combat with
Goliath.

Single combats were a common contemporary procedure in
the Near East. They may have been due to Greek influence, and
the Philistines were their warmest supporters (1 S 17; 2 S 21:15-
22; cf. 2 S 2:12-17), being as they were suitably armed for
hand-to-hand combat (cf. 1 S 17:4-7; vv. 38-39 which attribute
the same armor to the Hebrews are late). Rapidly, the single
combat became a cliché of epic literature and was associated
with the action of God as he triumphs over the forces of evil
(Jb 26:12-13; Ps 73/74:14; 103/104:26; Is 42:13).

In this instance the "welter weight's" victory over the "heavy
weight" seemed so marvelous that tradition discerned evidence
of God's presence (v. 47). The theme would soon become a
leit-motif in prophetic preaching against military expenditure.
Israel might remain weak in armaments and her equipment be
outmoded, but God would fight for her (Ho 1:7; Is 31:1; 2 K 19).

An important Christian tradition saw in Christ's descent to
hell the last decisive single combat of salvation history. It was
then that the enemy was definitively stripped of the power to
destroy the holy people, that salvation was seen to depend

absolutely on the victory of one only (1 Co 15:21-28; 54-57; Rev 9:13-21; 12:7-18). In the Eucharist we are reminded that agony means combat and that the agony of Christ was the combat of the unique champion for the salvation of the many.

IX. Mark 3:1-6 The ministry of the young rabbi Jesus, as
Gospel seen by Mark, took on a polemical character
Wednesday at an early stage. He was quick to inveigh
against the rigidity that characterized certain religious institutions such as purifications for meals (Mk 2:15-17), laws of fast (Mk 2:18-21) and Sabbath laws (Mk 2:23-3:6). All these were being observed without any proper understanding of their purpose and meaning.

a) On the *Sabbath* during the time of Christ the practice of medicine, or even care of the body, was severely restricted. The attitude seemed to be that it was better for the patient to suffer. (In this instance Matthew has Jesus quote 1 S 15:22.)

Jesus takes the opposite view that God is more honored by goodness (v. 4), and will not be restrained from doing good on the pretext of Sabbath observance. Is not the anniversary day of the liberation from Egypt made more holy when a victim is freed from the bondage of infirmity, than when he is left to languish for the supposed honor of God?

b) Mark gives us a personal note when he refers (v. 5) to Jesus' anger and dismay at the *blindness* of the onlookers. He often uses this phrase (3:5; 6:52; 8:17), resembling in this St. Paul (Ep 4:18; Rm 11:7; 2 Co 3:14). Doubtless he derives it from a dossier of anti-Jewish material that had been gathered in the primitive communities. Blindness of heart for him indicates man's incapacity to understand certain divine signs, not because God prevents this, but because things are inaccessible to man unless he gets, and accepts, assistance from God.

Jesus thus perceives the stubborn bastions against which his mission will be directed. Man will refuse his message, and become incapable of reaching up to the level required by the Word that issues from his mouth. He is having the same experience that the prophet Isaiah had, who when confronted by a similar negative reaction gave vent to the same sentiments (Is 6:9-10).

The blindness theme here reminds us of the Christian concept of man. According to this a man's "ego" is as it were on two levels. There is the one that acts and thinks and interacts with others. Then there is that other more fundamental "ego," very rarely touched. It is the "ego" of the absolute, which reminds the other, in the midst of relativity and contingency, that transcendence is his true dimension.

The reconciliation of the two egos is an extremely difficult task. People achieve it only at times, and more rarely still does someone manage to harmonize the two in an admirable balance. In any case, because of our difficulty in reaching the deeper ego, we use abstract terms like "transcendence" and "absolute."

Such is the predicament of sinful man (the meaning of original sin in Saint Paul or blindness in Saint Mark). Man's first blindness is blindness towards himself; he fails to know himself. He is unaware that his deeper "ego" is a sharer in a divine person, the Spirit of God. It is because he is not personally integrated that a man fails to see the manifestations of God, in Jesus Christ for instance.

Christ was the first man to achieve perfect harmony of the two egos, to be always so much in communion with the deeper ego that he could name God. He offers each of us the opportunity to emerge from blindness, to "expiate" the "original" sin by touching that deep area of ourselves (a gratuitous and given thing) where God dwells, and the promise of glory.

**X. Hebrews
7:25-8:6**
1st reading
1st cycle
Thursday

Here we have the conclusion of the demonstration that Christ's priesthood is superior to the levitic. In particular, the author points out that Jesus belongs to the order, not of Levi but Melchizedek (Ps 109/110); that his priesthood depends on his Sonship and his Lordship (Ps 2:7); that it fulfills "God's oath" (vv. 20-22).

a) The oath theme (vv. 20-22) is central to the reading, and it is regrettable that the essential verses have been dropped. The author finds this oath, not now in the promises to Abraham (He 7:6-7), but in the promise of Psalm 109/110, cited for the fourth time (cf. v. 21 and references in vv. 24 and 28). Now however, for the first time, the text is abbreviated. We no longer have mention of Melchizedek; the emphasis is not on him, but on the Lord's *oath* (v. 21). Otherwise the argument is developed normally. A priesthood guaranteed by divine oath is a pledge of a covenant superior to the old, which was not based on any oath by God (vv. 20-22).

b) A priesthood based on such an oath must of necessity be eternal (cf. Ps 109/110:4; vv. 23-25, a recapitulation of vv. 15-17). The perpetuity of the "Risen Lord" guarantees the *eternity* of his priesthood (v. 24), by contrast with the passing nature of the former priesthood. Because it is eternal, Christ's priesthood is always operative, always interceding for us. Our new priesthood is that of Christ in glory (vv. 26-28), that of the Son (v. 28). Because he is the Son exalted for evermore, he is priest for evermore, having become this once for all.

Men are not capable of carving out a path to God. When they organize cults of their own accord, this is futile. There is no real encounter, no deliverance at a deep level from sin. Christ was able to lead men into real communion with God, because his ascension and his enthronement as Lord brought his human nature into intimacy with God. His entry into divine life was accomplished in the very moment of death and surrender of existence. When we celebrate the Eucharist which is the memorial of this offering, and do so under the presidency of ministers who guarantee its relation to the Lord's death and enthronement, we are giving priestly value to our own lives. We are establishing that encounter with God which is authentic and transforming.

XI. 1 Samuel 18:6-9; 19:1-7
1st reading 2nd cycle Thursday

This passage certainly emanates from a very old tradition concerning the career of the doughty David.

David had three considerable advantages which assured his *popularity*. In the first place his warlike exploits were numerous enough to discountenance Saul, who possibly feared invidious comparisons (v. 7). Secondly his good looks (cf. previously 1 S 17:42) doubtless won him over much female sympathy (v. 7, and previously 1 S 18:20-21). Finally, genuinely humane qualities brought him faithful friends like Jonathan (1 S 19:1-7). His popularity was a sign that Yahweh was with him, and it prepared him for his future responsibilities.

XII. Mark 3:7-12
Gospel Thursday

This could be regarded as a sort of "summary" of Christ's first ministry in Galilee (we may have another in Mk 6:53-56). We may then expect to find elements characteristic of the Galilean ministry, somewhat idealized.

a) One such element is the *crowd* surrounding Jesus. We have the phrase "many people" (or "a great multitude") in verses 7 and 8 (as against one such mention only in Luke and Matthew) and the word "crowd" again in verse 9, which is proper to Mark.

Then, in Mark, we have seven different origins for the crowd as against four or five in Matthew 4:25 and Luke 6:17. We have not yet the internationalism of Pentecost, but there is clear indication of growing success for the prophet and thaumaturge of Capharnaum.

Up to this point Mark has not had occasion to present the teaching of Jesus. He has confined himself to his powers as healer and his attitude to some legalistic practices. This gives his success with the crowds an ambiguous dimension. People come to be cured, not to be converted. They do not understand that the miracles are the advance signs of the messianic era.

Mark too is the only one to point out (v. 9) that Jesus adopts a certain reserve in his attitude to this immense crowd.

b) The *demons* (v. 11) know well who Jesus is; he is the "Son of God" (v. 11), a title that here indicates his royal and messianic mission, not his theandric nature. In this context Mark is a child of his time, which took the view that the "angelic powers" were *au courant* with happenings in the world, in particular with the advent of the Messiah who would deprive them of their influence (cf. Mk 1:24, 34). Unlike the crowds, the demons realize that the messianic age has begun, and each time they encounter Jesus they proclaim this knowledge because they are temporarily responsible for the principles governing history. The day will come when Peter will turn to his own account this messianic knowledge of the angels (Mk 8:29). This is the moment when the control of the principles will have changed hands.

c) Taking this gospel in its context, we notice Mark's evident anxiety to describe the different *knowledges* of Jesus. The Pharisees are "blind" and do not know him (Mk 3:1-6). The crowds do not know him either but they do not show the same obstinacy. Their needs are immediate and down-to-earth. The demons do know him, but Jesus imposes silence on them because they do not know that his Messiahship is to be accomplished in death itself. His parents (Mk 3:20-35) have as yet only a sentimental and carnal knowledge, without depth. Finally there are the Twelve who one day will understand (Mk 3:13-19).

This tableau of different attitudes prepares us for understanding of the sower parable where the seed encounters different receptions (Mk 4:1-20). The different knowledges of Jesus is a leit-motif of all this week's Gospels. Mark is developing an insight which will be deepened later by John.

In our day too the person of Jesus evokes all the different reactions it did then, extending from blindness on the part of some to full faith on the part of others. We have all the equivocal religious motivations, the showy professions of faith, the gropings for security, the systematizations. A believer has often indeed to impose silence on himself. He has to forego external manifestations of his faith that might be misconstrued. He too must wait for the manifestation of the Kingdom in agony and death.

XIII. Hebrews
     8:6-13
     1st reading
     1st cycle
     Friday

Chapters 8 and and 9 of Hebrews are clearly the central portion of the letter. Indeed in Hebrews 8:1 the author himself affirms that he is broaching his major topic. This is the superiority of Christ's priesthood to all priesthoods of terrestrial origin. He actually points out that Christ's priesthood depends not of the terrestrial order; on earth he would not even be a priest, but a "layman" (He 8:4; cf. 7:13-14). His priesthood depends not on terrestrial or human criteria, but on celestial ones. These the author analyzes against the background of Christ's "celestial" vocation, his membership of the divine world (He 8:1-5). Our reading actually stops short of the celestial criteria, which begin to be enumerated at 9:11. In this passage the author returns once more to the affirmation that the usual "terrestrial" criteria for the priesthood of the old covenant do not apply in the case of Jesus.

a) The criteria for the old covenant priesthood (or any earthly priesthood) cannot apply to Christ's priesthood, because it depends on a *covenant* that is superior on two counts (v. 6). In the

first place the first covenant was not without reproach (v. 7).
Because the Jews disobeyed (v. 8; cf. Jr 31:30-33) it deserved
God's disapproval. Secondly, the new covenant is not based as
was the old on exterior dispositions. It is based on the spirit
given in the heart of every man (lay or priest) which enables him
to adopt a free, personal attitude towards God's will (vv. 10-12).
The presence of the Spirit ensures that religion is no longer to
be a religion of authority in which a professional clergy manifests
exteriorly God's wishes. Everyone, even the sinner, can come
directly to knowledge of God (v. 11). There is no longer need
for recourse to exterior rites of ablution or sacrifices in order to
be rehabilitated. Interior knowledge of God brings repentance
and pardon, v. 12).

b) All this is to say that the priesthood of Christ is derived
from the Spirit of God within him, which gives him perfect
knowledge of the Father's will to love, a knowledge that begets
free, spontaneous obedience and pardon for the sins of all humanity. His *ministry* is of a radically new order (v. 6), a
mediation and a priesthood.

All these criteria of the new priesthood, which reaches in
Christ its plenitude, are verified too in every Christian. Each
one enjoys the interior presence of the Spirit, knowledge of the
Father's will to pardon, freedom where the exterior tables of the
law are concerned, etc. Something that the former priesthood,
now outmoded (v. 13) was unable to convey is communicated by
Christ. For this reason his ministry is an extraordinary mediation.

XIV. 1 Samuel **24:3-21** *1st reading* *2nd cycle* *Friday*	Having fallen into disgrace at the court of Saul, David takes to flight and begins the life of an outlaw, leading a motley group of mercenaries (1 S 22:2) drawn from among Hebrew or foreign sheiks. This episode in chapter 24 (which is taken up again in 1 S 26)

tells of a grave imprudence on Saul's part while in pursuit of David.

The story is told in an absolutely popular style. The purpose is to stress David's chivalric spirit of *greatness of soul* in face of an enemy. The lesson of pardon and forbearance is obvious. The victory over Goliath was great indeed, but victory over self is another sort of greatness.

XV. **Mark 3:13-19** For the compilation of this list of the
Gospel   Twelve Mark had at his disposal a series of
Friday   sources. He already knew the story of the
             call of five among them (Mk 1:16-20; 2:13-13),
and had as well a complete list of the twelve disciples. In his redaction we notice the anxiety to manipulate the different items of information. Levi for instance (Mt 2:14) did not appear on the list he had available, and he suggests that this Levi, the son of Alpheus, is the same as James the son of Alpheus (v. 18). Finding the name Peter in the list, whereas his other sources speak of Simon (Mk 1:16), he felt obliged to add to the ceremony of vocation one of imposing new names (vv. 16-17). This is historically improbable.

a) There is a solemnity (vv. 13-14) about this account of the vocation of the Twelve. Prior to this he had only given us the call of five among them. He thought it important to show that all had been called, and having no information concerning the other seven, he imagines the scene of a general *call* for the group.

b) The vocation theme nevertheless is fairly secondary with him, providing the general background. For him, Jesus has not merely called the Twelve, but *appointed* them (vv. 14-15) to be his companions, and *sent* (*apostelein*–apostles: v. 14) them to preach and expel demons. This phrase, an echo of Mark 6:7 (concerning the mission in Galilee) seems to have been inserted deliberately in this context by Mark himself, not without some awkwardness. We have the repetition, in verses 14 and 16, of the sentence "and he appointed the Twelve." Christ apparently did indeed appoint them, but it is doubtful that he did so with a general mandate of preaching in view. This note of an apostolic mandate we probably owe to the primitive community. Mark's use of it is apologetic. He wants to show that the missionaries of the resurrection are actually the eyewitnesses of what Jesus did.

c) However, if Christ actually appointed neither missionaries nor apostles, but merely the Twelve, what would be his purpose? An old tradition, which Mark does not use, had it that Jesus told the Twelve they would sit by his side at the judgment by the Son of man (Dn 7:22), and constitute the definitive people (Mt 19: 27-28). Just before Pentecost, the Eleven were concerned to raise their number to Twelve, as if they regarded this judgment as imminent (Ac 1:16-20). It needed the post-Pentecost events, when this expectation was not fulfilled, to bring home to the Twelve the missionary character of their calling.

At the time then when Christ "appointed" (the term has a very official, juridical flavor) the Twelve, he still saw his own mission in terms of the prerogatives given the Son of man by the Ancient of Days. For him the Twelve have value as a symbol. They are the living stones (as with the stones of Gilgal: Jos 4:1-6) of the new sanctuary, the patriarchs of the new people, the judges who will be entrusted with discernment of citizens for the future Kingdom.

The fondness of Scripture for the number twelve is to be explained by the fact that it suggests the priority of the divine initiative in choosing. The Jewish tribes were originally separate, and it was the exigencies of cult for the God they venerated that led them to live in twelve associated amphictyonies. This association took time to get properly shaped (cf. Jg 5:2-11), faith in the promises made to the twelve patriarchs (Jos 24; Gn 49, etc.) being the molding force. It was not the people who chose God; it was he who first associated himself with Israel. "Twelve" then was a term which appealed at once to national consciousness, and proved a reminder of God's transcendent liberty.

Christ, by retaining the symbolic number for his companions in founding the new people, follows this tradition which stresses the divine initiative. Belief in the apostolic church means affirmation of God's priority in choice and reconciliation (cf. 2 to 5:18-21).

The different gospel accounts of apostolic vocation really illustrate three successive stages in insight about vocation. The early accounts (for instance Mk 1:16-20 or Jn 1:35-51) show us a master of wisdom, a rabbi, making disciples (come, follow me), entering into a deep personal relationship with them, forging bonds of association, brotherhood and friendship. But Jesus is no more than a master of wisdom; he is followed because he speaks with authority.

A second series of accounts to which today's gospel belongs, places vocation on a different level. Jesus realizes that he is the Son of Man, entrusted with the reconstitution of a people of twelve tribes. He chooses and authoritatively "appoints" twelve persons for this task.

It is only after his death and resurrection that we have the third stage. Now Jesus appears as Lord of the universe and of humanity. The apostles, under the influence of people like Saint Paul, realize that they have a truly universal mission and special apostolic powers.

All vocations follow this pattern, corresponding to depth of insight about Jesus and his mystery. The first motives are often not the decisive ones. It takes long experience to come to the realization that the proper basis of any call to the ministry must be the death and lordship of Christ.

XVI. Hebrews
9:2-3, 11-14
1st reading
1st cycle
Saturday

This passage is taken from a chapter which should really be read as a whole. The topic is the superiority of Christ's priesthood to any other form of priesthood. Among the arguments brought forward is a contrast between the Jewish sacrifice of the great day of expiation and Christ's sacrifice. Our reading gives us the second part only of this comparison.

Judaism	Christianity
vv. 1-5 The terrestrial tabernacle and its appointments	vv. 11-12 A very different sanctuary
vv. 6-7 A rite reserved to the high priest, to be repeated each year	vv. 12-14 A priestly rite that is unique, including every Christian
vv. 8-10 Efficacy limited to purity	vv. 13-14 Sovereign efficacy

Conclusion (v. 15)
Leading to a new argument

Throughout this contrast the author is showing how the passage from the old to the new covenant goes by way of spiritualization and interiorization. The notions of exterior and interior sacrifice are fully blended in Christ.

a) In the old covenant the *tabernacle* was the place of encounter between God and his people; it circumscribed God's presence. Now there is another tabernacle, the human personality of Christ. John had already followed this same path of sublimation by making Christ's humanity the temple (Jn 2:13-22). "Passing through the tabernacle" then means passing into humanity, making his body the new tabernacle. The imagery stresses the salvific dimension of Christ's humanity. Through the tabernacle the Lord passes into the sanctuary, which is "localized in heaven," which is God himself.

b) Next the author turns to a comparison of the rites of *blood*. If in the old covenant these led to expiation, that could only be by God's decision, not any essential efficacy of blood (Lv 17). Its efficacy is limited to whatever God allows. Christ's blood on the other hand is of itself efficacious, because of the divine force it has, and because it is eternal (a term frequently on the author's lips: He 6:5; 9:14-15; 5:9; 13:20). It is not just infinite duration that matters, but the fact that divine power and energy are engaged. This is why the author can say that Christ has entered the sanctuary "once for all."

c) The efficacy is eternal, but it is also universal and interior. Christ's blood makes not only the priest but all the people capable of "serving the living God" (v. 14). It actually makes all the people a "priesthood of the living God" (Rm 15:1; Jn 4:24). It is an expression of the interiority of Christ, something that lasts forever, and touches the interiority in each person.

The new covenant means that there is a new place of God's presence and of assembly. It is no longer the tabernacle, but the humanity of Christ. It means that there is a new purifying blood. This cleanses even from sin and enables the new priest to offer a spiritual sacrifice.

d) In acomplishing his sacrifice Christ passed through the new tabernacle of his own *humanity* (v. 11; cf. Jn 1:14b the Greek term means: made his tabernacle). In the ascension then he entered the true sanctuary of God. He entered it once for all, without the necessity to have the value of his sacrifice reviewed each year. Whatever power ablutions had to purify the former high priest pales before the spiritual efficacy of Christ's own oblation (v. 14). Where the former high priest entered the sanctuary alone, the spiritual cult is open to all the people (v. 14).

The author is thus presenting Christ's life, from incarnation to ascension, as a sacrificial liturgy, the eschatological tension of the Church's spread. The old feast of Expiation is now brought to accomplishment in the new covenant, where the temple is no longer a temple of stone, but Christ's humanity. The partial efficacy of the former cult has been swept away in this new rite, because it is inspired by God's Spirit and establishes immediate presence before God and solidarity for humanity as a whole.

This change from the tabernacle to Christ's humanity is really a change from thing to person. Liturgy will be no longer a spectacle but a personal commission. Celebration will not be celebration unless each one is respected, aware that he is known, able to know others. Each one must find the ultimate area of his commission in the social and political structures of the secular world.

The trend nowadays towards celebration in small groups can become then the expression of a very ancient principle. Not that celebration in large groups is to be rejected. But these large celebrations should always be bringing together people whom small groups have already united. The small-group movement is not to be looked upon as a psychological symptom or a "malady of the time." It is the normal result of a personalist concept of worship and of the sacrifice of Christ as priest.

God gradually led his people from the original bloody sacrifices to the spiritual oblation inaugurated by Christ. We can discern different stages in this progress.

There was the "quantitative" stage when the Jews offered holocausts of the pagan kind, tithes and first fruits of their goods (Lv 2; Dt 26:1-11). The object was to sacrifice from riches. Riches and abundance had to be manifested in the offering, thus securing it greater importance (and consequently religious value, 2 Ch 7:1-7).

Yet offerings of this kind were made without really involving the offerer. The peasant would bring the victim to be disembowelled by the priest. Only the unwitting victim was involved. We are far from the ideal of sacrifice where priest and victim are one.

Prophetic reaction against this disregard for spiritual and moral attitudes was violent but unavailing (Am 5:21-27; Jr 7: 1-15; Is 1:11-17; Ho 6:5-6). It was not until the exile that insight began to dawn.

In the expiation sacrifice, one that came into vogue above all at this time (Nb 29:7-11), the quantitative emphasis began to yield in favor of sentiments of humility and poverty. The most clear trend in this direction is to be found above all in the psalms (Pss 39/40:7-40; 50/51:18-19; 49/50; Jl 1:13-14; Dn 3:37-43). Gradually people became aware that personal sentiment was the essence of sacrifice. Typical of the sacrifice of the future was to be that of the suffering Servant (Is 53:1-10).

Christ clearly fits into this final trend. The core of his sacrifice is his obedience and his poverty (He 2:17-18; Rm 5:19; He 10:5-7; Mt 27:38-60; Lk 18:9-14). His oblation was that of the suffering Servant (Jn 13:1-5; Lk 22:20; 23:37; Mt 26:3-5).

The sacrifice of the Christian believer too is patterned on that of Christ; a life of obedience and love, which derives liturgical meaning from its association with Christ (Rm 12:1-2; He 9:14).

XVII. 2 Samuel
1:1-4, 11-12
19:23-27
1st reading
2nd cycle
Saturday

Chapter 1 of the second book of Samuel is directly connected with chapter 30 of the first book. It combines two distinct traditions, of which the oldest only is followed in today's reading.

Its historicity seems doubtful. We find verses 2-4 with almost textual exactitude in 1 S 4:12-17. This suggests that we are dealing with a particular literary genre, an elegiac style designed to introduce David's lament for the defeat at Gelboe (vv. 17-27).

David's elegy is extremely old and the difficulties in translation and exegesis are numerous. It is in any case older than the context of 1 and 2 Samuel. Its author, unlike the redactor of 1 and 2 Samuel, takes no stand as yet concerning the death of Saul. He merely describes the death of a great hero, whereas the author of 1 and 2 Samuel attributes Saul's death to his infidelity towards God. He ought to have sacrificed himself for David's renown. For the author of the elegy on the other hand Saul continues to be God's anointed. He finds it scandalous that one chosen by God should encounter such a destiny. Many centuries would have to elapse before divine anointing and death in humiliation would be conjoined in Jesus Christ.

XVIII. Mark
3:20-21
Gospel
Saturday

This brief text deals so harshly with the family of Jesus that many exegetes have tried to identify in the phrase "his own" (v. 21) not his parents, but the apostles. Others have gone to the extreme of arguing that the remark about "being out of his mind" is addressed not to Jesus, but to the crowd. The truth however seems to be that Jesus' family did intervene (cf. Mk 3:31-35) and that they addressed the remark to Jesus.

Mark likes to show us Jesus in a context of crisis. He gives us this detail in view of the teaching later on at verses 31-35. Jesus is the center of conflicts and unbelief. Attachment to him means rising above fleshly considerations and depending on the spiritual insight that is forged by faith.

We do not yet have faith of this calibre. Jesus is in absolute *solitude*. Not only his avowed enemies (v. 22) but the crowds (Mk 6:1-5), and the disciples themselves (Mk 4:10-13; 6:49-52; 8:17-21; 14:26-32; 14:50) lack the faith necessary to penetrate the secret of his personality. His family too. When they come to "lay hands" on Jesus, it is to have him confined, and ensure that political reprisals directed against this apparent revolutionary will not extend to them.

The prophet is always alone. His mother, his sister or his spouse will generally find reasons for curtailing expression and hugging the security of home. That is why he often has to choose celibacy. He cannot find the helpmeet who will share his mission and dedicate herself wholly with him to its accomplishment. For one Mrs. Martin Luther King, how many families have stifled a prophetic message?

THIRD SUNDAY

A. THE WORD

I. Isaiah 9:1-4
1st reading
1st cycle

Overwhelmed in the invasion by Eastern armies, the Jews of the North were gradually deported to Babylon (around 732). There the darkness of captivity descended on them, sometimes literally, because frequently the eyes of captives were put out. In any case they were no better than people waiting for death, already dwelling in the "sombre land" (*sheol*). Against this gloomy background, Isaiah gives his oracle about the light of Emmanuel.

The immediate reference of the image of *light* is to the coming liberation of the provinces that had fallen into Assyrian hands, and is connected with the future king. Subsequent tradition referred it to the coming of the Messiah and saw it as a characteristic of the eschatological future (cf. Mt 4:12-17; Lk 1:76-79; Ep 5:8-14). Light was an essential dimension of happiness. It indicates then simultaneously a number of concepts; salvation, deliverance from oppression and from sin, participation in the "glory" of the Messiah.

The New Testament affirmations about Christ being the light of the nations and of those who sit in darkness stress the real essence of the liberation and salvation that Christ brought. He is a light because of the joy and deliverance he procured, because of the magnificence of the divine gift he gave. It was exactly as when those in darkness or in blindness behold the light.

But he is also the light because he offers the world a new ethic. Often, in Scripture, the light-darkness contrast is used to describe the opposition between good works (those of the law: Ps 118/119:105) and sin. Light is opposed to darkness just as the Kingdom is to paganism. Passage from darkness only becomes possible for a man, because a salvation is proposed to him which obliges him to "walk in the light," instead of wandering aimlessly in the darkness of his sin.

II. Jonah   Here is described the preaching of Jonah at
  3:1-5, 10   Nineveh, and the unexpected conversion of
  1st reading   the population of this immense city. The au-
  2nd cycle   thor, of the 5th century, has derived from
                        Jeremiah the lesson that Yahweh can "repent"
of his anger, if men are converted (Jon 3:9; cf. Jr 18:7-8; 26:3-19). We actually find the vocabulary of Jeremiah throughout the account: "from the greatest to the least" (v. 5; cf. Jr 5:4-5; 6:13; 44:12), "burning wrath" (v. 9; cf. Jr 4:8, 26; 12:13; 25:37-38), "men and beasts" (vv. 7-8; cf. Jr 21:6; 27:54; 36:29).

Jonah did not go to Nineveh as a missionary, but rather to execute God's inexorable judgment on the nations. The Jewish view was that this judgment would bring justice to Israel while punishing and destroying the Gentiles. God might conceivably pardon Israel instead of punishing her (Jr 18:7-8), but such a procedure for the Gentiles was unlikely.

Our author is the first to face himself from such narrow views. As he sees it, a Gentile king may be converted just as well as a Jewish one (Jon 3:5-8), even more so indeed than some kings of Israel and Judah who refused to acknowledge their mistakes (Jr 36:24). The account actually reproves the Jews for their slowness to be converted (cf. Jr 7:25-26; 25:4; 26:5), whereas the Gentiles were converted at the first summons, without receiving any particular sign.*

He is then concerned to show that the maledictions of the prophets against the nations are no more inexorable than the

---

* See the doctrinal theme: *evangelization*, p. 94.

oracles against the Jews. All men, whoever they are, are called to repentance, and God's pardon is open to all. Later, Christ will make this doctrine his too (Mt 12:38-42).

The reading stresses the psychological conditions necessary for encountering the other, for evangelization that is.

Jonah, the countryman, goes off, very sure of himself, to encounter the city folk. He is convinced that he will control the relationship between Yahweh and Nineveh. He possesses the truth about God and can explain everything as a result, as if God could be limited to the ideas that are formed about him. So sure is he of his theology that he thinks he knows in advance what the reaction of his audience will be. He will be able to control this and direct it in the required direction. Hence his chagrin at the unexpected attitude of the Ninevites. Deep down Jonah does not want either a free God or an independent audience. He has reduced everything to an elaborate theory, and ignores the person.

His attitude has a good deal in common with that of certain contemporaries; colonists who cannot understand why Negroes demand independence, factory owners who are astonished when the workers spurn their paternalism, ecclesiastics who suddenly discover that the world resents their dogmatism.

Jonah (and his modern counterparts) could have made a good missionary had he approached Nineveh in the belief that he would find God there—God precisely because Totally-Other, not the familiar God he wanted to preach, according to his own narrow and inadequate concept. He would not then have succumbed to the temptation of judging and condemning those who did not think like himself, or deciding that the best followers of God were those who thought like himself.

III. Nehemiah
8:1-4a, 5-6,
8-10
1st reading
3rd cycle

A description of the important Feast of Tabernacles in 444 (?). The people are convened to an assembly during which the Law will be read and interpreted and the convenant with God sealed anew to inaugurate Judaism properly speaking.

a) *Tabernacles* was the most popular among Jewish festivals, the end of the season providing the occasion for great rejoicing (v. 10). Biblical writers however spiritualized these manifestations, and the assembly described in today's passage could be taken as the first result of this movement towards purification. We see another such, emanating from priestly circles, in the same century (cf. Lv 23:26-43).

b) The movement consisted in a transformation of the feast so that it became an *assembly* of renewal of the covenant according to the prescriptions of Deuteronomy 31:9-13. The ritual (proclamation of the Law, acclamations of *Amen* by the people) fulfilled to the letter the requirements of Deuteronomy 27:9-26 (v. 6). The Word was of paramount importance. It convoked the people, was read during the seven days, translated and commented on. The organizers were concerned that it be understood (v. 8), and that the faithful should adhere to it (v. 6). Thus the Word, as in Christianity (1 Co 12:27-28), was the origin of assembly. It brought together the first assembly in the desert and would continue to assemble the faithful until the day it would be made flesh for the unification of all men.[*]

IV. 1 Corinthians
1:10-13, 17
2nd reading
1st cycle

This letter is the reply by the apostle to the Corinthians on questions posed by leading members of the community who had come to consult him (1 Co 16:15-16). First of all, however, he gives a little space to the problem of factions in the community.

[*] See the doctrinal theme: *the word*, p. 88.

a) The *factions* in the Corinth Church have been set up on the basis of allegiance to Paul, Apollos, Peter and . . . Christ. Doubtless it is a matter of members who knew personally one or other of the four, followed his teaching, and were even baptized by him perhaps. Numerous natives of Palestine were in fact to be found in Corinth, who could have encountered Jesus or Peter. All would tend to cling to some emphases that were traceable to their father in the faith. Some (disciples of Peter) would be judaizing, others (disciples of Jesus?) would evince a free, prophetic spirit; others the missionary, ascetic emphasis of Paul; others still the philosophic, dialectical tendency of Apollos.

Paul very quickly disposes of the faction set up in his own name by affirming that he has no pretensions in that way. He has baptized no one (vv. 14-16). The party of Apollos he deals with by his analysis of Christian wisdom (1 Co 1:17-4:21). Chapters 5 and 6 would concern the libertarian disciples of Jesus; while the judaizers are reserved for the second letter, by which time doubtless their influence had increased. But this of course is merely hypothetical reconstruction.

In order to nip the whole matter in the bud, Paul singles out the Master of his ministry. Only one was crucified and merited the title of Master and Savior. He alone instituted baptism in his name (v. 13). The disciple is merely a messenger and missionary of the cross (v. 17).

Factions come about if people place the minister before the master, the rite before the message. Paul is careful to replace the minister in his proper role of simple agent (1 Co 4:1-5), and the rite of baptism in its proper relationship with the evangelizing Word.

b) He actually shows some antiritualist bias, being more interested in the *ministry of evangelization* than the liturgical one (v. 17; cf. further Rm 15:15-16).* He lived of course at a time when rite was unduly prominent in all religions. We have the emphasis on Jewish rites in Israel, the controversy about different

---

* See the doctrinal theme: *evangelization*, p. 94.

baptisms as between disciples of the Baptist and Christians, the "mysteries" of the Greek religions, etc. He did not wish Christianity to become distinguished as a purveyor of new rites, and strove to make it above all a religion of the Word and of Mission. Not that he wanted a religion without rite. He merely insists that at the moment rite is subordinate to Word and Mission. Its efficacy is derived solely from the missionary and sacramental Word that accompanies it and the faith with which that Word is greeted.

Our worries today about the relationship between liturgy and mission on the one hand, and sacrament and faith on the other, find at once their origin and their solution in these verses. If pastoral authorities in the Church had abided strictly by the principles to govern liturgical reform and would have ensured a central place for faith in the celebration of the sacraments.

Let us see to it that today's Eucharist, by the Word proclaimed and its accomplishment among the faithful, shows fidelity to the principles.

V. 1 Corinthians
7:29-31
2nd reading
2nd cycle

This short passage is part of a long argument designed to show that, since Jesus Christ, marriage while still a good thing is not an absolute. The relationship of the sexes cannot be completely exhausted by conjugal union; the encounter of each member with the Lord is also crucial.

a) The principal argument by which Paul relativizes, so to speak, marriage as an institution depends on the new concept of *time* which is brought about by the incarnation. The "time is short" (v. 29); the "shape of this world passes" (v. 31).

In the Old Testament marriage was the ideal institution, whereby generation after generation man was enabled to continue the work of creation until it culminated in the re-creation of the last times. But now the last times have arrived. Since Christ, God is present with men and in the universe. He will gradually transform them to the point of divinization. Marriage continues to be the ideal way for man to collaborate in creation and history, because it is a sign of God's presence until the end. But, for Saint Paul, procreation is not the only means to signalize the time of waiting. Because God is now present in every man and every thing through the mediation of his Son, virginity also in a special way becomes a sign for man of eternity.

b) At this time every event in life, joyous or sad, loses a dimension of its gravity. During the time when *history* had not yet attained its end, each event had importance because it might advance or retard the course of history. Now that the key to history has been found in Jesus Christ, the event has become relative. The Christian, even while he lives it, should be in a particular way detached (vv. 30-31).

Ever since the man-God entered human history, history has reached its term. All events and institutions no longer look to the final times for fulfillment. They become a sign of God's eschatological presence. Having attained their end, they become relative. Man can adopt towards them an attitude of detachment, if he derives this liberty from the divine presence within him. There is no question of rejecting the institution or abstaining from the event. Paul is no stoic. It is merely a matter of lucid assessment of their meaning, a realization that now there is a new way.

VI. 1 Corinthians 12:12-30 *2nd reading* *3rd cycle* Here Paul is concluding his analogy about diversities of function in the body. The purpose is to show that local churches have particular functions that should be harmonized with others, and that there should be mutual respect.

a) The Pauline concept of ecclesial functions has several note-worthy characteristics. He is particularly concerned in the first place about the primacy of charisms or functions of the *Word*. Whether it is in 1 Corinthians 12:8-10; 12:27-30; Romans 12:6-8 or Ephesians 4:11, the three principal functions, with very slight variations, are those of apostles who bring the missionary word to the world; of prophets who proclaim the word in liturgy; and of teachers who transmit it in catechesis.*

These charisms of the Word take precedence of another category composed above all of extraordinary gifts: exorcism, healing and glossolaly (so popular among the Corinthians), and a third category concerned with the organization of charity (mercy, help) and liturgy (presidency) in the community. The most note-worthy feature of all this is that liturgy is subordinated to the missionary value, and rite to the Word (cf. 1 Co 1:10-17).

b) Paul does not really distinguish between *stable functions* and *extraordinary charisms*. He is doubtless anxious to reassure the possessors of the latter that they are an integral part of Christ's Body. The same single Spirit inspires all members of the Body whatever their functions or charisms are. Any opposition or separation between the Spirit's two modes of action would be a rending of Christ's Body.

Many ecclesial problems and tensions could be resolved, if each one would remember that there is a common source for all gifts and functions.

VII. Matthew
4:12-23
Gospel
1st cycle

These verses tell us of Christ's first ministry in Galilee. The ministry and message of John the Baptist proved an occasion for Jesus of perceiving the will of the Father. He underwent the baptism (Mt 3:13-17), because he realized that passage through the Baptist's school was essential to his

---

* See the doctrinal theme: *the word*, p. 88.

ministry. He would become an itinerant rabbi, taking up the torch that John had laid down (v. 12; cf. Mk 1:14). But he would leave Judaea and the Jordan valley dear to John, and go to the lost sheep of Galilee and the North, even so far as the Gentiles of Syria (v. 23; a detail proper to Matthew).

a) Thus, at the very dawn of his missionary awareness, Christ sees himself as a rabbi preacher, who follows the Baptist's message faithfully (cf. v. 17, with Mt 3:2), but brings it, if not actually to the Gentiles, at least to those Jews who were so involved with the *darkness of paganism* that they were no longer more than Israelites in name.

Matthew is particularly aware of this universalist note, and feels the need to justify it. His contemporaries believed that the Kingdom would be proclaimed only to those Jews who remained pure. For this reason he introduces verses 13-16 and the quotation from Isaiah 8:23-9:1. The latter however he modifies by the introduction of the word "seated" in darkness (v. 16, badly rendered in several versions). He wants to stress still more the fact that the Syno-Palestinian territories are really corroded by paganism. The chief thing is that by affirming access for the Gentiles to the light, he gives a new meaning to a text that had contemplated only the Jewish exiles among the Gentiles.

Thus Christ's fidelity to the Baptist's message is at the same time accompanied by considerable independence. He does not want to gather round him just the "pure" that John assembles, or docile disciples. His message will be extended to the whole world. This is why he does not hesitate to break with John, not with regard to his basic message, but with regard to his manner of preaching. He decides to leave Judaea. He does not impose any baptismal rite, and becomes itinerant in order to be sure of encountering all men in every situation.

b) The summons to *conversion* (v. 17; cf. Mk 1:15 below) is certainly part of primitive kerygma, but its actual proclaimer seems uncertain. Either Jesus repeats here what he has heard from the Baptist, or the primitive community, who heard this summons for the first time on the lips of Peter (Ac 2:38), wanted to give it some sort of authenticity afterwards by putting it on the lips of both the Baptist and Jesus? It seems certain in the first place that the Baptist's preaching called for conversion but did not make the proximate advent of the Kingdom an issue. Mark 1:4 and Luke 3:2 do not in fact refer to this advent; it is clearly Matthew who introduced the connection in the Baptist's preaching (Mt 3:2). The concept of advent belongs to the primitive catechesis of Jesus. We find it in Matthew 4:17 and Mark 1:15 (probably more primitive), and repentance is linked not only with the advent, but with the accomplishment of time. Peter's Pentecost address is actually much closer to the Baptist's catechesis than to that of Jesus (cf. for instance the connection between repentance, baptism and remission of sin, but the absence of any reference to the advent of the Kingdom or the accomplishment of the last times).

The conclusion seems to be that the Baptist is responsible for the idea of conversion and its connection with baptism (Mk 1:4). Peter follows this fully. Jesus retained the Baptist's notion of conversion, but he immediately associated it with the proclamation of the good name of the Kingdom, softening by the good news the severity of John (Mk 1:15). At a later stage Matthew associated all the catecheses, actually attributing to the Baptist something that was peculiar to Jesus' preaching (Mt 3:2 and 4:17).

Christ, following God's universalist design, broke with the Jewish communities of "pure" and "observers." Do not our parishes and eucharistic assemblies likewise have to strip themselves in order to become open to people who do not feel they are concerned by the Christian message?

VIII. **Mark**   The first two verses of this passage need not
1:14-20   detain us here (vv. 14-15). They are simply
Gospel   a resume of the Gospel of the first cycle (Mt
2nd cycle   4:12-17), where Jesus is seen to be at once
a follower of the Baptist and an innovator.
Without waiting for the crowds to come to him, he becomes an
itinerant rabbi. Verses 16-22, the second part of the account, will
be the subject of our commentary.

a) Matthew (4:18-22) and Mark (1:16-20) correspond in their
accounts of the calling of the first disciples, whereas Luke brings
in the episode of the miraculous draft of fishes (Lk 5:1-11). The
first two evangelists are more interested in the quality of the
people called by Jesus. Luke is concerned with their apostolic
function and its eschatological meaning.

We should note first of all the human aspect of the disciples'
vocation. They are bothers or fellow countrymen, joined profes-
sionally by common pursuits (cf. Lk 5:1-11), and natives of
Jesus' own territory. Vocation is not exclusively supernatural; it
follows the natural plane.

And yet it is also the master's initiative. These fishermen are
to be the messengers of God's judgment (Jr 16:16; cf. Am 4:2;
Ha 1:14-15). The call of Jesus is peremptory, as if to indicate
power, and the disciples respond without any delay. So imminent
is the Kingdom that any delay would be fatal.

The account has been so disposed by the evangelists as to
indicate a sudden summons that receives an immediate response
from the disciples. In fact they hesitated considerably and did
not definitely abandon their occupations until after the resurrection (Jn 21:1). But in telescoping the events into a single episode
the evangelists stress the essential point. This is the capacity of
God's call, once it is recognized, to mobilize all human energies,
and the authority with which Jesus actually chose his followers.

b) Jesus' procedure of calling his disciples to *follow* him (v.
17) is characteristic of the new style the young rabbi proposes

to adopt. He does not gather them around him after the manner of contemporary rabbis and leaders of schools. He is not going to be a professor of thought seated on his chair with fervent listeners at his feet. He will be an itinerant rabbi constantly journeying towards the poor and errant. He will demand from his disciples not so much willing ears or enthusiastic gaze, but the willingness to travel, the courage to encounter the other at the furthest limit. Evangelization is not a matter of closed circles, gathered in a common framework of thought around a common master. It is a going out of oneself to encounter the other.

c) The final portion of the passage (vv. 21-22) describes the method adopted by the young rabbi of making his message known. He enters the synagogue and uses the homily on the second reading of the liturgy (cf. Lk 4:16-37) to communicate his ideas. Of this incursion into preaching Mark stresses above all the impression given of *authority* (cf. Mt 7:29; Mk 1:27). At the beginnings of the ministry this authority is not yet that of the "Lord," to which Paul himself alludes with such respect (1 Co 7:10). Nor is it even that of the Son of Man, who realizes that he is the *vice-gerens* of God, as in Mark 2:3-12. It is that of a rabbi who, instead of referring to legal texts and school traditions like the Scribes, depends directly on his judgment and conscience.

It is this reliance on himself in his teaching which makes the fidelity of Jesus something deeper. It is the fidelity of the Son of Man to him who sent him, the fidelity of the Son of God to his own Father. It is the fidelity of the Word to the Thought which transmitted it. The apostles chosen to carry this message to the world will be obliged to a like fidelity, because they are bearers of a Word which is not initiated by them.* Fidelity will be the basis of their authority. The very derivation of the word authority suggests indeed something "creative" (*auctor, augere*). It indicates a message that does not necessarily consist in saying what

* See the doctrinal theme: *the word*, p. 88.

should be done, still less what should not be done. The message should be an invitation to creativity and responsibility. Ecclesial "authority," so far from being focused on predetermined texts, should be eliciting new ethical insights from Christians, and leading them to the moral standard the world expects from them. The problems posed by modern life should be the area contemplated; revolution of the poor, non-violence, peace, etc.

IX. **Luke 1:1-4** Where Matthew shows us Christ as an itin-
 4:14-21 erant rabbi (Mt 4:12-17), Luke is more li-
 Gospel turgically minded (Lk 1:5-23; 24:50-53) and
 3rd cycle has his ministry begin with a Sabbath liturgy
 in the synagogue.

This liturgy was based on two readings. The first, from the Law (Pentateuch), was read and commented on by a doctor of the Law. The second, more recent in institution, was taken from the prophets, and could be read and commented on by anyone over thirty years of age. Jesus, who was thirty, claimed this right. His first public discourse is a liturgical homily.

a) Luke does not give us the actual discourse, but summarizes its essential trend in one verse: "Today, it is accomplished" (v. 21). This really gives us all the *essentials of a homily*. The liturgy of the Word is not simple catechism lesson. Nor is it an affirmation of the eschatological hope of the prophets. It is a proclamation of the accomplishment of the Father's plan in the here and now of assembly. There should be no dwelling on the past, be it golden age or age of decline. There should be no gazing towards a miraculous future. The present should be lived as the acceptable time of the Lord's coming.

This homiletic style of Jesus was followed by the apostles in their turn (cf. Ac 13:14, 42; 16:13-17; 17:1-3; 18:4). To that extent the Christian liturgy of the Word stems from that of the synagogue, but it supersedes it in the "celebration of the here and now." We should never cease to ask ourselves the question whether our sermons of today follow the pattern set by Christ, or that of the doctors of the Law.*

b) Jesus (or Luke) seems to have deliberately ended the reading at the point where Isaiah 61 proclaims a "year of grace." The verse which proclaims judgment of the nations on the other hand " and a day of vengence for God" (Is 61:2) is passed over in silence, in order to emphasize exclusively the grace of God. These words of *grace* create astonishment in the listeners (v. 22) and bring about the incidents narrated in verses 25-30. Furthermore, to reinforce the fact that his mission is exclusively one of grace, not of condemnation, Jesus (or Luke) inserts in this context a verse drawn from Isaiah 58:6, about freedom offered to prisoners.

Thus straightway Jesus defines his mission as a proclamation of God's gratuitous love towards every man. Such an affirmation inevitably gave scandal to Jews. They were concentrated on the eschatological future in an intensity of hatred for the Gentiles.

The affirmation that the Word of God is accomplished here and now (the proper function of the homily) is not just to assert that an old prophecy has been fulfilled, or an inspired text suddenly clarified. The Word that is being accomplished is not that of prophets or theologians but that deeper Word of God which christifies the human even in its actual state. The affirmation is that in the here and now humanity is being reconciled to God in Jesus Christ. Our homilies ought not to be concentrated on applying inspired or prophetic texts to the actual experiences of the assembly. They should rather aim to show, as the gospel does for the Christ-event, how actual events in Christian and human experience reveal God's plan. This is to say that scriptural sources and biblical language should be augmented with the language of sociology and psychology. We have to try to isolate the work of Jesus Christ from its socio-cultural context, as described in New

* See the doctrinal theme: *the word,* p. 88.

Testament language. To set it firmly in the contemporary milieu, we must present it as an answer to the actual quest of our actual audiences.

The homily should always show us the today of man encountering the today of God. Then it will really be the service of God's Word.

B. DOCTRINE

1. Theme of the Word

Throughout Church history all efforts at *"aggiornamento"* have invariably been conceived to restore the Word. That is still the case today, as the results of Vactican II clearly indicate. The liturgical reform fostered by the Council had as object a restoration to its rightful place, which had been neglected, of the celebration of the Word. The contemporary biblical movement too is designed to give proper emphasis to the Word of God in Holy Writ.

The time in which we live has very special characteristics. At the very moment in which we are rediscovering the riches of the Word, a strong tide is setting in the opposite direction, which tends to make it remote. The faithful find that the cleavage between their everyday lives and the Word they hear in eucharistic assembly is widening. The message that should challenge and nourish their conscience seems stilted, bound up with another time and another culture. People who belong to a technological age find themselves at odds with a Word that has always been regarded as a "given," something exterior, something transmitted from age to age. It is respected and revered, true, but its relation to the actual exigencies of living presents difficulties. Deprived of existential actuality, the Word itself runs the risk of being devalued.

The gravity of this situation can hardly be over-stressed. If the Word is to lose its power of challenge, initiation to the very mystery of Christ is compromised. It is time we examined our conscience. Is the Word itself in process of devaluation, or merely the tradition associated with it? It is highly important that we find the proper answer to this question. There can be no doubt that our theology of the Word is inadequate. We need a larger perspective, something more profound than what we have regularly tended to be content with. Let us examine the matter.

The word in Israel, manifested in the event

Language is certainly a major achievement of man. He uses it to develop the whole tenor of his existence, with all the projects this entails. It is something collective, something that binds the group and gives direction to its history. Each individual is involved in a common task and a heritage is accumulated. Such importance in the anthropological domain readily explains, the primacy of language in the history of religious experience.

In ancient religions men tended to give sacral value to the ancestral message that was transmitted from age to age. Here could be found the ultimate meaning of existence. This feeling became more intense when the word of heritage was woven into the rites that brought men into touch with the world of the gods. The heritage would be considered a divine blessing, and thus a mysterious reality but it was nevertheless a product of human endeavor. The "secrets" it contained, which would be revealed in an initiation, were such as a man needed to know in order to have all possible security in the cosmic, social, and eventually moral, orders.

With the regime of faith came a considerable reevaluation at the religious level. Jewish man was more realistic than pagan man. He was ready to accept the event, with all its dimensions of unpredictability for man individually and collectively, as the point *par excellence* of encounter with God. And God was seen as the living God, who intervenes as he wishes in the life of his people. This being so, the saving word, the word which contains the secret of human destiny and can benefit man, must obviously belong to God. Only the gratuitous intervention of Yahweh in the event itself is capable of revealing his word to Israel. This is a saving word which demands a capital: it is the Word of the living God. There could be no question then of reducing his Word to ready-made human language. Whenever the prophets seek to bring its message to the people, they use disconcerting and disturbing language designed to shock the nation out of illusory securities, particularly those of cult. They had to be steered along the unpre-

dictable road of fidelity to the covenant. A day would come when
the efficacious Word of Yahweh would kindle the salvation so
much yearned for.

Jesus, Messiah, Word of the living God

The common Jewish view was that the Messiah's intervention
on the day of Yahweh would mark the end of earthly trails. With
the coming of a new heaven and a new earth, a paradisal security
would be finally regained, more marvelous than the first. The
unpredictable, suffering, death would disappear. The "divine
order" of salvation and happiness would enter in, and on this
day the sovereign efficacy of the Word of God would become apparent.

But when Jesus came what happened was very different. So far
from being reassuring, his word seemed more disconcerting and
peremptory than ever. Instead of turning man from the human
state, it laid all emphasis on fidelity to this state. Its demands
were vast. It summoned man to the greatest of all insecurities, encounter with the other regardless of all barriers, all privilege.
It demanded action, and involved one in the precarious enterprise of universal brotherhood. Sinful man never welcomes such
language, because love of this calibre requires total self-renunciation. Jesus himself provided an example of the fidelity he required.
He was obedient unto death of the cross for love of all mankind.

By the way he spoke and by the way he acted this Messiah
showed that he himself was the incarnate Word of the living
God, and thus he showed the true character of divine intervention.
In his case, in order to inaugurate the Kingdom of the New
Covenant as Messiah, it was sufficient that he accept totally the
human state. His human fidelity had a dimension that radically
transcended all human capacity. In him God himself had come
to dwell among men. The Word of the Living God is seen to be
actually a Person. Men reach through him that filial state which
fulfills beyond all expectation their yearning for the absolute.
This does not detach them from the creatural condition. On the

contrary; the children of the Father are urged to follow the footsteps of the Liberator and embrace this actively.

In the mystery of Christ God's Word is revealed once for all. It is a mystery that is always actual, the incarnation that is of God's initiative throughout history to bring about human salvation. To receive this Word, and be molded by it, all that is necessary is to follow Jesus. It is not a comfortable way because it is that of the paschal mystery. But it is the only way that leads man towards his proper dignity.

The Word actualized in the people of God

After Pentecost the primitive community was thoroughly convinced that it owed its being and its action to the intervention among his own of the Risen Lord. Day after day, in the pattern of events, the Spirit reminded them of the genuine meaning of Jesus' words. The Gentiles, who began to enter the Church in greater and greater numbers, obliterated the remaining vestiges of Jewish particularism in the Christian community. At this time the nature of the divine salvific initiative in Jesus Christ came to be understood in full, as well as the demands of brotherly love without limits. The decisive event of human history was accomplished. The principal actor is the Risen Lord. Revelation is at an end.

"At every time and in every place" the people of God must go on repeating this experience so that salvation history can follow its course. These are the conditions for success in the human pilgrimage. Success cannot be attained unless Christ comes to be recognized by all peoples as the only way. They too must have the experience of the early Christian community, and realize that it is only by being freed from sin, as children of the Father, that they can undertake human responsibilities here below. The encounter with the other to which all are summoned is an essentially religious experience.

Throughout Christian history however, the people of God have been bedeviled by the tendency to degradation. It has happened in the past, and it will happen again, that the Church became pre-occupied with herself. She became so powerful that mission was only seen in terms of annexation and there was no genuine openness to non-Christians. At such times the Word ceases to be a living Word and is petrified in formulas. The essence of the mystery of Christ is obscured. The gospel ceases to appeal and is systematized in precise moral rules. The people of God begin to consider themselves the sole proprietors of Truth. Under these conditions the Word cannot be operative.

We must hope that among the people of God prophets will arise who will bring about the sort of *"aggiornamento"* that will make us see the "signs of the times." We want the sort of Church that can recognize and overcome all particularizing tendencies. Then the Word will come alive again. The gospel will recover its appeal.

The Word in the daily experience of modern men

It must be admitted that today we are undergoing a profound crisis in language, especially religious language. It is as if the linguistic heritage of humanity over the ages has ceased to be adequate and fails to interpret the existential situation. Why is this?

Modern man of course is particularly focused on the realization of his destiny. He feels himself responsible for this, and he feels that he has the resources. Like his predecessor he needs language, but a language that is all-embracing. The language of his predecessor seems too rigid, too fixed, too sacral, too alienating sometimes, to interpret new dimensions of living. He needs one that expresses his grandeur and his mastery of the universe. It must be a language of science and technology.

Such is the attitude. But is it actually true that man's destiny now is bounded by science and technology? Very obviously, no. The destiny is what it always was, the adventure of liberty. Throughout all the multiple human projects, what is involved is the ultimate dimension of human existence, the freedom to choose, the option for spiritual liberty, For this too a language is required, the language of metaphysics, of morals, eventually of religion. But the linguistic heritage in this domain too needs to be up-dated. It must be submitted to the scrutiny of scientific knowledge and it must be related to the actual experience of men living today.

Do we then have any place today for the Word of the living God? Yes of course, perhaps more place than ever. As we have seen, the manifestation of the mystery of Christ, his intervention in the secular world, is essentially linked with the lived experience of his people and their struggle for universal peace. The language of faith in Christ is the language of lived experience. We have everything to gain from contact with the language of human science; it is the language which interprets the truth of man as he is.

The Word we proclaim and the Word we sense

Throughout all the centuries of Christian history, the theology of the Word has placed emphasis, almost exclusively, on proclamation. The Word has been made the object of preaching; it was a "given" that had to be explicitly transmitted. The lives lived by Christians were simply the application of the proclaimed Word. They did not "speak"; they were simply the terrain where the Word was put in practice. God spoke where the Word was proclaimed, where the Scriptures were read and commented on, where the priest gave the Good News to unbelievers. The reason for all this was an ecclesiology which tended to make the Church exclusively an ecclesial institution.

For some time now there has been a change, which is likely to influence for the better the theology of the Word and restore it to its biblical origins. We are discovering once more that it is in the event that the God of faith speaks, the lived experience of his people as they engage in the human adventure. His Word cannot be dissociated from the response of faith. We recognize it in the ever actual intervention of the Risen Lord in the actual

world, in the witness to this borne by Christian lives. The holy
Books themselves are holy, because they record that unique experience of faith which came with the intervention by Jesus
of Nazareth.

The rediscovery was necessary. The actual life of modern man
is no longer the application of a Word already elaborated; it is
the nation of the collective future. The practice of faith in the
future can no longer be the application merely of the proclaimed
Word; it must be a concrete vision of the Word. In these circumstances the Word burgeons and can be sensed. The Word that is
sensed should be explicitly preached, nourished as it is by the
lived experience of the people of God now. In such proclamation
of a Word that is felt to be relevant, the actuality of Christ in
our world will become manifest.

2. Theme of Evangelization

As its etymology indicates, evangelization means proclaiming
the Good News. It is probable that Christians in our day realize
rather better than their predecessors how membership of the
people of God entails the obligation to participate actively in
universal mission. For some decades now, in various ways emphasis has been laid on the apostolic dimension of the ordinary
Christian vocation, and this has borne fruit. Paradoxically though,
Christians now seem less sure than their predecessors about what
should actually be done in order to accomplish universal mission.
The problems posed seem overwhelming to some. And indeed
we might as well face facts. Whatever methods we employ, the
traditional ones are certainly not going to pay dividends in
the future.

How then are we to proceed? Realizing that with people nowadays actions speak stronger than words, many Christians take
the view that the greatest means of witness is the life actually
lived in the secular environment. Men will hear the call of Christ
simply by observing the lives of Christians. Is this not quibbling

though, in a sense? What actually happens in bearing witness to Christ? In a world where all men, more conscious than ever of the need to shape their own destiny, seek to build the future, Christians find themselves involved. They bring their own vision of man and they try to model their lives on the evangelic ideal. In this sense they certainly do bear witness to Christian humanism. But can we describe this as witness to the Risen Lord? If so, it would need to be demonstrated, because it is by no means evident. And Christians must ask themselves whether in the tenor of secular life they apply any special criteria, do acts that are specifically Christian. If not, how does their faith make any concrete intervention, how does their witness express the Risen Lord?

These are obviously important issues that require consideration. Vagueness about them leads to carelessness, and the faith itself might become impaired. And if the salt loses its savor, how can the people of God be the leaven in the mass, the vital force of the new world?

The good news in Israel

All human communities will tend to give some sort of expression to the dynamism that animates them, their deepest principle of living, their religious quest. The salvation they envisage, however, is not generally presented as a Good News. Pagan man did not see salvation in the event. Rather did it belong to the fixed and established sacral order, an immutable reality towards which one had to discover avenues. Thus there would be no preaching of Good News by pagan religions. They would share their own religious experiences with others; and if they became convinced that their path was the exemplary one for all men they would indeed send representatives to the ends of the earth.

In Israel the situation was otherwise. Salvation was here seen as an event to be anticipated, a Good News that would break on the day of Yahweh. The regime of faith brought Israel to recognize Yahweh as the Totally-Other God, who intervenes as he wishes in the history of his people. Salvation is the object of a promise, and only the personal initiative of Yahweh is capable of establishing this covenant. The promise was made to Israel, and the Good News is reserved to Israel. Salvation belongs to her. The Gentile nations will not be excluded from it but their association will depend on Israel. On seeing the marvels wrought by Yahweh for his people, they will begin to wend their way towards Jerusalem.

Thus Israel's concept remained essentially centripetal; the only religious quest that counted was her own. There was no question then of evangelizing Gentiles, or pointing out to them that Israel's Good News was what they themselves, all unknowing, were awaiting. The history of the Diaspora demonstrates this. Communities in Mesopotamia and all over the Mediterranean did indeed make proselytes, and the spiritual influence of the synagogue everywhere was considerable. But the overall purpose invariably was to swell the ranks of the chosen people. It was taken for granted that in order to share the hope of Good News reserved to Israel, one had to become part of Israel's religious quest.

The good news destined for all: salvation in Jesus Christ

When Jesus intervened in history he proclaimed the advent of the Kingdom that his people had awaited. He put himself forward not as the founder of a new religion, but as Israel's Messiah. He came to accomplish the Law and the Prophets, to bring to its culmination the religious pilgrimage of the Jews. From one aspect everything was taking place according to Israel's expectation. The Kingdom he was inaugurating in his person he proclaimed to the Jews. It was for them he came. Their salvation was his great preoccupation.

Yet, in fact, of course the accomplishment took place in a totally unexpected way. The realism of faith was carried to its utmost pitch; the Messiah was inviting his fellow Jews to become the neighbors of all men. The event *par excellence* for him was the encounter with the other, the other in all his otherness, the always possible enemy. The accomplishment of the Law and the

Prophets is seen to be brotherly love without limits, a love that is not an accepter of person, that demands radical self-renunciation even to the surrender of life. Only his disciples would be capable of such a love, by the renunciation of sin and by receiving from him the great gift of the filial state. The Good News is this: that God's initiative in Jesus Christ enables men to enter his own Family, and all children of the Father must display universal love.

It is a Good News that Jesus proclaimed to the Jews, yes; but that is destined for all men. Israel's Messiah is the Savior of the world. The Father's Kingdom will tolerate no particularism, and acknowledge no privilege. All people are bidden to it. They will be granted entry insofar as they are ready to recognize in Christ the one road to fulfillment, and accept from the unique Liberator the grace to overcome their own brand of particularism. Being as he was the Messiah of Israel, at the beginning Jesus thought his own nation would accept its mission of communicating to all nations the Good News that was their destiny. The Jewish nation rejected this, finding a Good News that ignored their privileges a scandal. At this very time, the Jesus indicated by his conversations with some Gentiles, the nations were in a state of readiness to receive the Word of salvation. Very soon the cross would make clear the essential newness of the gospel.

The today of salvation revealed in the Church

It took the disciples some time to understand the significance of the Messiah's death on the cross, and longer still to perceive the requirements of evangelization. The first decisive stage was reached at Pentecost, the second with the foundation of the Antioch Church.

The death on the cross seemed to spell failure, but it became the very touchstone of accomplishment for Israel's hope. A re-reading of the Scriptures demonstrated that the only right interpretation was the one which took account of the cross. This was the gesture *par excellence* which manifested the double love, for God and for men. It was by presenting himself as Savior of the world that Israel's Messiah fulfilled his mission. He was not at the right hand of the Father, and simultaneously intervening constantly in the world as Initiator of the Kingdom, in order to accomplish the Father's will. It was reason of the presence among them of the Risen Lord that the Pentecost community felt themselves to be the messianic community of the "final Times," the community which possessed the secret of the world's salvation, Jesus Christ. This conviction they disseminated round about them. They evangelized, because the Good News was life and breath to them. They could not but evangelize because their Good News was destined for all men and had to be transmitted to them. Their evangelizing act was the new salvation event, the never-ending today acquired in Jesus Christ.

Another stage was still in the future; the realization that the Good News destined for all may be encountered by all, without any preliminary initiation to the religion of Israel. This will be the beginning of mission strictly speaking. A succession of events will point the way for this primitive community. At an early stage scattered groups of Gentiles had joined the disciples, but one day in the great city of Antioch a Christian community came into being where convert Gentiles found themselves in the majority. That was the moment when the disciples clearly realized the new character of their religion, and when they took the name of Christians. Jewish particularism was at an end. The Christian community was now effectively open to Gentiles, and, under the action of the Spirit, found itself in a state of mission.

The importance of witness in the manifestation of salvation

At every stage of salvation history the Antioch experience must go on being repeated. Men of every race and station must gradually find out that the Good News is the unexpected fulfillment of their own spiritual yearnings. For them all, the accomplishment brought by Christ means a surmounting of all particularism. As adoptive children of the Father, they take on the ties of a limitless brotherhood, which is the sign of the one Mediator's constant intervention in the world.

Men's spiritual quests are extremely diverse indeed, but in this age they are all profoundly influenced by a common factor. In the past the dominant dimension was the strictly religious one, man's relationship with the sacral. Now, all men feel themselves responsible for the construction of a more habitable world. Attention is concentrated, not as in the past on comtemplation, but on action, on the historical task that confronts us. This task is one of colossal dimension, the goal being a community of peoples where the voice of each will be heard. It has its dramatic side as well; success will depend on the use men can make of their liberty.

In face of this profound mutation, can we say that Christianity is without answers? No, because the novelty of the gospel is not ultimately something "religious." The new commandment is basically concerned with relationships between men: "Love one another, without distinction of race, culture or station." Love of this calibre presupposes a love of God, which recognizes the salvific initiative in Jesus Christ as the ultimate source of a human brotherhood that knows no limits. In this sense the people of God cannot but feel at home in a world where the emphasis is on action. It is precisely in this domain that their faith in the living Christ is deployed; the service they can render to humanity is irreplaceable.

Witness for this reason is all important. The Good News, before its proclamation, must, if it is to make sense, be lived by the people of God. The gospel is a power for the transformation of the world, but this must be made manifest. In our day realization that the Good News really is destined for all men will depend on the extent to which the people of God really seem to be involved in the human struggle. Their witness, true, may give scandal; but it is only by fidelity to the new commandment that they can lead people to the recognition of Christ.

THIRD WEEK

I. Hebrews
9:15; 24-28
1st reading
1st cycle
Monday

These verses form the conclusion to the analysis of Christ's sacrificial role as a perfect fulfillment of the ceremony of Expiation (cf. Lv 16:11-16). The author has demonstrated chiefly how Christ has brought all humanity within the Holy of Holies, near to God (vv. 11-13), and how his sacrifice purifies and consecrates the believer as priest and victim of the cult in spirit and in truth (v. 14; cf. Rm 12:1-2). Following closely the ritual of Leviticus 16, he concentrates on two important elements of Expiation; the high priest's solemn entry into the Holy of Holies (vv. 24, 26, 27b), and the expiatory sacrifice strictly speaking (vv. 24, 28a).

a) *Christ's entry* to the Holy of Holies is no longer governed, like that of the high priest, by the annual cycle of feasts. He enters once for all (v. 26), in an eternal "now" (vv. 24 and 26), whereas the high priest had to follow the recurring cycle. Furthermore the sanctuary he enters is far more authentic than that of the temple (v. 24), and it retains this quality not for some moments only, as formerly, but always. Consequently men's prayers and petitions have at all times an attentive mediator who is before the face of God. The high priest could only exercise mediation before Yahweh on certain occasions. Finally, if the high priest by his entry could authenticate the enthronement of God for one year, Christ in himself exercises universal lordship. When he issues from the tabernacle, as the high priest used, and returns among the people (v. 28), this is to exercise a definitive kingship over them. The people themselves too, the assembly of the just, await his return with much more fervor than the Jewish assembly used. He is the new high priest, the Lord; and his reappearance is altogether more glorious than that of the old high priest, as he reappeared after the enthronement of Yahweh (cf. Si 50:5-7).

b) It is not the fact of shedding his blood that makes the *expiation* of Christ definitive, but the offering of his life. The value of an act is measured by the person who performs it. Christ's oblation has a double value. As Son of God, his sacrifice transcends those of the old covenant. As perfect man, his oblation has a spiritual dimension, unknown in the former worship.

The general preoccupation of the author of Hebrews with establishing a close parallel between the Expiation festival (from which his audience are not precluded) and Christ's sacrifice, leads him to concentrate on a single aspect of efficaciousness for Christ's blood. The purifying and expiatory value, that is to say. The point was made at the very beginning of the letter (He 1:3). It insists that Christ, by his death and resurrection, can blot out and remit sins, not in an exterior fashion like the blood of goats (v. 25), but radically. He was the first man to live a sinless life, the Lord who is able to abolish the reign of evil.

II. 2 Samuel
5:1-7, 10
1st reading
2nd cycle
Monday

David was an excellent politician. Anointed king of the Southern tribes at Hebron (2 S 2:1-4), he at once tried to be recognized as king by the Northern tribes who had remained faithful to Saul's dynasty. Through the connivance of Abner he managed to recover his first wife Michal, the daughter of Saul (2 S 3:13), and thus to represent himself as a descendant of Saul. After the death of Ishbaal, the son of the old king (2 S 4), the throne was vacant. Through his diplomacy David was able to take over.

The very fact that the Northern tribes made a special pact with David, and repeated the anointing that had already taken place in 2 S 2, is evidence that he is now king of two distinct peoples, not of a single realm. His political awareness enabled him to see that he could no longer reside at Hebron, a Southern town. He must have a neutral capital, belonging neither to North or South, and Jerusalem was the obvious choice. It was still at this stage a Canaanite town. His conquest would be an exploit that would reinforce his authority over the tribes, and obliterate the memories of the Gelboe disaster.

The ruse which brought about the capture of the Jebusaean town was seen by contemporaries as a sign of God's particular assistance (we have this interpretation in Jg 4:17-22; 1 M 7: 10-29). It appears that the town was taken without striking a blow by some soldiers who were able to scale the shaft that led from the fortress to the fount of Gibon. This is still visible today.

A political coup engineered by alert diplomacy, a military crisis that becomes the topic of the day: by such very human, even questionable, means, is God's choice of the holy city manifested. Truly, God is present everywhere; man cannot determine the acceptable manner of his intervention.

III. Mark 3:22-30 Here we have the discussion by the Jews
     Gospel   concerning the source of Jesus' exorcist pow-
     Monday   ers. The tradition is common to all the syn-
                 optics (cf. Mt. 12:24-32 and Lk 11:15-23),
though each places it in a different context. Curiously enough, Mark incorporates it in the account of an episode between Jesus and members of his family (vv. 20-21; 31-35). But in many ways his account seems very close to the original tradition. The exchange about Beelzebub (vv. 22-26) and the mention of blasphemy against the Spirit (vv. 28-30) seem to be primitive and belong to the common source. Mark however is anxious to contrast with the lot of him who allows himself to be led by the evil spirit, the happiness of those who obey the word (as in Lk 11:27-28). Thus he introduces verses 20-21. Verse 27 is an

addition in the whole synoptic tradition (cf. Mt 12-29). Altogether, Mark is more discreet than the others, all of whom
introduce more material of this nature to the primitive account
(cf. Lk 11:15-23).

The essential theme of the passage is the *combat between the
two spirits*. According to the Jewish tradition, which had been
already prominent in Qumran doctrine, the world was delivered
over to the spirit of evil by the will of those who followed this
spirit. In the last times would appear the Spirit of good, who
would redirect men towards good and give them access to the
Kingdom. The fact that Jesus is expelling demons is evidence
that the Spirit of good is already at work in the world (Mt 12:28).

The Scribes for their part do not deny that he expels evil
spirits; but instead of seeing here the presence of the good Spirit,
they put forward the explanation, at least original, that he is
expelling inferior demons in the name of the chief demon (v. 22).
Jesus sees this as blasphemy against the Holy Spirit, because it
confuses the Spirit with Satan. The sin against the Spirit is the
denial of his presence in the world, of his capacity to make the
world over new. This is the sin that cannot be forgiven, because
anyone who makes such an affirmation cannot be part of the
Kingdom. He is rejecting the role of the Spirit, the precise thing
that is necessary for the inauguration of the Kingdom (vv. 28-30).

The two spirits are indeed very real; the combat in which
Jesus is engaged is that of the "stronger" against the "strong"
(v. 27). The faithful share this combat when they opt for one or
other spirit. Choosing the Spirit of God means hearing his Word
and putting it in practice (vv. 33-35), being ready to accept
whatever ruptures, even those of family, it requires.

Man was created to respond in fidelity to God's loving initiative. He is however free; he can be unfaithful and betray his
vocation. That is to sin. The experience of sin is in some way

that of immersion in something antecedent to man, something that involves creatures other than man, demons, and nature itself. When we sin, we enter this quasi-cosmic universe.

But because man is created free, he cannot become the plaything of other creatures, even when they are spiritual. That is what Christ made manifest by liberating himself from the cosmic solidarity that threatened to engulf him as man, and by liberating his brothers from the sway of demonic powers. It was not so much his exorcisms which brought about this liberation. It was, in a more basic sense, his victorious confrontation of temptation and death.

Up to the moment of Christ's death the cosmic solidarity of sin embraced heaven, earth and hell. After that a breach was made; another solidarity became possible, that of love. The day will come when Satan and death will be thrown in the lake (Rev 20:10-14). From that moment sin will have no more solidarity.

In the meantime however, the Christian finds himself torn between two polarities. He may yield to sin and become engulfed at one extreme. Or he may hear the Word and obey it, thus opting for the solidarity of the new Kingdom. For us, the word is heard in the liturgy of the Word; the spiritual sacrifice we offer in the Eucharist is our daily fulfillment of the Word.

IV. **Hebrews**
   10:1-10
   1st reading
   1st cycle
   Tuesday

In the preceding chapter (9:24-28) the author of Hebrews had analyzed the ceremony of expiation in order to show how it was fulfilled and transcended in Christ's sacrifice. Now he contrasts Christ's sacrifice with the whole sacrificial economy of the temple.

a) To understand the passage properly it is necessary to keep in mind the theology of the *sacrifice of the poor*, which had been already elaborated in the Old Testament (cf. Dn 3:38-40). Trial and exile had put an end to the quantitative sacrifices of the old temple. A new, poor sacrifice was substituted, suited to the penury of the time, but charged with sentiments of thanksgiving, penance and humility. The essence of the sacrifice is the involvement of the person and his sentiments. Without the mediation of any animal he offers himself as victim. God is not now the God of bloody sacrifices; he requires obedience and love.

Among the psalms which reflect this doctrine, one of the most important is Psalm 39/40. Here we have the insight of a sick man. God does not require sacrifices from him in thanksgiving for his recovery. He requires obedience and total fidelity to the law. From now on, for the author of this psalm, moral attitude will be the basis of worship; rite and life have become fused (cf. Rm 12:1-2).

The author places the psalm on the lips of Christ and thus clarifies the nature of the sacrifice of the cross. It does not consist in the immolation of a victim, however choice. Its essence is obedience to the Father's will, and Christ has shown this (vv. 7 and 9). From now on religion will be confined to a religion "in spirit and in truth" (cf. Ep 5:2).

b) We should however be exact about the *will of God* concerning Christ and the reciprocal obedience of Christ. The Father did not ever will the death of his Son. That would make him a sanguinary God only to be appeased by the blood of a loved one. Nor is the obedience in question obedience to the law because this is passing (vv. 1-4). God's plan was rather that his Son should share the human condition with such an excess of love that this would be transformed. Because the human condition necessarily entails death, it was not excluded from the human state of the Son. His acceptance of the human state had to be coextensive with his love for the Father.

In order to clarify fully the Father's will concerning the Son, the author modifies (fashioned a body: v. 5) the psalm that he puts on the Son's lips at the moment of incarnation (v. 5: entering the world). In this fashion he introduces to the preexisting, trinitarian relations the motif of the Son's sacrificial intent. This throws into strong perspective the Father's will, the deep sources of the Son's obedience, and the fact that all the period of the incarnation had a sacrificial dimension that reached its culmination in the cross. In Jesus, life and rite were perfectly linked, and never ceased to bear fruit.

V. 2 Samuel
6:12b-15, 17-19
1st reading
2nd cycle
Tuesday

After the ark had been recovered from the Philistines (1 S 6-7), it lost all interest practically for the people. It was retained in places other than those of traditional cult, and the people no longer gathered round about it as they had been wont. Once installed in the land they had conquered, gradually, with the memory of the nomad state, reverence for the relics of that state began to fade.

When he had the *ark* transferred to Jerusalem, David showed himself, once again, an excellent politician. The city, which had been formerly neutral territory between the two kingdoms, had become the political capital. It must now become the religious capital as well. Thus the political power would be strengthened and sacralized.

The gesture brought the nomad era to an end. This procession which brought the ark to Jerusalem was to prove one of its final transferences. The warrior-God who had traveled at the head of his people would now be stabilized at Jerusalem. To nomadism was succeeding fixity. The city would replace the desert as the focus of religious experience.

It was also a gesture of fidelity to the purest form of Yahwism. Saul and his daughter Michal, behind whom we can discern already the Samarian dynasty, stood for a less pure concept of religion, one more open to Canaanite influence (cf. 1 S 19:13-17). This doubtless explains as well Michal's reproaching her husband for his over-enthusiasm in religion.

David's loyalty to Yahwism is evident in the exercise of royal priesthood, something normal in the period prior to institution of the levitic priesthood, and consonant with the ancient prerogatives of the Jebusean kings of Jerusalem (vv. 13-14; cf. Gn 14:18-20).

The installation of the ark at Jerusalem and David's exercise of a royal priesthood symbolizes the course of salvation history at all times. The Church for instance in our day may be nomad and a stranger in our sort of world, but she realizes that all the roads she travels lead to the "stable city that is in heaven." The Eucharist is the sacrifice offered by the true David. It is a pledge of our heavenly citizenship and the guarantee of our entry to the eternal city.

VI. Mark 3:31-35 This Gospel was commented on with that of
  Gospel   Monday, p. 102.
  Tuesday

Mark is about to give us the parable (4:1-9) of the seed which falls on different ground. He is giving a preliminary illustration of it by showing that the *family* of Jesus is not necessarily ideal ground. Faith has nothing to do with sociological circumstances, or with human sentiments, be they ever so familial and brotherly.

VII. Hebrews   This is the conclusion to the central portion
  10:11-18   of the letter to the Hebrews. The principal
  1st reading   arguments are recapitulated: the sanctuary
  1st cycle   into which Jesus has entered (vv. 12-13; cf.
  Wednesday   He 9), the uniqueness of his oblation (vv. 12
                     and 14; cf. He 7:12, 27; 10:10 etc.) and its
consequence, a new covenant (vv. 16-17; cf. He 8:10-12).

a) The entry of Christ to the *eternal sanctuary* symbolizes his ascent to the Father, beyond the heavens, which in the mythic language of Jewish cosmology are represented as a tent (Ps 103/104:2). Thus he has passed beyond a "tent" that was not made by human hands (cf. He 9:11-12), creation that is, and is now seated above it.

A new dimension is added to the theme. Not only is Christ's sacrifice more efficacious than that of the high priest when he passed beyond the veil of the tabernacle; it also constitutes a messianic investiture (vv. 11-12). The Jewish high priest could not pretend to this. It is the first time a priestly act becomes a royal investiture.

b) Three reasons are put forward to demonstrate the *uniqueness* of Christ's sacrifice. First, by offering his life and his blood he surpassed everything that had been previously accomplished (cf. He 9:9-12). Second, the sacrifice makes perfect those who benefit by it (v. 14), something no other rite could accomplish (cf. He 8:7-13). Third, it provides access to spiritual and eschatological blessings, whereas the former rites provided only material ones. The very fact that the Lord henceforth is "seated" (v. 12), and not erect in the sacrificial position (v. 11), shows that everything has been accomplished once for all. The Christian then who is ceaselessly preoccupied with obtaining pardon is an anomaly.

c) Finally we have the theme of *interior covenant*. Christ brings to each person a new heart and a new spirit (vv. 16-17; cf. He 8:6-13), the characteristics of the covenant foretold by Jeremiah 31:31-34. Previously, the Jew who offered sacrifice continued to be a sinner, always at odds with the covenant. Now Christ has by his sacrifice once for all reconciled all humanity to himself, enabling them to offer the spiritual, unbloody sacrifice of the new covenant.

VIII. 2 Samuel It had long been thought that Nathan's proph-
7:4-17 ecy was composed of a primitive account
1st reading which had been considerably interpolated
2nd cycle over the centuries. It was argued that there
Wednesday were attempts to give it a more exclusively
national and royalist dimension (vv. 10 and
11a); or to show the responsibility of the kings for the decadence
of the covenant (vv. 14-15); or again, to lay the basis for a certain
kind of messianism (v. 16). Today, however, such interpretation
is regarded as hypothetical and there is a tendency to revert to
the view that the piece is a unity.

a) The main point in the primitive tradition is the reassurance
of David concerning the future of his dynasty and his people. The
nation he ruled over was not homogeneous. This is evident from
the successive anointings; in the South (2 S 2:1-4), the North
(2 S 5:1-3), and at Jerusalem (2 S 5:6-10). The king was won-
dering whether his reign would outlast his death. Nathan answers
the question. God has always protected David (vv. 8-9), and will
also his successor (v. 12). Saul's failure will not necessarily
extend to the *davidic dynasty*.

David was also troubled about the future of the people, who
had been so unstable throughout the period of Judges and the
reign of Saul. Unity could be jeopardized by the Northern and
Southern factions, by royalist and antiroyalist parties. Nathan
reassures him (vv. 10-11a); and the people will find stability.

b) Thus the prophecy, the product of a court prophet, is the
result of contemporary circumstance. The *messianic* emphasis
comes from the deuteronomic influence of verses 14 and 15. The
davidic dynasty is promised perpetuity if its members are faithful.
We have the same affirmation "for always" in verse 16. The
authors of Psalms 88/89:30-38 and 131/132:11-12 will take up
this theme, which is much more significant than the original
promise of Nathan.

Consequently, while of itself the Samuel text cannot be considered messianic, under the influence of Jewish religious reflect-tion it becomes an important source of davidic messianism.

c) The particular selection for today's reading does not feature very well the *house* theme. In order to stabilize his dynasty and provide a center for his people, David proposes to construct a habitation that will shelter the ark of the covenant (vv. 1-3). However, Yahweh tells him that he himself will build a house for the king (v. 11b). The point is not that God is refusing his temple, but that the future of the people and dynasty must repose on a personal covenant between Yahweh and the kings, rather than on the material temple. Mutual fidelity will prove more important in Israel's history than temple sacrifices. Later, when Christ brought to unprecedented perfection the relationship of love between the Messiah and his Father (cf. Is 66:1-2; Ac 7:48; Lk 23:44-45; Jn 2:19), tradition, a Christian tradition now, would recall this insight and reject the temple. Verse 11b consequently is highly important. It provides the crucial insight concerning the value for the people's salvation of communion between God and the king.

Neither Nathan, nor redactors of the prophecy, could have foreseen the accomplishment that would come in Christ's person. He was the true "house" of God. He guaranteed stability for the people, thanks to his filial attachment to the Father. The eucharistic sacrifice is a fulfillment of the prophecy. It "re-presents" the attachment of the Son to his Father, through death and transcending death.

IX. Mark 4:1-20   Three problems arise in the interpretation of
Gospel   this parable of the sower; the meaning of the
Wednesday   parable as delivered by Jesus (vv. 1-8); the
                 emphasis given it by Mark by placing it in
this context; and the interpretation given it by the primitive
Church (vv. 13-20).

a) Between a mention of sowing (v. 3) and of harvest (v. 8) in the parable proper we have four scenes juxtaposed. The whole interest is concentrated on the fate of the seed in the four different terrains. The scenes follow one another on a rather optimistic note, and finally we have the impression of an extraordinarily bountiful *harvest*.

The harvest theme of course, as a symbol of the last times, is traditional in Israel (Jl 4:13). What is new is the emphasis on the laborious sowing by which it is prepared. Jesus is modifying the eschatological emphasis, the advent of the Kingdom (harvest), by concentrating on the toil by which it is realized. He proclaims the coming, yes; but points out the slow character of its maturation.

b) Mark's particular context (which could indeed be the original one) gives the piece a christological emphasis. What Jesus is actually facing are the different obstacles and resistances which oppose his message; the blindness of the scribes, the superficial enthusiasm of the crowd, the distrust of his relatives, etc. He is finding meaning in this lack of comprehension, and contrasting the seemingly futile labor of the sower with the abundant harvest that maturation brings. He thinks of the trials of his *mission* and sees it in the light of the judgment to come. The judgment indeed is already at work, in that the disciples, amid the general indifference, seem to discern the Messiah (vv. 10-12).

c) Finally, we have the interpretation of the parable by the primitive communities. For them, it was not Christ's mission that needed clarification, but the various motives for conversion among the first Christians. The final harvest was not the problem, but the daily difficulties arising from persecution (v. 17).

Thus, some allegorization took place. Each scene in the parable represented a different kind of *conversion*. The sowing was not the important thing, but the manner in which the seed was received. Even the eschatological lesson of the parable is obscured in favor of psychological and paraenetic considerations

(v. 20). Where Jesus had been optimistic about his mission, the primitive Church seems somewhat tense and anxious.

d) It is in verse 11-12 above all that we find Mark's personal contribution. As he sees it, Jesus is already carrying out God's *judgment*. If he uses parables, the purpose is to exclude unbelievers from salvation and contrast them with the believers to whom gradually he reveals his secret. He is giving his particular answer to the worries of the primitive Church about Jewish unbelief and opposition.

Whether we follow Jesus' own interpretation or that of the primitive Church, the parable certainly stresses the contrast between the time of sowing, the time of the Church, and that of the harvest which is the Kingdom. The Church, true, is the temple of the Spirit, the people of God and many other things besides; but it is not identical with the Kingdom. The Kingdom is in process of becoming, and is already partially present. But too much insistence on this leads to forgetfulness of the distance we have yet to travel.

Nowadays there is only one road open to the Church. Without ever forgetting the Kingdom that is being prepared, she must be constantly mindful too of the seed which dies and is squandered.

Her road must be the road of self-emptying, the one that Jesus chose (Ph 2:6-11) throughout his earthly life (Lk 4:5-6; Mk 10:45; Jn 13:12-17), he who had all the means of power at his disposal. It was at the very moment when he was assessing the effect of his decision to be a defenseless prophet rather than a royal Messiah, that the sower parable came to his lips.

Whenever people seek in the Church a solid bastion against the process of desacralization and secularization, they fail to discern her true visage. It is one of renunciation, exile and dispersion. The Eucharist itself will have its true meaning when those assembled at the celebration exhibit in their lives the kenosis of Christ.

X. Hebrews
10:19-25
1st reading
1st cycle
Thursday

The author has just shown how believers too, following Christ, have penetrated the Holy of Holies. They too exercise a priesthood, thanks to the union of their lives with the Lord. To-day's passage enumerates the privileges of this new state.

a) Thanks to Christ, the Christian can approach the sanctuary directly (v. 19), without any cultic priesthood or intermediary rite. This *approach* is described as "newness," because Christianity alone enjoys it, in contradistinction to Jewish and pagan religions. Likewise, it is "life" (cf. Jn 14:6) because it leads to eternal life (v. 20).

It is an approach beyond the "veil," which in the temple separated the faithful from the Holy of Holies. Now the veil is suppressed (cf. Mk 15:38), because there is no more distinction between sacred and profane. The path through the veil is none other than the life "in the flesh" of Jesus It was a profane life, including death, that became sacral and holy because of the love which animated it (v. 21).

b) The author then goes on to draw some moral conclusions. First, there must be fidelity to baptism, to its interior effects as well as its exterior (vv. 22-23), because God is faithful to his own promises. Secondly, there must be mutual charity. Salvation cannot be lived in isolation, but only in the community of mutual love (vv. 24-25).

The most remarkable point about these councils is the significance given to liturgical *assemblies*. These must not be abandoned. They are salvation at work, and contribute to its accomplishment, until the "Day" when it will be finally achieved. This is a very precious affirmation. It means that the author attributes efficacy in the order of salvation to the liturgical assembly. For so long as the Church continues on earth, while the Kingdom is not visible, the assembly will be the sign of the final reassembly of all men in the Kingdom. It is furthermore an efficacious sign and really brings about salvation for men. Hence its important, not to say obligatory, character.

c) The Christian must keep the *day of the Lord* (v. 25) in view. In Hebrews, as in Matthew 24, this day indicates the fall of Jerusalem and the destruction of the temple. This will put an end to the former priestly economy and make way for the new covenant which is based on the glorious person of the new mediator (Mt 24:24-30; 26:61-64; 23:38-24:2; Ac 7:48-56). Doubtless the fall of the city could be foreseen at the time of the letter's composition. The author actually announces the end of its term (v. 25).

As he sees, it, the celestial economy has been set up ever since Jesus once for all passed through the spiritual temple (He 9:11). He thereby showed the passing nature of the former covenant (He 8:13). Automatically then the fall of Jerusalem ushers Christians into the new age, already celestial, where their priest fully exercises his priestly prerogatives. The author does not of course reject the end of the world and judgment (He 10:30-31); but he regards the fall of Jerusalem as the most decisive element in the Lord's coming. From this moment on, in the priestly and sacrificial order, everything is made clear.

Christ placed the decisive sacrificial act once for all, and is himself the people of God, a priestly people with access to all the prerogatives of the old high priest. Can we for that reason say that the people of God are a people without priests?

Some recent trends would seem to point towards the disappearance of the priestly ministry. Lack of vocations and the sizeable numbers leaving the priesthood have tended to focus more attention on the priesthood of the laity. There is a feeling that some appellations, like "alter Christus" or "priest according to the order of Melchizedek," have often been wrongly limited to ministers, where they should describe the whole people.

It would be unwise however to draw any conclusions about the possibility of a "Church without priests." True, we are witnessing a "de-ecclesiasticization" of the priestly ministry; but the suppression of "ecclesiasticism" and the disappearance of priestly and episcopal function are very different things. The priestly people cannot fulfill its priestly function except by sharing Christ's priesthood. For this ministers are necessary.

We shall be faithful to the spirit of Hebrews if we accept the disappearance of that kind of clergy, who for historical and sociological reasons stood in the way sometimes of the people's priesthood. During this process numerous delicate problems have to be faced; priest-workers, the obligation of celibacy, etc. According to our success in solving these, we can hope to have the joy of rediscovering a vital Church. She will be able as a whole to assume the responsibility of manifesting Christ's priesthood, and demonstrating its influence in the world.

XI. 2 Samuel **7:18-19,** **24-29** *1st reading* *2nd cycle* *Thursday*	Having benefited by God's promise, David goes before the ark to give thanks. The main themes of his prayer we find concentrated in verses 18-19 and 26-27, which are probably its original nucleus.

David's title to kingship differed for the different tribes, but his prayer envisages the *unity of the people*. This unity will come about through the alliance of his descendants with the God of armies. He prays before the ark, because this is destined to be forever the sign and witness of the people's solidarity under the davidic dynasty, in covenant with the Lord for the fulfillment of his promise.

Verse 24 was added subsequently. It reflects the theology of Deuteronomy (cf. Dt 7:6; 26:17), and repeats the teaching that the people's future depends on fidelity to Yahweh. It is noteworthy however that there is no longer question of mediation by the royal dynasty. Deuteronomy showed some reservation concerning David's descendants, who were frequently careless about the conditions Yahweh had set for the fulfillment of his promise.

XII. Mark
4:21-25
Gospel
Thursday

Mark conjoins two parables in this text which were certainly not so associated originally. The parable of the lamp (vv. 21-23) is indeed in its original version. The interrogative style indicates a source close to oral tradition, and verse 23 is a repeated affirmation in this tradition, to stress the importance of a teaching (cf. Mt 10:27; 11:15; 13:9, 43; Mk 4:9; Rev 2:7, 11, 29; 3:6, 13, 21; 17:9).

The grouping of verses 21-23 and 25 we owe to the primitive community. The latter explains the former, in the same way as Mark 4:13-20 explains Mark 4:1-10. The explanation sought is: why among Jesus' hearers some listened while others did not (cf. the key word "understand" in vv. 12, 20, 23, 24 and 33).

The parable of the measure however, in Mark's form (v. 24), is probably added by the evangelist himself. In Matthew's version (Mt 7:2) it is closer to primitive tradition.

We shall examine each parable for itself and then consider the particular significance of their association.

a) The parable of the *lamp* (v. 21) is a simple proverb, originally meant to show the necessity of action. He who understands something cannot remain silent; all his activity must be marked by this. Mark, however, by adding verse 22 brings the parable into the context of his doctrine about hearing the Word and about the messianic secret (Mk 1:25, 44; 3:12; 4:12). In this perspective the lamp stands allegorically for Jesus' teaching. It is obscured now and misunderstood. However the day will come when it will be manifested, and "those who have not been able to understand" the "mysterious" words will be judged and condemned.

b) Verses 24b and 25 really belong it seems to the parable of the lamp (as in Lk 8:16-18). They describe the eschatological luminousness of the lamp. Those who have known the secrets of the Kingdom will enjoy its fullness (to those who have it will be given). Similarly those who have heard the Word will produce fruit thirty, sixty and a hundred fold (Mk 4:20, just preceding our passage, and concluding the sower parable). On the other hand, those who have never understood the secrets will be even deprived of what they have received, like the different terrains in the sower parable (Mk 4:13-20), which lose not only the fruit but the seed.

Thus the idea is clear, and follows exactly the teaching of the sower parable. The message of Jesus is a lamp which burns first under a bushel before being manifested on the standard of the Parousia. People can see its brightness already under the bushel, just as the witnesses must receive the seed. They must do so in order to reap the reward when the lamp shines in fullness.

c) Mark's introduction then at this point of the little parable of the measure (v. 24) is quite awkward. It refers to final retribution certainly but not with such an eschatological emphasis as the parable of the lamp.

The Word of God, for so long as it is proclaimed in the time of faith, is like a lamp under a bushel. Its brightness can only be perceived in the shade. It has to be approached with confidence and fidelity to give light. But the Kingdom is growing. One day the lamp will be on a standard, and will illumine those who, in the obscurity of the mystery, had confidence in its rays.

XIII. Hebrews
10:32-39
1st reading
1st cycle
Friday

The people to whom this letter is addressed were Jewish converts to Christianity. In their present state of exile and poverty they regret the splendors of the ancient cult. They are tempted to revert, all the more so because they are crushed by persecution, and the Jewish nation seems about to be annihilated by the Romans. The author has already responded to this by showing the specific difference between Christian and Jewish worship. He now passes to his second topic, the need for persevering faith if the temptation to revert is to be resisted. Three considerations are brought forward, designed to reassure the wavering. The first (our passage) points out the futility of sufferings and struggles endured if apostasy is to be the result (He 10). The second (He 11) cites the example of the patriarchs' fidelity. The third and most important (He 12) is the example of Christ himself and God's instructions to his children.

There is possibly an allusion to baptism in the word "illumination" (v. 32; He 6:4; Ep 5:14). Next we have a description of the sufferings which merit reward. The author points out the foolishness of those who would let all go after each struggles, on the eve of reward (vv. 37-38). His two arguments in this context are taken directly from two prophetic texts in the Greek version (Is 26:20; Ha 2:3-4). These describe the attitude of the just man under *trial*. The second citation has particular importance. It shows how trial separates the just from the impious, begetting fidelity (the sense here to be given to faith) in one, and unmasking the other.

XIV. **2 Samuel**   Chapters 9 to 20 of 2 Samuel come from a
    11:1-4a,   very early hand, perhaps contemporary with
    5-10a, 13-17   David himself. The section is marked by a
    1st reading   very strong sense of retribution. As the author
    2nd cycle   sees it each fault is punished here on earth
    Friday   and the fault of a king receives particular
                      chastisement.

The fault is that of adultery. Desirous of evading the unexpected consequences of his fault, David tries to make it appear that the legitimate husband is the father. One thing leading to another, he is brought to the point of crime. The author will subsequently evince satisfaction that David pays by the death of his children and his own exile.

We may well ask what sin really is. It is a concept about which men of our time find it hard to be precise. We more often speak of "fallings short" of some ideal contemplated, unity say, peace, brotherhood. But we do not call these failures sins. What then may we brand as sinful? Human limitations? Hardly, because this is the human condition, and the most authentic human being is the one who accepts the limitations. Is sin the guilt feeling that destroys the dream of innocence? Hardly, because we only grow through our transgressions.

Is not sin rather the refusal to grow, the refusal to be always open, the refusal to advance towards the path pointed by liberty? It means hiding ourselves from the real, avoiding confrontation and dialogue, taking refuge in the self-sufficiency of pride, rejecting in advance communion with others, the gift of the Other?

If, after the sin of Adam, David's fault became a biblical model for sin, was not this because it was seen not merely as a breach of regulations for purity, but as a refusal to take the loftier path to which the covenant summoned him?

XV. Mark
4:26-34
Gospel
Friday

The two parables in today's passage, that of the patient husbandmen and the grain of mustard seed, belong, with those of the sower (Mk 4:3-8) and the leaven (Mt 13:33), to a group of narratives that indicate the same conclusion. They justify the Messiah's attitude concerning opposition to his preaching. They may very well indeed have been composed with Simon the Zealot in view and Judas Iscariot (or Judas Sicarius). These were members of an extremist group, who wished to undertake a holy war against Rome and establish the messianic kingdom.

a) In the parable of the patient husbandman (vv. 26-29) the Kingdom of God is compared with the *slow growth* of the seed to maturity, and the husbandman's long inactivity with the feverish activity of the harvest (imagery based on Jl 4:13; cf. also Rev 14:14-16). The harvest, as always in the Bible and especially the Joel text, indicates God's judgment and the inauguration of his Kingdom. In other words, the husbandman is God, who will soon act in the same spectacular manner as a husbandman at harvest time. It is true that actually, and especially throughout Jesus' ministry, God does not seem to act. He leaves Jesus isolated, without success, more and more rejected by his own. However his silence is related to his future judgment in the same way as the husbandman's present inactivity is to his future business at the harvest.

Jesus was criticized by the Jews. If he claims to be Messiah, let him give the signs of the coming Kingdom. Jesus replies that there are no extraordinary signs. God lets the seed grow slowly. There is nothing to be lost by waiting. The continuity between the laborious maturation of the Kingdom and its final manifestation in plenitude is assured. Those concerned with the building of the Kingdom must not lose confidence. God has given the beginnings. Throughout all his silence he is accomplishing his work. There must be patience and no attempt to hasten the issue. On the other hand those who reserve belief in the Kingdom until the moment of its manifestation should beware. It has already come close to them in the person of Jesus. Even in the modesty of means and slowness of growth, it should be discerned.

b) The parable of the mustard seed strengthens confidence in God by pointing the contrast between the humble beginnings of the Kingdom (v. 31) and the ultimate eschatological grandeur (v. 32; the nest motif is borrowed from Jewish eschatologies concerned with the incorporation of the Gentiles in the people of

God; cf. Ez 17:22-24). The piece is probably Jesus' response to those who contrasted the *modesty of means* employed by him with the glory of the expected Kingdom. They ridiculed the poverty and ignorance of Jesus' disciples by contrast with the triumphal cortege that should inaugurate the final times.

In tiny beginnings something great is already at work. The Kingdom is present already in a world that does not know it. A little light burns in the heart of even the most hardened sinner which may become a devouring fire. Despite appearances we must take God at his Word.

Ever since the promises to Abraham (Gn 17:2-8) the notes of plenty and abundance characterized Jewish hope. In the fruitfulness of the promised land the people had always seen evidence of the overwhelming abundance to come.

The New Testament does more than merely spiritualize this abundance. It actually makes it depend on the long growth that comes through poverty and denudation. The fullness of the Kingdom is brought about through the seed growing secretly. True failure for the Church does not consist in the modesty of the measures she adopts. The failure would be much more grave if, in order to achieve universalism, she were to resort to merely secular power policies.

When they share the eucharistic body of Christ, men of the most diverse character have to realize that there is already a fraternal bond between them. They should live this in practice, and find in it the strength to conquer all obstacles.

XVI. Hebrews
11:1-2, 8-19
1st reading
1st cycle
Saturday

The author is addressing Christians of Jewish origin who have been driven by persecution from Jerusalem and are disturbed and discouraged. Will not this exile from the Holy City deprive them of the inauguration of the Kingdom? He summons them to such a spirit of faith as cleaves to the invisible only, and rests on the certitude of already possessing the earnest of heavenly things (v. 1). To encourage them he reminds them of the example of their ancestors. Today's passage is concerned with Abraham.

Just like these first century Jews, Abraham had experienced exile, rupture with his family and national background (v. 8), the insecurity of the "displaced person." However he used this experience as the occasion for an act of *faith* in God's promise. He, and his children too, lived as nomads (v. 9).

The believer is in fact a pilgrim. He is in the world but not attached to it, because he has the taste for invisible things. His wanderings led him not alone to a terrestrial city (the Jerusalem these Christians want to regain) and a land of material promise, but to that invisible city which is life with God. Faith is not to be satisfied with tangible goods or immediate hopes. Its true domain is that of waiting; what characterizes it is the distant goal, the nonmaterial nature of the end sought.

Lastly, Abraham had to endure Sarah's sterility and the absence of posterity (cf. Gn. 15:1-6) (v. 11). This was his greatest trial, because he had to face death (vv. 12-13) without receiving the object of the promise. Here is displayed the ultimate characteristic of faith, the readiness to encounter death, knowing that it cannot frustrate the plan of God.

Death, more than suffering, is the sign *par excellence* of faith, of the giving of the self to God. Abraham believed in something "beyond death." He believed that he would be given posterity, exhausted though his body was, because it had been promised. This is the essential faith of Christ when confronted with the cross. He too gave himself to the Father for the accomplishment of salvation; but he had to witness (and here lay his agony) the failure of his whole enterprise. He had been sent to reassemble all humanity. He found himself absolutely alone, placing all his confidence in something beyond death, that would become manifest at the resurrection.

In the Eucharist believers can develop such a faith and learn to view their own failures with the gaze of victory.

XVII. **2 Samuel** Chapter 11 gave us a description of David's
12:1-7a, sin with Uriah's wife. We have the sequel to
10-17 this in 2 Samuel 12:15-25, when the child born
1st reading of this union falls into agony. This suggests
2nd cycle that originally the death of the child was re-
Saturday garded as a punishment of the father's sin.
Little by little a more religious outlook gained ground and finds expression in the tradition of Nathan's visit to the king (2 S 12:1-14). This was subsequently, before the 8th century, inserted in the primitive account.

a) Nathan begins with a parable (vv. 1-4), a common procedure with the ancient prophets (cf. 2 S 14:4-17). David reacts passionately and even pronounces a death sentence on the protagonist (vv. 5-6), without realizing that he is voicing his own condemnation. Immediately Nathan abandons the role of storyteller for that of prophet, and addresses David in the second person ("it is you") in the style of the old oracles of Yahweh (cf. 1 S 2:27-30). Then he pronounces the *sentence of death* on David's child (v. 10).

This proclamation is not however clear. In verse 10 David is punished by the constant presence of the sword in his family. Actually three of his sons, Ammon (2 S 13:19), Absalom (2 S 18:14-15) and Adonias (1 K 2:25) will perish by the sword. It is a thoroughly Jewish concept of history, where the father's crime becomes an "original sin," the source of ceaseless degradation. Verses 11-12 give another version of the punishment. We are perhaps dealing with a later addition, which reflects another Jewish concept, that of the *lex talionis*. The prophecy however will not be carried out to the letter. Finally, in verse 15, comes a third version, the proclamation of the death of the child born of adultery. The mention of this punishment is doubtless due to the final redactor, who was anxious to connect Nathan's prophecy with the events that actually ensued.

b) These descriptions of David's chastisement are too numerous and too different to be original. Subsequent authors, rereading and interpreting the history of David's descendants, were anxious doubtless to find there the evidence of original chastisement, and thus tampered unduly with the primitive text. Such interference however has its price. We can take verse 13 with verses 7-9 and make David's *repentance* depend on Nathan's oracle, not on the threat of punishment. In other words it is the discovery of his crime that makes him repent, not the fear of punishment.

His repentance wins immediate and absolute pardon from God (v. 13b) "God does not will the death of the sinner but that he be converted and live." It is of course regrettable that the interpolation put the proclamation of the child's death (v. 14) immediately after the proclamation of pardon. As if God were withdrawing his promise and seeking after all an expiatory victim.

It would be wrong to be led, by the verses which describe David's chastisement, to think that culpability is measured by the material disorder caused by sin. On the contrary; the chief point of the narrative is that sin and pardon can only be understood in the context of a personal relationship between the sinner and God. Interpreted thus, the Nathan episode is one of the most important texts in the Old Testament. It is the first instance of emancipation from the exterior rites and legalism which had masked the role of liberty in the relationship with God. It begins the process of desacralization that never ceases to be necessary.

Confronted by sin, God would easily have been vengeful,

broken the alliance, and intervened immediately with his eschatological judgment. It is such a God that is evoked in the
proclamation of punishments in verses 10-15. The concept however would be a perversion of the God of love, who shows
himself larger than rejection, who replaces the heart of the sinner
with a new heart.

We often encounter a narrow notion of sacramentality which
makes the sacrament of penance an allocation by the Church of
the pardon God has entrusted to her. The truth is that there is
a penitential dimension to every eucharistic assembly. This is
realized by those whose personal relationship with God is sufficiently strong to break down the barriers that are constantly
being erected by over-preoccupation with security.

XVIII. Mark	The account of the stilling of the tempest is
4:35-41	given in the three synoptics with fairly im-
Gospel	portant variants. This requires an analysis of
Saturday	the common synoptic tradition where Mark's
	text seems to be the primitive one, and a study

of the genesis of the Marcan text itself.

a) All the synoptics give us the account before that of the
exorcism of the Gerasenian (Mk 5:1-20). The two episodes were
conjoined for doctrinal reasons: to demonstrate that Jesus had
the *power* which dominates evil forces in nature as well as in
hearts. Furthermore Mark 1:23-27 gives us an exorcism narrative
which corresponds exactly in schema to the stilling of the tempest
(compare Mk 1:25 with Mk 3:39: threats; Mk 1:24 with Mk 4:38:
reproaches to Christ for coming to destroy; Mk 1:27b with Mk
4:41: obedience of elements and spirits to Christ; Mk 1:27a with
Mk 4:41: fear). The stilling of the tempest then seems to be the
manifestation of One who is taking up again the creative work
that had been jeopardized by evil powers (cf. Jb 38:1-11). The
emphasis is christological. In Christ, by a decisive victory over

evil, God is bringing the cosmos to perfection. Men are rendering to Christ the fear and wonder reserved for the Creator-God (v. 41; cf. Ps 64/65:8-9; 88/89:10; 107:28-30).

b) However, Mark throughout his Gospel is concerned to show that, before the resurrection, the apostles were unable to have true faith. Accordingly he adds verse 40, which should be carefully translated; "do you not have faith *yet?*" They could not have faith before the Pasch because the only true faith is faith in the Risen Christ. Thus, for Mark, the only true meaning of the stilling of the tempest is that it already includes the *resurrection*. For this reason he associates it with the tempest undergone by Jonah (compare especially v. 38, proper to Mark, with Jon 1:5-6; v. 41a with Jon 1:16, etc.). We might even ask whether he is not finding in the episode the famous sign of Jonah (Mt 12:38-40). Christ, like Jonah, is triumphing over the "inferior waters" when he controls the storm.

c) In Matthew the episode forms part of an ensemble of miracles that have a *catechetical* emphasis. Christ wishes to train the disciples. Thus he does not hesitate to confront them with obstacles and terrors that test their fidelity (cf. Mt 8:23 theme of following; 8:26 men of little faith).

The boat in the tempest has frequently been regarded as an allegory of the Church. It is indeed a very opportune image now, when we consider the Church and priesthood of today.

Like the apostles then, the Church now has withdrawn from the crowds, taking Jesus with her (v. 35). She finds herself isolated in secure institutions, weathering a severe storm. The priesthood too is stricken. It is in isolation. Despite all the discipline, the faith, the dedication, it too is in grievous straits.

Wherein lies the solution? An appeal to the Lord's power, to his threatening word? His eleventh hour rescue? To the "supernatural" as such? Possibly, but we run the risk of hearing again the response "Do you not have faith yet?" Faith will not impel us to seek refuge in ecclesial and clerical institutions. It will lead us to contemplation of the dead and risen Christ, to involvement in a similar death. We shall return to the shore and mingle with the crowd. Fear drives the Church into isolation; faith will protect her from pre-occupation with her own problems. Her proper place is in the world and the priest's proper place is with the laity.

FOURTH SUNDAY

A. THE WORD

I. Zephaniah
2:3; 3:12-13
1st reading
1st cycle

Zephaniah wrote a century after Isaiah (about 640). The fall of the northern kingdom is no longer more than a memory. Judah, which has miraculously escaped Sennacherib's invasion (Is 37:30-38), is overcome by economic and political lethargy. Zephaniah sees in this a possibility of contact with God. If the people are "poor" before Assur, why cannot they be "poor" also before God (cf. Ze 2:3)?

Such spiritual poverty will enable them to escape the judgment of the nations which the prophet proclaims (Ze 1:14-18). Unlike many prophets, Zephaniah gives us the positive aspect of the "Day of Yahweh." The disaser will affect only the proud who do not have spiritual poverty in their heart.

After the disaster, among Gentiles as well as Jews, there will be found people sufficiently spiritual to survive. Such is the topic of the poem (vv. 11-13) read today.

a) Following Isaiah 19:1-25, Zephaniah proclaims the conversion of Egypt and Ethiopia (the land of "Cush"), but does not go so far in *universalism* as his predecessor. God will give these people pure lips (Is 6:4-7), worthy to offer the sacrifice of praise pleasing to God, but they must carry out their worship in Jerusalem (v. 10). The influx of Gentiles to the temple will not mean confusion for the Jewish people (v. 11). It will have been unified by the abolition of the proud and arrogant who regard Sion and its temple as their exclusive privilege (Jr 7:1-15). Universalism will not become a reality until Israel and its temple have purged themselves of all exclusivism and pride (v. 11b; cf. Mt 21:12-13).

For the first time in Israel, a prophet makes the purification of the people the condition for the reassembly of the nations. Any mission which seeks the humiliation of the other is doomed to failure. True mission begins with the conversion of the missionary.

b) The essential condition which will enable the people to become missionary Zephaniah affirms to be *poverty* (v. 12). He describes it in terms borrowed from the social vocabulary of the epoch and transposed to the religious plane: *ani* (poor) and *dal* (humble) (cf. Ze 2:3).

It is significant that the concepts of poverty and universalism are associated in the same passage. If the people are determined to hold on to the temple and regard themselves as the exclusive possessors of Yahweh, their material poverty counts for nothing. Universalism becomes impossible. A missionary displays his poverty by not seeming to "possess" religious privileges.

Christians who are concerned about the problems of evangelization do not hide their dismay when confronted by richness in the Church. Not all Christians indeed have the vocation for voluntary poverty. Yet all must somehow meet the challenge of a poverty necessary to keep the Church missionary. Otherwise she could become that sort of instrument of prestige and power which would deserve the condemnation of Zephaniah 3:11b.

II. Deuteronomy 18:15-20 *1st reading* *2nd cycle* This passage belongs to a section that is devoted to the institutions and ministries of the chosen people. After the rights and duties of kings and priests, the case of prophets is considered.

The matter is introduced by a precept which forbids Israel to have recourse to divinization like the Gentiles (Dt 18:9-14). The sole means of finding out God's will will be the prophet (vv.

15-20). The author then gives us the criteria for determining the true prophet (Dt 18:21-22).

Deuteronomy differs from the rest of the Pentateuch in presenting Moses as a *prophet* (vv. 15 and 18; cf. Dt 34:10-12). There is not much point in concentrating on the differences it establishes between the prophet, the priest, and the political leader. These three functions are really seen as parallel mediations between the people and God. The author shows clear preference for prophetic mediation. Doubtless he was writing at a time when the kingship and the priesthood were undergoing a grave crisis. The prophets were the only ones to proclaim God's will, a return to the Law, and the constitution of a new people founded on the Word.

Thus the prophet has distinct superiority over the king and the priest. The king is confined to the political sphere, the priest to the cultic, but the prophet is the bearer of God's Word in every domain of life, individual and social. Priest and king are concerned with a law already determined; the prophet is open to new demands, unforeseen situations. His God is a God of change and novelty. He is much more immersed in the profane, where the priest is altogether sacral.

Finally, he has the power to transform words into acts. Moses is truly a prophet, and the author, who writes probably during the age of the great prophets, is quite right in regarding him as the greatest (cf. Dt 34:10). But the greatest of all prophets is destined to be Jesus Christ (Ac 3:33; 7:37). He will liberate the Word from the possession of priesthood and power, until it becomes God's active presence in the whole texture of daily life.

III. Jeremiah
1:4-5, 17-19
1st reading
3rd cycle

The word of Yahweh is the course of Jeremiah's vocation. It is delivered in three verse strophes (Jr 1:4-10) and is confirmed by those short visions, which determine the direction of Jeremiah's ministry (Jr 1:11-16). Finally there is a description of the courage the prophet will need to achieve his mission (vv. 17-19).

a) What we have in today's reading is marked by the *predestined* nature of the prophet's call (vv. 4-5). This is found at three levels: preexistence in the divine thought; consecration in his mother's womb; official investiture as a prophet for the nations. The note of predestination is a way of affirming the absolute communion between God and his prophet.

b) The prophet's most important quality is *strength.* These verses (17-19) were composed by Jeremiah after he had ministered for some time. He had come to know the people's hostility towards him. That is why he compares himself to a soldier confronted by enemy troops, a city in a state of siege. His strength has nothing to do with violence. It is victory over the self and control of sensibilities.

IV. 1 Corinthians Here we have a continuation of the argument
1:26-31 elaborated in 1 Corinthians 1:18-25, to show
2nd reading that human wisdom of itself is incapable of
1st cycle knowledge of God's person and his plan of
salvation. The proof is that God's manifestation and the realization of his plan would seem foolishness on this standard. They belong to categories that transcend human intelligence.

a) Paul continues his demonstration by an argument *ad hominem.* God continues to act with *foolishness* because as a sign of his presence in the world, he actually chooses a community as little qualified by worldly standards as the Corinthians are (vv. 26-28). He points out to the Corinthians that they would be better occupied in following out their vocation (bearing witness to the foolishness of God), than in meddling with false philosophies, which they are unable to understand.

b) Though men never have the right to boast of God's grace (v. 29), the Corinthians may do so, provided they glory in Christ (vv. 30-31, drawn from Jr 9:22-23). Their titles to glory are many: the justice of God which has established them, the holiness which divinizes their being, the redemption that liberates them from all alienation, including sin and death.

What human wisdom could provide such blessings? To live in Christ (v. 30) is to find one's glory in him (v. 31).

The intransigent tone of this passage may be disconcerting for modern Christians, who wish to have dialogue with the world, and express divine wisdom in secular terms. Nor are they likely to be reassured by hearing that the section belongs to a particular literary genre, where apologia and arguments *ad hominem* distort the true state of affairs.

We are dealing with a problem that is deeper. Nevertheless in the very text itself we have the outlines of a solution. Saint Paul is actually putting Christ forward as *Wisdom* (v. 30). The Lord is Wisdom because he reveals the mystery of God (cf. Col 2:3; 1 Co 1:24) in totally unexpected terms. He is that Wisdom which organizes the world by which man can find his way back to God (1 Co 1:21; cf. Rm 1:18-22). He is the "foolish" revelation of the invisible God; but he is also the center of the cosmos, and the first born of humanity (Col 1:15-16; cf. Jn 1:1-18). That is to say that man's effort to comprehend the universe must be under the aegis of the Wisdom which is Christ.

The gospel is a gratuitous epiphany of God, an insight about the world and about man, the key to achieving a balance between them. Man uses every conceivable "wisdom" he can muster in order more fully to know himself and the universe. But no system of itself provides the key. There is no more an answer, for instance, in Marxism than in capitalism; we are always doomed to be plunged into "foolishness" by such nostrums.

We can never afford to ignore the point made here by Paul. Human wisdom is not the only sort of widsom nor is it the best means of manifesting Jesus Christ. Paul actually likes to discern in Christian inadequacy where wisdom is concerned, a sign of God's presence. Out of relative nothingness he brings his Church into being (cf. Mt 11:25).

Is it not so really even among human beings? It is the most abject and the least cultivated, who, despite their poverty, can bring home to us the truth that personal dignity is more important than the bread offered to them. Our weakness, our very inability to overcome sin; are not these in themselves signs of divine election?

Our eucharistic assemblies nowadays include many "well-born," many wise, many powerful. They must never forget that the Lord they are celebrating came in weakness and foolishness.

V. 1 Corinthians 7:32-35
2nd reading
2nd cycle

This whole chapter is concerned with Christian states of life. Paul has treated in succession of married folk who live together (1 Co 7:3-5, 10), discussing what meaning continence can have for them; of married folk who live apart (v. 11); of those who live together but are not of the same faith (vv. 12-16). He then goes on to consider Christians who are not married, among them "virgins." He discusses men and women (vv. 25-35), betrothed people who are considering cohabitation at an early stage (vv. 36-38). Lastly he deals with celibates and widows (vv. 39-40).

However, he himself introduces some confusion into what should be a fairly obvious classification. He mentions continence (his own as it happens) in the middle of his remarks to married folk (vv. 6-7), and when dealing with people not yet committed (vv. 27a, 28, 29b, 33) he mentions marriage. The confusion is probably due to the tensions in the Corinth community. Attitudes varied between Encratite continence (1 Co 7:1-5) and the greatest sexual libertarianism (cf. 1 Co 5:1-13; 6:16-20).

Paul is concerned with sustaining at once marital indissolubility and the charism of continence. He shows how both have their source in the Lord.

If he sometimes gives the impression of being dubious about marriage, the reason is that he wants to establish equal acceptance for the new state of *continence*. Marriage was already known and accepted as the only possible state.

The counsels given to the unmarried ("virgins" in v. 25 designates men as well as women), recommending continence, are based essentially on the "distress of the present time" (v. 26) and the "trials in the flesh" (v. 27). These phrases refer not only to the vicissitudes of daily life, especially conjugal life; the force of the word *thlipsis* is essentially eschatological. We can understand it as a sort of devaluation of the significance of time. Time does not now have the meaning it had before Jesus Christ, when, generation after generation, it was proceeding towards its term. Now, the term has been practically realized because God is present in all. Consequently marriage does not now have the absolute importance it had previously, and spouses must give themselves to God, who is present in them, as well as to one another. The eternal God being present, time is precarious (vv. 29, 31). The institution of marriage, which is so strongly linked to the temporal, has been relativized by the advent of the final times (vv. 33-34).

Since the advent of Jesus Christ, each person lives the presence of God in himself, and the Christian bases his whole life on this. It cannot however be lived in isolation from events and from other men. The married state, even though it has lost its absolute status for the perpetuation of the race, continues to be the normal means of living the presence of God through interpersonal relations. God's presence however in the relationship is implicit; only when the Kingdom of God is all in all will it become explicit. Because we cannot live by what is implicit only, spouses need sometimes to be alone before God. That is why Paul shows a preference for virginity.

The proper blending of implicit and explicit is indeed fundamental in the Christian life. Christ is present in the life of the Christian, who offers the spiritual sacrifice of Romans 12:1-2. Such worship however must be based on the worship rendered by Christ; implicit and explicit are interwoven in eucharistic cult. Throughout all Christian life the profane must be punctuated by the eucharistic. So it is with marriage and celibacy. For Paul they are not mutually exclusive states, but rather complementary. Celibacy aims at living explicitly what marriage lives implicitly. The two are as necessary, one to the other, as life is to rite and rite to life.

VI. 1 Corinthians 12:31-13:13
2nd reading
3rd cycle

We can regard this passage as a hymn in three strophes. The first demonstrates the dependence of charisms or charity (vv. 12:31-13:3); the second makes this truth personal (vv. 13:4-13:7 or 8a): the third (vv. 13:8-13:13) makes a sort of antithesis between charity and the other virtues. It endures, whereas they pass away.

The hymn, coming as it does in the heart of the letter, gives the composition indeed its whole unity. Many subjects have been treated: celibacy and marriage, a collection for the poor, the use of charisms. The hymn affirms that the answers to all the problems are subordinate to charity. It is more important than charisms (vv. 1-2), more important than the collection (v. 3).

a) The eulogy follows a literary pattern common in classical and Jewish literature (cf. Wi 7:22-30, of which Paul adapts several verses). One or other virtue is extolled. First of all, Paul takes up the more spectacular charisms among those which so attracted the Corinthians (2 Co 12): glossolalia, prophecy, assistance, even suicide by fire, which was recorded as the acme of devoted courage. All are as nothing compared with charity. He uses the word charity ten times, each time without article or complement. That is to say he not only personifies it, but makes it an absolute that nothing can modify or limit.

b) In verses 4-8a charity is *personified*. It is patient, with the patience which endures hurt and controls resentment (Mt 5:10-11, 21-24). It is kind. It does not envy (a common Jewish sentiment where other religions were concerned; Ac 5:17; 17:5). It is not boastful (1 Co 4:6, 18-19). It does nothing rude (1 Co 11:4-6; 5:1-6; 11:21-22). It is disinterested (in the sense that it takes care of the weak; 1 Co 8). Finally, it does not fail (v. 8a). Endlessly exposed to trail, it triumphs endlessly over evil. It is here that we notice particularly Paul's anxiety to praise charity after the manner of a philosopher eulogizing a virtue. The phraseology "it is not . . . it is not," "all . . . all" is characteristically stoic.

c) The third strophe contrasts the knowledge we actually have with that which will be ours after death. Paul is not undervaluing the order of theological virtues that has come into being. He says precisely that faith, hope and charity, all three, will *continue*, but that charity is the greater. Verse 13 should be translated very exactly. He does not mean to say that faith and hope will disappear in favor of charity. He is really concerned to emphasize the whole order of theological virtues, where charity has an overarching importance. The affirmation that faith and hope will endure with charity, seems perhaps to be in conflict with the two texts where he asserts that the first two virtues will cease (2 Co 5:7; Rm 8:24). They should however be taken in this context in the biblical sense of human attitude in welcoming the Word of God and cleaving to it. In the new covenant, the Word has become Christ and reveals love to us. Faith however continues to be the total engagement of the self to God. There does not seem to be any reason for saying that this total engagement will cease when faith passes into the fullness of the heavenly vision. Faith and hope will emerge from the present obscurity, due to the time of trial in which we live, a tension which frequently engages Paul's whole attention (Rm 8:24; 2 Co 5:7). This obscurity however does not basically affect the religious organism. We are, by the new covenant, children of God; rendered, by love, faithful to him and aligned to his will.

All considered then, faith, hope and charity are but different aspects of a spiritual organism, that is new and complex certainly, but above all a unity.

Very striking in the passage is the manner in which Paul rejects all human definitions of love, even the most spiritual, even the most heroic. He does not find that love is necessarily present in a large network of interpersonal relations. The fact that the love he celebrates is so very different from the human concepts, but nevertheless a human act, underlines the truth that our lives are not regulated by a catalogue of virtues or by legal obligation, but rather by Christ's presence in us.

VII. Matthew
5:1-12a
Gospel
1st cycle

The beatitudes, as originally delivered by Jesus, were doubtless short formulas in prophetic style. They proclaimed the advent of the Kingdom as foretold by Isaiah, for whom the poor, the hungry and the afflicted would be the beneficiaries of God's salvation (Is 58:6-10; 61:1-3; 49:8-13, etc.). They were an affirmation that the time had come when the privileges of the Kingdom would be accorded, not on the basis of merit or particular conditions fulfilled, but simply because of God's will to save.

a) Luke invested the predominantly prophetic and eschatological tone of these formulas with a sapiental teaching, which offers compensation here below to the afflicted. He interprets them in the light of Jesus' doctrine about poverty and the use of riches.

He makes them an apologia for the sociologically poor, the social class to which the first converts belonged (Ac 4:34-5:11).

Matthew's attitude is different. He is concerned to give the gospel a deeper moral dimension, and interprets the beatitudes in the light of the *new justice,*[*] and the spirit of the sermon on the mount. Where Luke distinguishes between a "now" and a "future," he suppresses this distinction. The Kingdom is already present for anyone who wishes to grasp it, by a life in conformity with its justice. Both evangelists have in fact superimposed on the prophetic tone of Jesus' words (God is coming to save), Matthew a moral emphasis, Luke one that is all at once sociological, logical, and eschatological.

b) The Isaian *poor,* who are the beneficiaries of the gratuitous salvation of God in the original (Is 61:1-3), become for Luke the sociological poor. For Matthew they are beneficiaries because of their spiritual attitude.

Luke regards as beneficiaries of the future Kingdom the persecuted, the victims that is of events which for the Jews augured the last times. Matthew goes deeper by making the precision that they be persecuted for justice's sake. He has a similar modification of the beatitude of the hungry. They were among the beneficiaries of the future Kingdom for Isaiah (Is 49:6-13). Luke takes them as those who are really hungry for bread (see the parable of the rich man and Lazarus). Matthew, with his moral bias, makes them hunger for justice.

As a further reinforcement of this teaching Matthew adds some further beatitudes to those of Luke, all of them with a similar thrust. Blessed are the "merciful" (charity and pardon); the "meek" (probably a doublet merely for "poor." The Aramaic word for both is the same, and Matthew by the doublet in translation passes from the sociological to the spiritual); the "peace-makers" (or better still: the carriers of peace); and finally the "pure of heart" (a reference to the legal purity that enabled people to

[*] See the doctrinal theme: *justice,* p. 144.

"see God in the temple," for which Matthew now substitutes a more spiritual purity, as in Mt 15: 1-20).

The three or four original beatitudes of Jesus were not a proclamation of the conditions necessary for entry to the Kingdom. They were rather an affirmation, in prophetic idiom, that some afflicted folk (the categories usual in prophecy) had finally touched the benevolent concern of God. Very soon, altogether gratuitously, he would inaugurate his Kingdom.

In Luke, this kerygmatic emphasis is profoundly modified. The beatitudes are not now concerned with God's initiative, but with man's predicament (cf. the interpellation "you"). The direct style reinforces this. Luke indeed gives us four maledictions which create the impression that salvation is attainable by some classes, but refused to others. His vocabulary is extremely realistic (have your fill, laugh . . .), the product of social and vengeful eschatological attitudes that were common in some communities ("now" . . . "then" . . .).

Matthew has another view. He, too, doubtless disregards the prophetic emphasis, and concentrates rather on the human conditions for access to the Kingdom than on the divine initiative. He interprets these conditions as an anxious catechist, altogether concerned with the moral improvement of his readers. His whole sermon on the mount revolves around the concept of a new justice. His whole Gospel seems to be put forward as a new pentateuch, promulgated by a new Moses.

That is why he introduces concepts like "in spirit," "for justice sake" to the beatitudes and doubles their number. He is altogether a moralizer (gentleness, pure heart, humbleness).

This indicates that there is no absolute, single interpretation of the beatitudes. It indicates too, that while fidelity to Christ's teaching was always unanimous, it was not uniform. The modern Church can learn a lesson from this. Finally, it indicates that the different interpretations of the beatitudes, to be faithful to Christ's teaching, must blend with moralizing, catechetical and eschatological viewpoints the prophetic and kerygmatic emphasis of Jesus himself. God really comes, and he comes gratuitously.

VIII. Mark The two miracles in this passage are the first
1:21-28 performed by Jesus according to the synoptic
Gospel tradition. They are presented however, espe-
2nd cycle cially the first, in terms of a literary genre often
employed in the narration of miracles. We
have mention of the condition of the sick person (vv. 23 and 30), the sovereign authority and power of Jesus (vv. 25 and 31a), the immediate efficacy of his word or gesture (vv. 26 and 31b), finally, the crowd's reaction (vv. 27-28).

a) The over-all purpose of the genre is to reveal Christ's *power*. Mark, in describing the miracles, will often concentrate on that aspect of the power which counters the influence hitherto exercised by demons. The current belief was that humanity was under the sway of "impure spirits" (v. 27) who brought about sicknesses, cataclysms and death. God would one day end their sway, by means of an envoy, a "holy one" of God (v. 24: the term indicates association with the world of God as against that of the "impure," and it is even possible that it is a word-play on "Nazarean" in v. 24). For Mark then the miracle is not principally, as in the other synoptics, a summons to faith. It is the power displayed by God's envoy, which counters the sway of the spirits precisely in their own domain of sickness and death.*

This is, as yet a very primitive manner of describing redemption and salvation, but it indicates the power of Jesus as he reveals himself to be the envoy of God (cf. the words: threats, obey, authority in vv. 25, 27, which will be found again in Mk 4:41).

b) Mark does however succeed in establishing a link between the power and the *resurrection*. Many of his miracle narratives

---

* See the doctrinal theme: *healing,* p. 149.

allude to the resurrection, the sign of Jesus' power over death. The miracles seem to be the preliminary skirmishes of a combat that will be fully engaged in only on the cross and in resurrection. Thus in the second cure (vv. 29-31) the word *egeirein,* translated "get up," is really the term which designates the resurrection itself in primitive catechesis (Mk 6:14-16; 12:26; 14:28; Ac 3:15). The word recurs often in Mark's miracle-narratives (Mk 5:41; 9:26-27), as if to suggest that miracle is only comprehensible in terms of the paschal mystery.

c) It may seem surprising that the first confession of Jesus' *Messiahship* comes from the lips of a demoniac, at a stage when the crowds and the leaders were hesitating (cf. further Mk 1:34; 3:7). Today however we realize that someone in a pathological state, simply because of his oversensitivity and unawareness of self-identity, will frequently show uncanny intuition about something that challenges his illusions. He can only recover balance by resolutely immersing himself in real relationships.

The Eucharist is the paschal mystery at work in those domains of human life that are still under the sway of evil. Would the following interpretation of Mark's episode be altogether allegorical? Peter's house (v. 29) is the place of ecclesial assembly as against the synagogue (v. 23), the place of the messianic banquet served by the Church, now cured of fever, in honor of the Savior. She is now discharging a service that had been previously the responsibility of the angels themselves (Mk 1:13).

IX. Luke 4:21-30   This episode comes immediately after Jesus'
    Gospel   first preaching in the Nazareth synagogue (Lk
    3rd cycle   4:16-21). He defines his mission in terms of
                   Isaiah's text 61:1-2.

a) By comparing himself with the Servant of Isaiah Jesus shows his preference for the poor and afflicted (Lk 4:17-20). He fails to read one important verse in Isaiah, which proclaimed a "day of vengeance" for the Gentiles (Is 61:3). He thus shows his desire not to condemn the Gentiles. His listeners, astonished at first by his "words of grace" (v. 22), became scandalized when they understood that Jesus preferred to live at Capharnaum. This was a commercial city of mixed population (v. 23). He was proposing to accomplish there a work of salvation that he was refusing to do for his own neighbors (v. 24).

Jesus' reply clearly indicates his *missionary* intention. The great prophets of Israel did not always make Jews the beneficiaries of their miracles, and actually sometimes turned exclusively to the Gentiles (vv. 25-27). He intends to imitate them in this (cf. Mk 5:1-20; Lk 7:1-10; Mk 7:24-30; Lk 17: 11-19).

b) In Luke's compilation of the account we can discern the influence of another idea. Jesus' discourse (vv. 23-27) is in fact too violent for the context, and does not really answer the misgivings expressed in verse 22. It was certainly delivered by Jesus (it is in fact heavily Aramaic in vocabulary), but at some later stage. Verse 23 alludes to miracles wrought at Capharnaum, whereas Jesus had not actually yet gone there (Lk 4:31). The discourse furthermore contrasts *Jews* and *Gentiles,* where the people were contrasting Nazareth and Capharnaum. Capharnaum could not be considered a Gentile city.

Finally, Luke certainly adds a remark of his own (vv. 28-30) when he describes the hostility of the people to Jesus. He is in fact investing the first episode of the public life with the general atmosphere of the public life as a whole. We have the breach with Jesus' own social environment, the mission to the Gentiles, the unbelief of Israel.

The missionary must expect challenge from every quarter. Paul endured affronts from Gentiles as well as from "false brethren." Eliseus' power was challenged by the Gentile Naaman, that of Jesus by his own compatriots.

Though he is by definition linked with the Church, the missionary belongs to the world that has to be evangelized. In this double loyalty his love without limits is forged, but he has to live under strained conditions. The non-Christian world will not accept him as its own, particularly when his culture is different. Nor will the Christian world always accept him because his stance is a threat to certain accepted standards. It is his business to question values that have been sacralized. He disturbs, and frightens. When ecclesiastical authority itself becomes uneasy, he may have to make agonizing retreats.

His very rupture however with his place of origin can become the opportunity for inestimable inner growth. He has given his life to Jesus Christ. Challenge will purify him, and make him more and conformed by persecution to his crucified Lord and Savior.

B. DOCTRINE

1. The Theme of Justice

A people's spiritual odyssey is a profoundly complex proceeding. It is an adventure that engages the very depth of their being and colors the whole texture of their daily life. In search of the great goal men will turn in various directions. Some directions will seem promising; other trails sooner or later will vanish in nothingness. Through out the whole pilgrimage a subtle bond gets forged between the group as a whole and the individuals who compose it, particularly certain individuals. Religious leaders get thrown up, who provide a new insight about the road to be traveled. The community will either follow them or reject them. Language is affected by the whole development. Terms are coined to describe experience and the idiom is powerfully enriched. Or on the other hand the religious terms themselves may grow old and tired and finally disappear.

When the quest finally penetrates to faith, the effect upon religious language is particularly noticeable. It seems indeed to be transformed utterly. The vocabulary of justice and justification is a case in point. Jewish history indicates that the journey towards faith was long and arduous, and language only adapted itself gradually to the insights. Likewise the spread of Christianity throughout the world was destined to reshape the religious language of many peoples.

Divine justice and human justice in Israel

Man's natural desire for security was translated, in all primitive societies, into a scrupulous respect for the norms and customs which traditionally governed both social relationships and relationships with the gods. To assure a sacral stability, the community would exercise judiciary power over its members. It exacted respect for law and justified the innocent. Thus juridical and moral norms governing behavior were developed in an essentially religious context.

It was so originally in Israel; but the gradual growth in faith slowly transformed this context, so as to make it almost unrecognizable. To begin with Yahweh was the supreme Judge; he rewarded the good and punished the wicked. What initiated the Jew to the order of divine justice and enabled him to share the holiness of God was observance of the Law. Deeper insight in faith begins to change the language about justice and justification. The basic structure was maintained; but an order of justice that answered to security needs begins to yield to an order of mercy that answers to faith. The religious horizons of Israel are widened.

The disconcerting discovery came, when it was realized that the event was the point *par excellence* of encounter with God. Yahweh is the Totally-Other and the Creator of all things. Man has no valid rights before him. Everything that Yahweh does for his creature is a gratuitous expression of benevolence. He alone can save man, and it becomes more and more clear that salvation is a gift beyond all human reach. God's intervention to deliver man from sin is not a recompense for merit, but a demonstration that he is a God of mercy, tenderness and pardon.

The recognition of the Totally-Other God goes *pari passu* with the realization that man cannot merit salvation. Such justice as can be achieved by observance of the law is empty by contrast with the salvation Yahweh has reserved for his people, and which alone can fulfill them. Man realizes that he is indeed a creature of paradox. The relation to God that is kindled by faith, and which is man's proper destiny, cannot be reduced to the moral order. Divine justice and human justice stand in contrast to one another. Only abandonment to God can bring a man to salvation. Thus all eyes are turned to the messianic future; who is the one who can resolve the paradox?

Jesus of Nazareth and the justice of the Kingdom

The Messiah's intervention did not, in that sense, resolve the paradox, but rather intensified it. It is true that the order of faith and the moral order have not a common basis; but when the latter is brought to perfection in the new law of universal love, it opens the way to the order of faith and salvation.

By contrast with the formalism and hypocrisy of the Pharisees, Jesus reveals the unexplored riches of the authentic Mosaic tradition. He has not come to abolish the law, but to fulfill it. The fulfillment is universal brotherly love, into which the law is transmuted, when it is observed with fidelity to the event, and constant acceptance of the will of the living God. The Beatitudes are the charter of the New Covenant. It is only for the poor, the gentle and the humble that the new law of love becomes possible. These are the people who do not seek to quench their thirst for the absolute with any created good, who do not seek to possess anything, but abandon themselves to God in absolute confidence.

Jesus demanded this total abandonment; but he also announced the advent of the Kingdom. Man was given salvation, the Father's gratuitous gift. If he had to abandon himself to God, it was in order to become God's adoptive son and have his yearnings satisfied. Fidelity to the new law of love is the fidelity of a member of God's own family.

The Father's Kingdom is inaugurated in the person of Jesus. The absolute renunciation he demands from himself, full acceptance of the creatural condition, he demands from his brethren too. Thus speaks the Savior of the World. The one who proclaims himself Savior of humanity is the very one who experiences the human predicament at its utmost depths. This could only be possible for the Son of God. God so loved the world that he gave his only-begotten son, and in him found the perfect creatural and filial response.

Justified by faith in Jesus Christ

It took the primitive community many years to see all the implications of Jesus' intervention. At first apostolic preaching stresses the eschatological dimensions of the Kingdom that goes on being awaited. Saint Paul's early letters reflect this mentality where the order of judgment prevails. Very soon however Christians began to see the real meaning of their link with the Risen Christ. Instead of the Kingdom to come, they see the Kingdom that has already come, and must be built here on earth. Christian waiting is translated from passivity into mission. All believers are called to be God's partners in contructing his Kingdom.

It was under Paul's influence that the vocabulary of justice and justification received a specifically Christian coloring. Justification, salvation that is, is an actuality here and now. It is not indeed the product of human justice, based on human resources, but neither is it a purely eschatological entity. The Christian is a man genuinely justified by faith in Jesus Christ. He is justified, because this faith makes him an adoptive son, and opens for him the way to the Father. His justification is God's gift, but it becomes for him the principle of filial activity.

The justification of all peoples in Jesus Christ

The terminology of justice and justification comes from Jewish religious experience. It served to clarify, in the hands of Saint Paul, the nature of the salvation we acquired in Jesus Christ. But its importance is not confined to this. The very development of this terminology describes the stages by which one comes to faith, and it is of great pedagogic value. The actual words of course are relatively unimportant; but the expression of the meaning they enshrine, in any new idiom, is a matter of the utmost delicacy.

All peoples evangelized by the Church are already at some stage in the spiritual quest, and it is the missionary's task to assess this correctly. The proclamation of the Good News must meet this precise moment. All the spiritual quests, when we examine the language that expresses them, are invariably attempts to articulate in some way the moral and religious orders. In the non-Christian ones, we can discern a notion of collective and individual morality, through which it is hoped human aspirations will be fulfilled. Moral conduct has an immediate religious reference; salvation will come by this means. The traditional pagan always sought thus to insert himself into the cosmic harmony, the stability of which was assured by the sovereign deities.

From this to the faith in Jesus Christ there are two stages, that we know from the history of Israel to be successive. First must come the recognition of the Totally-Other God, the God of faith, with all that this implies by way of adjustment in normal life and culture. This will gradually bring about an awareness of the radical distinction between the religious and moral orders, however closely they be linked. The religious order is essentially one of mercy. Man does indeed have an intuition that salvation depends on God's gratuitous initiative, that, at this ultimate level, moral performance is really without efficacy. His awareness of sin sharpens his sensibility; he sees that it is the ultimate blindness. When the first stage has been absorbed, then comes the second. This is the recognition of the mystery of Christ in whom the order of faith is thoroughly accomplished. It is only in him that the relationship between the religious and the moral orders is properly articulated. In him a new people is enabled to make a specific contribution to the building of the Kingdom.

Our experience of justification in the Eucharist

The Christian awareness of justification is deepest during the eucharistic celebration. Those assembled are conscious of responding to a divine summons to salvation, conscious that their thanksgiving depends on the ecclesial link with Christ that makes them members of his Body. The marvels of God can be properly changed only by the children of God.

Sharing the Word and the Bread proves the best channel of the grace manifested once for all in Jesus Christ. It should constantly draw the faithful towards conversion from their sin, and towards conduct as children of God in the tenor of their daily lives. It should summon them to that total interior poverty, with which as adoptive children they must follow the first-born Brother in the way of obedience. But at the same time it makes them conscious of the grandeur of their filial state. Because they are justi-

fied by faith in Jesus Christ, they are God's partners in the building of the Kingdom, and they must honor that responsibility here
below. The Eucharist too will strengthen the bonds of universal
brotherhood that are symbolized in the assembly itself. It is such
bonds that will bear witness to their constant fidelity day after
day. This ecclesial sign must never cease to glow before the eyes
of men.

2. Theme of Healing

In our day healing the sick is the province of medical science,
and each new step forward in this domain is felt to be further
evidence of man's increasing mastery over nature. Sickness does
not have for us the religious significance it had for the ancients.
If we get ill we call a doctor. Having recourse to God for a cure
tends to suggest indeed a religious sentiment that is still unpuri-
fied, or even tainted with magic.

Consequently modern man is somewhat taken aback by the
numerous healings attributed to Jesus by the evangelists. If he be
a believer, he will tend to see Jesus as the divine Thaumaturge
who proves his mission by such miracles. By and large he misses
the real meaning of such healings.

The matter is too important to be neglected. In fact it concerns
the basic essentials of Christianity. When seen in the context of
the salvation acquired in Jesus Christ, these gospel healings have
a very actual meaning for our faith. They provide insights indeed
that have been far too often ignored.

Sickness and healing in Israel

To begin with, one thing is obvious. Sickness and the distress
it brings makes for considerable insecurity. It illustrates the weakness and frailty of the human condition, which is exposed to
all the risks of the unpredictable. Israel, like all other peoples,
had this experience.

Sickness runs counter to the yearning for the absolute, for

something solid and stable, that is common to all men. The nations adjoining Israel looked upon it as a plague produced by evil spirits, or the visitation of a divinity whose cult had been neglected. Healing was invariably sought through ritual, because rite was the only avenue to the sacral. Exorcisms would be practiced to retard the influence of evil spirits. A god's pardon would be implored by means of victims or sacrificial liturgies.

Israel too was preoccupied with the religious import of sickness, not with its natural causes. To them it seemed a visitation from Yahweh, who was punishing men. Very soon it became clear that Yahweh's only reason for such punishment must be man's sin. Sickness is the punishment of the chosen people's infidelity.

If Yahweh strikes, he also cures. Because he is the Totally-Other, the absolute master of life, his healing has to be implored as a grace. The grace will be accorded the believer only when he humbly confesses his sin and turns confidently to God's all-powerful mercy.

Thus sickness is the consequence of sin. It is an evil, and like sin itself will find no place in the new world. When the final times come, when the Spirit of life shall have renewed the face of the earth, sickness will be definitively overcome. The prophetic oracles that describe the coming of the Kingdom tell of the healing of incurable diseases. The lame shall walk, the blind shall recover sight, and so on.

The question however arose whether sickness was altogether to be explained by divine disapproval. Was there a connection between it and personal sin? As the insights of faith deepened in Israel there came the hint of another explanation. Sickness is not necessarily the result of personal sin. It can be a trial sent by God to strengthen the loyalty of his friends. This is the case of Job. Another insight suggested that sickness might be shown one day to have expiatory value for the faults of sinness. Messianic hope becomes involved. The one who inaugurates the last times takes on the visage of the Just One suffering. He takes our maladies upon himself and cures them by his own bruises.

The salvific import of Jesus' cures

For Jesus, as for his contemporaries, sickness was an evil, the result of sin, evidence of Satan's power over men. Thus the expulsion of spirits or the healing of the sick were part of the great messianic act that was inaugurating the Kingdom.

Before he healed he demanded faith; the cure was a salvific initiative that summoned the response of faith. It was not the act of a thaumaturge, but the act of the human Savior. In a way it was the anticipation of the great paschal act. This was something the believer could share, the victory of the new man. By the action of the Holy Spirit all things, spiritual and corporal, would be restored to their true status in the Father's design. Healing has the value of a sign. It is the touchstone of the universal restoration that transforms the interior man, who is renewed in heart and cured of sin. Healing would have no meaning apart from faith; faith is the only living principle that can save a man, body and soul.

As we observe these healings by Jesus we should be very clear about the nature of his intervention. It is the man God who is acting. Because his whole human life unto death was one of perfect filial obedience to the Father's creative plan, Jesus overcame sin. Simultaneously he became the one and only source whereby man can hope to build a proper human future. The cures he wrought remind us of the basic unity of God's creative work; all life, that of the body as well as the soul, comes from above. The salvation Jesus brought frees us from sin and establishes us in a state of sonship. Indirectly, but inevitably, this affects the whole human enterprise. It is a veritable "healing" wrought upon humanity as a whole.

He came among us as the physician of sinners. Sin being a rejection of God, the unique Source of life, we can see how his salvific work is something that touches all creation, material and spiritual. The healing of sickness is principally a sign of that other, more universal, healing. We can see how he fulfills the prophecy of the suffering Just Man. Obedient unto the cross, he accepts the state of suffering humanity in order to triumph definitively over humanity's woes.

The Church and the human enterprise

The Church, which is the body of the Risen Christ, has been throughout her long history essentially a "healer." Today however, apart from very exceptional cases, we cannot regard this healing function as principally concerned with physical sickness. Modern man will tend to consider the natural causes of sickness, and will rely on medical science to overcome them. Sickness always continues to be of course an occasion of spiritual trial because it creates insecurity. But the believer who turns to God in illness does so mainly to deepen his acceptance of the Father's will.

How then can we describe the Church as a "healer"? By introducing the believer to the living relationship with the Risen Christ, by gradually attuning him to his state of adoptive sonship, the Church leads him to imitate Christ's acceptance of the creatural condition. The obedience unto death of Christ is a fidelity that reveals man's true potential. The believer is better equipped than any other person to devote himself to human projects, because he undertakes them with the guide-lines of the gospel. With this perspective the whole human enterprise becomes for him a veritable work of healing. There is no greater obstacle to the terrestrial city than the disequilibrium caused by sin, man's frenetic attempt, that is, to divinize himself.

The ecclesial task of healing, which is limited only by the task of human civilization, is the joint task of Christ and his partners in faith. The faith required for this healing is not a passive faith but the faith of partners. The ecclesial task is exceedingly long, something that must be taken up again and again. Sin, in our world, continues to be a reality; the victory of faith will always seem to be jeopardized by the wisdom of the world.

Such are the reflections that indicate, rather more than the miraculous cure of a sick person, how the whole human enterprise finds "healing" in the basic tenets of Christianity.

The great sign of healing: universal charity

Today, as in apostolic times, healing should be accompanied by the proclamation of the Good News. If what has been said hitherto is correct, the greatest sign of healing that Christians can offer to the modern world is the ideal they have of the human being, formed after the evangelic pattern.

We have many passages in the gospels which describe the healing of sick persons. All of them must be regarded as works of love, the most universal kind of love, if we are to grasp their real significance in Jesus' ministry. The person who is healed through faith in Christ, and who, imitating Christ becomes himself a healer of others, is the one who has made the new commandment his own. "Love one another as I have loved you" (as I have loved you, that is to say, to the point of giving my life for all). The whole human enterprise will be launched on a proper basis, when the human ideal formed by its promoters is that of the one who accepts the other in all the mystery of his otherness.

Charity of such dimensions is a scandal to the unbeliever. Such people will not see here the sign of healing, held out to them too, until the light of faith illumines them. Christ when he healed called for faith. The Church cannot do less.

Thanksgiving for healing

It is in the Eucharist that the faithful forge a living relation with Christ, the physician of souls and bodies. They become his partners in the healing task.

We need only mention two essentials aspects of the eucharistic assembly. There is the penitential one, which permeates the whole celebration; those who share the body of Christ are the bearers of divine pardon. Then there is the aspect of universal brotherhood. The believer, when he receives the Eucharist, receives all men as brothers in the faith. Returning to ordinary life he will do the work of peace. And so the Eucharist makes of its sharers healers.

FOURTH WEEK

I. Hebrews
11:32-40
1st reading
1st cycle
Monday

This is a continuation of the preaching argument (He 11:1-19), meant to encourage the Jewish converts who are so pressured that they wish to return. But there is never any turning back.

The author reminds his listeners of the example of their Jewish ancestors. These remained faithful under *trial* and did not turn back. They were always ready for the adventure of faith. He writes in terms reminiscent of the "Eulogy of the Patriarchs" in Wisdom (10-16) and Sirach (40-49). We have a series of heroes: Gideon, Barag and Samson, who subdued kingdoms (book of Judges) and practiced justice, David who achieved fulfillment of the prophecies. Prophets, like Daniel, who closed the mouth of lions (Dn 6:23; Jg 14:1-10), or the young men who overcame the rage of fire (Dn 3:49-50). Other prophets, like Elias or Eliseus, who restored resuscitated children to their mothers (1 K 17:23; 2 K 4:36). Others still, like Eleazar and the seven brothers (2 M 6-7) who endured without weakening torture, imprisonment (Jr 20:2; 37:15), mutilation (Isaiah?), assassination (Mt 23:34-35), exile in the desert (1 K 19), without ever losing hope for the future.

In verse 39 we have his argument. If our ancestors, who could not yet attain fulfillment of the promise, could endure all this; can we, who can attain it (He 10:36) be less faithful than them?

Faith is supernatural, but it is nevertheless lived as a human experience. It must be marked by a self-giving where the future is concerned, by a readiness to risk one's securities and be open to newness. The Jews showed lack of faith when they wanted to return to the fleshpots of Egypt. They should have trusted the future, even though at that moment nothing but death seemed to confront them. Abraham, on the other hand, showed faith. He abandoned his homeland, convinced that at the end of his journey a better land awaited him than the one he left. These first Christians would be deficient in faith insofar as they preferred to revert to Jerusalem, to judaize, instead of trusting the change. It was Jesus of course who brought faith to the pitch of perfection. He encountered death, convinced that the risk was worthwhile, in view of the new life beyond.

In our era of mutation, faith must never rest at the stage of acceptance of truth. It must be a real self-giving to the future, a realization that the last word is not said just because some concepts become outmoded or some structures falter.

The essence of Christ's sacrifice lay in his total faith in a Father, who was able to produce the unexpected, even on the other side of death. Similarly, our eucharistic offering should consist in a jettisoning of the past and a trusting of ourselves to the event. Thus it becomes a profession of faith.

II. 2 Samuel
15:13-14, 30;
16:5-13a
1st reading
2nd cycle
Monday

Public opinion regarded Absalom, one of David's sons, as the only likely heir to the aging king. However, as the result of a fratricide (2 S 13), David had exiled him from the court. A vague reconciliation between the two did not prevent Absalom from contriving a revolt against his father, relying on the general discontent of the populace. When the time was ripe, he had himself consecrated king at Hebron, the old royal seat of the southern tribes. The revolt was now in the open.

David on hearing the news immediately left Jerusalem. He could not cope simultaneously with insurrections in the north and south. He sought to gain time by retreating to Transjordania in the hope of recruiting mercenaries. His *flight* had an atmosphere of mourning. Friends wept for him (v. 30), and enemies cursed him (16:5-14).

History was to deal harshly with David. His senile weakness did not soften the memory of his severity towards the people, and his leniency towards the rebels. Not surprisingly, the people rallied to a new king. David becomes now no more than a hunted figure, doomed to finish his reign in bitter failure. This was regarded as part of salvation history because it was an episode that revealed the presence of God and contributed to the realization of his plan (witness the association of the ark with the king's flight: vv. 15-26).

The most important moral of the passage is that failure and weakness do not impede God's plan. On the contrary, it is in the most complete acceptance of the human predicament, failures, misunderstandings, death itself, that the plan comes to fruition. The Son of God himself would later have to encounter similar failure, similar isolation, even death, before attaining glory and salvation.

III. Mark 5:1-20 The cure of the Gerasene demoniac is one of
　　Gospel　　the strangest episodes in the gospel. Exegetes
　　Monday　　agree in accepting its historical basis (vv. 1-2,
　　　　　　　7-8, 15, 18, 20) as a piece with an essentially missionary emphasis. Verses 3-5, 9-10, 11-14 may very well have been reworked by Mark as a sort of midrash on some Old Testament passage such as Isaiah 65:1-5.

Jesus' encounter with the Gerasene is his first contact with the *Gentile world*. Mark is particularly anxious to record (Mk 7:24-30, 31, 37) these few encounters. Immediately too, we notice, the forces of evil challenge Jesus. "What do you want with me" (v. 7) suggests that the demon expects Jesus to respect the different domains. Why should the Messiah enter a territory that is not his province?

Jewish ideas about Gentiles were quite unflattering. They

associated them with pigs (v. 11), dogs (Mk 7:27) or other impure animals which they were accustomed to eat (cf. Ac 10:9-16). They were represented as the slaves of demons (cf. the mention of fetters, bonds, binding, chains in vv. 2-5; cf. Ac 7:25), who frequented such impure places as tombs (symbol of the death to which Gentiles are consigned).

In such a highly colored context it is not surprising that Mark presents the salvation brought by Jesus to the Gentiles in spectacular terms. We have the expulsion of a legion of demons, the casting down of a herd of swine from a cliff into the sea (the classic punishment for sacrilege, cf. Mt 18:6). The evangelist however is mostly concerned with the spread of the Good News to the nations. Jesus himself was not able to undertake this mission, and Mark is explaining why. The Gentiles themselves require that he return to his own territory (v. 17); but Jesus requires the healed man to preach him to his fellow countrymen (vv. 19-20; cf. Mk 7:36-37). Noting that Mark passes over in silence Christ's prohibition of the apostles from going to the Gentiles (Mk 6:6-13; cf. Mt 10:6), we realize his anxiety to stress all indications of a genuine missionary apostolate in Jesus' own ministry.

In Mark, Jesus' first steps as rabbi show fidelity to some essential principles. He does not await the approach of the crowd but goes to meet them, in order to address the poorest and most estranged. He does not allow himself to be shut in by the boundaries of family, city or nation; but crosses all barriers in order to approach the unclean Gentiles.

His success however as a young rabbi is poor. Each class of listeners adopts an attitude of reserve, more or less. Only the demons know his secret, and they will not become converts. The heart of the Scribes is hardened. His relatives are preoccupied with mundane matters. The Jewish crowd does not consider his mission messianic. The Gentiles want him to go home. When he triumphs over demons, it is men who reject him, like the inhabitants of Jerusalem.

The agony which led Jesus to isolation and the cross was to continue. In a world now which has become, it seems, the "tomb of God," the Christian is likely to encounter the same isolation, the same indifference, from the wise ones. They are not even curious enough to inquire the reasons for his faith. This is the mark of God upon his life, a sign that cannot be read by men. Very often his eucharistic sharing of the Lord will become a sharing of his agony too.

IV. Hebrews 12:1-4
1st reading
1st cycle
Tuesday

In the previous chapter (He 11) the author put forward the example of the pilgrim people who were their ancestors for the benefit of his disturbed Judaeo-Christian audience. He now applies the pilgrim theme to the Christian people, pointing out that Christians will always be nomads in this world.

a) The nomad image is blended with that of the *athletic stadium* (as in 1 Co 9:24-10:5). Christians are runners in the arena, and their ancestors (v. 1) occupy the spectators' seats, encouraging them to persevere. The race is lengthy, and it is necessary to lose weight ("throw off everything" v. 1) to survive to the end.

Not all spectators are "supporters" necessarily. There are the opponents, the "sinners" (v. 3), who have previously offered many insults to Christ, and reserve like treatment for Christians.

b) The dominant image however is that of a *pilgrim* people. We have it principally in the recommendation (v. 2) to consider the person of their leader. Christ now takes the place of the column of fire that guided the people in the desert. The Israelites were being led towards material blessing: Christ will lead his people to "perfection" and to the throne of glory. The "perfection" in question is the state of those who remain faithful at the end of the pilgrimage. Christ is the "perfectioner," if one may coin a term that will render the force of the Greek text. He will, that is, bring the earthly pilgrimage to culmination in the sanctuary of glory.

c) Even though the vocabulary here is not liturgical in a specific sense, we do have perhaps consideration of Christ's *priestly* activity too. Previously the author has used the expiation ritual to show how Jesus has gone from the earth as far as the throne of God (He 9; 11:10-17) just as the high priest used to penetrate to the Holy of holies. But, whereas the high priest entered alone, Jesus brings all the people with him (He 9:14). The avenue is that of his flesh delivered for us (He 10:20) on Calvary and, symbolically, in the Eucharist.

V. 2 Samuel
18:9-10, 14b,
24-25a, 30-19:3
1st reading
2nd cycle
Tuesday

King David had fled to Mahanayim, in Transjordania, and recruited a new army from the people of that region. Absalom had just crossed the Jordan. A confrontation must ensue very soon.

The two armies were quite unequal in strength. In numbers that of Absalom was apparently superior. However that of David was commanded by seasoned officers like Joab (v. 2). It was familiar with the territory, which was full of forests, treacherous places and gorges (v. 8) that were destined to claim more victims than the army did, among them Absalom himself (v. 14).

One might well wonder how God's plan could become manifest amid this clash of arms. Yet it is true that Yahweh continued to educate his people by means of events, military or other, so that they would learn to understand and transcend them. One of the first stages in this education was the lesson that victories were not due to superior force, but to stratagems or topographical accidents independent of human planning. Israel thus learned at least not to be proud of victories, but to attribute them to God. That is the chief moral of today's reading.

Thus, little by little, the people came to understand that they did not need military strength or political alliances in order to overcome their enemies. God fights his own battles himself (Ex 14; Dt 32:27-30; Jos 23:9-10 etc.). In battle all that is required from the people is fidelity to him, and prayer (Ex 17:1-16; Jos 1:1-10; I S 7:9-12). It was through this prayer and obedience that they would soon learn the nature of the only real battle in which God is engaged. It is the struggle against the forces of evil which alienate humanity, the struggle in which Christ one day would gain the victory (Mk 5:1-20).

The account of David's victory is merely the abc of this long lesson. It would take men a considerable time to learn that they must divest themselves of power, and become aligned to the divine will.

VI. Mark 5:21-43   All the synoptics include with the resuscitation
   Gospel   of Jairus' daughter (vv. 21-24, 35-43) the cure
   Tuesday   of the woman with the issue of blood (vv.
                     25-34). This blending of two episodes is then
quite old apparently; but we do not know the reason. The key-word "twelve" years (vv. 25 and 42) may be the cause for associating the two; or the historical circumstances may really have been so.

Mark gives us the most primitive version. In him, the woman with the issue of blood still takes a very magical view of Jesus' powers, whereas Matthew and Luke make her an example of faith. In the other episode he is not concerned about whether the child is really dead or in a coma (v. 39). Matthew and Luke see the event in the light of the paschal mystery.

a) Mark has the woman approach Jesus as a doer of magic. She believes him the repository of mysterious forces that are

available to the needy. Her object is to benefit from these, as a
challenge to doctors who fail to cure (v. 26), and priests who
excommunicate one for uncleanness (Lv 15:25). For Mark it is
another instance of the general *misunderstanding* of the crowds
concerning Jesus and what he is. Luke on the other hand, though
for this purpose he has to introduce some modifications, treats
it as a miracle in answer to the required response of faith. The
woman makes a public profession of faith (Lk 8:47), whereas
in Mark she touches Jesus' garment in the greatest secrecy
(v. 28).

b) In the episode of Jairus' daughter too we have this failure
to recognize Jesus even in his *miracles*. Jesus seems not yet to
have achieved control over his power. He is awkward and distant
with the crowd and leaves them abruptly (v. 40b). He brings
with him his three disciples only (precisely the number required
for authentic witness), and ignores the parents (v. 37; contrary
to Lk 8:51). His tone even is one of reproach (Why . . . ; v. 39).
It takes considerable manipulation on Luke's part to create an
impression of benignity for this scene.

Finally we have Jesus' gesture of healing (v. 41; more affec-
tionate in Lk 8:54), and an ambiguous formula which could be
taken by Mark's Greek readers in a magical sense (v. 41; strangely
similar to the formula in Ac 9:40: *talitha koumi*). Clearly, in the
Marcan version, Jesus is hesitant about his healing power. He
has not yet gained personal control over it (cf. vv. 30-32). He
has not yet determined the conditions of faith necessary for those
who benefit from it. Meanwhile he continues to impose silence
on them, and on the witnesses (v. 43).

VII. **Hebrews**	The argument begun in Hebrews 12:1-4, de-
12:4-7, 11-15	signed to comfort the audience in their exile
1st reading	from Jerusalem, is continued. A new point is
1st cycle	made. Trial is a correction, such as all children
Wednesday	receive from their father.

This idea of *paternal correction* is fairly new in the New Testament. The author is appealing to ordinary human experience. All fathers have been at some time extremely severe. At the time their correction seemed harsh and painful; but later it was seen to be benevolent and just (vv. 9-11). So is it, according to the author, with life's painful vicissitudes, when they are viewed as paternal reprimands or punishments.

He relies also on a sapiental argument (vv. 5-7). The rabbis were wont to correct their disciples quite severely, but were not prevented by that from regularly calling them "sons" (Si 4:17; 23:2; Pr 3:11-12; 13:24; 23:12-14). Old talmudic traditions are often concerned with such precisions in rabbinic circles.

The two images however (familial and rabbinic fatherhood) really emphasize a more profound notion. If God corrects his "sons" (v. 8) treating them as illegitimates, it is because he sees in them his own son nailed to the cross (v. 10: "in order to share the holiness" acquired by Christ). God is no monster. When he chastises, this is not through harshness. It is agape (v. 6), the highest form of love.

VIII. 2 Samuel   This very old tradition ought logically to ap-
24:2, 9-17   pear between chapters 6 and 7 of this book.
1st reading   The ark has just been brought to Jerusalem
2nd cycle   (2 S 6). David purchases a site in order to
Wednesday   build a sanctuary for the ark (2 S 24). The
    project gains dimension, and he now contem-
plates a temple for Yahweh (2 S 7). The chapter was doubtless transferred to the end of the second book of Samuel in order to give that book a single theme, the ascent of the ark to Jerusalem (a theme that will inspire Luke as he describes the gradual ascent of Jesus, throughout his life, towards Sion). Verses 11-14 are certainly a later addition. Verses 16-17, which blend badly with 18-19, may also be later.

a) Confining ourselves to the primitive account, the reason for building the sanctuary was an epidemic among the people. As they sought the reasons for this, the diviners doubtless had recourse to a military *census*. This sort of religious sociology was not greatly appreciated at the time. It was a human attempt to assess man himself, the tasks confronting him, and the means at his disposal. David was in advance of his time. He was attempting to "secularize" what was still considered to be strictly God's domain.

He acknowledges his fault (v. 10) and straightway the pestilence ceases. In recognition, he purchases the threshing floor on which the sanctuary is to be built.

b) The verses added to this primitive tradition emphasize its marvellous character. The purpose was to dramatize the account, and assimilate it to the numerous accounts of *foundations of sanctuaries* that were current in semitic circles at the time. Everything is stylized. The three plagues are based on a stereotype (Jr 14:12; 21:7; 24:10; 27:8; 32:34; Ez 7:15; 14:21) and have only literary validity (vv. 11-14). The perfect number of victims (v. 15) is also stylized. Then the intervention of the angel, in verses 16-17, adds to the episode the dimension of theophany necessary for any foundation of a sanctuary.

c) The author of the passage poses the important topic of the *solidarity* between king and people in fault and expiation. The fault of one brings misfortune on everyone (v. 17), but the prayer of one is sufficient to arrest the plague at the gates of the holy city.

IX. Mark 6:1-6
Gospel
Wednesday

In the course of a missionary journey Jesus passes by Nazareth, the village of his own family. In the synagogue, on a Sabbath, he addresses the congregation according to the accepted rules for the homily on the second reading (Lk 4:16-30). He encounters only distrust and rejection.

a) Mark is having his readers witness a new manifestation of the people's *distrust* for Jesus. Jesus mentions "authority" (cf. Mk 1:22) not only because his presentation differs from the traditional dialectic of the Scribes, but above all because what he says cannot be accepted unless there is previous attachment to his person. He presents himself not only as a "rabbi" before his disciples and pupils. He is someone who wants relations of mutual confidence (cf. the "follow me" of Mk 2:14) as a preliminary to any teaching.

Jesus then is shaping his role as rabbi. He does so decidedly outside traditional rabbinic procedures. His teaching has an unusual preliminary requirement: an openness and confidence that constitutes genuine faith (v. 6).

b) By what right does he demand this from his coevals and compatriots? He could never have acquired such education from his *family background* (v. 3; cf. Jn 6:42). His family was too poor to play a part in the fulfillment of God's plan! His family indeed refused him the trust he required (v. 4; cf. Jn 6:44, the allusion to his parentage is peculiar to Mark).

The Jews here refer to Jesus as the "son of Mary" (v. 3), with a suggestion of illegitimacy. Matthew, who is concerned to justify the "davidic" ancestry of Joseph, has retouched the Marcan text in order to soften the offensive suggestion (Mt 13:55). Even in instances where the spouses admittedly had relations, at Nazareth a premature birth was material for gossip. Mary must have undergone embarrassment (the meaning perhaps of Lk 2:35), and was often absent from Nazareth during the time of her pregnancy (Lk 1:56; Mt 2:21-22). Being mother to the Messiah was no privilege: she learned to endure oppobrium as Jesus learned to endure the cross.

c) To the proverb cited by Jesus (v. 4), in order to explain the general lack of understanding, Mark adds a precise mention of lack of faith on the part of "his relations" (cf. Jn 4:44). The point is that faith does not come through heredity or ancestry. The latent hostility of the evangelists, especially Mark, to Jesus' family (Mk 3:20-35; Lk 11:27-28) may be explained by the opposition in the primitive community between supporters of a *dynastic* succession to Jesus ("succession according to the flesh": James, the brother of the Lord) and supporters of a *charismatic* (succession "according to the Spirit": the apostles). Each time that he criticizes Jesus' family, Mark in fact refers immediately afterwards to the mission of the Twelve (here: Mk 6:7-13 and again Mk 3:13-19), as if to emphasize the contrast between the two, and the differing concepts of the Kingdom.

X. Hebrews 12:18-19, 21-24
1st reading
1st cycle
Thursday

Like Paul in Galatians 4:24-26, the author contrasts the mountain of Sinai with that of the free Jerusalem, so that his listeners will not be led by nostalgia back to the former. They are wrong in seeking to return to a material mountain, be it Sinai or Sion which succeeded Sinai. From now on there is only one place of reassembly: the spiritual Sion.

a) As in most traditional religions, in Judaism too *mountains* have an important role (cf. Is 2:2; 11:9; 25:6-7). Their very elevation towards the heavens, the supposed dwelling place of God, was sufficient to make them sacred, above all when natural phenomena gave them a supplementary halo (vv. 18-19).

The culture and religion which begets such an attitude is one where man feels himself to be dominated by nature, and sees God behind natural phenomena. Going on a pilgrimage to a mountain is an admission of one's fear of nature, a recognition of the God who is master of her mysterious uncontrollable laws.

Christ however freed man from such alienation. When he triumphed over death, that essential law of nature, he enabled man to see his new freedom from nature's dominance as a grace of God. That is why man must not now seek in nature the means of encountering God. No more will men assemble round a sacred mountain: no longer will their religion be dictated by their fear of natural phenomena (vv. 20-21).

That is why the place of cult of liberated man (i.e. first-born, v. 23) will no longer be a natural mountain, but a gathering of free men, side by side with the angels, who were thought to control natural laws and are now reduced to man's own level (v. 22); side by side too with Jesus the mediator, whose victory over death has enabled man to conquer evil and be purged of sin (v. 24).

b) The whole argument of the passage echoes the contrast, pervasive throughout the letter, between *celestial* and *terrestrial*. The author's hope is essentially based on Christ's entry to the "celestial" world (on his divinity, that is), where he appears as the precursor of humanity (cf. v. 25; He 4:4; 6:20; 7:26; 8:1-2; 9:12-14; 11:12). He wants to spiritualize a Christian hope that has been too linked with the terrestrial Sion. The assembly will no longer take place around a material mountain, but around the divinized Lord. The Hebrew people had acquired the title of first-born at Sinai (Ex 4:22-23; Jr 31:9; Si 36:11). It is a title (v. 23) which Christians can claim in their turn, as they gather round the new Sion, which is the one and only first-born, Jesus Christ (He 1:6). After the Sinai assembly, the names of the elect were written in the book of life (Ex 32:32-33) and then in the registers of the terrestrial Jerusalem. Now they are written in the "celestial" book (v. 23), in heaven that is. Finally, whereas the Sinai assembly was due to the mediation of the angels (v. 22; cf. Ac 7:38, 53; Ga 3:19; He 2:2), the Christian assembly is around the unique and definitive mediator (v. 24), with a covenant that is altogether superior.

XI. 1 Kings **2:1-4, 10-12** *1st reading* *2nd cycle* *Thursday*	Decrepit now for many months (1 K 1:1-8), King David at the moment of death has a spurt of awareness which enables him to dictate his last wishes to Solomon, the son of Bethsabee, whom he has already designated as his successor, and who has been consecrated

by Sadoq (1 K 1:28-40). His instructions are harsh. The *lex talionis* must be carried out against some of his enemies and false friends (1 K 2:5-9, omitted from the reading). The instructions will be carried out faithfully by Solomon (1 K 2:13-46).

To this primitive testament, deuteronomic influence added, some centuries later, verses 3-5. The purpose was no longer the vengeance to be exacted on behalf of the old king, but the future of the royal dynasty, and the conditions which would ensure this. Its future would depend on a promise, mentioned in the deuteronomic interpolation; but this promise would require *fidelity* on the part of each king to *God's law* (vv. 3-4; cf. Dt 7:14-20). The truth is that, for Deuteronomy, the Sinai covenant between Yahweh and his people is renewed between Yahweh and each king. The king in the ultimate analysis is responsible for the covenant. If he slips up, the whole people is involved and loses the privileges of the promise. If on the other hand he is faithful, God will be indulgent to the faults of the people. The salvation of all depends on one. We are not very far from the two Adams doctrine of Saint Paul (Rm 5:12-19). However, the beneficiaries of the new Adam's mediation are really free agents; whereas, in David's time, the people were passive participants in the king's positive or negative performance.

XII. Mark 6:7-13 The mission-discourse has been preserved by
Gospel the evangelists in two forms, one short (Lk
Thursday 9:3-5 and Mk 6:8-11), one long (Lk 10:2-16).
In Mark and Luke the short version is addressed to the Twelve, the long to the seventy disciples. Matthew (10:5-16), for his part, combines the two.

a) Jesus, as Mark presents him, is very conscious of his role as rabbi. However, unlike the contemporary rabbis who gathered their disciples in a school or at the gates of some city, he is determined to be an itinerant rabbi (v. 6, peculiar to Mark). He wanted to encounter men in the life-situation that happened to be theirs. When he accepted disciples, it was not to reason with them like other rabbis, but to involve them in his *missionary* tours, and thus extend his ambit.

b) The content of the apostles' preaching is still, in part, what Jesus received from John the Baptist, *conversion* and repentance (v. 12, peculiar to Mark). The Baptist, however, was content to preach the proximity of the Kingdom (Mk 1:1-8). The disciples of Jesus on the other hand are commissioned to proclaim it as an actual, visible reality. They expel demons and heal the sick (vv. 7 and 13). They persuade the people that they have been liberated from the forces of evil, and have passed under the dominion of a new lordship. What distinguished Jesus and his disciples from the Pharisees and other masters of wisdom was their concern for the poor. For the disadvantaged the others had little time.

c) Mark emphasizes the *poverty* required from the disciples who are sent. His requirements however are less harsh than those of Matthew and Luke. He allows the shoes and staff (vv. 8-9) that the others refuse (Mt 10:10; Lk 9:3; 10:4). Because he is wholly concerned with the coming Kingdom where all blessings will be available, the missionary cannot retain any attachment to the methods and techniques of a world already passed. He is dispensed from the necessity of providing for his earthly future: his poverty is a prophetic sign (cf. Lk 6:20).

d) A second quality of the missionary is seen in his attitude to his hosts (vv. 10-11), with whom he lodges as a *nomad*. When doors are open to him he is glad to find a resting place, but if doors are closed he is indifferent. Never firmly fixed, but always *en route* towards the Kingdom (1 P 2:11; He 11:8-10), he welcomes the hospitality offered, but never to the point of worrying about a prolonged stay, or about the food proffered.

Poverty is indeed the ontological state of the believer, the adoptive son of the Father. However, like any spiritual principle, it has to be exercised in the domain of actual life, individual and social. This exercise does not come automatically; every Christian must make his own contribution. As the world is evangelized, the sign of poverty must be visible to men. This means that it must be visible in the actual context of their lives.

Consequently the Church has to bear her witness of poverty at two levels: in the individual Christian life, and in the ecclesial community, her institutions and structures.

In relation to the first, many concerned Christians do not conceal their disquiet. Often well-endowed with this world's goods, Christians' witness to poverty is rendered ambiguous by their material wealth. Wealth makes people preoccupied with security and nourishes the power instinct. Does fidelity to the gospel call for a voluntary renunciation of wealth? Not all people have this vocation, but all should examine themselves on the dangers of enslavement, on whether their wealth (material or other) is used for the public good. The poverty that any Christian is required to profess does demand a definite attitude concerning wealth. The matter is quite important just now because in general the wealth of Christians exceeds that of the majority of human beings. The Spirit indeed seems at the moment to be calling for a greater measure of voluntary evangelic poverty. Each one of us should reflect about the matter.

The second domain is no less urgent and important. Institutions are always noticed. A bishop may live in poverty in a sumptuous residence, but the residence will be criticized. We must be very careful that ecclesial institutions strictly speaking (liturgical ceremonies, missionary projects, etc.) do not give the impression of prestige or power. We must carefully review always the institutional material we are using.

However, we do not become poor simply by deciding to be poor. Sacramental grace will be required to develop in us the sort of poverty which is above all a receptive attitude to salvation history. The eucharistic assembly is essentially the gathering of those who are poor in Jesus Christ, those sent into the world as witnesses of salvation.

XIII. Hebrews   Here we have the conclusion of the letter. It
13:1-8   is a sort of hortatory postscript concerning the
1st reading   conduct of Christian life in the community. It
1st cycle   differs considerably in tone from the initial
Friday   chapters, but there is no reason to doubt the
               authenticity of chapter 13. The Christian, set
free now from Jewish priesthood and Jewish sacrifice, is part of
a new priesthood and a new liturgy, which is the basis for a
Christian ethic.

a) First of all, the Christian priesthood is distinguished from
the Jewish by an attitude of fraternal charity (vv. 1-3). This
is seen above all in Christian hospitality and care for prisoners
(common law criminals, political prisoners, and doubtless also
victims of persecution). The reason is that, being ourselves
sharers of the earthly state, we are always possible victims of
political pressure or persecution.

b) Secondly, there is the attitude of Christians joined in
marriage (v. 4). The *marriage* bed is compared to a true temple.
The Jews were wont to use the phrase "not defiled" to describe
the purity associated with the temple (2 M 14:36; 15:34; cf.
Jm 1:27). For the Christian then marriage is genuinely a place
of worship. Marital chastity takes the place of the former regulations for legal purity.

c) Thirdly, we have the Christian attitude towards *money* (vv.
5-6). The Christian is an example of evangelic detachment. He
is content with what each day brings because he knows that God
will not abandon his faithful ones. It is noteworthy that the
verse cited to describe this divine providence is taken from a
liturgical Psalm (118/119:6) which conducted the people from
the temple gates to the altar of holocausts. The author's purpose
is to indicate that every ethical attitude is liturgical in a real
sense.

d) Finally, Christians show *veneration for the leaders* of the
community (v. 7) and attachment to their teaching. The term

"guide," used to describe the leaders, was applied by the Jews to the high priests.

These guides are respected as the representatives of Christ (v. 8). He is always behind them, encouraging them and inspiring their teaching.

XIV. Sirach
47:2-13
1st reading
2nd cycle
Friday

During his actual lifetime David was the man of God, but he was this preeminently, too, as he survived in folk memory. Ben Sirach is responsible in large part for the davidic figure of folk memory. His manner of handling the traditions concerning the king, omitting some characteristics or inflating others, gives us a picture that is perhaps far from the historical figure. It is marked by the author's particular bias (his love of miracles and his admiration for the priesthood for instance). Yet it is just as revealing concerning God's plan for man, and for the king, as the old royalist and deuteronomic traditions.

a) The *valiance* of the doughty David is Ben Sirach's first topic: his combats as a young shepherd with the lion and the bear (v. 3), his duel as a young soldier with Goliath (vv. 4-5), his battles as king against the Philistines (v. 7). All these victories are described in an apocalyptic language that is reminiscent of Daniel 2 or 8, contemporary pieces (themes of the little rock, the "horns" etc.). David's feats then are being accommodated to the contemporary situation of the people. These are delivered over to the arrogance of their enemies and dream of the definitive victory over the forces of evil. David thus becomes the poor man who depends on God alone for the victory that is not attainable by his weakness (v. 5).

b) Sirach does not say very much of the promise made to David (only v. 11b, which is inspired by Psalm 131/132:10-18). He does not consider that this promise will resolve contemporary problems or resuscitate national hope. Indeed he attributes to the priests Aaron and Phineas the benefits of the promise made to David (Si 45:15, repeating Ps 88/89:30). In fact, at the time of Sirach, the kingship had been replaced by the priesthood. The temple was for the people, a pledge of God's fidelity, even though the throne was vacant. In these circumstances, the best praise Sirach could give David was to present him as the one who initiated the temple with its liturgy, and set up there the *priesthood* (vv. 8-10). This semi-priestly concept of David is rather dissimilar to what we find in 2 Samuel 7. Its sources should be sought rather in 1 Chronicles 22:5 and 16:4.

Sirach, for his part, is consciously trying to depict a David that will answer the popular notions of his time. It was during the liturgical feasts of the temple only that national consciousness now found expression. Thus David's importance was safe-guarded by representing him as one of the bulwarks of national hope. He was the founder of the temple feasts, those precious moments when God still spoke to his people, and pardoned their faults, in view of the future restoration.

Thus Sirach, after his fashion, according to the ideas of his time, is portraying David in eschatological and messianic terms. The ancient promise of Yahweh, read in the light of past events, never ceases to be the seed of future history.

His manner of procedure, selecting only those elements in the history of David which will have meaning for his contemporaries, has an interesting moral for reading the Word of God at any time. It is never exclusively confined to ancient history and exegesis in these terms is never sufficient. The Word demands reciprocity; it is essentially dialogue. A purely exegetical approach tends to make it monologue.

This is to say that, if we are to understand Scripture properly, we must be able to discern the Word in the event. We cannot read the history of David properly (or that of Jesus), unless we have come to recognize the domains where God is present to us here and now. Sirach realized this; few enough exegetes and spiritual writers realize it. They ignore the human sciences, that are capable of transforming mere exegesis into veritable dialogue with the Word itself.

XV.   Mark 6:14-29 Mark's narrative of the Baptist's execution is
Gospel   designed to put an end to current rumors about
Friday   the reappearance of the Baptist in Jesus (v. 14,
                  cf. Mk 8:28). Herod himself, in his remorse,
had been affected by these (v. 15). John however is really dead; witnesses know the place of his burial (v. 29).

a) While the primary intention is to dispel all confusion between the persons of John and Jesus, the second Gospel incidentally provides many details, for the most part original, concerning the Baptist's martyrdom. Thus the guilt of the weak Herod, who was a sympathizer with the Baptist (v. 20), is mitigated, whereas the odious Herodias is impugned (v. 19). This emphasizes the parallel between *Elias* and the *Baptist* (cf. Mk 9:11-13). Each is confronted by an evil king (Achab, Herod), and by a still more evil queen (Jezabel, Herodias: 1 K 21). Frequently enough in the Bible misfortune falls upon a line when an idolatrous woman gains undue influence. Athalia, Jezabel, Herodias and suchlike brought many kings to disaster.

b) Mark's account has some elements borrowed from the book of Esther. It was customary at such royal feasts that the queen display her natural beauty. Vasthi paid with her crown for her refusal to appear before the court in such garb (Est 1:7-12). The young Esther doubtless, at a banquet which answered her own purpose, had fewer scruples (Est 2:18) so that the king on several occasions offered her the "half of his kingdom" (Est 5:6; 7:2; 9:12). Mark, in his description of Herod's banquet, is doubtless thinking of such oriental customs. Herod, though he was a simple tetrarch, is represented as a king, to liken him the more to Assuerus (v. 14). His step-daughter is made to dance, so that her beauty, like that of Vasthi and Esther, may prove a lure to the guests (v. 22). He makes his wife the same promise as Assuerus (v. 23). These items are all peculiar to Mark. They contrast the *license and luxury* of royal palaces with the poverty and purity of the prophet (cf. Lk 7:25).

This time the new Elias is well and truly dead, and with him the former economy. He is not even assumed to heaven like his predecessor. He dies a victim to the primacy of politics over the spiritual, of natural instinct over the spirit. In this he is a true precursor of Jesus with whom he shares the role of the "suffering Servant." He continues to live however in his disciples, who were among the first founders of the Church. He continues to live in Jesus, his principal disciple, the head of the Church. He continues to live in all Christians, who assemble in eucharistic celebration, the better to proclaim their witness against the power mongers of this world.

XVI. Hebrews 13:15-17, 20-21
1st reading
1st cycle
Saturday

The letter to the Hebrews concludes with some moral counsels. That is, if it is proper to speak of moral counsels, when one remembers that throughout the letter the author has been demonstrating a single great lesson. The ethical standards of Christ's life, his love for the brethren and his obedience to the Father, are genuine liturgical worship and constitute the spiritual sacrifice of the new covenant.

The author requires his listeners to do good (v. 16). Today this would be described as interest in the advancement of the poor and depressed classes. Next, obedience to the leaders (v. 17) and prayer for their intention (v. 18). Such attitudes he sees as the *spiritual sacrifice* (v. 16) in which the God of the new cov-

enant is well pleased (v. 20). They are the attitudes of his Son,
Jesus Christ.

XVII. 1 Kings From its very beginning Solomon's reign was
3:4-13 to take a direction altogether different from
1st reading David's. The period of conquest was con-
2nd cycle cluded. The new king's attention would now
Saturday be turned to organization and development.

Solomon goes to Gabraon to beg the *wisdom* of Yahweh. The
wisdom in question is not yet that which is later so prominent in
the sapiental book, but a practical *savoir-faire*. Solomon is still
but a young man. He has never before exercised authority and
now what he needs for his task is above all the ability to judge
between good and evil (v. 9a; 1 K 3:16-28). He is going to exercise sway, furthermore, over a kingdom that is not his but God's
(v. 9b).

His prayer accordingly is full of the misgiving with which a
novice confronts his task and full of the humility of a man who
realizes he is God's plenipotentiary.

He receives God's answer in the form of a promise. As well
as the discernment he requires, he will receive the personal
blessings necessary for his prestige and influence (vv. 11-13).
He will even enjoy a long life if he remains faithful to God's
commission (v. 14: of deuteronomic origin: cf. Dt 5:33).

We have in this very ancient narrative a characteristically
Jewish view of human life. Just as subsequent failures are to be
explained by the original sin, so too an original promise or
blessing will guide the whole life towards happiness. Today we
realize that God's gift is like a seed which grows slowly following
the pace of human growth. Jesus too knew this ("in age and
wisdom": Lk 2:40, 52), and assumed only gradually the Father's
gift to him.

XVIII. Mark
6:30-34
Gospel
Saturday

This passage begins a new section of Mark's Gospel. We are no longer dealing with the initial apostolic efforts of the rabbi Jesus, nor with his triumphs over sickness and demons. The new section is a unified whole, in which bread is the central theme: the multiplication of bread (Mk 6:30-44; 8:1-10); discussions about ablution before eating bread, and about false leaven (Mk 7:1-23; 8:11-20); a discussion with a Gentile about the crumbs of bread she begs, etc. (Mk 7:24-30). For this reason the section has often been called the "section of breads." In fact it would be more correct to say that we are dealing with a series of narratives that were already for the most part put together before the redaction of the gospels. The purpose was to initiate people into the mystery of Christ and the original elements in his religion.

The first portion of the first narrative, which is all we have in today's reading (vv. 30-34), serves as an introduction to the section by indicating the important place of the apostles in the catechetical plans of Jesus. Verse 34 however, peculiar to Mark, has very great significance. The image of sheep without a *shepherd* is taken from Numbers 27:17, where the context emphasizes Moses' anxiety to find a successor, lest the people be without guidance (cf. Ez 34:5). Thus Christ is putting himself forward as Moses' successor. He can take charge of the flock, nourish them with the food of life, and lead them to sure pastures. The whole section indeed tends to put Jesus forward as the new Moses who offers the true manna (vv. 35-44;; 8:1-10). He too triumphs over the waters of the sea (Mk 6:45-52); frees the people from the pharisaic legalism to which the law of Moses had been reduced (Mk 7:1-13); and provides access, even for the Gentiles, to the promised land (Mk 7:24-37).

FIFTH SUNDAY

A. THE WORD

I. Isaiah
58:7-10
1st reading
1st cycle

This comes from a long diatribe about formalism in cult. It is directed especially against the practice of exterior fast. Isaiah is proposing a new kind of asceticism; no longer the ostentatious fast of the man who dresses in sackcloth (v. 4) and wonders why he has not been answered sooner (v. 3), but the fast of the man who shares with the other and loves his neighbor.

Genuine *fast*, because it means encounter with the most disadvantaged (vv. 7 and 10), offers thereby the possibility of encounter with God (vv. 8-9).

Like most contemporary religions, Israel regarded fast as an essential, especially after the feast of Expiation (Lv 23:26-32) or in commemoration of the siege of Jerusalem (Ze 8:19; 7:3-5; 2 K 25:1, 4, 8, 25). Some prophets however looked askance at abstentions from nourishment on the basis that the food was impure, or fast that was over-formalistic (Is 58; Ze 7:1-14). Others approved of fast on certain occasions (Jl 1:13-14; 2:12-17), because they thought it a more sincere sign of conversion than, for instance, liturgical sacrifice. Fast indicated a desire for conversion. It was justified when carried out for love of God (prayer and worship: Ze 7), or love of men (almsgiving and social justice: Is 58), or in expectation of the final times (Jl 2).

Fast without charity is null. The Church shows herself faithful to this principle when she organizes Lents of sharing. It would however be desirable that the confessional aspect of this ceremony be suppressed, and it be integrated with secular programs of assistance, as indeed Matthew 6:2-3 suggests. In fact, what counts is not the deprivation of nourishment but faith (vv. 8-9). Thus it becomes a more living expression of service to God and men.

II. Job   For the first time, Job addresses himself to God.
  7:1-4, 6-7   He sees that his illness (v. 5) is leading him
  1st reading   straight towards death and oblivion (vv. 6-7).
  2nd cycle   Thus he compares the *human state* to the life
         of a slave or a soldier (vv. 1-4), with all the
alienation and failure that this implies. The text is so clear as to render commentary unnecessary.

III. Isaiah   Doubtless the prophet is taking part in the Ex-
  6:1-2a, 3-8   piation ceremony of 740. From the vestibule of
  1st reading   the temple his gaze travels to the Holy of
  3rd cycle   Holies, accessible on this occasion to the high
         priest. Colossal statues are set up there: two
cherubim five metres in height whose wings overshadow and protect the ark; two guardians like those in the Assyrian temples, who carry fire to consume the sacrifices and who reveal the presence of the awesome God.

As he views the cherubim, and the ark which is the seat of Yahweh, the prophet believes himself summoned to an audience with the all-powerful God (theme of "armies"). The voice of heralds proclaims the entry of the monarch.

a) The prophet's vision is concerned with the *holiness of God*. He associates Yahweh's presence with the Jerusalem temple, and accordingly he portrays the temple and the city in terms worthy of this presence. Because Yahweh is holy, that is to say, the Totally-Other, whatever he touches must be "totally-other" too. Isaiah then sees himself as the prophet of a "holy" people. These are the small Remnant, who, in order to share Yahweh's Kingdom, are ready to be converted and become "totally-other."

The Seraphim proclaim the holiness of Yahweh in a triple ac-clamation (v. 3) that was destined to become a liturgical formula in Judaism even before it did in Christianity (Rev 4:8). We should not of course see it as any presentiment of the Trinity. It was only later apparently that the term was tripled for liturgical purposes.

b) Yahweh is the Holy One *par excellence*. His *glory* extends to the temple but also to the *universe*. It is because of his essential monotheism that Isaiah is the prophet of universalism. God is one. Therefore his glory cannot be limited to the temple of Jerusalem but must be manifested in the "armies of the heavens" and cover all the earth. Every event everywhere is an item in salvation history; every man and every culture is a manifestation of God's glory.

c) For Isaiah this realization of God's holiness and universal glory cannot rest at the level of philosophic definition. It begets a *vocation* (vv. 6-11). It is of little point for man to define God, un-less God flows into his life. We may well say that Isaiah was formed by this vision in the temple, because his whole message is centered on the themes of divine holiness and universal glory. He calls upon everyone everywhere to experience a similar con-version. One cannot see God without radiating him.

The three passages in today's third cycle give us a similar con-cept of vocation. Isaiah saw God's glory before being launched on his mission. The apostles want to touch the body of the Risen Lord before going forth to the world (1 Co 15:3, 11). It was when impressed by the miraculous draught of fishes that the Twelve abandoned their nets to become fishers of men (Lk 5:1-11).

It all poses a problem perhaps for people nowadays who want to be "sent" too, as witnesses to the resurrection. They do not have previous visions, like Isaiah or the apostles. Where do they find the mystic experience to inspire their mission? Is it only in his glory that God reveals himself? Does he not do so too in the everyday round, in failure and in suffering? Would it not be more in keeping with the incarnation if Jesus had fished all night, catching nothing, with the Twelve, rather than appear in the morning to work a miracle?

He worked the miracle of course, but the whole of his message was a demonstration that God is to be found in the everyday round, in ambiguity, in suffering and in death. It was in fact a profound contrast to the glory of Isaiah. The God that Jesus portrayed is rather to be encountered in the ambiguous terrestrial state than in grandeur and magnificence.

When the disciples set down the first accounts of these happenings, the miraculous draught, the appearances of the Risen Lord, they had not yet perhaps quite grasped the real tenor of Jesus' message, and were still under the influence of Isaian concepts of glory.

IV. 1 Corinthians Having shown the superiority of the gospel to
    2:1-5 systems of wisdom (1 Co 1:18-25), Paul ex-
  2nd reading plains why he did not preach a doctrine of
   1st cycle wisdom. He had done much more by providing
          a supernatural foundation for the Christian way
of life.

He does not preach a wisdom doctrine;* he bears *witness* (v. 1). Witness derives its value from the event witnessed, not from rhetoric, and the eloquence of the witness matters little. Unlike the discourse of wisdom, witness is based on something outside itself.

It does seem however that Paul is selective about the events to which he witnesses. He insists more on the cross of Jesus than on his Lordship (v. 2), more on his humility than his wisdom. The choice is not necessarily the same for all the communities he has founded. It was thus at Corinth ("among you"), because he wanted to avoid the misunderstandings that might otherwise have arisen.

Because the weight of witness is measured not by eloquence but

* See the doctrinal theme: *The knowledge of God,* p. 191.

by the event witnessed, Paul has not feared to present himself in spite of his feeble and halting language (v. 3). Because of his failure in the Athenian arcopagus (Ac 17:16-34), he might very well have feared failure throughout Greece.

The witness however must have a minimum of proof for his affirmations. This he has furnished, not in oratorical style, but by a demonstration of spirit and power (v. 7). This does not necessarily mean miracles in the strict sense. Doubtless he is referring to the charisms that suddenly manifested themselves in the Corinth community, and above all to the change brought about in the lives of many of his listeners.

Paul's vigorous witness to the crucified Christ (v. 2) is probably due to the fact that, for him personally, the cross for a considerable time remained incomprehensible. He could not accept the fact that the expected Messiah would be a crucified Messiah. The vision on the road to Damascus suddenly made him realize that the crucified one was truly Lord, and that he continued to be present with persecuted men, ready to associate them with him in glory.

It is as if he told himself that if God could change himself, the fanatical Pharisee, so easily by showing him that divine glory could be associated with such folly as the cross, this pointed the best road to the conversion of men. They too must go through the Damascus experience. He would present the folly of the cross as the road to glory.

Thus his witness to the world is based on a concrete, existential experience. The missionary will only convert others when he himself has passed through the conversion experience. Otherwise he is no more than a propagandist; his message is not really witness.

V. 1 Corinthians 9:16-19, 22-23 2nd reading 2nd cycle   To the problems raised by the Corinthians Paul offers tactful and often elastic solutions. Concerning marriage and continence (1 Co 7) he affirms the superiority of continence, but in such fashion that married folk will not feel disquieted (cf. for instance 1 Co 7:28). Concerning meat offered to idols (1 Co 8), he allows these to be eaten, but not to the point of scandalizing people who consider them contaminated (cf. 1 Co 8:13). Likewise concerning the use of charisms (1 Co 14:39-40), though here he sets up general principles. Previously, in Romans 14:1-21, he had shown a similar elasticity, the fruit of concern for one and all.

Such malleable attitudes towards both Jews and Gentiles (vv. 20-21, not included in our reading) brought much opposition. It might seem that the gospel message was being rendered subjective and opportunist. Accordingly Paul explains himself by describing in exact terms his mission and vocation.

a) First of all he stresses the fact that his vocation is a *charge*. He did not choose it; he is at the service of a master who imposes a task. Because of this responsibility (cf. Jr 20:9) he must be faithful to his mandate. He must be detached where personal rights and privileges are concerned (vv. 16-18). This is true regardless of philosophies or options to which he may feel personal allegiance. If all this lead to opportunism, it cannot be interpreted as desire for personal notoriety or defense of acquired rights.

b) In verse 19 he explains. The apostolic responsibility is a replica of the mission of the *suffering Servant* (cf. Is 53:11, theme of the servant and the multitude). Indeed he has often compared his Corinth ministry to the mission of the Servant (2 Co 6:1-2 and Is 49:8; 2 Co 4:6 and Is 49:6-9; Rm 14:11 and Is 49:18; Rm 15:20-22 and Is 52:15). Any elasticity on his part has nothing to do with personal motives; it is the sign of his service to the Lord. His charge is to help all men by adapting himself to that which is good in them, so that they can be made stones of waiting for the Kingdom of God.

Because of his knowledge of God and Christ,* Paul's standpoint is at a much deeper level than that of casuistry. If the solutions he

---

* See the doctrinal theme: *The knowledge of God,* p. 191.

offers seem sometimes opportunist, that is because the questions themselves were often superficial. His knowledge was of that essential quality that could estimate any problem, recognizing essential elements and relativizing the rest.

Christ himself acted in a similar manner when he fended off people who wanted him to interfere in their arguments (Lk 12:13). A superficial reading might suggest that he was avoiding embarrassing questions. But his whole teaching showed that he had the sort of knowledge of God that rendered many human problems, including religious ones, relative.

VI. 1 Corinthians It seems that some self-appointed "sages" in
15:1-11 Corinth were calling into question some aspects
2nd reading of the final resurrection, the resurrection of the
3rd cycle body itself for instance (1 Co 15:29-34). By
way of reply to them all that Paul can do naturally is refer to the basic apostolic kerygma.

The text in fact seems to be translated from the Aramaic. Everything indeed suggests that it was compiled by the primitive community at Jerusalem as a resume of apostolic kerygma. Many years later than this first letter to the Corinthians, Saint Luke will give us different apostolic discourses (Ac 2:22-36; 3:15-26; 4:8-12; 5:30-32; 10:39-43; 13:27-41) that had been put together in this way according to a formula. We have the proclamation of the death of Christ (here, v. 3b); the appeal to Scripture (here, v. 4b); the enthronement (verse absent here); scriptural proofs (here, v. 4b); witnesses to the resurrection (here, vv. 5-8); summons to conversion (verse absent here).

a) Paul asserts that his kerygma is a *tradition* (vv. 1-3, 11). Exegesis confirms this; he probably owes the structure of his kerygma to the Jerusalem community. In any case his message has nothing to do with wisdom or human gnosis. It is tradition that goes back (1 Th 2:13; 4:1; 2 Th 2:15; 1 Co 11:23) to the person of

Jesus himself (who, in turn, is the echo of what he received from his Father: Mt 11:27). From the very beginning then the Church had a profession-of-faith formula that is practically given us in vv. 3b-4. Paul cites, without change, the three great events of traditional kerygma: the death, burial, the resurrection. In dealing with the proofs he takes some liberties. He alludes to them, but only cites one, concerning the third day (v. 4; cf. Ho 6:2; Jn 2:1). His audience in fact were less well versed in the Scriptures than the Jerusalem community. The proof by witness on the other hand was liable to have considerable weight for them. That is why Paul gives it in detail (vv. 5-8). He provides an ancient list of people who had witnessed an appearance: Peter, the Twelve and members of the Jerusalem community, the late testimony of the women and the Emmaus disciples being passed over in silence (vv. 5-6. The list we note is strongly hierarchical). We can discern here the mentality of the Jerusalem community, which rather ignored the appearances to the women and the disciples. The mention of James, the brother of the Lord (v. 7), was certainly added later, again in Jerusalem circles. Then Paul notes the apparition to himself on the road to Damascus (v. 8; Ac 9:17).

b) The faith transmitted to Paul is essentially centered on the *paschal event*. It is not so much the historical event of course, and the proofs for this; but the doctrinal meaning of the event. Christ died "for our sins" (v. 3), with the implication that since then we are dead to sin (Rm 6:1-6). It is above all the doctrinal implications of the resurrection itself that are contemplated, as is evident from the contrasted verbs: "died" (the aorist tense), "has arisen" (perfect tense, past action that continues to have present influence.) The construction is actually repeated seven times in 1 Corinthians 15. Thus Christ's resurrection is seen as introducing an unprecedented religious regime, which touches each person directly. It demands a new style of life (Rm 6:1-6), the sign of our own resurrection (1 Co 15:20; 2 Co 4:14).

On these three events then: the death, the burial, the resurrection, faith is founded. They are not merely past events but must in the fullest sense be grafted into our new life. We too must die to sin and be finally raised up.

Sometimes the faith of Christians in Christ's resurrection is shaken. They will look for an objective presentation that corresponds with rationality. Too many elements in the traditional formulation seem to them the product of a religious insight that has its own value, but is little related to modern ways of thinking.

All this is very well, provided that faith is not confused with knowledge, and that the "traditional" character of faith in the resurrection (as something that transcends experience and rationality) continues to be respected.

The Christian believes in the paschal event because he sees there Jesus taking on the full burden of human contingency (death) on the one hand, and on the other realizing to the full the human yearning for the absolute by his response to God's initiative. The death on the cross was more than the death of a condemned man. It was the death of the man-God, who never ceased in his full fidelity to the human condition to be the Father's Son. The paschal event is the greatest moment of encounter between God and man, the perfect human response to divine intervention.

The Eucharist is the memorial of the paschal event because it renews at once God's intervention on behalf of his children, and the perfectly adjusted response to that intervention.

VII: Matthew
5:13-16
Gospel
1st cycle

This passage, one of the most structured in the first gospel, contains the three themes of salt, light, and the city. To understand it properly, we have to determine what Matthew took from oral tradition and what is due to his own redactional work.

a) The *logion* about salt has been interpreted differently by the synoptics and placed in three different contexts. Mark 9:50 gives us the primitive formula and includes the *logion,* with other sayings about the key-words salt and fire, in an eschatological grouping. In Luke 14:34-35 it becomes a parable. This evangelist wants to convey that, where the Kingdom is concerned, one must go the full way and not lose savor (cf. the parable of the king who embarks on a war).

For Mark and Luke then salt indicates the new religion and the demands imposed by it. For Matthew however, the *logion* becomes a missionary allegory: salt represents the disciples ("you are the salt . . . ").

To be salt is to be the most precious element of the earth. The earth cannot subsist without it. With it, on the other hand, the earth can pursue its destiny. Likewise a Church which is no longer faithful to herself, not alone loses herself but makes the world savorless.

b) The saying about *light* has been considerably reworked by Matthew in the same allegorizing fashion. In Mark 4:21 the light which is taken from under the bushel to illuminate the whole surroundings designates the teaching of Jesus, as it is gradually discovered and understood. Matthew becomes allegorical and moralizing. He concocts verse 14a (you are . . .) to set up the parallel with salt. Likewise he adds the image of the city on a hill (v. 14b) and ends with a moral application. Each disciple can be a light insofar as his actions are signs of God for the world. Christian witness then is something destined to be seen by all. It is a response to missionary demands. Sanctification is not exclusively an interior matter. On the other hand one must never so belong to the world as to be totally conformed to it and neglect to bear witness to transcendence.

VIII. Mark
1:29-39
Gospel
2nd cycle

We have two things in this passage. First there is a sort of "summary" of Jesus' thaumaturgic activities (vv. 32-34) which follows the description of a particular miracle (vv. 29-31). Then there is a description of his missionary activity (vv. 35-39).

a) The summary of *miracles* belong to a particular literary genre (cf. Mk 3:10-12; 6:53-56; Mt 15:30-31; 19:2; Lk 5:15-17; 7:21, etc.). In this genre generalizations, not to say exaggerations, are frequent. For instance, the large numbers of those healed (in Mark, v. 34, we have the term "many," whereas in Luke 4:40 and 6:18-19 we get mention of "everyone"). Or again, the names of the different maladies (here in Mark, diverse maladies simply; but in Matthew 15:30-31 more elaboration and precision).

b) However, even within the limits of a summary, the redactor's hand can make itself felt, and Mark cannot refrain from insinuating a favorite theme, the *silence* Jesus was wont to impose on demons (cf. Mk 1:25, 34; 3:12) or those healed miraculously, at the beginning of his ministry. This is a very understandable reaction when a man feels that something higher than himself has been channeled through him. Adam and Eve wanted to veil their sex when they discovered they had the divine power of giving life (Gn 3:7). Jesus wanted to conceal his miraculous power because it was something which exceeded the human. The mystic will want to conceal within his room the extraordinary experiences he has.

Mark however regarded Jesus' desire for silence as a defense against the misunderstanding that surrounded him. The word he was disseminating might kindle an overly nationalist enthusiasm. So many dangerous misconceptions about his mission were possible that he distrusted any sort of open, fanatical publicity.

c) Mark's first chapter gives us the spiritual and apostolic development of Jesus during the first weeks of his ministry. He went first of all to Judea and to the desert to become a disciple of the Baptist (Mk 1:9-13). It seems likely that he spent some time in the Baptist's group, only quitting it after the latter's arrest (Mk 1:14). At this stage he makes a decisive turning. He will not be, like his master, a rabbi to whom disciples come (Mk 1:5), but an itinerant rabbi. He will go forth to meet the crowds, and precisely the most forsaken among them, in Galilee. He goes to Galilee and has his initial experence in his own town of Capharnaum (Mk 1.21).

Success now seems to be assured. The sick are brought to him

continuously and the whole city is at his doorstep (Mk 1:33).
However he refuses this highly ambiguous success (cf. Mk 1:34b)
and makes a new decision. He will abandon the city (v. 38) for
the neighboring villages. The *missionary* ideal is the one which
dominates his life and the criterion by which everything must
be judged.

It was in seeking the will of God that Jesus took this decision
which was to affect all his life. His self-awareness as rabbi was the
fruit of prayer (v. 35).

Mark is alone in stressing Jesus' anxiety at this stage to form
his disciples in the missionary way ("let us go . . . " v. 38). He is
imposing on them a task which few of the contemporary rabbis
demanded of their disciples.

It is only at the resurrection that the messianic secret of Jesus'
mission will be revealed. Then the real power of the Son of Man is
seen (Mk 14:62). Jesus has to die and be raised up to accomplish
to the full the messianic mission entrusted to him. The injunction
of silence prepares people to understand his death. True understanding of miracles requires faith, and this can only come after
the resurrection to those who have found the key to the personality of Jesus, at once human and divine (cf. Mk 9:9-10). It is
necessary, all considered, to share the mystery of the Eucharist
in order to see the Christ who lies behind the thaumaturge.

IX. Luke **5:1-11** *Gospel* *3rd cycle*	Here, Luke combines two distinct traditions: the call of the first disciples (as in Mk 1:16-20) and the miraculous draught of fishes (as in Jn 21:1-11). He concludes the passage with an allusion to the special role of Peter.

a) Already, in Mark 1:17 and Matthew 4:19, Jesus had said, in
reference to the disciples' avocation, that he would make them
fishers of men. It was a play upon words, substituting men for fish.

In Luke, however, the fact that the title is given after the miraculous draught of fishes indicates that the evangelist is going further than the word play, and describing the efficacity of the apostolic function itself.

The whole meaning of the miraculous draught will be clearer if we remember that water for the Jew, above all the sea, was the habitation of Satan and of forces opposed to God (Gn 1:7, 17-24; Pss 73/74:13; 23/24:2; Jb 38:16-17; Jon 2:2-4; Rev 9:1-3; 20:3; 13:1). Until the advent of the Savior, nothing, except a miracle such as that of the Red Sea, could be undertaken to rescue those that the enemy sea had engulfed. With the coming of the Savior however, the task of fishing for men and withdrawing them from the power of evil could go forward. That is in fact the basic meaning of the descent into hell (*inferi* = inferior waters) in 1 Peter 3:19. Christ goes down specifically to save those engulfed by the waters of the deluge. Fishing for men then means being engaged in the project of rescuing all those engulfed by evil. Jeremiah 16:15-16a had foreseen this task.

For Luke the Church is an institution charged with the rescue of humanity from the inundation that threatens it. For the success of the task some, in the Church, are entrusted with a specific apostolic function. Success in their "fishing" however, and the ardor with which they pursue it, they owe to Christ alone.

b) To induce the apostles to accept their roles as fishers of men, Jesus presents himself as the veteran fisherman who knows where the shoals of fish are (v. 4). Fishermen generally guard closely this particular secret or reveal it only to genuine friends. Peter is aware of this and hastens to benefit from the secret conveyed by someone he regards as a seasoned fisher. During the actual course of the fishing however, his sentiments change and *faith* is kindled. It is the Messiah that he recognizes, on his return to the shore (vv. 8-9). He sees God himself behind the lineaments of this Jesus whom he had first taken as a simple fisherman rather more competent than the others.

One does not then become a fisher of men through competence.

The essential thing is a faith that has encountered God and communicates with him.

During the centuries immediately preceding ours, the phrase "fishers of men" had tended to take on the narrow significance of recruiting agents. The missionary was a fisher of men to the extent that he saved them by administering baptism. The ordinary Christian merited the title to the extent that he brought about conversions and recruited souls into the Church. This individualist view scarcely corresponds either with Luke's thinking or the thinking that would be acceptable now.

Behind its mythic associations, the miraculous draught seems to have a deeper meaning. Humanity is challenged by powers that threaten to engulf it. Jesus sees himself and his disciples in the role of liberators who stem the downward process toward catastrophe.

Humanity indeed in our day is held back from overwhelming itself by such a slender thread, that we need posit no demonic forces other than selfishness and lust for power. A fisher of men now is the one who cooperates in every project that seeks to stem this catastrophe. A greater measure of equality, more stable peace, a greater opportunity for the small people of the universe to improve their lot: these are the things needed to rescue humanity from the flood which threatens to engulf it. The Church can never win credence as a fisher if her members abstain from such projects, or join them only in the morning, rather than labor throughout the night with the rest of humanity. She cannot manifest the love of God unless she shares that love with men. The only proper witness to the world of the presence of Christ is the meaning that Christians give to the projects for human progress. This will channel such projects finally towards divine life.

B.   DOCTRINE

1. Theme of the Knowledge of God

Knowledge, for modern man, connotes an intellectual activity that does not necessarily involve the whole person, either where God, or other persons, are concerned. The current concept is a Western one that has been reinforced considerably by the devolpment of science and technology. By definition scientific knowledge is abstract and impersonal.

With biblical man it was otherwise. Knowledge for him overflowed the domain of the abstract; it set up an existential bond. To know something was to have concrete experience of it; to know somebody was to have a personal relationship with him. In the religious sphere then the knowledge of God must obviously be central.

This is not to say that the two concepts of knowledge are mutually exclusive. But for a biblical understanding of faith the existential concept is the important one. The God of faith is not the God of philosophers or savants, and faith itself must never be confined to abstract, impersonal knowledge of objective truths.

Jewish man and knowledge of Yahweh

Pagan man had a spontaneous urge to communicate with the sacral world which alone could bring fulfillment. Liturgies and mysteries offered him ways of gradually reaching this supreme knowledge.

For Jewish man on the other hand, who preceived God as the Totally-Other, the sovereign master of human history, the basic step in this domain was the affirmation of the divine initiative. God knows us before we know him. It would be impossible to know God unless he allowed himself to be known. The knowledge of God to which faith gives access is a gift of grace, the fruit of election. God knew Abraham. He knew his people. He knew his prophets. He makes himself known to those he has chosen. He reveals his name and manifests his solicitude, fidelity and love.

In fact, of course, the Jewish people did not reach to the sort of knowledge of God that was offered them. They misunderstood the "ways" of Yahweh. They were unfaithful to the requirements of the law and the covenant; they fashioned idols. They deluded themselves often by fancying they knew Yahweh, whereas the existential relation implied by such knowledge ought to have penetrated to the heart and overflowed into the texture of life. The prophets never ceased to point this out, with emphasis. The people did not listen, would not allow themselves to be taught by Yahweh. Thus "for lack of knowledge" (Is 5:13; Ho 4:6) they would be chastised.

In failure, ruin and exile Yahweh would make himself unknown. Such events destroyed the illusions of Israel.

Confronted by infidelity in their own day, the prophets turned towards the future. When the day of Yahweh dawned, when a new covenant would be inaugurated, then the knowledge of Yahweh would be shared by all. Yahweh would multiply his initiatives. He would engrave his Law in the heart (cf. Jr 31:31-34), producing "a new heart" as the work of the Spirit (Ez 36:26). Then, when all would have knowledge of Yahweh, they would become his witnesses before the Gentiles, so that these in turn would come to know him too.

The Man-God, the Savior, and knowledge of the Father

The last times were inaugurated by Jesus and they were the times of true knowledge of God. Jesus of Nazareth was the only person who could say in very truth "I know the Father." The whole mystery of Christ is concerned with this knowledge of the Father, and we have numerous passages in the fourth gospel which illustrate what it was and how much it meant. Very often Jesus refers to this knowledge in a polemical context. It becomes a source of scandal and provides the motive for condemning him to death. Let us consider why.

When Jesus insists that he knows the Father, this can only

mean one thing. He is altogether faithful to the Father's will, is accomplishing God's plan for man, and is the expected Savior. Simultaneously he lets it be known that this perfect response to the divine will is not elicited from merely human resources. He preaches absolute self-renunciation for the love of all men. There is only one way of explaining all that he affirms; he is God. His salvific "yes" is the yes of the Son of God. His knowledge of the Father is perfect because it is the retention on the human level of the knowledge he had as Son of the eternal Father. When he insists that he knows the Father as the Father knows him he causes scandal. He is implying his divinity. The Jews chose to accuse him of blasphemy rather than acknowledge the man-God. This would mean acknowledgement of man's basic incapacity to achieve of himself the salvation which alone could satisfy him.

The Jewish fear that Jesus would go to the Gentiles is a proof that they were aware of this demand for radical poverty. If the salvation he preached was something of universal dimension, based on a love that was commensurate with the Father's love for humanity, then the privileges of Israel were in jeopardy. The traditional concept of the covenant was overthrown. We can understand how the special knowledge of the Father that Jesus claimed proved to be a scandal for the Jews.

Knowledge of the Father, and of his envoy, Christ

In the sacerdotal prayer, as preserved for us by John, Jesus says: "This is eternal life, that they should know you, the only true God, and him whom you have sent, Jesus Christ" (Jn 17:3). For Saint Paul, everything is summed up in the knowledge "of the love of Christ which surpasses all understanding" (Ep 3:19).

The synoptics, and above all the fourth gospel, insist that it was only after the resurrection that the disciples acquired true knowledge of the Father and his envoy. It was then that they received the Spirit who revealed to them the full meaning of Jesus' words and deeds. Because death was the supreme expression of Jesus' obedience to his Father's plan, the death on the cross in some sense accomplished and brought to perfection the knowledge he had of the Father. From this moment onwards the disciples were enabled to know the Father's envoy and through him the Father himself.

Thus, for the Christian, there is a very close link between knowledge of God, knowledge of Christ and the gift of the Spirit. When, through baptism, we enter the Church, we are involved in the great stream that springs from the heart of God and flows back to him through Jesus Christ in the Holy Spirit. This is what knowledge means. Our whole life should be permeated with this knowledge that saves us, that makes us, with Christ, saviors of humanity. The knowledge is not based on human wisdom; it is faith in Christ crucified, and in divine wisdom.

To know God is to embrace the way of obedience unto death in universal love, as adoptive children of the Father, in response to the initiative of the Spirit. Saint Paul sums up Christian life in these terms: "to know Christ and the power of his resurrection and to share his sufferings by reproducing the pattern of his death. That is the way I can hope to take my place in the resurrection of the dead" (Ph 3:10-11).

Knowledge of God the basis of missionary witness

The missionary must attach himself heart and soul to the knowledge of God that is offered to him by "the unfathomable riches of Christ" (Ep 3:8). This is absolutely essential for his witness to be authentic. The more he knows God, the more he will be conformed to Christ in his death; the more will he, like Christ, become a living witness to the Father's initiative, and to acceptance of the salvific plan.

He will not acquire this knowledge ready made, at once. It will develop through contact with the people he evangelizes, sometimes in unforeseen and disconcerting ways. If he merely remains on the fringes of this people, he will not bear true witness to the crucified and risen Christ. He must share their lives, endeavor to penetrate to their inner dynamism, thus deepening the dimensions of his knowledge. Thus he will begin to realize what it means to be conformed to Christ in his death. It may be a new test for his faith, but it is also a deeper insight into the treasures of wisdom and knowledge hidden in the mystery of God and the salvific plan.

We must not of course minimize the risk involved in mission. Nowadays, and very rightly, there is great insistence on the need to become adapted. The missionary must be "present" to those he evangelizes, share their language, formulate the message in terms suitable for them. But this presence will only be of value when it is a sign of the mystery of Christ. However well adapted he is, he will be false to his charge if the knowledge of the Father is not central for him as it was for Christ. This may lead him to confront death in obedience, something that will inevitably run counter to the wisdom of the world. The apostle, like his master, is summoned to encounter challenge, perhaps persecution. His lot is never an easy one.

The Eucharist, the source of knowledge of God

The eucharistic celebration is the occasion *par excellence* for acquiring knowledge of God. It involves its members in Christ's own thanksgiving, his sacrifice, his obedience to the divine plan, in a word in his own knowledge of the Father.

To achieve this purpose, proper place should be given to the liturgy of the Word. The Scripture readings and the celebrant's homily should lead each member to make the here and now of his own life, and that of the whole world, what the sacrifice of Christ, and his knowledge of the Father, was once for all.

It goes without saying that this knowledge of God will be disseminated effectively among the members present, only in that proportion to which their spiritual sacrifice is expressed in their daily lives.

2. Theme of Imitation of God

Men have always imitated models and modern man is no exception to the rule. But the models change visage, or name. The extent of imitation varies. It may be exterior merely (the hair-do or clothes of a movie star), or at the other extreme it may be concentrated on spiritual or moral style (imitating a master of wisdom for instance). But the reason for imitating is invariably the same; it gives some sort of expression to the universal. Something becomes tangible and approachable, and consequently provides security. If we can have within our grasp the "exemplar" of an action or an attitude, we feel we are touching something solid. The exemplar appears to have generated some "value" or "universal" and provided concrete means of attaining it.

Christianity makes the imitation of Christ a pivotal matter. It has actually been the subject of a celebrated spiritual classic. If Christians of our day do not feel altogether enthusiastic about this little book, it is just because they feel that the horizons of the topic are vastly wider than the book allows. No one has any doubt about the centrality of the theme. Christ is the Way, the Truth and the Life, and we must all try to follow in his footsteps.

A problem arises perhaps concerning the exact content of imitation. What do we mean by imitating Christ? He is not in the first place a master of wisdom. He is the Incarnate Word, who died and rose again for all humanity. He is the unique mediator of universal salvation and imitation of him cannot be confined to imitating his behavior. He lived at a time and in a culture that is no longer ours, so that a slavish copying of what he did and how he reacted would be quixotic. There is plenty of reason then for attempting to plumb the real meaning of imitation. We shall be dealing with something that is altogether crucial in our faith.

Imitation of Yahweh in Israel

Ancient pagan religions attached great importance to the imitation of divine models. In their quest for the absolute, men, who find themselves in a fluid and precarious existence, will only find security in actions that seem to bring the gods to earth. There is a constant thrust to achieve contact with the divine archetypes, to penetrate to being itself, apart from which all seems empty and chaotic. Imitation seems the means *par excellence* of divinization. Liturgies are developed which offer ways of access. In ritual men can share mysteriously in divine activity; they are snatched from the hazards of existence and rooted in the stability of the gods. All important activities in life become ritual so that they can have meaning. If the ritual is scrupulously observed, a man can truly "mime" a divine act and absorb the energies it deploys.

It was natural then that the Israelites should see imitation of Yahweh in terms of cult to begin with. Cult imitates a divine model. As faith deepened, however, this whole concept was destined to be altogether transformed. Yahweh is the Totally-Other, the Inaccessible. Between him and the creature the gulf is unbridgeable. Cult does not divinize. The one way of salvation is fidelity to the Covenant. Yahweh will gratuitously save those who depend on him for everything and faithfully observe his Law. Yet because man is created in the image and likeness of God, the fidelity demanded by the Covenant has some resemblance to Yahweh's own action. And it is actually by meditation on Yahweh's action that Israel gains more and more insight into the concrete requirements of the Covenant. The path of Yahweh is always one of fidelity and love, and the prophets never cease calling upon the recalcitrant people to follow him in this path.

In the hinterland of all this however is a vague awareness that the moral ideal of imitation of Yahweh is never going to fulfill man's deepest aspiration. The negative feelings about sin are revealing. It is man's dream that he can somehow have a dimension of the absolute in his response to God. But is not this negatived by the creatural condition? It was out of the yearning to bridge the impasse that messianic hope was born.

Christ and the perfect imitation of God

Israel's hope was fulfilled in the intervention of Christ, beyond all expectation. Yet it was the very unprecedented character of the fulfillment that brought about rejection by the Jews. Let us examine why.

Jesus actually put himself forward as the perfect imitator of the Father. His response to the divine initiative was the adequate one. He is indeed the Messiah, the one who can communicate with God as genuine interlocutor. Saint Paul will rightly describe him as the Image of the Father. But at the same time he demands from himself and from his future disciples absolute self-renunciation, that obedience unto the death of the cross which is the condition of universal brotherly love. What is essential is absolute fidelity to the creatural condition, acceptance of the human predicament. In order to imitate the Father, Jesus does not seek to elevate himself in any way from the creatural state. On the contrary he views this state with the maximum of lucidity and embraces it with the maximum of obedience.

It is because he is man-God, the incarnate Word, that he can reconcile the two extremes of the paradox: the Image of the Father and the full creatural state. Because he is the Son "he can do nothing of himself that he does not see the Father doing" (Jn 5:19); whatever he says is "what he has seen with his Father" (Jn 8:38). Because of the hypostatic union the perfect harmony of his activity with that of the Father overflows into his humanity. Thus he is the man who imitates the Father perfectly, without ceasing to be man. This is the secret of human salvation.

The great expression of his imitation of the Father is the event of the cross. We recall that pagan man in his attempt to imitate divine models sought security. He sought through his liturgies to evade profane time and space. Now, there is no such attempt at evasion, no gasping at security in human terms. There is simple acceptance of the event that leads to lucid self-renunciation, the event that immerses in radical insecurity. In the sacrifice of the cross Jesus carries imitation of the Father to its peak point; he reveals the essential nature of double love, which is the source of salvation.

The Church and the imitation of Jesus Christ

What Jesus accomplished once for all on the cross he continues to accomplish in his Church through the members of his Body. Salvation history and that of imitation of the Father has been begun in the New Adam. It goes on through generation after generation, but the shape it takes will depend on the quality of active contribution by Church members. For the members, imitation of the Father necessarily comes by way of imitation of Christ. There is no salvation except in Christ, and he who wishes to be saved, or play his role in the salvation of humanity, must follow Christ in his Passion (Jn 13:36 and 1 P 2:21).

What do we mean by this imitation of Christ? It will be necessary first of all to become conformed to his image, which presupposes ecclesial intervention in baptism. This is what introduces us to Christ's Body and enables us to act as adoptive children of the Father, through the link with Christ. The Church's function however does not cease there; it will be constantly required for our proper development. To act as adoptive children we must be always in touch with the sources of interior grace and be modeled by the sacraments and the Word.

The effect of ecclesial action upon us is constantly to protect us against the temptation of evasion, to make each one open to the event and to what God wishes from him. These will be the events of daily life, of whatever kind, which prove a challenge to our faith and are our means of demonstrating acceptance of the creatural condition. Imitation of Christ does not consist of following a predetermined schedule. It means a total acceptance of what happens; it means traveling the road of the Passion which is the event *par excellence*.

Our imitation has nothing to do with conformism. There is no question of trying to reproduce exactly this or that attitude of his. It means taking his lucid view of reality, being open as he was to the event. In a way it is more inventiveness than imitation. The event will always be unique; so too the believer's reaction will have to be. We should always be asking ourselves whether our response has this quality.

Imitation of the Father and missionary witness

Just because modern man has ceased to be the religious creature he used to be, Christians in their witness are sometimes tempted to subordinate their imitation of the Father to the service they must render humanity. There are indeed colossal human tasks confronting us all; peace, world development, social and international justice, etc. If we are to have impact as Christians, must we not first assume our responsibilities in the collective effort for which modern man knows himself to be equipped?

This is a subtle temptation of which we must beware. If we succumb, Christian witness runs the risk of losing its whole *raison d'etre,* and indeed it loses its savor even for modern man himself. If imitation of the Father is to be the essence of our witness, we must behave as sons of God, and at the same time show superlative acceptance of the creatural condition. We must demonstrate that Jesus Christ the man gives an eternal dimension to human activity, without ever changing its human quality. For that matter we are often wrong in thinking that modern man is so preoccupied with earthly responsibilities that he has smothered his yearning for the absolute. He just differs from his predecessor in channeling his sense of the absolute into the human tasks themselves. For him they are not purely "temporal" tasks. When we assume our due responsibilities in this field, we should show by our attitude the true state of things. Far from wishing to curb the deployment of purely human resources to the full, the child of God will be absolutely open to the task of human progress.

We should also remember that the men of our time will appreciate the quality of our work for human progress only if we show a scrupulous respect for the rules of the game. The task depends not alone on the inspiration behind it, but also on the manner of its execution at various levels: political, social, economic, etc. Here we Christians, like everyone else, should undergo the necessary training. If not, we can have little hope of accomplishing the ultimate objectives.

Imitation of the Father in the eucharistic celebration

The great eucharistic prayer is concluded by a joint recitation, on the part of celebrant and faithful, of the Our Father. All express their desire to imitate the Father by imitating the Savior: "As we have learned from the Savior . . . we dare to say" "Father, forgive us our offenses as we forgive those who have offended against us." Which is to say "Father, allow us, in Jesus Christ to extend to all men the pardon You have granted us."

The eucharistic celebration should as a rule make everyone conscious of the unending actuality of God's pardon. We should feel the urge to make his gesture towards us a blanket for all wrongs. When we partake of the Eucharist, we are established in the charity of Christ, which is the perfect imitation of the Father. This result will not come automatically. Proclamation of the Word will be highly important; Scripture readings and the celebrant's homily must make the message actual. The actual structure of the celebration is likewise important. All present should be conscious of their diversity in unity, should feel the dimension of openness, and take their group as a microcosm of the whole.

FIFTH WEEK

**I. Genesis
1:1-19**
1st reading
1st cycle
Monday

The postexilic priestly editor to whom we owe this first chapter of Genesis has behind him the whole history of the chosen people, and a whole style of expression that has been forged by the events of salvation history. Not only does he tell the story of creation; he reads it in the light of God's other salvific interventions.

a) Creation is a *victory* over chaos (*tohubohu*), in the same sense as the return from exile was (Is 35; 40:1-8; 43:16-20). It is a victory over darkness, in the long tradition of manifestations of God's glory (Is 60:1-2; 49:9; 50:1-10; Jn 1:5); a triumph over the sea, like the victorious passage of the Red Sea (Pss 103/104:5-9; 105/106:9; Ha 3:8-15; Is 51:9-10; Rev 20:1-13); a separation of night from day, moving towards the definitive victory over darkness (Rev 21:25). Creation thus is not seen as the beginning of a history where everything is given once for all. The author writes out of his lived experience. For him there are not two distinct orders, that of creation and that of redemption. There is just the realization of the divine plan of salvation.

b) We should also notice the *universalist* dimension of the account. One of the most important insights in the whole history of Israel is that of God as creator of heaven and earth. Yahweh now is no longer the God of one small localized people; he is the God who controls the universe (Is 45:12-13; 40:27-28). We can see this influence in the author's anxiety to extend to the universe the cultic environment of the Jerusalem temple. Like the temple, the world has its "firmament" (Ps 150:1; Ez 1:22-26) over which God has placed his throne. "Luminaries," the name given to the lamps in the sanctuary, are to be found now in all creation (v. 14; cf. Ez 35:8, 14; 25:6; 27:20; 39:37; Nb 4:9-16); and they are provisional only, because one day the glory of Yahweh will be sufficient to illumine the definitive temple (Rev 21:23). Even the blessings which God lavishes on creation (vv. 22-23) parallel those which the priests give in the temple (Pss 132/133:3; 127/128:4-5; 23/24:5). Finally, at the very center of this temple of creation we find the "image" of God, man (vv. 26-29; Ps 8:5-6), which replaces the statues of gods, and which will be perfected in Christ, the image of the Father (Col 1:15-17).

c) The structure of the whole account indeed is essentially cultic, designed to support the institution of the *week* and the Sabbath rest. During the author's time Sabbath observance was the distinctive mark of the chosen people. The institution of the Sabbath is for him something not merely social (as in the ancient sources), but the privilege of imitating God. Like God, man frees himself at least one day of the week from the constraints of work.

The classic schema of Christian catechesis, a creator God who is destined to become a Redeemer God in Jesus Christ, is not essentially biblical. Even in the New Testament, reflections such as those of John (1:1-18) or Paul (Col 1:15-17; Ep 1:3-14) consider creation in relation to the person of Christ. It is in him, not only Word but man-God, that all things were made; creation was for him. Similarly, the Genesis author only considers creation in relation to salvation history.

For them faith in a creator God has nothing to do with philosophical proof or religious intuition; it is faith in Jesus Christ. Creation begins with the man-God; he is the alpha and omega. It is not the work of a cosmogonic God like Zeus or Mardouk, but of Jesus Christ himself. The life of Jesus is not a mere episode in the life of the Christian God; it is the substance of that life. There is no point whatsoever in equating faith in Jesus Christ with the philosophic belief in a creator God.

II. 1 Kings
8:1-7, 9-13
1st reading
2nd cycle
Monday

On the completion of the temple, Solomon as king of Jerusalem and thereby a priest of the Most High, less in a functional sense than as a general organizer of worship, proceeds to the consecration. The definitive account of this ceremony was compiled by someone under the influence of the Deuteronomic reform (6th century), on the basis of earlier data. We find here two of the most important principles of deuteronomic reform; commemoration of the desert marvels and the covenant, and maintenance of the principle of a single religious center in Israel.

The main elements of the account tend to make the temple the memorial of the *Sinai covenant*. For this reason Solomon chooses the feast of tabernacles for the consecration (v. 2). Because it celebrated the completion of harvest, and this was the most popular of all festivals; but from Deuteronomy onwards it commemorated the desert sojourn (Dt 16:13-16). He also solemnized the inauguration by a formal translation of the ark (v. 3) which contained the instruments of the Sinai alliance (v. 9). In his fashion Solomon was continuing and stabilizing the desert economy. Having led the journey through the desert the ark was placed in a fixed sanctuary, not with the idea of setting a term to the history of the liberation. On the contrary it was to be a constant memorial, designed to keep foremost in worship the desert blessings.

The final, and most important, reference to Sinai is the manifestation of God in the cloud (vv. 10-11). The reference clearly is to some cultic representation of the Sinai theophany (cf. with v. 10 Ex 13:21-22; 19:16-19; 40:34-38; Nb 12:4-5; with v. 11 Ex 19:22, 24; 33:18-23). Thus, stable though it was, the temple was not opposed to the desert economy. Sion institutionalized, but did not destroy the Sinai event. It would indeed be frequently judged, and criticized, by the prophets, on the basis of fidelity to the covenant.

So we see Solomon perpetuating the memory of the outmoded nomad culture in the midst of a stable city society. Are we to take this as evidence that one culture is more favored by God than another, that we must go back to the principles of nomad society if religion is to flourish? Solomon does not demand this. He used the technology and materials of his time in order to build a temple. But he placed the tabernacle in the center of this structure and entered it, as if to indicate that, for all the stability of urbanism, one could be nomad at heart.

Our contemporary culture offers many opportunities for the exercise of nomad faith. It coexists with forms of nomad culture (bedouins, gypsies) that teach us many lessons about God and his grandeur. It is characterized by frequent displacements of population; from village to city, from Europe to America, from living place to place of work, to weekend lodgings, to holiday camp. It creates dramatic, and traumatic, uprootings that cast people into profound isolation. So that nomadism in the material sense is by no means an uncommon experience for many people. Nomadism in the spiritual sense is also possible for us all. We must live in our culture with the determination to transcend it, not being content with the blessings it provides. Our gaze must be turned towards the future, towards realization in God, whatever this cost in terms of renunciation and self-abandonment.

III. Mark Here we continue the "section of breads," that
6:53-56 portion of the gospel where Jesus is particu-
Gospel larly concerned with the formation of his
Monday apostles. They have been involved in the multiplication miracle (Mk 6:30-44). He has
shown them his power over evil, which he intends to communicate to them one day (Mk 6:45-52). But they do not yet under-

stand (v. 52); and doubtless it is in order to find a quiet corner where he can converse with them that he wishes to retire to Bethesaida (Mk 6:45). Contrary winds, however, bring them towards Gennesareth, territory that is altogether Gentile.

a) Though he had been looking for solitude, immediately Jesus finds himself victim of his reputation as thaumaturge. He performs a series of miracles, the elements of which reflect the somewhat magical religion of the *Gentiles* (touching of garments in particular: v. 56; cf. Mk 5:27-28).

However, this particular "summary" (parallel to Mk 1:32-34) transcends the thaumaturgic dimension and gives us the universalistic thrust of the section of breads. For the most part, in Mark at least, the section is localized outside Palestine (Mk 7:24-37; 8:22-26). The blessings brought by the Messiah go beyond the national frontiers. Gentiles are admitted to a share, and Jesus is willing to prolong his sojourn among their sick, so that the apostles will realize that the baskets of bread they gathered after the multiplication for the Jews, are destined for the nations. Thus we have a foreshadowing of the "for you and for the multitude" dimension of the bread at the supper (Mk 14:24) and in the Eucharist.

b) A very powerful wind (*ruah*) drives Jesus and the apostles towards Gentile territory, an irresistible force as it were (Mk 6:48). They could always retort to those purist Jews who would reproach them with contamination by unclean soil, that they were driven there in spite of themselves. The force was more than natural, and must then come from God.

Later when the apostles, without the Lord this time, would go among the Gentiles, they would again be driven by an irresistible force which was also called "*ruah.*" It was the *Spirit.* It would take this powerful force to impel Peter towards the centurion of Caesarea (Ac 11:12), though there is no mention of it when he goes among the Jews of Lydda or Joppe (Ac 9:32-42). Likewise it would take this force to send Philip towards the eunuch of

Candace (Ac 8:29), and subsequently into the Gentile territory of Azot (Ac 8:39-40).

Not least then among the functions of the Spirit is the destruction of the barriers erected by selfishness and particularism on men's journey towards the Lord. Sometimes of course selfishness is strong enough to confine the force of the Spirit within powerful structures.

IV. Genesis
1:20-2:4a
1st reading
1st cycle
Tuesday

Compiled after the exile, chapter one of Genesis recounts creation in the context of the great oriental cosmogonies that the Jews had come to know through contact with Babylonian culture. Yahweh is presented as the victor in a mighty combat with chaos. Like any victorious chief he divides among his followers the spoils and booty taken from the enemy. Herbs, plants, animals, stars, all possessions taken by God from chaos, share one after another the blessings of the conqueror (Gn 1:4-25). Finally man is summoned to receive the best share of the booty.

The account has another dimension, which reflects more directly the priestly mentality of its redactors. Creation is seen as a temple of cosmic proportions. The stars are the "luminaries" (v. 14). A "firmament," like the one on which God is enthroned in the temple, divides the universe in two (v. 6; cf. Ez 1:22-26; 10:1; Ps 150:1). It only remains to install the statue and image of God. Man will be that.

a) There is little point in assigning special significations to the terms *image* and likeness (v. 26). Theological analyses which see one as a natural mission, the other as supernatural, are unquestionably an abuse. The author's use of two words is simply the Hebrew poetic style of doublets and parallels.

Image has often a cultic sense in Scripture. It designated the replica of God that was set up in pagan temples (Nb 33:52; 2 K 11:18; Ez 7:20; Am 5:26). Priestly writings were the most un-compromising critics of these images of wood and stone and the most ardent proponents of man as the only valid "image" of God (Gn 1:26-27; 5:3; 9:6). Thus God, who rejects all man-made images of himself, himself sets up in the temple of the universe a live statue made in his likeness, man himself. Man's highest dignity is to be on earth the creature who is "scarcely less than a God" (Ps 8:5-6), the point of contact between God and the universe.

"Likeness" suggests the same thing as image. It too is a term often used in the liturgy, with perhaps a more mysterious nuance. It is, as it were, that veil which shelters the glory of God from indiscreet gaze (Ez 1:26-36).

b) Man, made in the image of God, becomes a *pair*. Verse 27 would seem to suggest that the author sees in this the fullest realization of divine life. He does not say, as in Genesis 2-3, that women is taken from man's body. Here man and woman are partners, come simultaneously to life, and share as a couple the one great enterprise: mastery of the universe. They both enjoy God's blessing in common (v. 28). Whereas, in Genesis 2-3, Yahweh seems an outside force, a constraining and somewhat vindictive force; here he is the model for the couple's life, and their collaborator. Parentage is no longer a curse (as in Gn 3:15), but the fruitfulness of a couple blessed by God.

c) The *blessing* of the human couple (v. 28) is deliberately different in phraseology from the preceding blessings of the animals. The animals could "multiply" (Gn 1:12, 24, 25); but their fecundity is limited to the species ("according to the species"). Human fecundity on the other hand is directed towards mastery of the earth ("subdue" . . .).

The domination of the earth is indicated by a verb which means "trample under foot." The reference is to the gesture by which the victor took possession of enemy territory (2 S 8:11; 1 Ch 22:8; Nb 32:29; Jos 18:1; Ps 109/110:1). Yahweh has triumphed over the abyss, and he is giving man the right to use his victor's privileges. This is not the action of any semitic God. The Babylonian cosmogonies envisaged man merely as the guardian of God's territories and flocks. Genesis 1 is alone in treating man as God's image, even in the exercise of creative power. In Yahweh, there is nothing at all alienating.

d) The blessing of the couple is precisely that which Abraham and Sarah will receive at their entry to the promised land (Gn 17:3-6). By this transference of the patriarch's blessing to the father of all humanity, the author wishes to convey that all men will share what has been hitherto jealously guarded for the seed of Abraham. He is demonstrating a *universalism* almost unknown in the Scripture of his time. Indeed he confuses two orders that have perhaps been far too much distinguished: that of creation and that of salvation, the natural and the "supernatural."

As he sees it, God's will is unique. The dimensions of salvation are those of creation as a whole. This reaching out to all the people of the universe we find throughout the whole first chapter of Genesis. The characteristic of the Jerusalem temple (luminaries, firmament, glory) are made characteristic of creation as a whole.

Indeed creation finds all its meaning in this deliberate mingling by the redactor of the natural order and that of salvation. When God created Adam, he was already thinking of the one who would be this veritable image (Col 1:15-17). He realized that the universe to which he was giving his life would one day be the spiritual temple of the only cult agreeable to him. His combat against chaos, the fruit of which he was committing to man, would one day have its culmination in Christ's great combat in the desert and on the cross against the powers of evil.

Man of course will betray this project and try to turn to his own profit the great liturgy of creation. However, as long as he remains fruitful and multiplies, his posterity will again one day be turned towards God in a new creation.

V. 1 Kings
8:22-23, 27-30
1st reading
2nd cycle
Tuesday

When God had taken possession of his temple by the apparition of the cloud (1 K 8:1-11), Solomon addressed a brief discourse to the people reminding them of the significance of the dedication (1 K 8:14-21). Then he made a brief prayer of thanksgiving. The redaction of this that has come down to us is profoundly deuteronomic in inspiration (6th century). We have the classic schema of Jewish thanksgiving: thanks to God for his benevolence (v. 23), anamnesis of the fulfillment of the promises (v. 24), a very long epiclesis in the form of multiple petitions (vv. 25-40), a concluding doxology (vv. 52-61).

The reason for the thanksgiving is the covenant, to which God remains faithful (Dt 4:37-38; 6:23; 7:8-10; 8:15-18), provided the people remain faithful to him. Verse 27 is awkwardly placed, and is either a later addition or should be attached to verse 23, the actual thanksgiving. It praises the transcendent God for agreeing to come so close to his people (cf. Dt 4:7). Herein lies the greatest mystery of the temple (cf. 1 K 5:15-20).

Before enumerating the petitions the king specifies what *prayer* means to him (vv. 28-30). He uses three different terms: *tephilah* which has a suggestion of pain, it supposes agony of suffering; *tchinnah* which means trust, a perception of God's mercy which leads to repentance and good resolutions; *rinnah* which is joyful prayer, certain of response.

Prayer is associated with the place where the name of God is found (v. 29; cf. Dt 12:5, 11). Solomon's prayer makes no mistake; God is in heaven (v. 30) and it is there he receives the petitions addressed to him.

The interesting aspect of Solomon's prayer is that it indicates the link with the temple, and the necessity of mediation in order to encounter God. Here mediation comes through the temple because of the presence within its walls of God's glory. The

Jewish feeling about the necessity for mediation was strong; but it was as yet too material and localized. When Christ put himself forward as the temple of the new covenant (Jn 2:18-21), he maintained the principle of mediation, but by absorbing it totally into himself he liberated prayer from any association with a temple or a place (Mt 6:5-8; Jn 4:21-23). Christ's mediation is accomplished by alignment of the petitioner's will with his in such fashion that his lips seem to pronounce the very prayer of Christ himself, and the Spirit, to the Father (Rm 8:26-27). The eucharistic assembly, insofar as it is the body of Christ, provides that mediation necessary to the Christian's prayer. But the Christian should realize that it is here "the name of the Lord resides" for the accomplishment of his will and his sacrifice.

VI. Mark 7:1-13 *Gospel Tuesday*   Christ continues the training of his apostles. He has instructed them in their missionary and eucharistic role (Mk 6:31-44). He has manifested his power over evil (Mk 6:45-52). He has introduced them to universalism (Mk 6:53-56). They realize immediately that the structures of the old religion will not be adequate for the missionary and universalist demands of the new. A discussion begins which is focused on the pharisaic traditions. It is not of course here in proper historical context; it takes place in Palestine (v. 1) whereas Jesus is just now outside the frontier (Mk 6:53). By so placing it Mark is stressing its importance in apostolic training and Christian initiation. After the eucharistic and missionary aspects of Christian life, comes the ethical aspect.

a) The discussion about the *Pharisees* is concerned with two concrete points: ritual ablutions before meals, concerning which Mark provides frequent information for his non-Jewish readers (vv. 3-4), and the ritual offering of goods which dispensed one from the support of parents (vv. 10-11). There is little point in analyzing these customs. They are only described in order to illustrate the point of verse 8, which is curiously repeated in verse 9, and emphasized by quoting Isaiah 29:13 (v. 7). Men's tradition kills the Word of God.

The Pharisee is the type of the ancient Adam who thought to have wrested from God the knowledge of good and evil. This he would use to develop a life of holiness. However, this constant discernment between good and evil led in fact to a life of tension. Each detail had to be judged good or evil, and such a man found himself torn by a knowledge that was not proper to him. Furthermore, he tortured all humanity because he claimed to know those who practiced good and those who are the slaves of evil. God alone can judge this (Mt 7:1; cf. Rm 12:14-21).

Jesus challenged the Pharisees to transcend this anxious discernment between good and evil and recover contact with the actual Word of God. Instead of judging men's actions on these principles, they should endeavor to know God himself and be known by him.

b) It is in this sense that we should understand verse 8, where he contrasts *commandment* and tradition. Tradition is purely juridical. It considers "cases" and enjoins "attitudes." It regulates exterior behavior.

Commandment on the other hand is personal. As in the decalogue it uses the second person. It emanates from a person, and can only be obeyed in communion with that person. It touches the very depths of one's being. It does not as such provide new precepts that counter men's tradition. It is not quantitative. What it does is introduce a new manner of freely accepting traditions and living them in faith and communion with God.

The story of the Pharisees is that of a whole humanity which pretends to a knowledge it cannot master, presumes to discern good and evil and judges men, without taking account of God who is the only one capable of judging. Christ was the first man to subordinate his knowledge of good and evil to that deeper knowledge of God and the divine will. His life in conformity with that will delivered him from all casuistry about good and evil. It made him completely open to the sinner. When the Christian in turn examines his conscience, it is not to sort out there and analyze good and evil. It is above all to discern there the Word of God, and the person of Christ living in him and for him (1 Co 4:3-4). Each day in the Eucharist he is reminded of God in him and of what it entails.

VII. Genesis In approaching this ancient creation narrative, **2:4b-9, 15-17** we should keep in mind that Genesis 1, of *1st reading* more recent origin, gives a rather different *1st cycle* account of the world's beginning, thus rela- *Wednesday* tivizing in large part the details of Genesis 2-3.

This account is much less universalist than Genesis 1. The author never transcends the horizons of the Palestinian peasant of his time. He is concerned to find the origin of his own daily experience, its vicissitudes and its joys.

He is more egocentric than the author of Genesis 1. He does not consider creation as a whole, to celebrate it and give praise. He takes from the old popular traditions only that which will serve his moralizing intent.

The geographic ambience of the account is that of the Palestinian peasant: the rainless steppes where he lives a nomad life (v. 5), the fertile *adamah* watered by the rain where he turns to agriculture (v. 9). In the rainless areas (v. 5) the curse of God weighs heavily on the soil (Jr 14:1-7; 5:22-24; Am 4:7; Is 5:6). Where the rain falls God brings blessing and prosperity (Dt 11:11-17). However, the lot of the Jewish people was to pass from one domain to the other, endlessly, by God's will (Dt 28:63; Jr 4:1-33). Why?

The peasant of this time, if he were a believer, no longer

attributed the fruitfulness of trees and soil to nature divinities. He realized that Yahweh was behind all the forces of nature. It is he who makes the trees burgeon, makes their fruits delectable, above all in the promised land (v. 9, cf. Dt 8:7-10; Ez 47:12; Rev 22:2). Why then should the Palestinian sometimes find his trees barren and fruitless? Why should his garden resemble the steppe with its withered shrubs?

To such questions about the predicaments of life the author replies with the parable of the tree of life and the tree of the knowledge of good and evil (vv. 9, 17). The life given by the first is the happy terrestrial existence. When man eats its fruit he escapes death. The knowledge offered by the second is the faculty to decide oneself what is good and evil. Such knowledge is forbidden to man (v. 17). It would mean rejecting the creatural condition and pretending to an autonomy which is reserved for God alone.

Placed in the garden of Paradise, man is a servant merely, obliged to maintain the garden (v. 15) and bounded by restrictions (v. 17). At the same time he enjoys the well-being that the Hebrew slave enjoyed from the family he served (v. 16b). Man is a *servant*; he cannot aspire to a higher condition and must accept the limitations of his state. The drama which is about to unfold, which will explain to the Palestinian the reasons for his wandering in the steppes, is the prideful revolt of the servant who rejects his own state and looks for autonomy.

Man is basically dependent. His temptation is to forget his state and look for absolute autonomy. The first man to live in total dependence is Jesus. He reestablished humanity in its proper creatural place; but simultaneously he communicated the secret of life that would be filial and friendly. Man would no longer be called a servant but a friend (Jn 15:15). He would once more taste of the tree of life.

The Eucharist is the paradise where Christ, even in the hour of death, refuses all personal autonomy. He makes the cross the tree of life.

VIII. 1 Kings   Thanks to the exertions of his father David,
10:1-10   thanks to luck and an acute political sense,
1st reading Solomon achieved a prominent position among
2nd cycle   near-Eastern peoples of the time (1 K 5:18), a
Wednesday relatively tranquil time. He followed a policy
of openness towards foreigners. He contracted an alliance with Pharaoh (1 K 3:1). He called in foreign artisans for the construction of the temple (1 K 9:10-24). He made a commercial treaty with Tyre (1 K 9:10-28). But, over and above everything else for biblical writers, he tried to integrate human wisdom with the Hebrew genius (1 K 5:13).

It is against this background we must see the visit of a queen from south Arabia, or, more accurately the regent of one of the Sabaean colonies in Arabia.

The passage in today's liturgy indicates the king's ardent interest in all *human values,* which are here symbolized by wisdom (vv. 3-4). His interest of course did not stop short of idolatry (1 K 11); but in general it was of great importance in the regime of faith. He, like all believers after him, realized that human values have direct bearing on the quest for God.

The Church today should take a similar view. She should open her doors and enter into debate with all contemporary currents of thought. She too should glorify God by interesting herself in all his works, by welcoming all forms of men's spiritual search. The attempt to reconcile the faith and human wisdom carries its risks of course, but they are risks that should be fearlessly faced. There is no reason for instance for failing to use the findings of social science concerning human relations, particularly in our missionary enterprise. There is no reason for ignoring the mass media, psychoanalysis, the psychology of religious freedom.

Openness in these domains is really based on a fundamental conviction. It is this. In the salvation plan the divine initiative encounters men as they are, where they are. They are called to become God's partners with whatever religious and cultural values they possess. The encounter is a demanding and purifying experience, but it has no elements of rejection. The classic tradition of theology has always insisted that grace elevates nature but does not destroy it. Our attitude then as Christians towards human values must invariably be positive. Any sifting that becomes necessary ought to make for clarification of these values in themselves

IX. Mark   Here we have a resume of one of Jesus' numer-
   7:14-23   ous diatribes against the Pharisees. It is con-
   Gospel   cerned with cleanness of hands. Judaism had
   Wednesday   carefully developed a thousand and one legal
            prescriptions for cleanness in eating. Jesus begins with these, but he immediately widens the debate by referring to the prescriptions of the law itself (Lv 11) and contrasts legal and moral uncleanness (cf. Ac 10:9-16; Rm 14:14).

His criticism of prescriptions does not extend to the law itself. The inner dynamism of the law ought indeed to have brought about the spiritualization he requires. The Jews however, and particularly the Pharisees, had blocked this dynamism by their overly material concepts. As a consequence, *pharisaism,* which used to be a synonym for piety and perfection, because of Jesus' polemic, became a synonym for hypocrisy. Yet Christianity owes much to it: several apostles to begin with, among them Saint Paul, the important doctrine of the resurrection, and the canon of Scriptures which were the base of apostolic preaching. And even if the Pharisees were responsible for the complicated legal prescriptions, they were at the same time responsible for stressing the importance, in the law, of charity. They were the scrupulous guardians for observance of the law, at a time of all-encompassing pagan influence, and thus really saved the soul of the people. In doing so however they deemphasized messianism considerably. It was too dangerous politically. They over-emphasized cultic procedures, subordinating to these the demands of human brotherhood and social justice.

Because Jesus based religion on person rather than on law, and presented a purified messianism, attaching greater importance to brotherhood than to cultic practice (Mt 15:18-20), it was inevitable that he should clash with pharisaic integrism and intolerance. He pressed for a return to the spirit of the primitive law, removing the rigidity that stood in the way of spiritualization. All this stops considerably short of dismissing pharisaism as complete hypocrisy (a fault that was in fact severely reprimanded in pharisaic circles), and even though some primitive Christian communities in the heat of polemic did go this distance, we should avoid doing so.

Isaiah, inveighing against temple formalism, and Jesus, against the priority given by the Pharisees to cultic procedure over behavior, present a new ethical ideal. Here, the vertical relation to God cannot be maintained apart from the horizontal relation to all men. What was new in the Christian moral ideal was not the injunction to love God, nor yet to love the neighbor, but the combination of the two in one. God is apprehended in the dimension of his universal fatherhood of all men, and all men in their inviolable dignity as adoptive children of the same Father. That was the attitude of the man-God and should be that of the Christian. When we are absorbed by baptism into the love of the Father, we simultaneously receive all men as brothers.

It is in the eucharistic celebration that we gain insight into this indissoluble link between the love of God and the love of men. It is insofar as it assembles men, that the celebration is worship of the Father, insofar as there is sharing of the same bread and sending on the same mission that it is thanksgiving.

X. Genesis **2:18-25** *1st reading* *1st cycle* *Thursday*	Woman's creation takes place in an essentially masculine world. Man had already become self-conscious, and had taken possession of the things round about him, naming them (vv. 18-20). Then he discovers in woman the "help-meet" he seeks.

For this particular biblical tradition then, the world came into being male. Woman has a place there only in her relation to man (v. 23; cf. 1 Co 11:9; 1 Tm 2:13). This is corroborated by the legend of Adam's rib (v. 21): woman is the flesh of her husband. It is a far cry from the equally sharing couple we find in Genesis 1 (Gn 1:27-28).

The tradition should be qualified by the other biblical traditions, particularly that of Genesis 1. It presents the couple as turned in on themselves, at the mercy of forces they do not control (cf. v. 25; Gn 3:10-16 . . .). The later account of Genesis 1 on the other hand shows us a blessed couple, turned towards the conquest of the world (Gn 1:27-28).

The misogyny of Genesis 2-3 was to influence the *state of woman* throughout biblical history. She was the "other" in a masculine world. Her femininity found no proper place in structures that had been pre-established by males. Her behavior was regarded as foolish and witless. She was accused of being possessed or demonic. She was alienated, made a perpetual minor, subject to the mediation and authority of the male. We still have the vestiges of this tradition in the letters of Saint Paul (1 Co 11:7-9), even though he is careful to introduce correctives.

Jesus, however, really delivered woman from these alienations, not sociologically, but by pointing to his person as the new-Adam and the First-Born of creation. He is the only mediator for reconciled humanity (1 Tm 2:5). All other mediations, such as that of the male for the female, cease and are relativized.

XI. 1 Kings
11:4-13
1st reading
2nd cycle
Thursday

Having reached the heights of renown and riches, Solomon was able to people a harem of 700 princesses and 300 concubines (v. 3). Tradition of course may have somewhat exaggerated the figures, but there is reason to accuse Solomon of sexual license. At the time the possession of numerous women indicated position and riches rather than depravity of morals. No one can really "possess" another human being in whatever way.

a) The *woman* however was still considered at this time a mysterious being, subject to the uncontrollable forces of fruitfulness and sterility. She readily had recourse to magic in these domains, requiring to remain in contact with the divinities of her particular clan (Gn 31), so that no confusion of divine jurisdiction would interfere in this regard. Her association with mysterious forces turned her almost inevitably to magic and idolatry, not to say sacred prostitution (Ho 4:12-14; Dt 23:18-19; 1 K 14:24; 22:47; Ba 6:42-44). The fact that she had to maintain loyalty to the gods of her people meant that idolatry could make inroads among the chosen people.

Deuteronomy in particular is quite severe about marriages with foreign women, precisely because of the danger to Jewish monotheism (Ex 34:15-16; Dt 7:3-4; Tb 4:12-13).

b) The contemporary concept of *retribution* would entail condemnation of Solomon's foreign wives (vv. 9-13). Deuteronomy in fact promises prosperity to the Hebrews only to the extent that they succeed in destroying all the Canaanite tribes in the Promised Land (Dt 7:1-2). Royal marriages with foreign women were a flagrant violation of this divine command (1 K 15:13-15; 16:30-33). In the deuteronomic tradition all the misfortunes decreed by Yahweh for foreign associations come from a sort of original sin of the kings. The philosophy of history is that any regression or bad turning in the pattern of events must be traced to the king's behavior. One man's fault affects the whole people and distorts the course of history .

Not until Jesus' intervention in history would the full dignity of woman be recognized, and her basic equality with man. This was part of the universalism which characterized his messianic consciousness. True universalism is demonstrated by interest in the little ones and the poor. In Jesus' time woman was still subject to numerous interdicts. She was not yet fully a part of the chosen people. It was this inequality that he challenged by his attitude to women. He did not directly attack the regulations, but each time the opportunity arose he accepted women as authentic persons, called in the same way as men to take their part in the construction of the Kingdom. They too benefitted in precisely the same way from the divine initiative of love and pardon. Saint Luke particularly, in his Gospel, stresses this attitude to women, with the purpose of showing the Savior's universalism.

It is remarkable by contrast that the development of Chistianity in the Graeco-Roman world failed for many centuries to focus attention on the status of women. In general, on this point, it was as if paganism had succeeded in maintaining itself. Monogamy, true, and the indissolubility of marriage were extolled; but the civilization of the Christian West remained up to our own day a masculine civilization. Woman was only accepted as a second-class citizen. Perhaps it was the white man's attitude to sexuality that has held back for so long a development that Christianity of its nature would be bound to support.

Nowadays proper status for women is the order of the day. It is indeed a matter of major importance that is only beginning to be properly charted. Christians, one hopes, will not be absent in this struggle where the dignity of all humanity is at stake.

XII. Mark   Although Jesus had offered bread to all who
7:24-30   wished to have it (Mk 6:30-44) twelve baskets
Gospel   of fragments had been collected. The purpose
Thursday   of the present passage is to show the meaning
                       of such a quantity.

It appears that at the earliest stage of the tradition this episode
was limited to the proverb in verse 27 which affirms that proper
charity begins at home. This reflects the time when Christian
communities still considered themselves a Jewish sect among
others. Like the others they did not believe that the coming of the
Messiah meant the end of Jewish election.

During a second stage, the Christians began to withdraw from
Judaism. The account of the cure of the Canaanite woman's
daughter was added (vv. 25-33). It was an episode fairly similar
to the cure of the centurion's son (Mt 8:5-13) or the Gerasene
demoniac (Mk 5:1-20) which reflect a further development, an
awareness that the Jewish people do not have a monopoly of
salvation (cf. Ac 15:8-11). Nevertheless, during this stage there
was still some acceptance of persons. Gentiles, even convert
Gentiles, were not admitted to the same table with Jews, because
of the cleanness regulations Christians did not yet dare to
suppress.

The third stage comes with the actual redaction of Mark.
Verses 24, 27a and 31a were added to show that Jesus was the real
founder of the mission to the Gentiles. During this stage the
primitive community became aware that Israel is rejected, that
the Kingdom has passed to others (Mk 12:9).

The miracle at Tyre is given by Mark and Matthew (15:21-28)
only. The differences between the two versions point up Mark's
particular purpose in the narrative. Matthew has the Syro-
Phoenician woman come into Jewish territory (Mt 15:22; as
Naaman the Syrian came to the Jordan: 1 K 5:12-14). But in Mark
Jesus goes into *Gentile territory* to proclaim salvation (v. 24; cf.

Mk 5:1; Mk 6:53). He also omits the extremely harsh remark which Matthew has Jesus make on the occasion (Mt 15:24). Nor does he have this Gentile woman confess the Messiahship of the Son of David as Matthew does (Mt 15:22). The conversation, however, about the crumbs of bread (vv. 28-29) he does retain, because he finds in this play upon words an allusion to the fragments after the multiplication.

His purpose is clear. The Gentiles too have a right to the bread of salvation, because they in turn benefit from the Lord's kindness (cf. Mk 6:34; 8:2).

It is probable that at the time of encountering the Gentile woman Jesus did not yet fully realize his universal role. He was a Jewish rabbi concerned with the instruction of his own people. It took this unexpected (more unexpected in Matthew than in Mark) entry of a pagan woman to develop his insight. He now extends his role as rabbi by developing genuinely missionary horizons.

Similarly, it would require a hint of the same kind, in the person of the pagan Cornelius, to induce the apostle Peter to extend his function as president of the Judaeo-Christian community and go to the Gentiles.

Incidents like those of the Canaanite woman and Cornelius show that mission is not merely centrifugal. The missionary urge does not just arise from a desire to make propaganda and have influence. The important thing is the encounter between Christian and unbeliever, between the Church and the world. The believer must welcome the other, and show himself ready to listen, to receive before giving.

When the eucharistic celebration sets up in its members this sort of urge, it is fulfilling its function.

XIII. Genesis
3:1-8
1st reading
1st cycle
Friday

The most plausible explanation of the sin of Adam, which is described in this passage, is that it was sexual. In the near-East the serpent was the god of fruitfulness, for the land and for women. Many women, Jewish as well as those of neighboring nations, had recourse to the cult of the serpent to ensure a fruitful marriage.

From the 8th century onwards, the Jewish prophetic tradition inveighed against such sexual cults (Gn 31; Jr 44:15-18; Ho 4:12-14; Ba 6:42-44; 6:27-29) and claimed Yahweh alone as the true source of fruitfulness (Gn 17:16; 25:21, etc.).

By resorting to idolatrous practices and a serpent cult, Adam and Eve were trying to secure by their own efforts a fruitfulness that was God's province, and thus become independent of him. The result is sudden and decisive: they find themselves aware of a new knowledge. Where previously they had seemed simple and adolescent (Gn 2:25), they now know sexual attraction and shame (v. 7). There is nothing unusual in this. They reach an adult awareness but they reach it through transgression, a basic ambiguity in the human state.

The interest of the narrative, as it has emerged from the author's rehandling of the primitive myth, is not as such the precise nature of Adam's *sin*. It may well be that he has chosen sexual rather than another type of fault in order to condemn the idolatrous practices of his time.

He stresses very clearly the essential content of sin: that is to say, pride. By raising himself up against God, man rejects the dependent state. In this instance, the source of transgression is no longer taken to be influences exterior to man (as in Gn 6:1-4, 6 for example). It lies in the very heart of man (Si 15:11-20). That is the meaning of the dialogue between God and Adam concerning the latter's fault (vv. 10-13). Because man has a determining function in the universe, it is normal to regard his urge to transgress as partly responsible for the world's disorder.

The passage is the most important scriptural text concerning original sin. It should, however, be properly understood and some elementary things ought to be made clear. We cannot expect a text of the 8th century B.C. to give answers to the questions raised by modern science. Our passage neither contradicts nor affirms monogenism from a single couple, or polygenism from several ancestors. Science only can broach this problem, and if today it seems to lean toward polygenism, we need not feel bound to read into Genesis 2-3 what it was not meant to say.

Furthermore, any text has to be interpreted according to the intentions of its author. The Yahwist author is trying to explain why the Jewish people was set apart from other peoples. He does so by pointing out that this was not God's original purpose. He blessed "man" ("man" in general that is, not a particular person), but man fell into sin. Subsequently, in Abraham, he again blessed man (all men). The Yahwist traditions were not concerned with the question whether mankind was descended from a single couple, and man's sin traceable to this single couple. They were concerned with affirming that God wished to bless mankind, but that, because of man's transgressions, he was led to a course other than that planned.

Indeed it is quite possible to regard original sin as a sinful state, an ambiguous slumber of transgression into which every man born is cast. It is a state developed during secular growth and ratified when the child, grown adult, himself transgresses (Rm 5:11). In other words, it is perfectly possible to maintain that original sin is transmitted by generation. Provided, that is, we regard generation, not as a biological phenomenon linking us to a primordial couple, but as a cultural, social and historical phenomenon which involves us in a history of transgressions that preceded us, and influences our free decisions.

Thus, each man comes into the world deficient in divine life because the mediation that would link him to salvation in Christ has been blocked by the sin of the society into which he is born, which he in turn ratifies. That this sinful state was initiated by a first sin is indubitable. But this first sin was followed by other, sometimes much graver, sins, the cumulative weight of which was decisive for all humanity.

Society deprives the man born into it of Christ's mediation by not living the divine life, because of all the sinful decisions. If society does live the divine life, mediation is restored. Such a society is provided by the Church. That is why, through baptism, which admits to the Church's sacramentality, a man is liberated from the sociological milieu that shuts him off from salvation.

XIV. 1 Kings 11:29-32, 12:19 *1st reading* *2nd cycle* *Friday*	Jeroboam became known as an architect during the construction of the temple, with the result that Solomon made him one of his principle ministers. One day he encountered a prophet who mimed before him the approaching schism of the people and his own responsibility in this.

The prophet's mantle is new, as recent as the kingdom of David, and already it is rent. What Saul could not do when he tried to snatch the mantle of Samuel (1 S 15:27), Jeroboam could. He received practically the whole of the mantle, but in shreds. It is a tragic symbol of the coming *schism*.

But God's fidelity is at once evident. Even in the dismemberment of the people, simply for love of David, he retains the promise made to him. He retains his attachment to the holy city by having the tribe of Benjamin veer to the land where Jerusalem is, beside the small kingdom of Judah.

Thus, at the very moment when hopes for unity were disappearing, and with them one of the signs of the covenant, there remained in Jerusalem, and among David's descendants, sufficient evidence that God would be faithful to his initiative across the hazards of death and failure.

It is very significant that Benjamin follows Judah. It was one of the northern tribes and had, indeed, often headed movements of revolt. Now it is side by side with Judah, as if to prevent this tribe from turning in upon itself, to remind it of unification and its destiny for dialogue. Their coexistence demonstrates that tribalism has been overcome. There are excellent hopes that one day a descendant of Judah and of David will successfully undertake the reunification of the people and of all peoples.

XV. Mark Mark's account of the cure of the deaf-mute
7:31-37 (*mogilalos*) has quite original elements. For
Gospel instance he establishes a close parallel between
Friday this cure and that of the blind man (Mk 8:22-26), that is already indicated indeed by the inclusion of both in the so-called "section of breads" (Mk 6:30-8:26). There is the same insalivation (7:33; 8:23), the same imposition of silence on the subject (7:36; 8:26), the same imposition of hands (7:32; 8:22-23), the same approach on the part of the friends who "conduct" the subject (7:32; 8:22).

Both narratives teach a similar lesson. Not hearing and not seeing are signs of chastisement (Mk 4:10-12; 8:18), a cure of these ailments a sign of salvation. This salvation which is a gift of God presupposes a break with the world. When Jesus brings the deaf and the blind "aside" so that they will hear and see, it is because the crowd as such is incapable of hearing and seeing.

a) It appears that the cure of the dumb man is a replica of Isaiah 35:2-6: The prophet had announced to the people exiled in Babylon an undreamed-of destiny. It would be invested with the "glory of Lebanon," and the dumb themselves would cry out for joy.

Jesus is in Gentile territory on the frontiers of Lebanon, and there miraculously gives speech to a dumb man. The people are going to return from exile, enriched by the renown of foreign lands, filled with unspeakable joy. The miracle is proclaiming the imminence of *salvation*.

b) Doubtless Mark incorporated this miracle in a pre-existing ritual for baptismal initiation. The gesture whereby Jesus raises his eyes to heaven before the cure (v. 34) is found again only in the multiplication episode (Mk 6:41). This seems to suggest a liturgical dimension.

So that we seem to have an echo of the first ritual for *Christian initiation*. The most ancient rituals we have already make provision for a rite for the senses (eyes in Ac 9:18; nose and ears in the Tradition of Hippolytus, no. 20, etc.). If we take the view that saliva, for the Jew, was a sort of solidified breath, it could signify the gift of the Spirit that was characteristic of a new creation (Gn 2:7; 7:22; Wi 15:15-16). And Mark doubtless gives us the Aramaic term used by Jesus, *ephphata* (v. 34) because it was in the traditional ritual.

We could reconstruct the ritual perhaps thus: an exorcism (Mk 7:29, which just precedes our passage), sponsors—those "who conduct," imposition of hands (v. 32), a "setting aside" (v. 33, not the later *disciplina arcani,* but indicating insight into the originality of the faith), a rite for the senses (v. 34), three days of preparatory fast (Mk 8:3; Ac 9:9), and then participation in the Eucharist.

In concluding the episode, Mark returns to the synoptic tradition (vv. 36-37), and mentions the praise of the crowd, who saw in the miracle the advent of the messianic era (Mt 15: 30-31), because it was a fulfillment of Isaiah's oracle 61:1-2, that had been already interpreted in this sense by Jesus himself (Mt 11:5).

The initiation to faith, which is the main theme of this passage, reminds us of the whole topic of healing *mutes* in the Bible. Most accounts of prophetic vocations, of people, that is, who are going to be bearers of God's Word, are associated with healings of mutes or stammerers (Ex 4:10-17; Is 6; Jr 1). We are dealing with a literary procedure designed to show that the prophet is incapable by natural faculty of even beginning to speak. The word he is to transmit he receives from Another. That is why the healing of a mute person who proclaims the Word is considered an excellent symbol of faith, an infused virtue which does not depend on natural qualities.

Another characteristic of the mute-healings is noteworthy. During periods of divine chastisement, the prophets were struck dumb. The Word of God was no longer proclaimed, because the people blocked their ears so as not to hear it (1 S 3:1; Is 28:7-13; Lm 2:9-10; Ez 3:22-27; Am 8:11-12; Gn 11:1-9). Muteness is associated with lack of faith; the mute person is often deaf as well.

When the prophets speak, and speak copiously, it is a sign that the messianic times have arrived, that God is present and faith ubiquitous (cf. Lk 1:65; 2:27, 38). We have one very important text in this regard: Joel 3:1-2. Pentecost is its precise fulfillment (Ac 2:1-3).

The impressive number of healings of the deaf and mute wrought by Jesus is a sign of the inauguration of the messianic era (Lk 1:64-67; 11:14-28; Mt 9:32-34; 12:22-24; Mk 7:31-37; 9:16-28). The sending of the apostles, at the end of the gospels, to bear the Word to the world, is thus presented as a prophetic vocation. A new speech is given to them (Mt 10:19-20; Rm 10:14-18), as if they too had to emerge from dumbness.

This healing of a mute makes us aware that faith is a messianic blessing. Mark, however, in recounting it, wants to stress also the Old Testament theme which associates dumbness with lack of faith. Several times he points out that the crowd has ears which do not hear, eyes which do not see (Mk 6:4, 10-12; again in 8:18). The whole "section of breads" (Mk 6:30-8:26) can be regarded as the section of non-understanding (Mk 6:52; 7:7, 18; 8:17, 21). In order to effect the cure of the deaf-mute Jesus withdraws him from the crowd, as if to stress the fact that dumbness is characteristic of the crowd and that it is necessary to be apart in order to be open to faith.

The distinguishing feature of the last times is that men are in a filial relationship with God, are capable of hearing his word, responding to him, and speaking of him to others. The Christian then is in some sense a prophet, a specialist of the Word, the familiar of God. He should be able to hear the Word and proclaim it, requiring for this the ears and lips of faith.

XVI. Genesis These verses give us the maledictions which
3:9-24 followed the original sin in the garden. A
1st reading malediction of the earth (vv. 17-19) comes
1st cycle after those on motherhood and the powers of
Saturday evil (vv. 14-16). The curses then are concerned with those elements that for the Jew constituted prosperity; fruitfulness of the woman (v. 16), of the land (vv. 17-18), the influence of angelic supra-terrestrial powers (vv. 14-15) and life itself (vv. 17-19).

a) In its attempt to explain the tenor of events, the mythic *curse* can be regarded as a kind of embryonic science. The contrary, or abnormal, is featured; an animal that moves without paws, childbearing that is agonizing, work that overwhelms . . . death itself. It would be wrong however to polarize myth and science in this context as if they were simply two corresponding aspects, one being the shadow of the other. In fact myth here is more existential than science, its level is deeper and more universal. So that if science be justified in "demythologizing" the curses, it should not altogether displace the myth. The religious message must be respected.

The author's attitude is that human history develops well or ill, is one of blessing or of curse (cf. Dt 28:15-19), according to the religious and moral choices of man. The secret of history lies within the heart of man. Curse characterizes the state in history where man tries to be equal to God (v. 22); blessing that state where he accepts himself as the image of God, something that Christ alone accomplished (Ga 3:13-14). In Genesis 2:8 the curse never has the last word. Curses may be piled one upon the other (Gn 3:14-20; 4:11-14; 6:5-7; 13), but blessing triumphs in the end (Gn 8:21) and rectifies the course of history. The enmity between the seed of the woman and the seed of the serpent, which we had in verse 15, will ultimately cease. One day man will be delivered from the idolatrous cult of the powers and the alienation this brings.

b) Such a philosophy of life implies of course as an underlying principle the Hebrew doctrine of *retribution* in earthly existence. If man is buffeted between prosperity and misfortune, the reason must be a religious or moral one. Sin disrupts the harmony of things by blocking entry for fruitfulness and life. If man's most noble activity becomes the source of woe, that must be because some rupture between God and man has distorted the system.

Another conviction also underlies the thinking. For peoples who have as yet no sense of history, of the possibility of change and reexamination, all situations are given "from the beginning." If woe destroys prosperity in man's lives, the cause must be something at the beginning. As a sense of history began to grow in Israel, she freed herself gradually from this notion of an original "given." She discovered the possibility for each generation to question its origin and its past by the path of conversion. In salvation history there is no fatalism.

The original curse then is only understandable in the doctrinal context of its proclamation, a retribution doctrine limited to the present, devoid of a sense of history. Unfolding revelation will gradually remove this ambiguity. The people will be educated to the meaning of history, to the fact that the past is reversible by the grace of God (compare Ez 28:24 with v. 18; 1 Co 15:20-23, 45-49 with v. 19). Eventually, overly material concepts of retribution will be modified by faith in something beyond death, that is ratified by Christ's resurrection.

Following the cross, the Eucharist finally lifts this initial curse. It gives the key to history, celebrating that decisive "hour" when humanity found it could be delivered from the inevitability of death and evil, and enter the glory of the final times.

By attempting to wrest from God the knowledge of good and evil, by refusing to trust someone greater than himself in discernment of persons and things, man introduced curse to the world. He wanted no god other than himself and his own egoism. Things would no longer have the goodness with which God had invested them, but that which man would bestow. Good and evil, life and death, became locked in combat because man, now knowing them, could not, like God, pardon evil to make it good, heal death to make it life. Making himself like God, he had no access to divine life and could not change evil or death. However godlike he thought himself, inevitably he proved ludicrous. He knew good and evil, life and death. But he did not, like God, control them; and was forever tossed like a puppet between ambiguities.

It was thus that death, which is simply the natural lot of man, came to be seen as the result of God's anger. The human agony is not so much dying, but dying with the feeling that there is no way not to die, unsure that there is someone who was there before we were born and will be there after us. It is precisely because man can form a concept of the everlasting that death appears a punishment rather than a natural phenomenon. It is the overwhelming challenge to human limitations, and it restores the balance between man and God, which man, with his knowledge of eternity and his pretensions to self-sufficiency, is always trying to disrupt.

Jesus Christ only was capable of knowing good and evil, of passing from life to death in triumph. He vanquished death by his own divine life which nothing could take away, and he vanquished evil by limitless pardon.

To members of the human race, who, after Adam, know death and life, good and evil, the Eucharist offers the fruit of the tree

of life which Adam could not pluck (v. 22). This spark of divine
life within them enables them to overcome both evil and death.

XVII. 1 Kings The tribes, which were already divided poli-
12:26-32; tically, now become separate in the religious
13:33-34 domain by the construction of two new tem-
1st reading ples for the northern kingdom, one at Bethel
2nd cycle and one at Dan (v. 30). These were two an-
Saturday cient sanctuaries that retained the reverence of
the majority of the people, despite the recent
period of unification at Jerusalem (Gn 12:8; 13:3; 28:19; 35;
Jq 18).

The north at once yielded to the urge to represent Yahweh in
sculpture and constructed a golden calf identical to the one of
Sinai (Ex 32). The Israel king, for the cult of the two temples,
chose priests from among the people, not the Levites (v. 31).

At the time these measures could not be regarded as grave
faults. The people were not really accustomed to a single temple;
this was a dogma only developed two centuries later under
deuteronomic influence (Dt 12:1-12). Nor was the setting up of
a nonlevitic priesthood matter for scandal; because the king was
still considered the chief organizer of cult, responsible for the
choice of priests. The legislation about the levitic monopoly of
the priesthood of Aaron was also much later (Nb 16). The law
forbidding sculptured images of Yahweh was indeed known (Ex
20:4); but as yet, doubtless, it was not absolutely binding. In the
Jerusalem temple itself, as well as the ark of the covenant, was
preserved the famous serpent of bronze. In any case, cult at
Bethel and Dan was not idolatrous; it was directed towards the
true God. It was not a nature cult, because God's intervention in
history was acknowledged (v. 28). It may have been somewhat
influenced by Canaanite worship and syncretist tendencies.

Thus in today's reading Jeroboam is charged with a fault the meaning of which only becomes clear some centuries later. His sin was later seen as the original sin of the northern tribes. They never ceased to ratify it, during a time when prophetic voices called for conversion and spiritualization.

The mistake of Jeroboam and the northern tribes was in seeking a religion without faith. One could believe in the existence of God, in providence; one could set up a worship and a priesthood, without being in the least open to God's plan, or faithful to his Word. There is always a tendency, late or soon, to make God in the image of man and reduce him to human categories. Obedience will only be rendered to a God whose requirements are translated into human terms. Religion and nationalism (or any other sort of humanism) are confused. When engulfed by the secular, without any element of the transcendent, religion becomes degraded and dies the death of all things human. The history of the northern tribes is there as a reminder.

XVIII. Mark 8:1-10 *Gospel Saturday*   The "section of breads" (Mk 6:30-8:26), which has been read now for several days, can be arranged, from the point of view of composition and purpose, in two parallel portions. A comparative table will illustrate this.

6:30-44 and 8:1-9: multiplication of bread
6:45-52 and 8:10-13: Christ on the waters
7:1-23 and 8:14-18: discussions about pharisaism
7:31-37 and 8:22-26: the senses opened (deaf and blind)

The whole section is possibly assembled from two different traditions that were put together independently, featuring more or less different episodes, which point to the same teaching. The discovery, that is, of the mystery of Christ's personality, the sacramental and missionary dimensions of the new religion. The two traditions were later combined in a single section, which is reproduced by Mark with certain modifications.

Today's passage begins the second part of the section. We are given another multiplication narrative. The miracle was probably a single occurrence but is recounted twice because it was preserved in two different sources.

a) It is worth noting to begin with that both multiplication narratives use the vocabulary of the eucharistic liturgy of the time (Mk 14:22; Ac 4:41; 20:7; Mk 8:19). The reader could not be mistaken about the meaning of a miracle in the "desert" (v. 4). It indicated that manna was being supplanted by the eucharistic bread.

The author however does not confine himself to the eucharistic rite (v. 6). He gives us data which present the Eucharist as the *sacrament of faith* and mission. The first aspect is seen in the dialogue between Jesus and the apostles (vv. 4-5), with emphasis on the latters' lack of understanding (Mk 8:14-21). It is also evident in the very context of the multiplication, where the lesson is that the Eucharist can only be shared when the senses have been opened (Mk 7:31-37).

b) The Eucharist is also the *sacrament of mission*. This we see in the reference to the fragments (v. 8), showing that not all the guests contemplated by the Lord were present. Furthermore the number 7 (by contrast with the number 12 in Mk 6:42) could very well be a symbolic number in the Greek tradition which preserved the episode. Similarly the number 12 was the symbolic number in the Jewish tradition which preserved the first multiplication (Mk 6:30-42). Finally we have the missionary dimension in the actual context, where there is question of rites of initiation and of conversion of Gentiles (Mk 7:14-38; 8:22-26).

This multiplication narrative then served the primitive communities as a symbol of total reassembly in the actual local assemblies (Ac 20:1 Co 12:13; Col 3:11; Ga 3:28). There would be reminders of the road leading towards faith and acceptance of attitudes other than the Jewish.

These particular nuances in Mark's account suggest reflections about similar aspects of the Eucharist in the 20th century. Remembering the different cultural milieus in which people live, what sort of aspect ought the eucharistic celebration present that would enable people to express their faith and feel at home?

In this hour of the Church's catholicity, when the Second Vatican Council has made provision for an authentic diversity in the total unity, sacramental liturgy is about to undergo acculturation in unprecedented terms. This will enable the young churches of recent development to be really present to their members. The previous existence in the Church of oriental liturgies was a good precedent. The substitution of vernaculars for the Latin liturgy is no more than a first step. It is an important one indeed, but it will be necessary to go further as soon as possible, following the rhythm of the living organism. How far can or should we go? In Asia can the Lord's supper be celebrated with rice and water? It will be the task of the Church itself to decide of course, always maintaining the "substantial" quality of the rite. What the theologian can say here and now is this: from the liturgy of the apostolic communities we must preserve all that is necessary to make Christian initiation an alignment of the total man, body and soul, with the historic event of the cross.

There is another point. The very fact that the necessity of Christian ritual is now being reexamined shows that the risk run by the Church in encountering the contemporary world is not inconsiderable. Her very existence is at stake. Without always realizing what they are doing, some missionaries tend to reduce the Good News of salvation to a moral ideal, a universal brotherly love that is divine in name only. They are the victims of overanxiety for adaptation to modern man. Christianity is gravely threatened by such attitudes. The gospel ceases to be a Person, the man-God who is the unique mediator. Salvation loses its gratuity, and its historical dimension. The Church is not the Body of Christ but a school of wisdom founded by a Master. If we accept the fact that faith is altogether based on the person of Jesus Christ, who died and rose again 2000 years ago, who is always living in his Church, the necessity for sacramental initiation goes without saying.

It is probable indeed that rite will be less prominent in the life of the modern Christian than it used to be, because he is more conscious of finding the sacrament of the Church in the texture of actual life. But he can never abandon all rite because he can never abandon Christ's mediation or the gratuitous salvific initiative of the Father.

SIXTH SUNDAY

A. THE WORD

**I. Sirach
15:16-21
1st reading
1st cycle**

Ben Sirach is the first Jewish author to reflect on the first chapters of Genesis and in particular on the account of the fall. He is sufficiently informed about stoic philosophy to refer to it (v. 11 is inspired by a verse of Euripides that Chrysippus often quotes), but he is not necessarily an adherent. We might say that Genesis provides this Wisdom writer with the topic of his mediation, the origin of sin, and stoicism helps him to seek an answer in the nature of human liberty.

He gives us two reasons for *death*. One is biblical, the sin of Eve (Si 25:23); the other stoic, the corporal condition of life (Si 41:3-4). Because man is a material composition, death comes, but man's lot might have been otherwise had he obeyed God. The author does not commit himself or seem indeed to have attempted to reconcile the two viewpoints. He simply juxtaposes fragmentary attitudes without synthesizing them. Man he says is mortal (v. 18), but it is possible for him to so behave that he will escape death (vv. 14-18, inspired by Dt 30:15).

Yet he seems fully to realize that, sinner or not, man cannot avoid death. His concept of what lies beyond death is still too vague to be any sort of affirmation of a life stronger than death. Can we go any further in our search for a synthesis? Man is mortal; that is part of the creatural condition, human freedom notwithstanding. And yet freedom changes everything. We can accept the human predicament or reject it in pride.

Death is not really the consequence of our ill-use of human freedom, but yet it is profoundly associated with freedom. When freedom is only used to bolster self-sufficiency and egoism, death makes it ludicrous. In this sense death is truly a punishment.

II. Leviticus
13:1-2, 45-46
1st reading
2nd cycle

This comes from the regulations concerning cleanness, particularly those for the treatment of *"leprosy"* (Lv 13-14). There is no reason to believe that we are dealing with the disease known to medicine by this name. The term was used for most maladies of the skin.

The underlying mentality is extremely primitive, not to say superstitious, and reflects the thinking of the postexilic priesthood about cleanness. Fears about uncleanness must have been especially intense after the exile, when we find people seeking prescriptions in murky oriental sources that even the former legislation had not seen fit to include.

III. Jeremiah
17:5-8
1st reading
3rd cycle

This is actually a psalm, which probably served as a model for Psalm 1.

It treats in lyric fashion an ancient deuteronomic theme. Man is at the crossing of the ways between *malediction* and *beatitude*. After the proclamation of the clauses of the covenant, the people were confronted with their responsibilities. Happiness would be the result of consent, misfortune of refusal. The psalm of Jeremiah (or more probably of one of his later redactors) spiritualizes the deuteronomic dilemma. It is no longer a question of material happiness or misfortune. The just man will not only possess the numerous fruitful trees promised by Deuteronomy; he himself will be a tree that will not cease to give fruit (vv. 7-8). Likewise the wicked man will be punished not only by the sterility and aridity of his fields; he himself will become a desert where no one will seek to live (v. 6).

The man who "trusts in himself" tries to construct a happiness tailored in his own terms, backed by the sort of securities he

seeks: love, money, a profession . . . The human "heart" however
has unsuspected depths and spurs a man beyond the horizons of
this calculated well-being. It makes him seek communion with
the absolute, and penetrate to him who can provide a more total
happiness in altogether different terms.

IV. 1 Corinthians Paul continues with his apologia for Christian
    2:6-10 wisdom, and shows its superiority to human
   2nd reading systems of wisdom (cf. 1 Co 1: 26-31; 1 Co
    1st cycle 2:1-5). Doubtless he is thinking of the homily
in Baruch 3:9—4:4, concerning the superiority
of Jewish wisdom. It was delivered in the synagogue each year
on the anniversary of the destruction of the temple.

Baruch shows there that foreigners, sages or merchants (Ba
3:22-23), do not have God's wisdom any more than the giants
or angels had (Ba 3:26). God's temple may have been destroyed
but his true dwelling remains untouched by the disaster (Ba
3:24). By his wisdom and his law he does not cease to dwell in
the hearts of those who remain faithful to him (Ba 3:38—4:4).

a) Paul's argument is developed on this model. For the destroyed temple, now is substituted the crucified Christ (v. 8).
Neither sages nor angels (the meaning to be given "The princess
of this world" in vv. 6 and 8, as in Baruch 3-4) had that knowledge of God's plan which brought Christ from death to glory.
Their *wisdom* was confounded and God accomplished his plan
unknown to them.

He continues to follow Baruch. Baruch had explained how,
once the wisdom of men and of angels was confused, that of God
would directly manifest itself to men (Ba 3:38). This is in fact
what God has done, by sending the Spirit (v. 10). The wisdom of
the princes of this world was confused on the cross, and God sent
men his own Spirit to reveal to them the depths of his *mystery*
(v. 7). That is to say the project, for long kept secret, of man's
delivery through the cross of Christ.

The "princess of the world" may have known all the laws governing the universe and humanity. They knew the meaning of matter, the meaning of history, and were so capable of putting things in proper perspective that they could sometimes discern absolute values. What they did not know was that this absolute was a Person, with all that this implied in unpredictability and gratuitousness. So, when God is about to give man not only an understanding of the universe and of history but also an understanding of eternity, together with the urge to participate in it and judge all things by it, they are completely unaware.

People seek in "wisdom" an explanation for the world and find themselves confronted by a destiny.

V. 1 Corinthians As will be the case again in 1 Corinthians
10:31-11:1 11:23-29, Paul is not so much concerned with a
2nd reading defense of the sacramentality of the Eucharist,
2nd cycle which his correspondents do not seem to doubt
(cf. 1 Co 10:16, where an affirmative answer is implied). He is stressing the repercussions that the Eucharist has on the "body" of Christ, which is the assembly and the Church.

a) One of the key-notions in Saint Paul is the *unity of each person with Christ* which is brought about in the Eucharist. The blood is the covenant (1 Co 11:25; cf. Ex 24:3-8), the common life, that is, between God and man. Bread and wine give communion (*koinonia*: a being in common) with God (1 Co 10:16). The term "communion," in this sense, replaces the Old Testament term "alliance" (cf. 1 Co 10:18). It is contrasted with the so-called union with pseudo-divinities that could be brought about by idolatrous sacrifices (cf. 1 Co 10:20).

b) This unity however implies another union, that of each with all.* And the union in question is more than a simple jux-

*See the doctrinal theme: *double love,* p. 250

taposition of individuals: it is, on the contrary, organic. It constitutes a "body" (1 Co 10:17; cf. 1 Co 11:29) which is the Church. The Eucharist then, by the blessing pronounced over the bread and wine of the new covenant, is the sacrament which builds up the Church.

c) As well as being communion with God and the brethren, the Eucharist is also the *convocation* of non-Christians (vv. 31-33). It is the sign of God's glory confronting the world. Thus every measure should be taken to make the sign clear, a manifestation of the unity of the members with God and among themselves, and also a manifestation of welcome to others, "all things to all people" (v. 33; cf. 1 Co 9:22).

The consecrated bread that is reserved in the tabernacle of the most insignificant Christian community is not confined in its mystery to that spot. It represents the power of the Church, the power indeed of a humanity regenerated in the Body of the new Adam. The reserved sacrament stands for the unique Body of Christ, of universal and cosmic dimension, and enables that Body to go on being built as hearts are converted to greater love and greater unity.

VI. 1 Corinthians 15:12, 16-20 Many Corinthians doubtless were troubled by the resurrection of the body (v. 12). They *2nd reading* probably did not doubt this in the case of *3rd cycle* Christ, but they saw no link between the paschal event and the general resurrection of the body. Such people may well have been either disciples of Sadducean Jews who denied the resurrection (Mt 22:23), or people tinged with Platonism. For the latter there would have been no necessity to posit the survival hereafter of a body to partake of the anticipated spiritual bliss.

Paul's argument is deployed on two complementary levels. On the one hand, if Christ arose, it is evident that we too are promised the same *resurrection* for the simple reason that we have the same nature as he (v. 20). On the other, Christ's resurrection is only comprehensible in relation to that of men generally, not the other way round (vv. 13-18). He is not affirming an internal link between the two resurrections in the philosophic sense. He is arguing from the plan of salvation. If the dead do not rise again, that would prove that Christ did not succeed in saving them. Salvation means victory over corporal death.

Unconsciously, a modern Christian might easily find himself thinking exactly like the Corinthians. For apologetic reasons, the resurrection of Christ has to be accepted. It is an extraordinary miracle, which ratifies his mission and teaching. But how does this include one's own resurrection and that of men generally?

There is furthermore some difficulty in grasping how the buried and decomposed body can recover life. The average Christian tends to disassociate soul and body. This is a heritage of Greek philosophy, a dichotomy which is barely reconcilable with the unity of human personality.

In fact the opposition between the Corinthians and Paul arises largely from two different anthropological views. On the one hand we have Greek dualism, which allows a quasi-autonomous existence to the soul; on the other the unified Jewish concept, where body and soul together make up the person.

VII. Matthew   In this passage we have the greater portion of
    5:17-37   the antitheses of the sermon on the mount (Mt
    Gospel   5:21-48), preceded by an introduction from
    1st cycle   the hand of Matthew (vv. 17-19).

a) The three first verses touch on the deepest meaning of the new religion. Verse 17 doubtless belongs to the oral tradition that Matthew is reproducing, but he gives it a new interpretation, corresponding to the idea of *fulfillment* which pervades his whole gospel. His essential theme is the fulfillment of Scripture (Mt 24:34-35; 6:26, 56). All that is written in the law, down to the least detail, has the value of prophecy and must have "fulfillment" in the eschatological era. To emphasize this, he borrows from the synoptic tradition (but in another context: Lk 16:17) the beginning of verse 18—the saying of Jesus, that is, which affirms that no detail of the law is without point (Mt 23:23; 15:6). The phrase "until all be fulfilled" however is Matthew's own, reflecting his basic preoccupation (Mt 1:22; 2:15-17; 4:15; 8:17; 13:35, etc.). For him, not only has Jesus come to bring the law to perfection by supplying what was wanting; he fulfills all its details also (understanding it in the Old Testament sense of prophecy). Furthermore, the Christian's moral life (v. 19) must be more than a fulfillment of the general recommendations of the law. All the details must be included, because the law as a whole has the value of prophecy. It was accomplished in the life of Jesus and must be similarly accomplished in the life of each Christian, so that the inauguration of the last times, the time of fulfillment, may become manifest.

It is perhaps surprising to find such a precise eulogy of legal observance in the New Testament, when we remember the diatribes elsewhere of Jesus and Paul against the law (cf. also Jr 9:23-24). The explanation lies in Matthew's eschatological preoccupation.

Pharisaic justice in fact was limited to observance of the law. It was not communion with God and would always tend to divinize the law. Christian justice on the other hand did not depend basically on legal observance but on the fact that the last times are fulfilled in Jesus. He was the first to obey the law in communion with God. In Matthew the placing of verse 17 before verses 18-19 is important. From now on, between the law and the Christian there is a mediation, the justice, that is, accorded by Jesus. The Christian who obeys the law does not find therein his justice. He is manifesting the justice acquired in Jesus Christ, which is a sign of the last times, because it is communion with God.

b) The first antithesis concerning the new justice has to do with the fifth commandment. To understand the full import of

Jesus' teaching, it is necessary to remember the refinements introduced by the scribes and commentators to the law concerning homicide. To determine whether homicide had taken place a whole series of conditions had been developed each as extraneous as the other. Jesus established a new criterion: *personal intention*. This could be judged more severely than murder, even if there was no more than a simple injury exteriorly.

In fact the first portion of our passage gives us two distinct sentences. In the first (vv. 21-22a) Jesus asserts that a simple injury may be matter for the "tribunal" just like homicide. In this instance the tribunal designates the community council, which, on the national level (the Sanhedrin) or the local (at Qumran, for instance), had the right to excommunicate erring members. It had then in a certain sense the right of life and death, determining those who deserved to belong to the community (Mt 10:17; Jn 16:2). It is certain that the primitive Christian communities exercised a similar sort of jurisdiction (Ac 5; 1 Co 5:1-4; Tm 20; Mt 18:15-17).

The second statement (v. 22b, c) is not a qualification of the first. It simply reiterates the same thing in different terms. The "tribunal" is neither more nor less grave than the "Sanhedrin" or "Gehenna." What is being contemplated is the expulsion by the community of the guilty from its midst. Where Jewish jurisdiction judges only the exterior, Christian will have to examine the intention, as God does.

Two principles are implied in this new jurisprudence of Jesus. First, that God "examines the heart" while man is confined to the exterior (Jr 11:19-20; 12:1-3; 17:9-11). Second, that from those who belong to the new covenant, because it "changes the heart" (Ez 36:23-30; Jr 31-34), more will be demanded.

c) The second section (vv. 23-24) deals with the necessity of *love in sacrifice*.* The Jew, if before offering sacrifices he suddenly realized he was unclean (Lv 15-17), had to undergo prelim-

---

* See the doctrinal theme: *love and sacrifice*, p. 255.

inary ablutions. Jesus is requiring the Christian to have the same reaction if he remembers that he has some dispute with another. His is not referring to the prescriptions on homicide, but to those on ritual cleanness. Thus, while the two pieces are different in inspiration, they both indicate the anxiety to establish a new justice. It will be based on interior attitude and opposed to all formalism. Furthermore the bonds between the individual and the Christian assembly will be of the interior order.

d) The teaching on *divorce* is clear (Mt 19:9; Mk 10:10-12; Lk 16:18; 1 Co 7:10-11). This procedure does not dissolve the union set up by God, or restore liberty to either of the separated parties, or to anyone who marries them. The teaching is completely new; Judaism had never spoken thus. Doubtless it is to stress the novelty of his doctrine that Jesus speaks in particular, rather than general terms. He immediately mentions the concrete situation of the divorced woman and the man who wants to marry her.

Verse 32 however differs from the other gospel texts in mentioning the responsibility of the husband who divorces the woman and thus exposes her to adultery. The conclusion nevertheless is identical. No divorce can dissolve the conjugal bond.

e) The phrase "unless it be for fornication" in verse 32 is peculiar to Matthew (cf. also Mt 19:9). The reference is to Deuteronomy 24:1-4 which, however, has to be properly interpreted. *Divorce* here is not a matter of law, but of fact. The law is that God has united the couple indissolubly. Two facts, however, can break that: the death of one of the partners, and the sin of adultery which is spiritual death. The law indeed forbade the injured husband to take back his wife. She had contracted such a stain as to make it impossible now for their union to witness the union between God and his people (Si 23:24-27; Ho 2:4). Thus Deuteronomy did not permit divorce on the basis of law but took a pastoral attitude. Once it was certain that the husband was wronged, he was required to disengage himself, and to release his wife from all his rights over her, in such fashion that she should not belong to two men, or he to two women. Jesus is not reproaching Moses for this particular edict; he regards it as a genuine precept, precisely designed to combat the hardened sinner who chooses troubled situations. In normal divorce, the initiative for separation came from the man. This is what Jesus is firmly condemning in rejecting all excuses for divorce. He is clearly telling the Pharisees that the law of Moses cannot be invoked against the primordial precept.

Yet, once separation has taken place as a result of the woman's fault, the man who sends her away does not necessarily commit adultery, particularly if his intention is to obey a precept, not to covet another woman. This special case of the Jewish man who subjects himself to the detail of the Mosaic law (a case that is not repeated in Christianity) is taken into consideration by Jesus. He will not condemn such a man before God, and excuses him from the fault of adultery. That does not necessarily imply that a second marriage on his part would be judicially valid.

f) *Oath* is the evidence for the existence of lying. If there was no lie, there would be no need to resort to oath. Yes would be yes, and no would be no (v. 37). The Old Testament had campaigned against the lie by enacting legislation about the oath and forbidding the lie, at least in this case (v. 33; cf. Ex 20:7; Nb 20:3). Forbidding a lie however, when an oath was being taken, was an excessive recognition of the lie. Jesus transcends this legislation by forbidding a lie in any circumstances, so that the oath becomes redundant.

VIII. Mark
1:40-45
Gospel
2nd Cycle

This cure of a leper is recounted in the three synoptics. They all seem to agree in making it one of Jesus' very earliest miracles, manifesting the power over evil of the young rabbi. They also agree in placing it in Galilee. Luke actually adds the detail "in a town" (Lk 5:12), something that is quite improbable, when we remember the severe Jewish legislation (Lv 13:45-46) which excluded lepers from inhabited centers. In any case, Matthew 8:5 corrects this by placing the episode at the gates of the town.

Matthew adds to the episode the cure of a Gentile and a woman (Mt 8:1-15), showing that Jesus is the assembler of classes that had been hitherto excluded from full membership of the chosen people. Luke is content to see it as one of the Lord's first miracles which kindled the admiration of the crowds (Lk 5:15). Mark too makes it an early miracle.

The account is heavily laden with indications of Jesus' growing awareness of his *power as thaumaturge*. He is seized with pity first of all for the suffering he encounters, and it is rather unfortunate that Luke does not mention this as well as Mark (v. 41). The "emotion" and "compassion" are important. It is through these human sentiments that Jesus channels the powerful and healing love of God. Humanly speaking, he desired the cure of these sick people that he encountered, and without this urge there would have been no miracles. He realizes that his love for his fellows is the channel of God's love for men.

Moreover Jesus is still a novice in the exercise of his charism. He fears it even. He urges the person healed to keep the secret (note the quite firm tone of v. 43, proper to Mark). He is particularly anxious to impress upon him that he must not omit the legal examination (Lv 13-14). Then, he avoids insofar as he can the admiration of the crowds who would be liable to misunderstand his miracles (v. 45). It is noteworthy too that he does not appeal to the faith of his petitioner, something that he does regularly afterwards. He is just at the stage of discovering the divine power within him and he is looking for the best circumstances in which to exercise it.

The contemporaries of Jesus tended to associate body and soul much more closely than Greek thought. For them every physical malady must be the consequence somehow of a moral one. Thus in healing the body Jesus quickly came to see that his preaching was in a real sense the inauguration of the messianic times and the age of consolation. Several months later it was clear to him that the coming of the Kingdom was concerned with his own person; that faith in his mission must be the condition for partaking of the healing and pardon he was bringing.

Whether we are dealing with his first cure or those at the end of his life, we realize always that it is the man-God who is at work. By structuring his human life around love and compassion for his fellows, while at the same time showing perfect obedience to his Father's plan for creation, he vanquished sin and gave us the first instance of a man without any evil. Simultaneously he became the one concrete foundation on which humanity can attempt the construction of a better future. His healings of the sick tell us more about his personality than about sickness. They are but significant indications of the total healing he was accomplishing throughout all creation.

Today healing has become the province of science and civilization and there are many marvels to show. The Christian should cooperate with this whole-heartedly. But he must never forget that he cannot be a true healer of his fellowmen, unless the liberation from evil is realized in himself as fully as possible by his fidelity to the Father. In the building of the terrestrial city, there is no greater malady than that introduced by man's pretensions to be self-sufficient in the quest for happiness.

IX. Luke   Luke's version of the beatitudes has been
  6:17, 20-26   analyzed in conjunction with that of Matthew
  Gospel   5:1-12 (see p. 137). His *blessing-curse* formula
  3rd cycle   may appear somewhat shocking. However, it
  is simply an Old Testament literary procedure
of which we have an example in the first reading of this third cycle (Jr 17:5-10).

These beatitudes are not extended to the poor simply because they are poor, nor the curses pronounced on the rich simply because they are rich. Jesus is praising the poor because they live in two worlds, the present and the eschatological. He is threatening the rich because they inhabit only one, the comfortable life that inevitably enslaves.

The rich man is he who is so satisfied with his possessions that he never journeys to the depth of his being. Nothing summons him there. He lives in a rich, super-industrialized society, where everything is made super-secure and established.

The poor man possesses only his solitude, but his courage in living takes him to the very depths of himself, and there he finds another world. He may be solitary in one world, but in the other he is rich, that world of which he senses the proximity and the triumph. He stands as witness to that beyond which is achieved through pain, by means of blows and misfortunes, successes and failures, victories and betrayals.

B. DOCTRINE

1. The Theme of Double Love

The relationship between love of God and love for men is basic in Christianity. Jesus combined the two commandments in the New Testament in such fashion that there can be no doubt about the association. Both sentiments ought to be combined in the single Christian act.

Any misunderstanding about this can lead to grave perversions, that jeopardize the very essence of the faith; and we should never be under any illusion about the fact that throughout Church history there has often been imbalance which had to be corrected. Today for instance Christians are very concerned about the demands of brotherly love without limits; they are less concerned about the association of this with love for God. Sometimes too the nature of brotherly love itself tends to be misunderstood. When God is not included in the picture, it can very quickly be perverted.

Such misunderstandings can be very damaging in the area of mission. If we Christians cease to be witnesses of God's love when we serve our brothers, our witness is invalid. It conveys a wrong notion of brotherly love because it does not display the source.

Consequently it is important for us to understand the link between the two loves. He shall then be getting very close to the meaning of Christianity.

Love of God and love of neighbor in Israel

Jewish history is knit up with religious tradition. The discovery of the Totally-Other God was crucial for Jewish man, individually and collectively. Moral insights developed side by side with this religious experience, and the two orders, religious and moral, become inextricably intertwined.

The reason is not far to seek. The believer had to seek all his security in God without any recourse to human resources. If one belonged to the regime of faith, it meant that one ceased to regard oneself as central. One deliberately chose a "justice" that was of God, not of men. One accepted the creatural condition, with all this meant in terms of relationship to the Creator and to other men.

Thus Israel's experience led to insight about love of God and love of one's neighbor. If Yahweh loves his people, and displays particular benevolence towards the little ones and the poor; if he maintains fidelity in spite of sin on the part of his faithful, man's duty is to follow this example in dealing with his fellows. It is by following God's example that one comes to know him. One cannot love God without being interested in men, respecting them, being concerned about the poor and disadvantaged.

But, in the very concept of the neighbor, we can discern the limits of Jewish universalism. Because of Israel's conviction about being a people apart, her consciousness of election in terms of privileges, the neighbor had to be one of the chosen people. Her attitude towards the Gentile was different. She recognized God as Creator, master of the destiny of all nations, but not to the extent of universal fatherhood. She did not learn the lesson of brotherly love without limits. Without total renunciation the lesson cannot be learned.

The indissoluble link, in Jesus, between the two loves

In Jesus, the two loves came together. The inadequacies of the old covenant were surmounted. The true dimensions of human salvation were clarified.

The key to salvation, it became clear, was love; not any sort of love, but love that was immersed in the mystery of God. The basic principle of this love is the perfect reciprocity between Father and Son, which is expressed in the person of the Holy Spirit. It was in the name of this love that the Father sent the Son to reconcile all humanity into his own Family.

Jesus was the perfect exponent of this love. He loved the Father with the love with which he was loved, and thus became God's partner in the realization of the divine plan for humanity. Because of the Incarnation this love was spread to all humanity, who were his brothers. In the Father's Family the same law governs all relationships. All are recognized by the man-God as adoptive sons.

Such are the dimensions of the love manifested in Jesus Christ. By his Incarnation the love he demonstrated became rooted in humanity. Filial love for the Father and universal brotherly love were fused in his way of obedience even to the death of the cross. The total self-renunciation required by this obedience springs from filial love that is creatural, and from a total acceptance of the other, in all his otherness, even if he be an enemy.

It was by demonstrating this indissoluble link between love for the Father and love for men that Jesus brought about salvation. He invites us, in him, to enter the Family of the Father, to live there as sons, and to find there our fellowmen as brothers. It is thus that we come to see what our creaturehood really means, and what its possibilities are. When Love became incarnate the order of creation was seen for what it truly is in the mind of God.

The Church the sacrament of double love

The link with Christ is of primal importance for every man. It is the only avenue to saving love. Our destiny is to love God with the filial love of partners and all our fellowmen as brothers. Love of such quality is only possible for the man-God, and we can only reach it on this earth by joining ourselves to him as unique mediator. This we do by entering the Church which is his Body. Our baptism gives us the capacity, provided we take the means, of loving as he loved.

We should be very clear about this. The love to which we are summoned has a definitive exemplar. We are asked to love *as* Jesus loved. We go before the Father as adoptive sons, realizing that to him we owe everything, including our filial state, and that our filial response makes a contribution to the divine plan. We realize too that all men are our brothers and that we must cement bonds of brotherly love with them. This will require from us a fidelity to the creatural condition that excludes sin; because the kind of double love we have to manifest is impossible without self-renunciation. It is also impossible without full respect for the order of creation and a desire to promote it.

The commitment then is one that exposes us to all sorts of demands that we can never previously anticipate. It is an adventure of which we cannot chart the way. The order of creation is not something fixed and established. It is something that must be constantly shaped, something that must be invented as it were day by day. The requirements of yesterday are not going to be those of tomorrow. Where love is concerned, we can never go on automatically repeating ourselves.

The witness of love in the world now

It has always been the task of the Church to exhibit to men the love which saved the world. Being as she is the Body of Christ she never ceases to be a sign of this, but at any given time the intensity of the sign will depend on the fidelity shown by believers. The Church must be present to the people to whom she exhibits the sign, and must always be concerned about the actual means to be employed.

What are these in our world now? Like all men indeed at all times, modern man dreams of more peace and more justice. But he is much more conscious of the need to muster all human resources for this purpose. If we will the end, we should will the means, and mere good intentions are not sufficient. Precise plans have to be made, on the individual and collective level, that will tackle the problem at its roots in all its complexity.

The witness of love in the world today must be particularly concerned to articulate supernatural charity with man's creatural responsibilities. This charity which is infused into each Christian soul can become the source of a great dynamism in the human sense. One who, following Christ, loves God and all his fellowmen will feel the urge to bring about a transformation in human relationships. That transformation calls for lucidity and inventiveness; it requires the dedication of individual liberty and responsibility. From this aspect it seems that we do need a re-evaluation of traditional procedures in Christian charity, especially collective charity.

On the other hand, in a world which is preoccupied with service to humanity only, the Christian must beware of settling for an ideal of universal brotherhood that falls short of the gospel. God must always be part of the evangelic ideal. Self-renunciation is essential to it, and the only basis for this self-renunciation is the relation between creature and Creator. What the world needs more than anything else is the witness of double love. If we Christians fail to love God with the creature's filial love, we cannot really love our fellowmen as brothers. We shall very quickly find ourselves turning from the gospel towards other alleged solutions.

Eucharistic initiation into love of God and men

The link between the two loves is best cemented in the eucharistic assembly. The initiation here is always on-going. When we respond to the Father's initiative of love by giving thanks, we feel the urge to bind ourselves to those who are our brothers in Jesus Christ. The actual celebration consists of a fraternal sharing of the same bread, and is a constant reminder of the duty of mission, which is the expression *par excellence* of love for all men.

All ecclesial assemblies have in fact as purpose the proper disposition of the members towards God and towards all men. The two thrusts must always be in evidence; they provide a basic "structure" for everything the Institution does. Whether it be a eucharistic celebration, a simple liturgy of the Word, some Catholic Action meeting, etc., there is never question of emphasizing now the love of God, and again that of men. Everyone present is always summoned to deepen the quality of his double love, that of God and men together.

2. Love and Sacrifice

We still have too many practicing Christians, even attendants at daily mass sometimes, who participate in the Eucharist without realizing the demands that it makes in fraternal charity. And, at the other end of the scale, one frequently encounters Christians who are deeply concerned about fidelity to the gospel, but who never set foot at Mass, because they are scandalized by the lack of charity they detect in the eucharistic community. And of course, also we have those who are so aware of their own short-comings in charity, they do not consider themselves worthy to share the Eucharist.

The first group have really failed to grasp the fundamental meaning of the eucharistic assembly. There is an essential link between Christian cult and the exercise of charity. Can we be so sure the second group are wrong? There is a saying of Jesus which seems to be on their side: "So then if you are bringing your offering to the altar and there remember that your brother has something against you, leave your offering there before the altar, go and be reconciled with your brother first and then come back and present your offering" (Mt 5:23-24).

What then is the true nature of the link in Christianity between sacrifice and fraternal love, between the cult of the New Covenant and universal charity? As we shall see, the answer to this question involves consideration of the most profound dimensions of faith. Our meditation can prove the beginning of an inspiration that will color our whole life. The effort is very well worth while.

Sacrificial cult in Israel, the demands of the covenant

Pagan man of the ancient world was in search of the one happiness that could satisfy him, participation in the sacral world. Seeing that he did not belong to it, that it was superior to him and dominated him, he turned naturally to sacrifice as a necessary measure, and the history of sacrifice is as old as humanity. When he offered sacrifice to the gods, he recognized his dependence and hoped for favors in return. Because liturgies were the accepted means of communication with the sacral world, sacrifice would naturally tend to be cultic. Results would be obtained, provided that the cultic rules were scrupulously observed. Hence sacrificial rites became the great source of security in pagan religions. They were the infallible means of winning the gods' favor, and the complexity of the ritual prescriptions was a constant reminder of the gods' demands.

The Jewish people also had their sacrificial rites. Some were of native development; some they had borrowed over. Israel's accession to the regime of faith, however, brought a thorough reexamination of her worship. For one thing, cult gradually passed from the cosmic plane to that of salvation history. Henceforward the ritual sacrifice commemorated the major events of the Exodus: the going out from Egypt, the covenant, the gift of the Law, etc. Furthermore, the salvific dimension of the cult was judged by the criterion of the covenant.

In this domain the great prophets played a predominant role. If convinced that the people of the covenant were resorting to the security of sacrifices while neglecting the prescripts of the Law, they did not hesitate to inveigh against a cult that was formalized, and therefore without salvific efficacy. They would not reject the notion of sacrifice, but insisted on its veritable dimension. The cult pleasing to God must be the expression of genuine fidelity to the requirements of the covenant. "Steal, would you, murder, commit adultery, perjure yourselves, burn incense to Baal, follow alien gods that you do not know? And then come presenting yourselves in this temple that bears my name, saying: Now we are safe. . . . I, at any rate, am not blind—it is Yahweh who speaks" (Jr 7:9-11).

Jesus Christ, high-priest and apostle

In Jesus of Nazareth the prophetic message found its full accomplishment. The sacrifice of the New Covenant was offered on the Cross and its content was the complete gift of self for the love of all men. "Jesus, knowing that his hour was come to pass from this world to the Father, having loved his own who were in the world, loved them to the end" (Jn 13:1).

The very concept of worship is renewed. The prophets had been right in discerning the close link between sacrificial cult and a moral and religious life that conformed to the prescripts of the covenant. Fidelity to the Law was the touch-stone of cult pleasing to Yahweh. In Jesus all is unified. His exemplary moral life is not alone the preliminary condition for his sacrifice; it *is* that sacrifice. The cult in spirit and in truth that he inaugurates entails essentially the sacrifice of the "heart." It entails, that is to say, recognition on the one hand of the Totally-Other God, who is gratuitously summoning men, in Jesus, to adoptive sonship. And, on the other, it entails full acceptance of the creatural condition, in self-renunciation and limitless love of the brethren.

Jesus' sacrifice of his life to the Father, which concerns all humanity, is indissolubly linked to his mission to all men. The love which inspires him is authentic love of the Father, and authentic love for all men. Both loves are really one. They blend into one another, and both presuppose full acceptance of the creatural state and of the absolute self-renunciation it necessarily implies. Jesus is both high-priest and apostle. His perfect response to the Father's love, and his exercise of universal brotherly love, spring from the same source. One is guaranteed by the other.

So that sacrificial cult in the New Covenant is inevitably a cult that relates the worshiper properly to God the Father, and at the same time to all men. It is a cult altogether directed towards the evangelization of the world. Its high point is the sacrifice of the Cross. There, Christ offered himself once for all to the Father, for the love of all, and he is forever the Father's unique Envoy to all nations.

The Church, a priestly people in the act of charity

What is true of Christ is obviously also true of his disciples. Their living link with him enables them too to render to God the spiritual cult that is agreeable, the offering of oneself as a living and holy sacrifice.

The Church is the priestly people of the New Covenant, and the fundamental law of Christianity is charity, the double love for God and men. The worship to which this priestly people is committed is the exercise of charity, even to the total gift of self for the salvation of all men. To affirm that the Church is a priestly people is to discern where the leaven is in the mass. It is to affirm that Christians, mingled among men, must carry out in the texture of their daily lives the mission of gradually assembling the dispersed children of God. Such affirmations, be it noted, because many Christians are unaware, distinguish Christians completely from the levitic priesthood of the Old Testament. The Christian priestly people is not assembled in a temple for prayer and sacrifice, separated from the rest of men, and dedicated exclusively to religious activity. On the contrary, Christians are fully merged in the human mass. They are men and women indistinguishable from other human beings, except by their membership in the Body of Christ, their partnership in that great act by which Christ, today as yesterday, builds from human material the Kingdom of his Father. The priestly responsibility of Christians is carried out by the dissemination of the charity of Christ to the very limits of humanity.

It is in order to fulfill this function as priestly people in the human mass that the Church herself takes on an institutional visage, and assembles her members. Assembly is necessary, if people are to realize their priestly quality and become more and more rooted in the charity of Christ. The constant sacramental initiation into salvation history gradually molds the believer after the model of Jesus Christ. And, basic among all assemblies, is of course the eucharistic celebration. It is here that the faithful live the act of charity and experience all the richness of the worship pleasing to the Father.

The missionary witness of the priestly people

It is regrettable that terms like worship, priesthood and sacrifice do not immediately suggest mission and evangelization to the average Christian. The link between them in the New Testament is so close that they can only be properly understood when their association is discerned. When Saint Paul wishes to describe the worship he renders to God, he does so in terms of evangelization. "I render a spiritual cult by proclaiming the Gospel of his Son" (Rm 1:9). And when he describes the mission to the Gentiles that has been confided to him, he does so in cultic terms: ". . . the grace which God has given me, to be a minister of Christ Jesus among the Gentiles, a minister of the Gospel of God, so that the Gentiles may become an agreeable offering, sanctified in the Holy Spirit" (Rm 15:15-16).

To bring the Good News to all the nations is to guide them towards the true spiritual cult. Better still, it is to exercise the cult of double love for God and men in such fashion that it becomes contagious. By faithfully carrying out their priestly function, the people of the New Covenant fulfill their missionary responsibility. And *vice versa*: when missionary, they discern the full dimensions of their priesthood and the full dimensions of Christ's charity.

The evangelization of the world we know requires great realism on the Christian's part. Modern man will only acknowledge the validity of Christian witness to charity on one condition. That is, that the Christian seem fully aware of, and involved in, the great human tasks of the day. These call for inventiveness, constant research, effective means, and collective action. It should be very clear that the lucid exercise of Christ's charity, far from removing us from such areas, must tend to make us more intensely aware of human responsibilities.

The eucharistic celebration and reconciliation with one's brother

Tradition is unanimous on this point. The proper fruit of any eucharistic celebration is that the charity of Christ be developed in the assembled community. Sharing the Word and the Bread reinforces the bonds that unite the faithful to Christ in the offering of this worship which alone is pleasing to the Father, the worship of universal reconciliation. By being present in the Eucharist, Jesus associates us with him in this universal reconciliation. He continues to accomplish, through the members of his Body, the work of the cross. He is the only one in all history capable of performing the task; the only possible reconciliation is that which was brought about once for all on the cross.

There is then a sort of logical priority of the cross over the Supper; the latter only gets meaning from the former. Jesus' saying in Matthew 5:23-24 "if then you present your offering" has a striking application in his own life. We must, however, be careful of interpreting this text as if the eucharistic celebration were secondary in the Christian life to reconciliation with one's brothers. We cannot really practice reconciliation without first being established, indeed rooted, in the charity of Christ. The proper fruit of the Mass is precisely: that the worshiper be invested with the power of reconciliation that is Christ's only. We should be wrong in thinking that our participation in the Eucharist is merely the expression of the charity we exercise. When we say that, for us, the celebration is logically prior to our exercise of reconciliation, we are simply affirming the absolute priority of Jesus Christ.

SIXTH WEEK

I. Genesis
4:1-15, 25
1st reading
1st cycle
Monday

The Qenite tribe (cf. Nb 24:21), neighboring the Amalecites, the Madianites and the Hebrews, had an oral tradition concerning their eponymous ancestor, Cain. Doubtless it recounted the massacre of Abel (v. 8), Cain's nomad state as a result of his crime (vv. 9-14), the origin of the talisman-tatoo of the Qenites (vv. 15, 23-24), and finally the genealogy of the tribe's patriarchs (vv. 17-22).

It is not surprising to find some Qenite traditions in Scripture. The tribe had in fact rendered sufficient services and contracted sufficient alliances with the Hebrews to merit the honor. The two tribes seem indeed to have shared the sanctuary of Hebron in common. Furthermore Moses married a Qenite (Jg 1:16), and David also (Abigail: 1 S 25). It was a Qenite woman who one day saved the people from foreign oppression (Jg 5:24).

In an agricultural and pastoral world, they were an artisan tribe, representing a technological mentality among rural folk close to nature (cf. Gn 4:21-22). This doubtless explains the biblical redactor's reserved attitude towards them.

Another tradition told of a sort of clash between two types of sacrifice, the one of nomad origin (first-born of the flock: v. 4), the other agricultural and settled (produce of the soil: v. 3). Doubtless there is an attempt to explain to people, who are in the full course of social and economic mutation from the nomad state to the agricultural and urban one, that God prefers the nomad type of sacrifice.

The Yahwist redactor combines the two traditions in one, and places the whole after the history of Adam and Eve. Cain is made their son (v. 1), and his brutal and wicked life furnishes tangible evidence of the curse that fell on men and on the earth. Here is new fuel for Yahwist pessimism. From Adam to the flood, human history was regressive. Each generation added to the curse, and accumulated guilt, of the preceding one. The universe was precipitated towards ruin and unexpected salvation in Yahweh.

However, all is not wickedness among this blighted folk. Abel is presented as a gentle, pious creature. But he quickly disappears from a scene where good is excluded.

Subsequent traditions did not fail to emphasize the figure of *Abel*. He will be made a prophet, a witness to God's will in a world which pretends to its own knowledge of good and evil (Mt 23:35), or a martyr who offers to God not alone his lambs but his own life, like Jesus Christ (He 11:4; 12:24). He will seem an avenger, whose blood, covering the earth, ceaselessly calls on God to condemn evil (He 11:4b). He will be made a sage, who participates in the divine life, whose knowledge transcends that which Adam stole from God (Wi 10:10).

The image of Abel most suitable for our times, however, is that of the pastoral nomad, by contrast with Cain, the settled tiller of the fields.

The Church will offer a sacrifice as pleasing to God as that of Abel, whenever she abandons stability and immobilism to become nomad. She is living in a world where the rapidity of movement summons her to abandon institutions and strip herself of all possessions, except those which will enable her to enter into dialogue.

II. James
1:1-11
1st reading
2nd cycle
Monday

The author of this passage, according to exegetes, is James, the "brother of the Lord" (Mt 13:55; Ga 1:19; Ac 12:17, etc.), not to be confused with the two apostles of the same name. He rallied the infant Church after the resurrection (Ac 1:14) and became the leader of the Jerusalem community, doubtless because of his blood relationship with Jesus. He represented the "dynastic" faction which was soon to be displaced by the "charismatic," favoring Peter. In any case it is evident that the author is a Christian with a

Jewish, even a legalist, bias. He is so concerned about "works" that he can be regarded, with some straining of the text, as opposed to the Pauline doctrine of "salvific faith."

The people he addresses are Jewish Christians, who have been scattered among the Diaspora (v. 1) and who are victims of the persecutions in 55-60.

His correspondents are undergoing trial (vv. 2-4), they seem to lack wisdom (vv. 5-8), and they live in poverty (vv. 19-11). Thus they exhibit all the characteristics of the Israelitic "poor of Yahweh." James proclaims salvation for them in the language of the ancient prophets. "The humble shall be exalted and the proud humbled" (1 S 2:1-8; Ps 71/72:4, 12; Lk 1:52; 6:20-26).

In recompense for their trial he proclaims joy (vv. 2 and 12), the joy of knowing they are on the road to perfection (vv. 3-4). To those devoid of knowledge he promises the wisdom of God (vv. 5-8), provided it be sought with full simplicity of heart. For the poor he proclaims exaltation, for the rich humiliation (vv. 9-11).

What we have is a paraphrase of the *beatitudes,* but in a tone more kerygmatic than moralizing. The Kingdom is imminent, and the sign of its proximity is the end of trial for the unhappy and the ignorant. The piece is perfectly in accord with the Old Testament prophetic tradition.

III. Mark
8:11-13
Gospel
Monday

After the multiplication of bread, Jesus embarks on the waters, and during two crossings (vv. 10 and 13), begins a lively discussion with those blind Pharisees who were demanding a sign. Then, in the boat itself, we have another conversation with his disciples, who did not properly estimate the miracles he had accomplished (vv. 14-21).

The motif common to the two episodes is the *unbelief* of Christ's hearers. In the case of the Pharisees it is blindness, in the case of the leader of the apostles lack of attention. Thus Mark is remaining faithful to his initial theme: lack of receptivity in depth to the message of Jesus (cf. Mk 4:1-20). In pursuit of this theme he does not hesitate to modify somewhat the account.

The discussion with the Pharisees (vv. 11-12) was probably concerned with the sign of Jonah (cf. Mt 16:1-4), the sign of the resurrection, by which Jesus in turn would triumph over the sea (Mk 6:45-52 and 8:11-13). Mark, however, here suppresses mention of the Jonah sign, because he is not yet concerned to give presentiments of the passion, and above all because he is concerned to focus his readers' attention on the Pharisees' blindness (cf. Mk 4:15). His central purpose is the analysis of negative reactions to Jesus' message by different strata of the population.

On the other hand, to verse 14 he adds: "And they had with them on the boat only one loaf." The phrase is not primitive. Matthew 16:5 does not know it, and it contradicts verse 16, where Mark himself clearly says that the apostles had no bread. We might explain it by saying that Mark, anticipating the interpretation of John 6:26-27, 32-33, in thinking of that symbolic bread which is Jesus himself. The apostles fear that they have no provisions, forgetting that they have the bread *par excellence*. The discussion which follows then takes on meaning. Jesus tries to make them understand that he is this bread (vv. 17-21).

Perhaps Jesus spoke of the "word" of the Pharisees and Herodians (*amira*) which the apostles understood as "leaven" (*amira*). They would then unwittingly have disclosed their materialist preoccupations, by contrast with Matthew 8:3; 4:4, etc. We should have an explanation thus of Jesus' serious reproach: how can they still think in these terms after what has just been "signified."

Mark thus we see to be concerned with the different types of unbelief. This is real in the case of the apostles, but it is more than anything else the inattention of people who are unduly worried by material considerations (cf. Mk 4:19).

IV. Genesis
6:5-8,
7:1-5, 10
1st reading
1st cycle
Tuesday

Here we have an extract from the preliminaries to the flood. There are some highly colored verses due to the Yahwist bias of the author. Prior to the Bible, there were Babylonian traditions concerning a catastrophic deluge. Doubtless the reference was to an inundation of the Tigris and Euphrates valleys which spread to the known world.

The original contribution of the Yahwist tradition is to set this event in the context of salvation history. Although man's sinfulness has reached its height, the mercy of God intervenes to retrieve the situation. Humanity escapes and re-begins its history under better conditions, having a covenant with God.

Today's reading is altogether concerned with the *dramatis personae* of the flood. We have a humanity which, since Adam, has been continuously decadent, and which now reaches the peak of misfortune; a just man wandering in this universe, whom God will save from the disaster; finally, God himself. God is unique. He is responsible for prosperity as for misfortune, for the life of the just and the death of the wicked. He is a just God who punishes, but who does not sacrifice the pious man with the others.

In this fashion the oriental deluge sagas are rehandled in Hebrew thought. There is a more delicate moral approach: they are absorbed into salvation history and made to convey an uncompromisingly monotheist doctrine.

V. James
1:12-18
1st reading
2nd cycle
Tuesday

The structure of this piece is fairly simple. A crown of glory is offered to him who withstands temptation (v. 12). Temptation certainly does not come from God but from man's desire (vv. 13-15). Nothing but grace can come from God, who makes us the first fruits of his creation (vv. 16-18).

The thought of the passage is still extremely Jewish. The beatitude for those who endure trial was already formulated in Daniel 12:12; and the statement that temptation does not come from God we find in sapiental literature (Si 15:11-20; Pr 19:3). In the affirmation that every gift comes from the Father, we have the Jewish faith in one God, and even the title given to God recalls the creation of the luminaries (Gn 1:14-18). Finally the phrase "first fruits of his creatures" probably ought not to be taken in the Pauline sense of new creation in Christ (cf. Ep 2:10; 2 Co 5:17; Ga 6:15), but in the sense of Wisdom 9:2—man made to dominate creation.

a) The *crown* which symbolizes happiness for the tried man indicates, in Scripture, joy (Ct 3:11; Wi 2:8), or victory (1 Co 9:25; 2 Tm 2:5). As a "crown of life" (Rev 2:10; Wi 5:16) it probably indicates a messianic reward of the last times. Verse 12 is inspired by Daniel 12:12, and it affirms the eschatological value of trial and temptation.

b) *Temptation* thus is a necessary stage in the advent of the final times. But though it is included in the plan of God, it cannot be regarded as willed by God. God does not tempt (v. 13, cf. Si 15:11-20; 39:33; Pr 19:3); he disseminates blessing only (vv. 16-18).

To support this argument the author recalls that God is holy, inaccessible to any evil (v. 13). He cannot will any evil or propose any evil to man. On this point there is some divergence from the Old Testament (Gn 22:1; Ex 15:25; Dt 8:2). God who is the creator of the stars does not know their changes or vicissitudes. Being the source of blessing, he is that unchangeably (v. 17). In God, the father of lights, there is no shadow; he cannot pass from day to night. He is endlessly light and can will nothing but good, since he decided to create man and communicate his Word to him (v. 18).

Temptation then can only spring from man's desire (v. 14). On this point too he transcends the Old Testament (cf. Gn 2-3;

Wi 2:24; Mt 4:1-10). He no longer sees the source of sin in an exterior tempter, but in man's own passion. If there are children of God, children by the Word, there are also children of sin (v. 15).

The order of nature, or of "luminaries" as James might say, because it preceded man, could be looked on as a gift coming from God and thus matter for authentic thanksgiving. But the sign of creation is ambiguous, and man does not easily discern behind it the Creator.

Because he controls and dominates it, nature seems to be something within man's measure. Why should he not then take himself as a god, and himself provide this nature that he enjoys? Forgetting that he is merely the first fruits of creation, his interest in creation is measured by his capacity to control it. But such thinking is always idolatry, or magic, or some form of atheism. Temptation is indeed always there for man. The one who has a pure faith to guide him through his trial is blessed.

VI. Mark 8:14-21 Gospel Tuesday — This passage was analyzed in commenting on the passage preceding it, Mark 8:11-13, p. 263.

VII. Genesis 8:6-13, 20-22 1st reading 1st cycle Wednesday — The biblical account of the flood is a juxtaposition of two distinct traditions: the Yahwist (8th century), which is highly colored, realist to the point of anthropomorphism, concerned to have all animals, clean and unclean, in the ark, and the priestly (6th century), where the covenant theme enters, the notion of pairs of animals, and some chronological precisions. In the first, the rain falls for forty days and forty nights, and it falls in winter (*gesem*). In the second the waters remain on the earth for fifty days, after a spring rain. The material in today's reading is principally Yahwist.

a) What distinguishes this biblical account from the parallel Babylonian ones is the concept of a *unique God.* The Babylonian flood is the result of rivalries between gods and their desire to be rid of a humanity that is too demanding. The biblical on the other hand, whatever its origin or its extent, is the work of a unique God, who freely decides to punish the guilty and save the just. History is not seen as subject to the fatalism or unconcern of the gods; in the smallest detail it is controlled by a God who assumes responsibility for prosperity and misfortune.

It is, however, true that Noah's attitude throughout the story is highly ambiguous and somewhat shabby. Nothing can justify his self-righteousness as a pious man, anxious to save his little family and his personal virtue, while leaving the wicked world to its fate. A man, as long as he lives on earth, is responsible for the world and should not allow any exterior judgment to relieve him of the responsibility. Moses understands this better than Noah, when he refuses to be separated from his people, to leave them exposed to divine wrath, while he himself has favorable terms (Ex 32:10-13). Jesus goes further still. He refuses to be disassociated before the Father from sinful and mortal humanity. Primitive Christian theology indeed reacted against the biblical account of Noah's delivery, by imagining Christ delivering also the victims of the flood (1 P 3:18-21).

The Christian is responsible not only for himself but for all humanity. This was the responsibility Jesus assumed by relinquishing his life for all men. Since he has reconciled the world to God, no Christian can make distinctions between a Christian world and a secular world. The former destined for happiness, the latter cursed. His object should be to make Christ co-extensive with the whole world; not to sacralize it, but with full respect for the autonomy of the profane, and not of course, on the other hand, reducing Christ to the stature of the human.

b) The original feature in the account is God's *promise*, given in anthropomorphic terms, never again to rage in this fashion against humanity (v. 21), and to restore the normal laws of nature (v. 22). God knows that the heart of man is wicked, but man's sin will no more impede the normal, harmonious development of creation. And yet this solution stops short of the actuality. The Jewish author does not know that God cannot contemplate a creation without man. When his Son presents him with a restored humanity, it will be evident that creation participates in this restoration, and is destined for the same transfiguration as man (Rm 8:18-26).

VIII. James   The whole letter of James is a collection of
1:19-27   eight schemes for homilies in the primitive
1st reading communities. Our passage today is the third.
2nd cycle   Having considered trial (Jm 1:2-12), and the
Wednesday   origin of temptation (Jm 1:13-18), the author
now goes on to a third topic: the Christian's attitude to God's Word (Jm 1:19-27).

He is very concerned about moral life, and tries to establish a series of specific Christian attitudes in the midst of trial and weakness. A fundamental idea of his is the necessity that faith should issue in works (Jm 1:22-27; 2:10-26).

All the catechesis is extremely ancient. The communities to which it is addressed are still recruited exclusively from Jewish milieus, and their problems are typically Jewish.

a) Such communities were destined to undergo endless discussions and complaints about the problems which arose during the transition from Judaism to the religion of Jesus (Jm 3:18; 4:11). The author tells them they must *hear the Word* and put it in practice. This will solve many problems and put an end to much discussion.

The "Word must be welcomed" then (cf. Pr 2:1) and "kept" (Pr 7:1-3): the teaching, that is, of the gospel. The Word is not merely a doctrine, it is God's mysterious presence among those who hear it. That is why it is "planted" in a man when he welcomes it (v. 21). In this context James resorts to the ancient maxims of the sages to their disciples. One should not give way to anger in order that the Word can work (Pr 14:17; 14:29; 16:32). Teaching should be accepted with "docility," with the modesty, that is, of the humble which confounds the arrogance of the proud (Jm 4:6; 3:13-14; Si 1:27; 45:4).

So that the Word is like a seed, drawing from itself its own efficacy (cf. Mt 13). No obstacle must be placed in its way and suitable ground must be provided where it will fructify. Silence characterizes that ground (v. 27) because God cannot speak in intemperate human language. Devotion also (v. 27), which is worship and prayer, but above all charity and love.

The Word being nothing other than the divine life in man, "keeping" it does not mean burying it like a treasure in some empty vault. It must expand into trinitarian life, as subsequent New Testament writings will have it (Jn 8:51-55; 14:21-24; 17:6-19; 1 Jn 2:5; 5:2-3). It must issue in works (vv. 22-25; cf. Mt 7:21-26). It has nothing in common with Corinthian gnosis, speculation without any moral involvement. It has nothing in common with Jewish reasoning, where discussion leads to no longer doing the will of God. God judges the efficacity in a man of his Word by the "works" it produces (Tb 12:9; Jb 34:10-11; Jr 17:10; 31:29-30). This is religion pure and without stain.

c) He uses the image of a *mirror* (vv. 23-24) to illustrate the connection between reception of the Word and works. Looking at oneself in a mirror suggests a close, careful inspection. There may be some blemish or fault that has to be eradicated. What would be ridiculous is, seeking by the mirror to have a closer view and discern defects, yet quitting it, and forgetting to clean away the blemish. Such is the folly of the Christian who anxiously scrutinizes the Word, discusses about it, discovers even his own faults, but goes away without correcting them.

The essential theme of our reading then is the connection between faith and works, or more precisely, between faith and charity towards our brothers. We can see how fundamental in Christianity is this combination of "faith-brotherly love." Stoics and atheists often have an extremely acute moral sense, and will push love for men to its very limits. Such an attitude will make for inner harmony in a man.

But biblical revelation adds to this, harmony with God, the product of faith and fidelity. The Jews, however, were unable to retain this harmony. They distorted it into a search for security and an arid legalism that undermined the original dynamism of the covenant. All harmony was restored by Jesus. The love for the other that he displayed was the highest expression of his own creatural liberty. It was impossible for him to love the other in his otherness, that was heightened by sin, unless he refused to make self a center or an absolute. Such was the price he paid in order that human liberty, restored to its proper stature, should be the source of brotherhood among men. But that love, in him, demanded the theological dimension. It is at once fidelity to the Father and respect for the divine filiation in all of his brothers.

By giving his life for the love of all men, he bore decisive witness to the "law of liberty" (v. 25). This is none other than the law of unconditional love, where moral prescriptions become relativized in the light of God's love. This charity of Jesus inspires the whole moral life of the believer by means of the Eucharist. Here the believer becomes a hearer of the Word (v. 23) and by his commitment puts it in practice.

IX. Mark
8:22-26
Gospel
Wednesday

Mark is the only one to give us this cure of the blind man after the second multiplication, just as he was the only one to describe the cure of the deaf-mute after the first (Mk 7:31-37). Both accounts are very similar. The content is similar: the cure of a sense by which the exterior world is perceived. So with the purpose: to demonstrate that understanding and knowledge are the gift of God. And finally, the ritual followed. In both instances the sick man is "conducted" (7:32 and 8:22) as if he were a catechumen. He receives an imposition of hands (7:32 and 8:23-24). He is brought "apart," as if to show that one cannot know God while remaining with the nonunderstanding crowd (7:33 and 8:23). Jesus uses saliva in both instances, a sign of solidified breath and of his Spirit (7:33 and 8:23), because only the hearing of the Word can save a man from his apathy. He uses it twice because the journey towards faith is always slow and tortuous. Finally, in both cases he imposes complete silence (7:36 and 8:26).

The similarities are so striking that we can conclude that Mark, or the source he was using, wanted to represent faith as a gift given to the poor, by contrast with the incredulity of the crowds, the Pharisees and the apostles.

Possibly too he wanted to provide two miracles, that conformed to the development of the *catechumenate* ritual. He wished to stress the importance of initiation to the mystery of Christ's person, to the requirements of the eucharistic assembly, and of mission.

Today's passage, and, in a general way, the whole "section of breads," raises the question of initiation to faith. In the modern world this is a matter of very great moment. Numerous "Christians" approach the sacraments under some security-seeking impulse that is more or less religious. Others on the contrary, very conscious of the process of desacralization, try to exhibit a faith that is divorced from all religiosity.

Pastoral theology over recent centuries was based above all on the efficacity of the sacraments, signs of God's salvific intervention in human life. There was perhaps though insufficient stress on the fact that the sacrament is a point of encounter, where the actual presence of God must be met by adequate motivation of the recipient.

X. Genesis
9:1-13
1st reading
1st cycle
Thursday

Here we have an extract from the discourse, of priestly origin, which God was considered to have held with Noah after the deluge.

a) The essential theme is that of *covenant*. Noah becomes, like Adam, the father of humanity. God makes a covenant with him, as he did with the first man (Gn 1), and blesses him in the same fashion.

As in the other covenants sealed by Yahweh according to the priestly tradition (Gn 1; Gn 17), the initiative comes from Yahweh. Only he can bind himself. The covenant is a sign of his goodness and is cosmic and universal in dimension. All covenants are characterized by a sign: blessing for Adam, circumcision for Abraham, the sabbatic economy for Moses, the rainbow for Noah. The rainbow is the instrument whereby Yahweh launches his lightnings on the earth (Ps 7:13; Ha 3:9-11). But this weapon is now over the clouds and he will not use it any more.

b) In fact the admission of the deluge narrative to their Scriptures by the Jews was due less to their interest in the catastrophe itself, than to a wish to stress God's promise that there would be no deluge any more. The promise was in any case the main thing that distinguished the biblical from the pagan accounts. No other god had made such a promise, because no Gentile god is a creator. It is only the *creator* who can ensure stability for his work and the security that humanity needs on earth. The Gentile gods wanted the deluge in order to destroy a humanity that had become too numerous and too threatening. Scripture however shows Yahweh as anxious to bless man, that man should be fruitful and multiply. Here again we have that optimism of the priestly tradition concerning God and the world, that is found in Genesis 1.

c) Oddly enough, in the covenant with Noah, we have a new prescription, by contrast at least with the primordial covenant with Adam: permission to eat the flesh of animals. It is given however with considerable reservation concerning *blood* (vv. 4-7; cf. Lv 17:11-14; Dt 12:23).

Experience had taught the Hebrews, as well as other peoples that blood was the principle of life and soul for animals, just as breath was for man. Any living thing which lost blood or breath lost life. There were, however, several considerations militating against the use of blood. A natural repugnance, first of all, to drinking the life of an animal. Blood seemed to be the vehicle of a mysterious power and thus fell within the sacral domain of tabu. Finally, there was the Hebrew distaste for Gentile practices, especially the idolatrous custom of drinking blood (Ps 15/16:4; Ze 9:7; Ac 15:20, 29; 21:25).

Murder is a crime in a double sense, and blood does not cover the earth (Gn 4:10, Is 26:21; Ez 24:7) because the soul of the victim wanders over the earth unable to enter sheol. The primitive obligation of spreading the blood of the immolated animal over the earth (Mt 12:24) must be seen in the same context. Only in a second stage of priestly legislation was it enjoined that this blood be spread over the altar so as to enter the domain of God (Lv 17:11).

This right to eat meat, accorded by the covenant with Noah, may be an echo of the ancient view that man passed from a vegetarian stage, living from the fruit of trees like Adam, to a hunting stage, when he lived on the flesh of slaughtered beasts. It was a decisive transition. Man had to perfect his technology, and his native urges to aggression and violence were developed. Sexual roles were affected, the man now having to seek outside, often at a distance, sustenance for his menage. A new idea of divinity was developed. No longer is God only present in the stars and at origins; he is present in life and makes blood sacred. The transition is interesting because it makes God the God of life rather than nature. We are nearing the concept of a presence of God in the human person even though the effect as yet was to over-sacralize blood and the clan. Since Jesus Christ, and especially in our time, personal freedom has become the sacral domain, the seat of God's presence.

XI. James
2:1-9
1st reading
2nd cycle
Thursday

The immediately preceding passage in the letter of James (Jm 1:27) had concluded with a summons to practice religion pure and without stain, that succored widows and orphans. The author wants to find evidence of this attitude in the liturgical assemblies themselves.

Previously the prophets had condemned a worship that was carried out amid social injustice (Am 2:6-7; Is 1:23; Ez 22:7). The God who is being praised loves the poor with a love of predilection (Ho 14:4; Jr 5:28; 7:6), and worship must take account of this. Christian assemblies reserve a special place for the rich and outrage the dignity of the poor (vv. 1 and 5). James roundly condemns such an attitude in the primitive Jerusalem community, which does not respect the spirit of poverty (Ac 2:44; 4:36-5:11). His thinking of course is still too colored by an overly sociological view of poverty. Subsequent generations will modify the concept of spiritual poverty. Pauline churches in particular will prefer to have rich and poor live together in harmony, than to insist on a monopoly of salvation for the poor. James' essential point, however, is not so much the defense of poverty, but the link that ought to be evident between the cult of worshipers and their social attitude. Now that cult is spiritual, the link between *rite and life* is more close than ever. It is forged in the very texture of liturgy.

Later on (Jm 2:14-16) he will return to the topic. If we address to poor brothers the liturgical greeting "go in peace," without doing anything to make that peace genuine and concrete, we are being false to the basic demands of Christianity. Ever since the cross, the content of sacrifice is mercy and love. Goodness is better than ritual offering (cf. Mt 15:1-10; 23-1:26). The liturgy of our assemblies is not a true enactment of the Lord's sacrifice unless it show itself to be a service of others.

Poverty is indeed the ontological state of the believer in the Church, the state of the Father's adoptive child. But, like every spiritual principle, it must be manifested in the concrete circumstances of life, individual and collective. This does not happen automatically; each Christian must play his own part. In the process of evangelizing the world, men must see the sign of poverty. It will only be recognizable in the context of their actual lives.

Thus ecclesial witness to poverty must be borne at two levels, by each Christian in his individual life, and by the ecclesial community itself, in its institutions and apostolic action.

In the first domain, Christians who are concerned about evangelization do not conceal their disquiet. Possessed of goods in abundance, they sense the ambiguity of such riches, which bring security and nourish the power instinct. Does fidelity to the gospel demand voluntary renunciation of wealth? Not everyone has this calling, but everyone should ask himself how he can be delivered from enslavement, how his riches (material or other) can be used in the service of everyone. The poverty demanded of the believer does enjoin a concrete attitude towards riches. The commandment is a grave and urgent one, because in general the material wealth of Christians today is greater than that of most of humanity. There can be no doubt that in the actual circumstances the Spirit is calling for voluntary evangelical poverty. Each one of us should review his attitude in the light of this.

At the second level, the demands are no less great; institutions always attract notice. A bishop may live in poverty in a palace, but the palace itself will be criticized. We must then be careful not to give the impression of prestige or power in strictly ecclesial institutions (liturgical celebrations, missionary projects, etc.). All of our institutional apparatus should indeed be subjected to thorough reexamination.

XII. **Mark**
8:27-33
Gospel
Thursday

For Mark, Peter's confession at Caesarea marks a turning point in the life of Jesus. Prior to this he had adhered strictly to a policy of secrecy concerning his messianic mission, forbidding the beneficiaries of his miracles to speak, and the demons to acknowledge their defeat. Now, suddenly, he abandons this attitude, demanding openly a confession of faith from his disciples (v. 29).

The apostles of course had often the opportunity to discuss Jesus' personality among themselves and they were convinced that they were not following a simple rabbi. Peter's confession expresses this: from now on they know they are associated with the Messiah (v. 29).

In Mark, Jesus does not appear to respond to this expression of messianic faith. He continues to be reserved, and confines himself to enjoining *silence* on his apostles (v. 30, peculiar to Mark). Mark, however, continues the narrative with the first prediction of the Passion (vv. 31-33), explaining the kind of Messiahship Jesus has in mind.

Here we have an important transition. Jesus is no longer the rabbi and thaumaturge. He accepts recognition as Messiah, but has yet to convince his followers that this is a sorrowful mission.

In this, Mark is omitting the ecclesial dimension which primitive tradition had accorded the confession at Caesarea. He omits, for instance, the account of Peter's investiture (Mt 16: 17-19). More than the other synoptics, he is preoccupied with the mystery of Christ's personality and its slow discernment by his followers.

The importance of Peter's confession lies in its contrast with previous responses. For the crowd, Jesus is no more than a precursor; it is not he who will accomplish the Kingdom. For Peter however, Jesus really *is* accomplishing the Kingdom of God, at least provisionally as Messiah. He has yet, to be adult in faith, to deepen his insight into the humiliating aspects of Messiahship, but his first response is decisive.

In fact, many Christians are still at the stage of the crowd's response, regarding Jesus as merely a precursor. Because justice and peace are not triumphant yet, because suffering and conflict

278 GUIDE FOR THE CHRISTIAN ASSEMBLY

continue to dominate the world, nothing, they think, has been done.

Such people cannot conceive how Jesus can be Lord amid the prevailing confusion and deceit. Faith however does not really begin until we can recognize not alone Christ, but the crucified one (vv. 31-33). Until one has faith of this calibre, it is better to be silent and say nothing of Jesus (v. 30).

XIII. Genesis   In the account of the tower of Babel two
11:1-9   Yahwist traditions are combined. In the first
1st reading (vv. 1, 3, 4a, 6a, 8b, 9), men want to construct
1st cycle   a city to which they will give their name. They
Friday   all speak the same tongue, but God dislikes
           their enterprise and comes down from heaven
to confound their language. The construction is interrupted and
what has already been built gets the name of "confusion."

In the second (vv. 2, 4b, 5, 6b, 8a), men want to build a tower
after the model of Babylonian ziggurats to reach the heavens,
which will be their sign of assembly wherever in the world they
find themselves. God confounds their project and disperses them.
The builders' intention however is not to mount to the heavens
but to have a rallying point which will prevent their dispersion.

It is probable that some ancient story of the construction of a
Babylonian ziggurat, which was violently interrupted, lies behind
this tradition. Hebrew folklore absorbed it into another tradition
of Babylon, that cosmopolitan city of many languages, in order
to explain the origin of different languages and the lack of communication in the world.

The interest of the narrative is manifestly religious, concerned
with the meaning of *technique*. The author, who recounts the
legend without concern for its historicity, wants to demonstrate
the dangers of a technique by which man tries to promote himself,
not receiving everything from God in the nomad fashion. To build

a city and give it one's name, like the kings and emperors of the time, is to try to control time, to survive into the future, things that the author sees as not prerogatives of man. To use bitumen and brick made by human industry for erecting a city, instead of cement and the stones of nature (v. 3) is an affirmation that man can procure for himself what God provides. It is to prefer the "artificial" and "technological" order to the natural. To attempt to overcome the lot that leads man to dispersion, by building a rallying point (v. 4b) is a universalist ambition, which only God is capable of realizing.

The Yahwist is true to his thesis. Man's sin has always been to set himself in the place of God (cf. Gn 3:6). He sees technology as a diabolical means of undertaking such a project (cf. further the malediction of Cain's technocrat descendants in Jn 4:17-22).

These Yahwist misgivings have relevance today. Certain religious phenomena are ridiculed in the name of a technological progress, from which man expects what he formerly depended for on God. It is indeed true that modern civilization sometimes gives the impression that man is becoming equal to God. But it is also true that human efforts can result in "failure" and confusion, that man can build a world devoid of communication.

The pessimism of Genesis II however has to be corrected by the optimist vision of Genesis I. Man cannot make himself like God, but he is the image of God, commissioned to stamp that image on creation. There is a difference between being "like God" and the "image of God." To be the former is to arrogate divinity in seeking human progress; to be the latter is to seek this identical progress, but in reference to God. God is apprehended not in a utilitarian sense, but in faith, in spontaneous welcome, and in dialogue.

XIV. James   This is one of the most important passages in
    2:14-24, 26   the letter of James. It is so in the first place
    1st reading   because it is one of the most Christian pieces
    2nd cycle   in a work strongly marked by Judaism, but
    Friday   above all because in discussing the relationship
    between faith and works it seems to contradict
the Pauline reading.

It is undeniable that James seems hostile to the abuses that
can arise from certain Pauline affirmations. The spies that he
sometimes sent to follow Paul could inform him, not only about
what Paul thought and said, but also about the manner in which
it was interpreted.

The fact is that, across all the hazards of personal problems
and "hangups," Paul and James clearly share the same faith, and
have the same view about *faith and works.* In the first place,
James accepts the law of liberty (v. 12), probably in the sense
given to it by Paul, an abrogation of the law of Moses (2 Co
3:17; Ga 4:23-31; 5:13). Then, both have the same concept of
faith, as something which is not adherence to the formulas of a
credo, but concerns and transforms the whole of life (v. 14; cf.
Ga 5:6). James is certainly less mystical than Paul. His religion
is horizontal and practical, where Paul stresses the vertical and
personal. Their attitudes are complementary but by no means
opposed.

James of course modifies Paul's interpretation of Genesis 15:6
(Abraham believed in God and this was imputed to him for
justice, v. 23; cf. Ga 3:5-7; Rm 4:2-3). He shows that Abraham's
faith was expressed in a "work" so heroic as that of sacrificing
his son (vv. 21-22). But the two are not really in opposition; they
simply give very different meanings to the term "work." Paul
understands it exclusively in reference to the means of salvation
offered the Jews by the law of Moses (circumcision, temple, etc.).
He wishes to be finished with such works, because now he relies
on a "law of liberty." Nor does James, who also believes in the

law of liberty (v. 12), deny him this. But James takes "works" to mean activities that are based on faith (vv. 14-20, 26), and we can scarcely maintain that Paul rejects these (Ep 2:8-10).

The supposed opposition between Paul and James is based on the view that both allow the same meaning for "works." The truth is that they have an identical doctrine but a different vocabulary.

Modern activism runs the risk of subordinating faith to "works." "When I work I pray." Those who react against such activism on the other hand often rely on a supernaturalism that is inadequate. Between the priest who spends all his time visiting the sick and the one who prays for them in his room, there is a middle way. We must moderate our expressions of faith by the engagements we undertake; everything must be judged by the standard of personal communion with Christ.

We shall not be judged by pharisaic standards, by the quantity, that is, of our works. We shall be judged by the harmony we achieved between the observance of God and the observance of the world.

XV. Mark
8:34-38
Gospel
Friday

Jesus has just elicited a profession of faith from his apostles and emerges from the reserve and secrecy he has observed since the beginning of his ministry as a rabbi. Peter has said that the apostolic group accept him as the Messiah (Mk 8:27-30), and Jesus' immediate reaction has been one of silence and reserve, as if the answer of Peter did not fully satisfy him.

a) Jesus gradually came to a full awareness of his messianic role. He could not fulfill it by being the missionary rabbi and thaumaturge that he was at the beginning of his ministry. He must become the suffering Messiah. He and his apostles had been convinced of his Messiahship by certain events, but other, more sombre, circumstances made it clear that he was threatened by suffering and persecution. The attachment of the crowds was too superficial for lasting fidelity. The elite would now no longer tolerate so iconoclast a rabbi. Accordingly he proclaims his approaching *Passion.*

The text of this prediction is formal. The synoptics, or the primitive tradition, recognized its importance. It is accordingly reproduced three times, in quite stereotyped fashion (Mk 8:31-33; 9:30-32; 10:32-34). The three days motif very probably belongs to the primitive tradition. It must be admitted, however, that Jesus really did, at this stage, foretell his resurrection. So keen a sense did he have of the necessity to succeed in his mission that he could see no other issue. In the midst of the persecutions that were developing, his only recourse was the total commission of his life to the Father, who was able to raise him up again to accomplish his mission.

b) Peter's insight is still far from being that of Jesus. He is still thinking of a political Messiahship, but realizes that the Twelve are not now, as at the beginning, just disciples of a Master. They are the collaborators of the King-Messiah. For this reason he does not hesitate to reprimand Jesus for his pessimistic sentiments. How can a Messiah endure suffering (v. 32), seeing that Elias has already come to arrange everything (Mk 9:9-13)? Jesus treats this rejoinder as a new diabolical *temptation* (cf. Mk 1:13), which is jeopardizing his mission, and weakening his resolution by considerations of a human order.

c) The prediction is introduced by the phrase "he must" (v. 31) which generally in the gospels, and above all in Saint Luke (2:49; 4:43; 9:22; 13:33; 17:25; Ac 1:16; 3:21), indicates the very special *will of God* for Jesus.

The phrase is probably apocalyptic in origin (Dn 2:28-29, 45 according to LXX; Mt 24:6; Rev 4:1; 22:6), indicating the inevitability of the final times. There is no question, however, of blind fatalism, but of God's plan to accomplish salvation history with man's free collaboration. Likewise the use of the phrase interprets the Passion of Christ as the sorrowful destiny of the

Son of man, on which the eschatological future of humanity depends. The Father does not, of course, will the death of his Son; he wills his Son to bring love to the world. It is a mission that cannot be accomplished without trial and without fidelity to man's mortal state. The love that will illumine the final times cannot come upon the earth unless channeled through pain.

At each new turning point in his mission Jesus encountered temptation. It assailed him at the outset when he began as a rabbi, following John the Baptist. It returned when he had to choose a Messiahship of suffering and death. It would come finally at Gethsemane when he was about to fulfill the role of the suffering Servant.

We can discern temptation in the very arguments used by the Christian to justify his calling and mission in the world. The arguments are not necessarily sinful; on the contrary they are full of good intentions and seem conclusive. All the same they can prevent the man who yields to them from penetrating to the core of his vocation, and fully accepting the responsibility laid upon him by God for the salvation of the world. We have a tendency to emphasize, reasonably, the value of what we are leaving. We have first to bury our father. We find niceties which enable us to evade the issue. We talk about the "neighbor" we must love. We accept the compromising assistance of some secular source, as if only God were powerless. We must depend on the Eucharist, that great sacrament of Christ's victory over his temptations, to enable us to overcome ours.

XVI. **Hebrews**	The author is addressing Christians of Jewish
11:1-7	origin who have been driven by persecution
1st reading	from Jerusalem, and are in consequence dis-
1st cycle	turbed and discouraged. Will not their exile
Saturday	from the holy city preclude them from the in-
	auguration of the Kingdom?

He summons them accordingly to a spirit of faith that relies only on the invisible and on the certainty of already possessing the "earnest" of the "heavenly" realities (v. 1). Being as they are of Jewish culture, their ancestors can provide the model for such faith.

The beginning of this "Eulogy of the Patriarchs" is a fitting conclusion to the first chapters of Genesis, which appear in the liturgy from the seventh week onwards. Wisdom 10:1-4 has already provided us with a conclusion; but where the author there was concerned with God's mysterious action in events, the author of Hebrews is more concerned with the spiritual meaning of the attitudes adopted. This is the first time that a biblical author chooses, instead of stressing God's pedagogy of men by means of events, to describe the free attitudes of men. It is an important change. It is a desacralization of nature and of the "signs of the times"; the only sign considered of God's presence, is man's own liberty.

Faith was already required in the reading of the creation narratives (v. 3). It is only by faith indeed that we perceive that visible things emanate from a Word, and are the reflection of a mysterious design. Faith is required if we are to live creation and history as the continuous unfolding of the Word and of God's plan. We contemplate, in the light projected by the invisible on all visible things.

This is precisely what the ancestors of the chosen people were able to do. They discerned, in the pattern of events encountered by their liberty, the Word of God, and the summons to a particular attitude. Thus did Abel (Gn 4:1-26) separate himself from his brother through the faith he manifested in his sacrifice (v. 4) at the risk of his life. The faith of the just man kindles the hate of the unbeliever. Obeying the Word of God he had heard, Abel is thus led to abandon everything, life included, in order to obtain an eternal life "where he still speaks."

Thus Noah, reading in events the invisible, discerned the urgency of quitting his fellows (v. 7; cf. Gn 6-7) and condemning their attitude. He too had heard the Word and obeyed it, by giving his time and effort to the construction of the ark of salvation.

The believer is convinced that God is present in history and that his will can be discerned in the event. It is a particular attitude. The unbeliever does not hear this "Word" of God; he challenges and mocks the attitude of the believer. The Bible shows us that believing and unbelieving attitudes are as old as man, and will continue to the end of time.

XVII. James 3:1-10
1st reading
2nd cycle
Saturday

In this passage James turns to one of the most destructive things that the primitive communities encountered: adulteration of the word and syncretism. Paul frequently clashed with false teachers, sometimes from Judaism itself, who through contact with dubious wisdom distorted the gospel (1 Tm 1:3-7; 2 Tm 4:1-8; Tt 3:8-15). Everything suggests that James had the same people in mind.

He begins by recommending his listeners not to take lightly the task of teaching (vv. 1-2). The *tongue,* for all that it is small, is a mighty instrument for controlling the lives of many, just as the bit in the horse's mouth is sufficient to control him, or the rudder which is so small controls a ship (vv. 3-4).

Sins of the tongue he treats in the manner of the sages (Pr 11:12; 29:20; 10:19; 12:13; 13:3; 16:27; 18:21; Si 5:11; 32:8; 19:4-17, etc.). Man may tame the animals (v. 7), but he cannot tame his own tongue (v. 8). He may use his tongue to praise God, but he also uses it to curse men (vv. 9-10). He concludes by recommending listeners to have mastery over the tongue (v. 10).

Speech is part of the person. If it is not controlled, the integrity of the whole person may be affected. In our consumer society, language is in constant danger of being depersonalized. Words no longer transmit truth, but are manipulated solely for their publicity value. Language ceases to be the instrument of dialogue between two persons; it is a monologue directed at an object. In our day commercial publicity and political propaganda take the place of sophistry in the time of James.

XVIII. Mark Mark's contextual placing of the Transfigura-
9:1-12 tion, rather more noticeably than the other
Gospel synoptics, becomes an affirmation of Jesus,
Saturday presentiments of his death and glory. Jesus has
just foretold his approaching Pasch (Mk 8:31-32), but Peter immediately rebukes him. He cannot conceive that the kingdom of glory and power foretold by the prophets is destined to come through suffering and death (Mk 8:32-33).

The first verse falls into this context. Despite rather confused translations, what Jesus is saying, in somewhat sorrowful tone, is this: "they are expecting a kingdom of power; but not one among them is ready to pay with his life for its coming." Mark thus sees the Transfiguration above all, as a revelation by Jesus of the whole paschal mystery to the elite among the apostles (the very ones who will be close to him at Gethsemani: Mk 14:33).

That is why Elias gets precedence over Moses (v. 4). If John the Baptist is Elias, he is proclaiming by his own sufferings those of the Messiah (cf. the explanation by Jesus in Mk 9:12-13). Clearly, what is basic in Mark's gospel is the concept of the *suffering Messiah*.

Other points which arise in the narrative are discussed in the commentary on Matthew 17:1-9.

The Transfiguration then is really a special exhortation for Peter. He must listen to Jesus (v. 7) when he speaks of suffering and death. But all the time he must continue to see him as the definitive Messiah, the ideal Servant (Is 42:1).

The faith demanded from the witnesses of the Transfiguration gives today's Church a reason for not avoiding the involvements and self-renunciation she must face. She must not seek a kingdom of power, but one that comes by the way of death. It also teaches her that this has its corresponding Transfiguration. The only reason she is called to be present in secular structures is to transfigure them. She will do that by being ready to die to all comfort and security. She will encounter the vicissitudes of glory and humiliation, realizing that her victory will only be achieved when, broken by death, she looks upon a world she will have transformed.

SEVENTH SUNDAY

A. THE WORD

I. Leviticus
19:1-2, 17-18
1st reading
1st cycle

This comes from a legislative compilation that was made after the exile (Lv 17-25), and is called the "Law of Holiness," because it is particularly concerned with God's holiness, and with the obligations imposed by his transcendence on the people who have a covenant with him.

These obligations are in the main liturgical (sacrifices, ablutions, priestly character), but are also concerned with the purity of the race by precise rulings concerning sexual relations. Like most previous legislation the section assembles texts from various sources. It is, however, rather surprising to find in this ensemble concerning cult and sexual purity a passage concerning social brotherhood (vv. 9-18), the high point of which is a summons to love one's neighbor as oneself (v. 18).

The passage stems largely from deuteronomic legislation (Dt 24:7, 14-15; 19:16-21) which was concerned about social relationships. Was it perhaps inserted in the cultic regulations of Leviticus, because it was already realized that fraternal charity was more important than all the rules for sacrifice, and was the real sign of God's holy presence among men?

a) A comparison between Leviticus 19:13-14 and Deuteronomy 24:14-15 is revealing. The second text contemplates only the humiliated poor man, the first extends the law of charity to every *neighbor*. Deuteronomy, however, shows concern for the stranger, whereas Leviticus unfortunately is too concerned with purity of the race to have this interest.

One would say that the *raison d'etre* of the law of Deuteronomy is pity for the poor, the victims of injustice; whereas the *raison d'etre* in Leviticus is blood solidarity and bonds with the "neighbor." Times have changed in fact between the two strata of legis-

288

lation. The deuteronomic belonged to a period of profound social mutation; in Leviticus nationalism has come to be the only bulwark against paganism.

b) Blood solidarity appears as a main consideration in the regulation concerning trials and *false witnesses* (vv. 15-16). Injustice in tribunals seems to have been a recurring abuse in Jewish society. The law constantly returns to the problem, endeavoring to set up a regime of honesty. The psalms and the prophets are always complaining about the venality of judges and witnesses (Ps 81/82; Jr 21:11-12; Am 5:10-15). The argument put forward by Leviticus, however, for justice in tribunals is original. National brotherhood ought to be sufficient to prevent suits between Jews ("your compatriot" v. 15; "your own" v. 16). A simple brotherly reprimand ought to produce the same result as a tribunal (v. 17b).

Clearly then the intention of the section is to create an awareness of national solidarity. Ethical attitude is determined by brotherly union; one does not hurt one's own kin. The earliest Christian legislation finds its inspiration here; suits among Christians are decided by the community itself (Mt 5:25-26; 18:15-22; 1 Co 6:1-8; Rm 12:17-19).

Yet this is quite an inadequate concept of love. If we may borrow the language of Tillich, it belongs to space-religion rather than time-religion, or, more correctly, the religion of liberty.

Love of the neighbor only is more or less deliberate cult of the self, with all that this embraces, blood and kin, race and family, the nation. There are other soils and other places; but these are at best tolerated when there is not open conflict with them. The terrifying destructive force that is latent in racism and nationalism does not need to be stressed. A limitation of love to spatial frontiers is indeed basically a recrudescence of that polytheism which limits gods to special territories.

Christian love has nothing to do with space, or for that matter with the limitation of time. God required Abraham to go out beyond the frontiers of his family and his race, to embark on a free adventure that was to mold history. That is why all nations were promised to him. He required his own Son to offer his life, not alone for his own, in the spatial sense, but for the multitude. This is the multitude that transcends the limits of the visible Church, and that it will require all history to unite in love, across the hazards of tribalism.

II. Isaiah   The prophet, charged with the duty of consol-
     43:18-19,   ing the exiles during the Babylonian captivity,
     21-22,   sustains their morale by brief affirmations and
     24b-25   oracles of hope. He has, however, to use a sym-
     1st reading   bolic style in order to be understood without
     2nd cycle   being discovered by the enemy.

a) One symbol that is clear for Jews but arcane for others is that of the *new exodus* (vv. 18-19). Let the exiles be consoled. The God who freed their ancestors will soon free them too, in quite spectacular fashion.

Thus, by reading the history of the past, the Jews learned to discern the future. Their God is unique, the same in the future as he was in the past, the same at the end as at the beginning of history. The beginning of a true sense of history is the monotheism of Second-Isaiah.

b) The lessons to be learned from history were not always heartening ones. Just as in the past the people had murmured, the new people too would encounter the same temptation to *forgetfulness* and revolt (vv. 22-25). Sin, in itself, is such a sinister re-beginning. God is the same throughout history, but the man with whom he deals is also the same. He is more concerned about himself and his comfort than about thanksgiving to God and communion with him in worship.

We cannot become unburdened of the past. Remorse is constant, and hope, in agony, is aborted. We cannot be unburdened indeed, but we can absorb and assimilate the past. We can do so because God's pardon, without changing our past, gives it new meaning by the assurance that we were loved and continue to be loved.

III. 1 Samuel David has quit the court of Saul and become
26:2, 7-9, the leader of a band. The country is still feebly
12-13, 22-23 unified, and the central government too weak
1st reading to deal with these armed mercenaries, who live
3rd cycle on the country, harass the regular troops with
ambushes and avoid full engagement. All new
states know the phenomenon, and it is by no means unusual to see
the central power seized by some such group.

Often in the leader of such a band there is a *chivalric spirit* which transcends the mentality of his men, sordid hirelings and adventurers (like Abishai, v. 8). David's biographers seem to have been conscious of this. Two different traditions record examples of his magnanimity (1 S 24; 1 S 26). Sparing one's enemy at the time was not necessarily evidence of charity or pardon. It might merely be an indication that the chief in question was so certain of his strength that he could seem weak and relaxed. David's gesture however is more than this, because God is the reason for his pardon (v. 9). He foreshadows the theological basis that Christians will provide for their love (2 Ch 6:27-36).

Why does the Bible, which is salvation history, preserve such anecdotes of the lives of predators, which, chivalrous though they be, nevertheless fall far short of true pardon* and love?

The reason is that God is present not only where there is perfect love and accomplished virtue. We find him, when there is no more as yet than foundation stones and the preambles of faith. The viewpoint of David's biographer is extremely open. He discerns

---

* See the doctrinal theme: *mercy*, p. 301.

an attitude in his hero, which God can transform and bring to perfection. His chivalry is seen as a respect for the other because he is the image of God (v. 9). Under this aspect David's gesture really belongs to salvation history; God can shape it towards fulfillment.

The chronicler's sympathy for David as a guerilla is paralleled in our day by the feeling in some quarters for people like Camillo Torres or Che Guevara. The activities of these particular heroes have certainly been sometimes ambiguous, but can any more be said for those of David? To preserve one's independence, respect persons, even enemies, give one's life for something greater than oneself when others suffer round one, are these not perhaps foundation stones to the Kingdom that we must respect as such? Such was the price David paid so that one day he might provide an approximation to the Kingdom of God. May not a Torres or a Guevara have been on the same road and be pursuing it beyond the barrier of death?

IV. 1 Corinthians   The Corinthians were avid for intellectual wis-
3:16-23   dom and reproached Paul for his over simple
2nd reading   presentation of the message before them (1
1st cycle   Co 3:1). They were contrasting him with more
                                    philosophical and more intellectual preachers.
Today's reading gives us the conclusion of Paul's argument in response.

a) He compares the work of a preacher to that of a builder. When the work is completed, the builder is judged by the quality and durability of his materials (1 Co 3:10-15). Good workmen will be recompensed (1 Co 3:14), less good put aside for a while (1 Co 3:15); but those whose work has destroyed the *dwelling of God* in men's hearts will be punished (v. 17). In Paul's thinking the dwelling is destroyed when its basis, Jesus Christ, is removed, when his cross (1 Co 1:18) and resurrection (1 Co 15) are denied.

b) Turning then to Scripture he cites two texts (vv. 19-20; Jb 5:12-13; Ps 93/94:11) which confirm this viewpoint. God is not to be found at the end of a human *philosophic* quest. He confounds the sages, because, without waiting for them to discover him one day, he reveals himself to men and tells them, in Jesus Christ, who he is.

c) The third argument (vv. 21-23) is quite unusual. Why should Christians follow the school of this or that master of wisdom and become infatuated, seeing that the truth, in Christ, had delivered them from all slavery. They had become masters of the secret of all things.

This is an argument that must of course be delicately handled. It is true that the revelation of himself made by God in Jesus Christ is *liberating*. Why should one be concerned with what men say about God when God speaks of himself? But his revelation is not in competition with philosophic systems; it does not offer a new interpretation of reality in conflict with existing views. God's Kingdom is not of this world, nor is his "philosophy." What we *can* say is that Jesus reveals what any ideology discerns more or less dimly. He fulfills all ideologies by enabling them to transcend their limits, insofar at least as they are open.

There is no question of denying value to the quest of men according to their culture. We Christians indeed should further all such quests. It is only thus that we ourselves can clarify who God is, and tell others of him. Indeed it is probably because the Church has remained too entrenched in a single framework of thought, that she has become incapable of talking about God to people of other cultures.

**V. 2 Corinthians
1:18-22**
2nd reading
2nd cycle

Relations between Paul and his Corinthian disciples were not always smooth. In 57, in particular, a grave crisis in the community required the apostle's presence (2 Co 1:23-2:1). During this visit he undertook to return for a longer stay (2 Co 1:15-17). However, so as not to give the impression of "ruling their faith," he canceled this journey, thus drawing on himself the reproach of using a "yes and no" language (vv. 17-18).

He devotes a few verses to a response to this accusation of duplicity. He recalls that he is a minister of Christ, who is altogether "yes" (vv. 19-20), and he concludes the argument with a short trinitarian formula (vv. 21-22).

a) In Christ there is no trace of duplicity. He said yes to the Father without the slightest reservation (v. 19) and because of this obedience God was able to be faithful and accomplish his promises (v. 20a). It also enabled all men who are united with Christ to say yes to the Father in their turn (v. 20b), and thus practice *sincerity*.

Being as he is a minister who proclaims Christ and a Christian who lives by Christ, he himself can have no duplicity in his heart when he makes promises. Every Christian indeed should follow suit; his yes to men should echo his yes to God.*

b) In verses 21-22 we have the *trinitarian formula*. To the Father belong anointing and the seal; to the Spirit, the earnest of glory; to the Son the strengthening of faith. This division of functions is literary rather than doctrinal. Unction and the seal probably indicate baptism; earnest of glory the Spirit himself, considered as the pledge of future eternal life. The strengthening given by Christ is the sharing of his yes, in an obedience which brings about fulfillment of the promises.

Sincerity in modern times is valued on an unprecedented scale. Sociology and psychology combine to unmask previous false tabus. Art strives after the greatest simplicity and rejects all ornament to the point of becoming abstract. Public opinion is more tolerant of mistakes and errors in individuals and systems than of falsity or hypocrisy. If a new catalogue of cardinal virtues were possible, sincerity would clearly be placed among them.

The Second Vatican Council made away with a series of ec-

---

* See the doctrinal theme: *imitation of God*, p. 195.

clesial institutions that hindered sincerity of conscience. This reform however will not be complete until each individual applies it to himself, educates his conscience, and follows it openly and unswervingly.

VI. 1 Corinthians Paul is trying to explain for his readers the
     15:45-49   manner of final resurrection. His own early
     2nd reading   years had been passed in a Jewish environment
     3rd cycle   where opinions were quite divided on this
topic. A party of pharisaic inspiration, during the Seleucid persecution, had imposed the doctrine as a normal stage of the coming of the Kingdom (2 M 7:11-23; 12:44). Others, of Sadducean persuasion, adhered to biblical traditions where survival was never mentioned in other than hesitant terms. Others still, influenced by Hellenistic thought, believed in the immortality of the soul only, set free of the body (for instance, the Book of Wisdom).

Jesus at once ranged himself with the pharisaic tradition, and the primitive Christian community based its faith in the resurrection on the paschal event itself. When Paul writes to the Thessalonians he reflects the thought of the Pharisees and the Judaeo-Christian communities (1 Th 4:14-17; 2 Th 1:10; 2:14). As he sees it, bodies recently placed in tombs will be resuscitated; there is a real corporeal life both before and after death.

The Greek world found this doctrine too simplistic (Ac 17:32). Paul found himself confronted by a series of grave objections, above all in the Corinth community. His answer is found in this chapter.

He makes a distinction between humanity before Christ (the first man, v. 45) and humanity after (the new man). The vital principle of the first man was his soul (*psyche, nephesh*), something that could not give corporeal resurrection. The new man on the other hand has received a new vital principle, the Spirit, which can spiritualize his body and give it resurrection. This principle is a gratuitous gift ("heavenly," vv. 47-48), in the sense that it cannot be reduced to a natural level.

This "spiritualization" of the body, which begins in this world and is perfected in *resurrection* and incorruptibility, does not necessarily, for Saint Paul, entail immaterialization. God's Spirit is of course different substantially: he is light and holiness. Saint Paul, however, does not define the Spirit philosophically (that would mean immateriality) but in a religious sense. The Spirit makes us share in the divine. He inspires the man who is not limited to human means alone (flesh and blood, v. 50). He puts man in touch with the divine life within him.

The human body accordingly is not incompatible with the Spirit. It can on the contrary share those religious qualities which manifest here and now the gift of divine life to the human person. They will always be known as glory and incorruptibility.

When the natural body becomes a spiritual body, this is not an escape from matter; it is a bringing of the privileges of divine life to those who have always lived them corporally. Such a view would be inconceivable apart from faith in the resurrection of Jesus, who issued from the tomb. Without shedding corporeity, he became the vivifying spirit. The body of the risen Christ has the prerogatives of the Spirit because, corporally, he completely shared the divine life. In the Eucharist, our communion with this spiritual body gives us a share of the Spirit. We experience it now within the limits of corporeity, but it is an earnest of what our future resurrection will mean.

VII. Matthew
5:38-48
Gospel
1st cycle

In this passage we have the last of the six antitheses that the evangelist groups in the sermon on the mount (Mt 5:21-48), to illustrate the "new justice" (v. 20). The conclusion in verse 48 refers not to the last antithesis, but to the antithetic section as a whole.

Luke 6:27-36 gives us another version, not antithetic in structure. The antitheses are probably peculiar to Matthew, though Matthew is more likely to give us more primitive sayings than Luke. Luke for instance substitutes for the precise diatribe against publicans and Gentiles (Mt 5:46, 47) one against sinners in general (Lk 6:33-34), doubtless to avoid offending his readers.

In Matthew 5:48 we find the Jewish theme of perfection, regarded as the fulfillment of all the prescriptions of the law, and practiced indeed, according to rabbinic lore, by God himself. Matthew confines himself to superseding such formalist perfection by the gratuitous perfection which the Father sends down from heaven (Mt 5:17, 20; 19:21). Luke actually goes further by disregarding the ideal of perfection, and speaking only of goodness and mercy (Lk 6:36).

Matthew's account is just as carefully studied as that of Luke. He gives us the legalist precept, drawn from both the law and rabbinic tradition (v. 48); and at once he contrasts with it the new commandment, which is gratuitous. The new commandment is given in the form of a triad (vv. 44-45, as in Mt 5:22, 34-35 and 39-41). Then we have two concrete examples, one Jewish (v. 46), one Gentile (v. 47), indicating the independence of the new ethic as against legalist or philanthropic systems.

Luke's procedure on the other hand is concentric. The same idea is repeated several times in different fashion (vv. 27-28, 29). The triad structure appears in his examples ("and if . . . and if . . . and if . . ." vv. 32-34). In concluding he resorts to antithesis ("on the other hand," v. 35), but it is not so much an antithesis between Jewish and Christian justice as between interested and disinterested love.

Whatever may be the differences between the two evangelists, in either case the lesson is the same. Love must transcend the limits suggested by nature and sociological or psychological considerations. It must extend to the frontiers of all humanity, including enemies. Christ then is disjoining love from the sacral boundaries of family or nation. Love has its own religious dimension that is not confined to preestablished sacral domains. God is not to be found in family, or race, or nation; he is to be found in the act of love (Mt 5:48; Lk 6:36). This is what the gospel means in speaking of "imitation" of God* in brotherly love without limits. Today, instead of imitation, we might use the term "communion"; but the idea is the same. Given that God exists, love must be the avenue towards him, not the sacral nature, greater or less, of the object loved.

Love of this calibre transcends the natural limits of one's community. It goes in search of the person and his divine secret. Nor is it merely a matter of enlarging horizons in the quantitative sense. The love itself is changed essentially by a personalization and a deepening.

VIII. Mark   This piece is very probably the result of con-
  2:1-12   siderable manipulation of previous material.
  Gospel   Two different traditions seem to be combined.
  2nd cycle   The first (vv. 1-4, 11-12) recounts the cure of
         a paralytic before an admiring crowd. The second (vv. 5-10) gives us a discussion between Jesus and the Scribes concerning the power to pardon given the Son of Man.

a) The combination was made perhaps, because the cure of the paralytic was regarded by the primitive community as a sign of the *pardon for sins* now offered. According to Isaiah 33:23-24 paralytics and sinners are associated in the same salvation. Such a doctrinal interpretation of the miracle would have recalled the discussion about power of pardon. The conclusion of the discussion was to show that Jesus was indeed the Son of Man foretold in Daniel 7:13-14, and that instead of condemning his principal mission would be to pardon and justify.

* See the doctrinal theme: *imitation of God,* p. 195.

The juxtaposition of the two traditions suggested a new insight: that pardon for sin depends on the faith of the sinner and the community around him (v. 5; as in Lk 7:48-50; Ac 10:43; 13:48; 26-18).

b) The discussion about pardoning was certainly later, belonging to a stage when Jesus' thaumaturgic power had assumed radical dimensions. It was that of the Son of Man (Mt 26:64; 24:30; 13:41; 19:28; 12:8), whose power was particularly wide where judgment was concerned, a power that could not be exercised without delegation from God.

The phrase "on earth" in verse 10 can only be understood as a contrast to the future glory of the Son of Man, when he will come on the clouds (Dn 7:13-14). Jesus is affirming the fact that he is already invested, during his earthly mission, with the power over sin which he will exercise in plenitude when he is seated as judge. The power is discretionary. He can pardon as well as condemn, by virtue of his delegation from God who alone can pardon and judge.

Consequently the apparition of the sovereign judge at the end of time is being foreshadowed now by the exercise of pardon and mercy.* The faith required to benefit from these gestures of the Son of Man is recognition of this anticipatory judgment on earth.

c) Jesus delivers the paralytic from the *trial* to which his contemporaries, regarding his malady as due to sin, would subject him. However, it is only by oneself undergoing trial that human kind can be delivered from all trial and judgment. The crowd who witness the healing of the paralytic suddenly harden against Jesus. The paralysis is now on the other side, and he finds his own trial begin by hearing the accusation that very soon will bring about his death: "he blasphemes" (v. 7; cf. Mk 14:64).

Insofar as modern man has lost the sense of God, he has stifled the sense of sin and consequently the meaning of a Messiah who

---

* See the doctrinal theme: *mercy,* p. 301.

pardons and dies for the pardon of sins. The Christian will only be able to bear witness to God's pardon and its necessity insofar as he purifies his own notion of sin. He must disengage it from overly materialist associations, and recover the concept of a liberty that commits itself or refuses itself. Pardon is not an individual, paternalist procedure but a community enterprise of love for the building of true peace and justice in the different domains of human life.

Christians are dispersed throughout the world to proclaim and offer this pardon to men. In the Eucharist they will be able to become aligned with the merciful initiative of the Father. He shows his pardon by giving us the bread that has been consecrated by his Son's victory over sin and death.

IX. Luke
6:27-38
Gospel
3rd cycle

This passage, which is parallel to Matthew 5:38-48, was dealt with in commenting on Matthew (Gospel, 1st cycle), p. 296.

B. DOCTRINE

1. The Theme of Mercy

Insofar as modern man has lost the sense of God, he tends to query Christian ideas about sin and divine pardon. However to the extent that the God he rejects is a mere substitute for the God of Jesus Christ, it is possible that his notions of sin and pardon are a deformation of the true Christian notions. For that matter the judgments that Christians, increasingly, tend to pass on their non-Christian brethren are based, not on valid concepts of sin and pardon, but on the erroneous concepts that have gained currency.

What in fact did happen? The relationship between supernatural and natural, which has been analyzed theologically since the 13th century, has been very slow in influencing the everyday routine of Christian life. Sin, which doctrinally speaking is essentially a personal rejection of the God of love, tends in fact to be understood in natural terms, in terms of the disorder which it creates. By emphasizing the material act in the objective order, one runs the risk of obscuring the encounter of two liberties, and the notion of guilt becomes encumbered with material elements that do not properly belong to it.

And as for the notion of pardon, the images frequently used to illustrate it do not go to the heart of the matter. Quite certainly, the distaste evinced by modern man suggests that our notions in both domains need to be purified.

Yahweh the God of pardon up to the day of judgment

Man has been created in God's image and likeness, and he is called by his Creator to a supernatural destiny that he can only accomplish by responding to the divine initiative. Man is a creature and only God can divinize him. Yet, in fact, man has tried to divinize himself, to satisfy by his own resources his thirst for the absolute, to touch somehow the sacral world that keeps eluding him. In other words, he is a sinner. At the very beginning of hu-

man history we have original sin, at the very beginning of the
history of the chosen people the sin of the desert. The Bible,
which recounts all this, sees human history and Jewish history as
a constant recrudescence of these two great sins. Instead of following God's way, man turns away and follows his own.

Thus, in the perspective of faith, sin is essentially a rejection of
love: Jewish man sees the relationship of the people to Yahweh
as a personal one. If man blocks this channel of love which links
him with God, he destroys himself.

What is Yahweh's reaction to sin? Unquestionably he could
exercise vengeance, break his covenant and intervene at once
with his eschatological judgment, letting man condemn himself.
But to take that view simply would be a misunderstanding of the
God of love. Yahweh is a God of mercy and pardon. His love
shows itself altogether larger than the rejection which challenges
it: even in his state of sin he reaches out to man. When he pardons, Yahweh shows himself superior to hate.

Man however, to be pardoned, must turn away from sin and
be converted. Little by little sinful man becomes aware that even
this conversion depends on divine love, that man in every single
detail depends on this gratuitous divine initiative. When Yahweh
pardons he replaces the sinful heart with a new heart.

A final insight was the believer's realization that his own
pardon depended on his pardoning in turn. The just man should
model himself after the mercy of God. The extent to which he
pardoned would be limited by the frontiers of Jewish universalism, but there was a deep realization of the link between this
and divine pardon.

The messianic pardon of the Son of Man

When John the Baptist proclaims the imminence of the Kingdom he summons people to conversion in view of the judgment
that is to be. But when the Messiah comes, he affirms that he
has come among men not to judge but to heal and pardon.

The unexpected revelation showed the true character of divine pardon. God pardons by becoming incarnate; he so loved men that he gave what he most loved, his own Son. It was the infinite generosity of this gift that made possible a total response by man. Jesus of Nazareth made that total response. God's pardon became fully effective when he in his humanity set in motion the same pardon, a human pardon of divine dimension. He manifested this pardon, this total gift of himself, by a love for men that vanquished all hate, that reached out to man in his rejection. Concretely it took shape in his pilgrimage of absolute obedience unto the death of the cross "for the remission of sins." On the cross sins were remitted, because the love displayed on the cross was stronger than hate. Divine pardon had found in man its perfect response.

So that it is with Jesus of Nazareth that the history of pardon begins. His victory over hate was destined to be extended bit by bit. When others, in dependence on him, followed in their turn the path of obedience, God's partners were multiplied. The pardon of the cross began to flow through history. The history of pardon in other words is the history of true love, the history of salvation. Because he is the only mediator, the man-God is the only one among man to have the power of pardon. But by our link with him we all in turn become capable of limitless giving and limitless pardon.

The history of pardon then links indissolubly divine pardon with our pardon for one another. It could not be otherwise; it is the lesson of the whole life of Jesus. His supreme moment on the cross was a manifestation of God's pardon for men, and of the man-God's pardon for all his brothers.

The Church of mercy

Because the Church is Christ's Body, it is the establishment in history of the task of mediation. By virtue of this the Church can forgive sins. If it were otherwise she could not be the Church of Christ, nor would he be present in her. She would not be the sacrament of human salvation. And when we affirm that she has the power to forgive, we are saying that in her the history of pardon is being continued. The exercise of God's pardon requires an agent on earth. She is that agent.

To his apostles Jesus communicated the power of pardon, to those people, that is, whose responsibility it is, throughout the time of the Church, to ensure ecclesial presence in the world. And when the apostles or their successors pardon in the name of Christ, it is in fact the whole people of God who find themselves involved in the mystery of the cross, and in the act of pardon which is at once divine and human. The existence of the whole Church indeed is an act of mercy for the benefit of all humanity.

However true it is that the whole Church is engaged in the act of pardon, it also remains true that all members without exception are obliged to subject themselves to the ecclesial channel of pardon. All are sinners and must have recourse to what we call the power of the keys. By baptism we are all marked with the inviolable sign of divine pardon. Yet the baptized person is still a sinner and knows his need of the power of the keys.

All sacramental activity on the part of the Church is an exercise of mercy, but this is particularly true of the sacrament of penance. Here God encounters the confessed sinner as the father did the prodigal son. His whole concern is the preparation of the family feast. At this moment the whole Church should join with God in restoring the penitent to ecclesial communion.

The penitential dimension of the eucharistic assembly

Over-narrow ideas about sacramentality have tended to make people restrict the ecclesial power of pardon unduly to the sacrament of penance. The eucharistic celebration has been losing its penitential dimension. This is a serious matter, because it is in relationship to the Eucharist that the real character of the sacrament of penance can best be discerned.

It is only necessary to survey the actual Mass formularies to realize what a prominent penitential dimension the Eucharist does have. There is constant exercise of ecclesial pardon. It could scarcely be otherwise indeed, when we remember that the eucharistic assembly is the best symbol of the assembly of the Father's family, which is altogether based on mercy. The great moment of ecclesial pardon comes when the celebrant invites people to approach the holy table. Very evidently the Church cannot summon members to share the Bread unless she is also offering pardon. The universal brotherhood into which the communicant is ushered was set up by Jesus on the cross in that great act of divine pardon "for the remission of all sins."

SEVENTH WEEK

I. Sirach
1:1-10
1st reading
1st cycle
Monday

The Siracid wrote his book about 190 BC. He wrote in Hebrew. His nephew, a member of the Egyptian Diaspora translated it into Greek about 110 BC. The Hebrew original has been lost and such fragments of it as have been recovered are quite dissimilar. The Greek version is not very much better; it has very many variants. Despite these obstacles, the thought of Ben Sirach is clear enough. What we have are the reflections of a cultivated bourgeois who wants to live his life with God and feels happy that he is achieving this.

Today's passage is the introduction prefixed to the work and sets the tone for the whole book. Ben Sirach is a sensitive soul. When he contemplates nature or reflects on his experience of life, he discerns a mysterious transcendence which he calls the *wisdom* of God, a creative wisdom that contains the secret of all things.

He has come to this concept as a result of human wisdom and common sense. He has traveled a good deal and seen many wonderful human works. His thoughts move from the work itself to the energy which created it. Behind the material he discerns some genuine wisdom, a combination of good taste and skill.

The sage or scribe, however, is the person who leaves everything else aside in order to analyze things and people, to discern behind them the artisan who inspires them. Such *savoir-faire* is no longer human, but divine, as unmeasurable is it.

It sometimes happens that human works outlast the artisan who made them, and we are sorry that we no longer know a person of such genius. Likewise with nature. How one would have wished to assist at creation, see the manner in which God shaped it, know his thought as he worked (v. 4). But all this escapes man; the wisdom of God had accomplished everything before man's gaze could fall upon it (v. 6).

One possibility, however, remains open for the man who wishes to seek out the secret of this wisdom. The artist who has created a masterpiece brings with him at his death his wisdom. But God can communicate his wisdom to those he loves (v. 10).

II. James What James has just finished saying con-
3:13-18 cerning good and bad use of the Word, he now
1st reading repeats in different terms concerning true and
2nd cycle false wisdom. His realist cast of mind makes
Monday him disinclined for abstract principles. As he
sees it, the criteria for distinguishing the true sage from the false one are extremely concrete and tangible, and he proceeds to enumerate some of them.

The test of true wisdom is good conduct (v. 13), just as that of faith is works (Jm 2:12-24). And the most important elements of good conduct are gentleness (cf. Si 3:17), absence of intrigue (vv. 14 and 16; cf. 2 Co 12:20; Ga 5:20) and bitterness, and that boastfulness which seeks to advance oneself and leads to fanaticism.

True wisdom is pure (v. 17) in the sense that it is without flaw. He proves this by showing that wisdom opposes intrigue and bitterness by its anxiety for peace (Pr 3:17; Rm 8:6), for tolerance and docility. It enables sages to live harmoniously at once with brothers, adversaries, and superiors. It is generous towards the poor (mercy: v. 17), impartial towards subordinates. It will be seen in its capacity to create round about it a large network of varied interpersonal relations. In the end the real criterion of wisdom is charity.

III. Mark   The cure of the epileptic in Mark is rather dif-
  9:14-29   ferent from the version in the other synoptics.
  Gospel   He is more attentive to detail, as for instance
  Monday   when he dwells on the discussion between the
                   crowd and the disciples (vv. 14-16, 28), or
stresses the importance given by Jesus to this miracle (v. 25). The
details he gives, for the most part, suggest doctrinal points of
importance.

a) The first group are concerned with the diagnosis of the
child's *malady* (vv. 17-18, 21-22, 26-27). It is doubtless a case of
epilepsy and the diagnosis of Luke, the physician, is much
briefer (Lk 9:39). Mark's details, however, have less to do with
medical science than with the demonology and apocalyptic genre
of his time. The tableau he draws describes the enemy's assault
against the chosen people, represented here by the child.

Dumbness (v. 17), which is not mentioned by Luke or Matthew, indicates the absence of the Word of God among the
people. Passage through fire and water (v. 22) indicates the trials
to be undergone by the people for their purification (Ps 65/66:12;
Si 15:16; 1 K 17:1-7; Dt 32:3-4; 20-24). The grinding of teeth
(v. 18), also peculiar to Mark, recalls the classic punishments
for peoples and nations (Mt 8:12; 13:42, 50; 2:13; 24:51; 25:30;
Lm 2:16), or the spite of the wicked at the salvation of the just
(Pss 34/35:16; 36/37:12; 111/112:10; Jb 16:9). Foam is another
symptom he records (vv. 18, 20). The impious are often compared
to this evanescent substance (Wi 5:14). All of these details are
sufficient evidence that what is being diagnosed is not epilepsy
but the people's incredulity. Finally, Jesus describes the crowd
as an "unbelieving generation" (v. 19).

b) The people then are ailing, but Mark proclaims proximate
healing by some other details, which he borrows from a *catechumenal liturgy*. Three times he repeats that the child is "conducted," a phrase that indicates sponsorship in primitive Christian
language (cf. Mk 7:32; 8:22).

The healing takes place after the pattern of a death and resurrection (vv. 26-27) to indicate that there is no healing except by communion in the paschal mystery, the source of delivery from evil. The fast and prayer required by Jesus (v. 29) refer to the current practice for catechumens.

c) It would not be surprising if, among the many accounts of healings or resuscitations of *children,* tradition preserved this one too with a view to solving the pastoral problem of infant baptism. Judaism had excluded children from benefit of the Kingdom. By fixing attention on all the instances where children had been the beneficiaries of Christ's miraculous power, the early Christians were doubtless anxious to provide a basis for their baptism of infants and admission of them as full members of the Kingdom. How could the Church be a sign of universal salvation if she excluded from her fold even those who were not responsible?

Sometimes sacramental practice in the Church has been based too exclusively on the *opus operatum,* without sufficient regard for the faith of the sacramental candidate and the surrounding community. Pastors have tended to rely too readily on the certainty of the active presence of Jesus and neglect the formation of the candidate. In fact they should guide his steps all along the way and be concerned also about the warmth of his welcome among the Christian community.

In today's Gospel we have an excellent model for pastoral conduct of the sacraments. We have the rite in which the paschal mystery is communicated to the candidate in the faith, the dispositions of the ministers themselves who preside over the prayer and the conversion by being personally involved. For the efficacy of the sacrament none of these dimensions should be neglected.

IV. Sirach
2:1-11
1st reading
1st cycle
Tuesday

This book, which was excluded from the Jewish canon, was written in Hebrew about 200 BC by a certain Ben Sirach, and translated into Greek by his grandson about 130 BC. Ben Sirach (or "the Siracid") is a mixture of bourgeois and pious man, of sophisticate and traditionalist.

Like his predecessors in the tradition of wisdom, he is particularly concerned with individual retribution. The book of Proverbs had given an overly materialist concept of this, which Ecclesiastes and Job, as a result of reflection on suffering, had called in question. Accordingly Ben Sirach does not feel he can contemplate personal retribution without giving an explanation of *trial*.

Misfortune can fall upon the just man as well as the impious (v. 1). But the just man who is confident in the Lord (v. 6), or lives in the fear of God (vv. 7-9), can encounter trial with the assurance that God is accompanying him and purifying him (v. 5) in view of the day of retribution (v. 3).

This teaching was previously put forward by Job. Ben Sirach, however, adds a new note by alluding to the experience of the people and the patriarchs (v. 10; cf. Si 16:5-10; 40-50). This shows that confidence in God under trial has invariably been rewarding.

To fear God under trial does not mean that one sees misfortune as the product of God's power, in the sense that he wills evil or allows it to come as a chastisement and purification of man. Biblical fear of God means a sense of God's presence. Fear during suffering is an interpretation of suffering. It gives suffering a meaning in that God is concerned in it, not by power but by love.

When we have confidence in him during suffering, we are not waiting for him to deliver us. We are accepting the companionship he offers us. We are affirming that despite the ambiguity in the existence of evil and suffering, some meaning can be found in communion between God and man. The Eucharist, following upon the cross, schools us in this fear of God and confidence in him.

V. James   James is disturbed by the evidence of growing
4:1-10   conflicts in the Christian communities and he
1st reading   tries to discern the reasons.
2nd cycle
Tuesday

One of the reasons for *discord* is the desire for pleasure (v. 1; cf. 1:14-15). Doubtless he is thinking of the desire for material goods, money or influence. A second cause is envy (vv. 2-3). One covets what one's neighbor possesses, and in order to get it attacks him. Envy sometimes will even deform prayer. God is used in order to get as much as one's neighbor, as if prayer could be utilized for such selfish ends.

A third cause is love of the world (vv. 4-6). This makes man an "adulterer," because it makes him break the link that binds him to God (cf. Mt 12:39; 16:4). It binds him to earthly goods instead of life with God, as if it were possible to serve two masters at once (cf. Mt 6:24). He reinforces his argument with two scriptural texts (vv. 5-6), the first in a form that is quite difficult to understand. Doubtless his text is corrupt. The second reminds us that God's favors are given only to the humble (cf. Pr 3:34; Si 10:14-15; 1 S 2:7).

He continues his list of causes for discord by mentioning pride (vv. 7-10). This can only be overcome by resisting the devil, drawing near to God like Moses on Sinai (Ex 24:2) or the priest in the temple (Ex 19:22), and purifying the heart (2 Co 7:1; He 9:14). And for all this, humility is necessary (v. 10). A final source of discord is slander, but this is not included in the reading.

We exhibit endless hypocrisy when we allege ideology as the reason for the oppositions and conflicts in the world. It is of course true that different groups have different ideas and views more or

less opposed. When we reflect upon it, however, it is not these
ideas or rival solutions which bring about the conflicts, but the
manner in which they are propounded and the hidden and perhaps unconscious motives that inspire protagonists.

Being human, all of our ideas have their limitations, but, of
themselves, they are neither opposed nor complementary. They
become so because of the personal element. Discords are not between ideas, but between protagonists of ideas. James is perfectly
right to remind us of our psychology, and our inner motivations:
power-seeking, pride, attachment to property, envy of the other's
possessions. Instead of setting up commissions to seek solutions for
many conflicts between men and nations, we might do well to
have the rival groups examine themselves.

VI. Mark
9:30-37
Gospel
Tuesday

For the second time, Jesus tells his disciples of
his imminent passion (v. 31). Simultaneously
he abandons his preaching to the crowds (v.
30) who are definitely incapable of understanding, and devotes himself to the final training of his disciples.

a) The apostles, however, understand scarcely better than the
crowds. A few verses earlier (Mk 9:9-13), Mark has a precise
echo of one of the apostles' discussions. It is the business of Elias
to prepare everything, so that the Messiah will merely have to be
enthroned. Why then a Messiah destined for suffering?

The *incredulity* of the apostles, however, could be resolved.
Scripture could show them how the passion was indicated by a
series of antecedents. Christ's predictions are so thoroughly im-
pregnated with Old Testament allusions that we can actually
identify the texts. The verb "to be delivered" (v. 31) comes from
Isaiah 53:6 and 53:12, implying the whole doctrine of the suffering Servant. The phrase "into the hands of men" (v. 31) is from
Jeremiah 33:24 (or 26:24), thus associating Jesus with the first
great persecuted prophet.

"To suffer much" (v. 31) also probably refers to Isaiah 53:4 and 11, according to an Aramaic targum (to crush), and suggests again the suffering Servant. "To be rejected" (v. 31) recalls the stone rejected by the builders in Psalm 117/118:22 (cf. Ac 4:11; Mk 12:10).

The apostles must have had fairly considerable scriptural knowledge, which enabled them to understand the course events would take.

b) The second topic of the apostles' discussion concerned the imminence of the Kingdom. They were anxious in advance to reserve their places as ministers and counselors to the Messiah (v. 34; cf. Mk 10:35-40). Jesus uses this discussion to point out the conditions for entry to the Kingdom. Not alone must the Messiah suffer to inaugurate the Kingdom; his disciples in turn must present themselves as *servants* (v. 35) and poor (v. 36: the child at that time was considered negligible, the Aramaic word for child being the same as that for servant).

c) We should not, however, get the impression that all these allusions make the discourse artificial. Underlying all the sayings is the common topic of conditions for entry to the Kingdom, and of life within it.

To *enter the Kingdom* one must be as docile as a child. One must be modest (v. 36), that is to say, and not seek the best places (vv. 33-35). Within the Kingdom one must become the servant of all (v. 35), offering one's love to the most despised (v. 37, where we must remember that children were negligible in Israel). This charity will be of special importance for the leaders of the Christian communities. They must not scandalize the little ones, those Christians, that is, who are less knowledgeable concerning the subleties of casuistry and doctrine (v. 42), whose faith could be undermined by theories that are too advanced (cf. Rm 14:1-15:8).

Jesus certainly did not wish to reduce to an infantile level the ethics of the Kingdom. He has in mind a community which respects the child and considers his reactions, but above all he wants his apostles to resemble children in being ready to depend on others. Men, least of all the Christian, cannot pretend to save himself.

Finally, the disciple will be despised as someone feeble without importance, just like the child in Jewish society. He should remember this for him is the way of following Jesus on the journey towards Jerusalem (Mk 9:29-32).

VII. Sirach
4:11-19
1st reading
1st cycle
Wednesday

If it is true that divine wisdom, the secret of things and persons, is attainable (Si 1:10), how can one know it?

In the schools of the sages is the author's answer. He is thinking of these when he makes his eulogy educative wisdom (vv. 11-15). No book, however, and no teaching can supply for the existential experience of *search* (vv. 16-18), across the hazards of confusion and anguish, blind alleys and tortuous ways. Nothing is worse than believing that one is born with the truth, or that one can acquire it once for all. To be a sage is to be ready to learn, but to be also ready to question everything, to see one's certitudes vanish without dismay. It is to accept one's limits and confusions without succumbing to false solutions or resting in false security. Instead of believing, at each wrong turning, that one has reached the limit of search, the sage will continue the struggle. Wisdom beckons in front; it will not fail the one who remains faithful.

VIII. James
4:13-17
1st reading
2nd cycle
Wednesday

James continues with his examination of the attitudes adopted by different Christians to discover the obstacles presented by living to the faith. From the beginning of chapter 4, he has in view the poor who have nothing and want possessions (vv. 1-12), merchants who have possessions and want more (vv. 13-17), the rich who possess much and yet are incapable of aiding the poor. Our reading today concerns the second group.

James is addressing himself to Christian merchants of Jewish origin, who since the Babylonian exile had within their number a large group of international dealers (for instance: Priscilla and Aquila, Ac 18:3). James does not condemn their avocation, but he does condemn the *presumption* on which it rests which induces people to invest and arrange dividends without remembering that life is short (vv. 13-14; cf. Lk 12:16-21).

The concept of the transience and vanity of life is deep in wisdom literature (Jb 14:2; Ps 101/102:4, 12). The presumption which ignores these facts is no more characteristic really of business than of other professions. It consists in a lack of dependence on God, which is basically opposed to the spirit of faith (v. 15). Where one's treasure is, there is the heart also. If discussion of one's business has no reference to God, then one ceases to take account of God. A hardening in this attitude will mean that sin is entering our life (v. 17).

James of course is addressing all Christians, whatever their state, as well as the merchants. If attachment to one's profession, one's social state, one's work, becomes an absolute, then the horizon is limited and there is no place for the attitude of faith. Faith is something adventitious in one's life that does not color the whole. There is not really any Christian ethic of business. All Christians nowadays are capable of determining the just conditions for the people and principles involved. The Christian, in other words, does not bring any new solutions for the ethics of whatever profession he follows. His witness is on a broader basis: that of salvation, and openness to the Kingdom of God. His faith does not dispense him from terrestrial obligations. On the contrary, it increases the ambit of his cooperation. He is armed against selfishness, and can see all things in relation to the final end.

IX. Mark
9:38-40
Gospel
Wednesday

In the midst of a particularly composite discourse, concerning the conditions for entry to the Kingdom, these verses form a parenthesis, which stands by itself. Probably it was the theme of the "name" of Jesus in welcoming little ones (v. 37) that gave us this series of sayings about the name of Jesus in preaching.

Our passage is concerned with the supernatural efficacy of the *name of Jesus* in exorcisms (cf. Lk 10:17; Mt 7:22-23; Ac 3:6; 16:18, 19:13). Throughout the apostolic age this usage in expelling demons is particularly well attested. It is not a magical formula; calling on the name of Jesus always presupposes faith (v. 39; cf. Lk 4:7-12). It is an affirmation that the thaumaturge is not acting in his own name but is relying on the salvific power of Jesus. To call upon Jesus' name with faith makes his actual person present and active. Faith, not particular formalities, releases this power. That is why the apostles must not be scandalized to see the name of Jesus produce effects outside their own particular ambit.

X. Sirach
5:1-8
1st reading
1st cycle
Thursday

Ben Sirach is convinced of God's presence in the texture of human life. On this point he is less pessimistic than Qoheleth and less troubled than Job.

The presence is particularly important where the sinner is concerned. If God leaves him unpunished and does not chastise his infidelity in this life (v. 3) it is to grant him a respite, so that he will be converted and able to lead a happy life.

But the sinner must not fall into any *presumption.* He must not ask himself what sin he could have committed in order to suffer as he does (v. 4), or challenge the limitless patience of God by trust in his riches (v. 1), or over-bidding in evil (vv. 5-6).

Sin becomes definitely irretrievable when it is coupled with presumption. Scripture constantly stigmatizes hardened and presumptuous hearts, while, especially in the New Testament, it displays extraordinary benevolence towards the sinner who acknowledges his weakness. Indeed presumption seems to arise precisely from the fear of lapsing. The sinner will not recognize himself for what he is and prefers the false security of his own resources to the humble avowal of inadequacy. Failure, even moral failure, is part of the human predicament. Which of us would dare claim the ideals of the sermon on the mount (Mt 5:21, 28, 39; 6:19; 7:1)? Failure or success are really relative terms, relative to ideals. If one fails according to the standards of one's hopes or ideals, at least it can be said that one is confronted by the basic lesson of one's poverty. And this lesson of failure (even if it is as decisive as the divorced person remarried) makes room for a new start.

Presumption lies essentially in the refusal to open ourselves up to the poverty that can bring renewal. It is also to be found in those people who judge the sinner incapable of surmounting his failure, and excommunicate him. The combination of the two presumptions, the sinner's own, and that of society which excommunicates him, creates a situation of death from the failure of a moment. The sinner grows more hardened, and all possibility of recovery is lost. Christ was the first to reject the notion of a situation of death (Lk 19:10). Would there were many more to follow him.

XI. James   With a vehemence worthy of the ancient
    5:1-6   prophets, concerning injustices by the rich.
   1st reading   James now turns upon those who are so at-
   2nd cycle   tached to their goods (vv. 2-3) that they will
   Thursday   not even pay their workers properly (v. 4)
                 and oppress people less fortunate than them-
selves.

The style he adopts is that of prophetic invective. He tells the
rich to howl, so overwhelming are the misfortunes that threaten
them (v. 1). Less strong language doubtless would be insufficient
to penetrate hearts so hardened (cf. previously Am 8:3).

The chastisement is already here; James uses verbs in the perfect. Disaster is imminent and it is only the rich who are unaware.
The corruption of gold and riches, however, (vv. 2-3) will yield
to the devouring fire of the consumer.

The sin of these rich was failure to pay their workers (v. 4),
despite the pressing injunctions of the law (Lv 19:13; Dt 24:15)
and the prophets (Ml 3:5; Si 31:4; 34:21-27). At the time, this
was one of the quickest roads to wealth, and often tribunals (v.
6), because of shabby procedure and the venality of judges,
allowed the just and the innocent to be despoiled in favor of large
fortunes (cf. the vineyard of Naboth, 1 K 21).

Chastisement will be proportioned to the fault. For the life of
a poor man taken the rich man will pay with his own life; like
an over-fattened swine he will be disembowelled (v. 5).

Though James is very extreme in his sarcasm and invective, he
is only repeating a classic teaching of the gospels (Lk 12:16-21;
16:19-31; 6:24). He is not dealing with the moderately wealthy
who have increased their holding slowly, by fair means and by
hard work. These are the great money-magnates. Such people are
no different today. We have huge proprietors in Latin America
and Africa, who have been enabled to batten on the backs of the
poor by a little political intrigue. They will shout (v. 1) to the

heavens about persecution because a "leftist" regime confiscates their property. We have capitalist companies who dictate the economy of a country at a distance and keep workers under stone age conditions so that some wealthy may prosper. We have social-ized states who appropriate all the wealth of a country, and use it to promote interests that are not always those of human beings.

XII. Mark   The whole discourse from verse 33 to verse 50
    9:41-50   is particularly composite. Jesus has spoken of
    Gospel   the necessity for the apostles to become "ser-
    Thursday   vants" (v. 35). This word suggests the idea of
    "child" (v. 36), because both words were the
same in Aramaic; and Jesus speaks of the need to welcome chil-dren "in his name" (v. 37). From this comes the topic of the use made of the name of Jesus (vv. 38-41). The theme of "children" returns, and we have a new development about the scandal of little ones (v. 42). "Scandal" again brings in the matter of pun-ishment for those who cause it (vv. 43-48). The punishment is one of "fire," which suggests the *logion* about the faithful "salted by fire" (v. 49); and finally comes the saying about "salt" itself (v. 50).

We are clearly then dealing with a series of *logia* that oral tra-dition has combined in a more or less coherent whole. In order not to lose the thread of thought, it had to rely on associated key-words. There is no doubt of course that these are the very words of Jesus, but they are organized to illustrate the topic of *entry to and life within the Kingdom.* Attempts have been made, not with-out some success, to reconstruct the discourse anterior to oral tradition. It would be somewhat as follows.

To enter the Kingdom one must have the disposition of a child —littleness and dependence, that is. One must also be converted and pray to the Father. Within the Kingdom, one must continue to practice *littleness* by becoming the servant of all (Mk 9:33-37), and being humble as a child (v. 35). One must extend one's charity likewise to the weakest (children, v. 37), and to disciples (v. 41), to whom hospitality is due in particular. In determining who is the true disciple one must not be too severe in criteria (vv. 38-40). Charity must also be extended to the little ones, ordinary Christians who are not versed in the subtleties of casuistry and doctrine (v. 42). Scandal given to these is particularly reprehensible, above all if it be given by the leaders of the community.

Finally, the disciple in the Kingdom must be merciless towards himself if he discovers in himself any moral failing (vv. 42-48). Everyone will be tried at the last judgment. It is better than to test in advance what is good in oneself (the salt of charity, v. 50) than to wait for the judgment.

XIII. Sirach **6:5-17** *1st reading* *1st cycle* *Friday*	Ben Sirach finds the theme of friendship congenial. Wealthy and cultivated as he was, he doubtless came to know many friends who veered between loyalty and interest. Thus he knows the pitfalls of friendship, but can be greatly moved by it. There is no doubt that he

has had much personal experience in this domain, but he is also otherwise informed and uses occasionally a book that he knew well: the Wisdom of Ahigar (cf. v. 7; Ahigar no. 17 and 178).

He knows that wealth attracts friends. He tests friends, and sifts out the interested (vv. 5-13; cf. Si 8:18-19; 2:8-13; 37:1-5). His criteria for true *friendship* are two: loyalty during trial (v. 7; cf. Si 9:10; 22:23-26) and above all common love of God (vv. 16-17).

All this is rather a far cry from the depth of some great spiritual friendships of the Christian era. Ben Sirach clearly remains on the exterior level and only gives himself to his friends after the manner of a proprietor prudently sharing his goods. Though he rightly discerns that the horizontal dimension of friendship must be complemented by a vertical, the fear of God that he expects from his friends is more a guarantee of probity than a source of sharing. Jesus will reveal that there is no true friendship unless one is able to die to oneself and to life itself for one's friends (cf. Jn 15:13).

XIV. James   Having dealt with the rich, James now turns
5:9-12   toward his "brothers" (v. 7), the poor. He re-
1 reading   quires them to be patient in awaiting the com-
2nd cycle   ing of the Lord (vv. 8-11), and counsels them
Friday   not to swear (v. 12).

a) He asks for *patience* from the poor. He does not urge them to revolt, because, as he sees it, the economic system of the rich is already so corrupt that very soon it will collapse. This catastrophe will seem like a coming of the Lord (v. 8) because the wicked will be condemned and the poor enabled to recover liberty and happiness. Perhaps he is referring to the actual fall of Jerusalem (70 AD), of which there were premonitions at the time of writing.

The future is a motive for patience; but so is the past, with its numerous examples of courage and endurance under trial (v. 10). Here he uses a consideration classic in Jewish and Christian writing: a eulogy of the patriarchs meant to encourage the faith of his contemporaries (Si 40-50; He 11; Mt 5:12; 23-34, etc.)

b) The *judgment* destined to overwhelm the rich can fall upon the poor too, unless they show themselves charitable (v. 9), keep their engagements (v. 12; cf. Mt 5:34-36; 23:16-22), are, in a word sincere in all their social relations.

XV. Mark   Mark's version of the discussion between Jesus
10:1-12   and the Pharisees concerning divorce differs
Gospel   slightly from that of Matthew 19:1-9. He in-
Friday   sists rather more than Matthew on the law of
                  nature, taking account doubtless of readers

who would be insufficiently familiar with Jewish jurisprudence or
the Word of God. He thus says (v. 6) that "God *made* them male
and female," where Matthew refers to a "word" of God to Adam
and Eve (Mt 19:5). And, while Matthew distinguishes the law
of Moses from that which is merely tolerated by Moses (Mt
19:7-8), Mark gives us the direct will of God (v. 9). Finally, by
disregarding the precision of Mt 19:9, he avoids a serious difficulty in interpreting Jesus' meaning, as he sees it man cannot
destroy a unity that is part of nature.

There are three stages in this version of the discussion. In commenting on Deuteronomy 24:1, the Pharisees had considerably
widened the reasons for separation, but they did not agree about
the list of causes (cf. Mt 19:3). The evangelist does not give us
these discussions. He merely assumes that the Pharisees came to
ask Jesus if it was permissible to repudiate one's wife. That would
be a fairly astonishing question, seeing that Deuteronomy 24:1
admitted the possibility. On this point Mark does not have the
original text.

He takes the Pharisees to be referring to the law itself (v. 4).
Jesus tells them that this prescript should be abolished and a solution sought in God's will, which is written in nature (Gn 1:27;
2:24). According to this, man and woman must stay together. No
man, not even Moses, can interfere with the *fundamental unity
of the couple* (vv. 11-12).

Mark's doctrine then is clear. Marriage is more than a free contract between two persons. It involves the will of God which is
inscribed in the complementarity of the sexes; the mere will of the
spouses is not sufficient to explain the unity of marriage; God's
will is there too. That is why divorce is not merely a wrong against
the forsaken spouse; it is an injustice to God himself. We can
always ask the question, of course, whether the human wills are
to that point lucid that they really undertake a genuine natural

union with all that implies, and thus engage too the will of God.

XVI. Sirach   Here we have a reflection by Ben Sirach on
  17:1-15   the first chapters of Genesis. He is the first bib-
  1st reading   lical author to treat them so extensively.
  1st cycle
  Saturday   His principal idea appears to be the *unity* of
        the cosmos around about man (vv. 2-4) which
is guaranteed by man's submission to the law (vv. 5-8, 11, 14).
The viewpoint is probably of stoic origin. Where Greek philosophy, however, made human reason the nucleus of cosmic unity
(cf. intelligence theme in v. 7), Ben Sirach introduces the notion
of fidelity to the law. He makes reason the instrument of submission to God's will and the means of ratifying his covenant.

Man's role in nature furthermore transcends that of reason and
the law. He lends his voice to all creation for the praise of God
(vv. 10, 13).

His vision of creation and of man's role in creation is optimist.
The human role is at three levels. First of all he is the organizer
of nature over which he has all power; by virtue of this he is
image of God (v. 3). For Ben Sirach, the technique employed by
man to dominate the world is a presence of God in the world, the
sign of his energy, and the object of that "wonder" which creation
manifests before God himself (v. 4). If he lived in our time, he
would have no difficulty in seeing God's presence in the triumphs
of science and technology.

Secondly, the human role is ethical. It will not be sufficient to
conquer space and install gas and electricity in every house. The
annihilation of distance will mean little if man continues to be
separated from his brother, if violence issues from his heart and
guides his hand, if peace is but a myth of which people talk without result. It is not by intelligence that man will spiritualize the

world, but rather by a victory over himself, by the free exercise of love.

Ben Sirach adds a third dimension to man's role in creation, that of religion. It is his business to "bind" creation to God by praise and thanksgiving. Praise in this sense is already implicit at the previous levels (Rm 12:1). The Christian is convinced of his royal priesthood and of God's participation in his endeavors. But there are times when it should be explicit, times such as those when the liturgy proposes a "Mass for the world."

These three human functions in our day are rather overturned. Man is about to succeed in the first. He has humanized the universe, liberated himself from the sacral, and triumphed over things, time and space. This victory, however, has proved alienating even when it seemed to have reached the goal. Technology has not given us corresponding humanism; humanity is still in its alienated, infantile stage. For the humanism we need, some profound revolution, a reshaping of human structures, especially cultural structures, will be required.

The third human function is religious. Here too we are in crisis, to some extent because the liturgy offered man, shaped by men themselves, is still too associated with an epoch when man had not mastered nature. We shall only recover man's true liturgical medium when he comes to realize the basic character of his new existence in the world and his stature before God.

XVII. James
5:13-20
1st reading
2nd cycle
Saturday

This is the conclusion of James' letter. He is considering the circumstances of prayer, joyous or painful, as for instance sickness (vv. 14-15) or sin (v. 16), individual or collective.

a) His treatment of the topic of *prayer* resembles considerably, in viewpoint and language, that of Matthew (cf. Jm 4:2-3 and Mt 7:7-8). First he considers the case of sickness. From now on this is subject to Christ's messianic power, exercised by the community through anointing and prayer. Anointing (v. 14) was a procedure well known in all Mediterranean countries (cf. Mk 6:13; Lk 10:34 for the New Testament), and formed part of the magic ritual of many religions. In Christianity the efficacy of the oil is not magical. It depends on the invocation of the name of Jesus (cf. Ac 3:6) and is accompanied by the "prayer of faith." The power lies in the faith of the petitioners (Jm 5:14) rather than in the formula pronounced.

Next he considers the case of sin. The mutual confession and prayer to which he refers can be understood in a cultic context. We have numerous prayers which confess to God the sins either of the psalmist or the people as a whole (Dn 9:1-19; Ba 1:1-52; 8; Jdt 9:1-14), and they are often concluded by a thanksgiving for the pardon received (Gn 32:9-12; 152:1-10; Is 38:9-10; Tb 8:15-17; Si 51:1-12; Pss 21/22; 31/32; 39/40; 50/51; 115/116; Jb 33:26-28). What is original in James, by contrast with the Old Testament, is the concept of public mutual confession.

James sees this kind of prayer as efficacious, as the prayer of Elias was (cf. Jm 5:15-17); it is a means whereby the believer can bring to bear the very power of God.

b) Prayer for sin is accompanied by *mutual confession* of sins (v. 16). The community then, the Christian assembly, itself had the power of pardon, and this is perfectly in accord with Matthew 18:15-18. There are other texts, however, formulated in the same terms, which seem to contradict these two, the power being reserved to the apostles (Mt 16:19; Jn 20:23). In the case of the Supper, we have a similar apparent contradiction. 1 Corinthians 11:23-28 envisages it as a community ceremony without any reference to ministers, while Matthew 26:26-29 contemplates action by a minister with the necessary gestures.

The opposition of these two groups of texts has sometimes been used to the detriment of the power of the assembly as such. A false notion of the relation between the priesthood of the people and the ministerial priesthood has been the reason. Today it seems better to say that the two traditions are really complementary, both in their fashion contemplating the same reality. The assembly as such, living and structured, is the repository of the Messiah's powers, including that over sin. But this has to be communicated through the "service" of priests. Thus when an assembly gathers for instance for a penance celebration, as recommended in verse 16, it does not come merely to witness the exercise of powers exclusive to the minister or the president. It is rather a matter of the minister requiring the assembly for the exercise of his charism, so that the presence of the pardoning Messiah may be assured.

James' teaching about prayer is the primitive teaching and resembles in its simplicity that of the synoptics. Many details are lacking concerning both prayers, that of the sick and that for sinners. It may be that little attention was paid to this aspect because the last times were iminent and the only proper means of living them and being saved was prayer.

Nowadays the average Christian does not have a particularly good sense of the link between prayer and actual living. Very often he prays in established formulas that have no reference to daily life.

Jesus of course has given us the true key to prayer; he is always praying as his Father's partner (cf. Jn 11:41-42; 17). The Christian too can always be in prayer insofar as he considers himself the partner of God. He will discern God's presence in the pattern of events and recognize his own role in salvation history.

The greatest evidences of human frailty are sickness and sin. Yet once they are associated through prayer with the death of Christ, they can lead a man to the discovery that he is God's partner in universal salvation. In the Eucharist above all we can give thanks and confess sins, intercede for the sick and pray for the general pardon of sin.

XVIII. Mark
10:13-16
Gospel
Saturday

All the synoptics give us, between the second (Mk 9:30-32) and the third (Mk 10:32-34) predictions of the Passion, a series of texts concerned with the conditions of entry to the Kingdom. In that Jesus himself only enters it by the road of suffering and death, clearly his disciples too must be denuded in order to achieve it.

The principal beneficiaries of the Kingdom are voluntary eunuchs (Mt 19:10-12, not in Mark), children, those negligible beings (Mk 10:13-16), the poor (Mk 10:17-27) and those who have learned detachment (Mk 10:28-31).

Mark's vision of the scene is extremely personal. He is the only one to show us Jesus becoming offended with the disciples (v. 14) and embracing children (v. 16). These traits doubtless seemed too human for Matthew and Luke.

As Matthew sees it entry to the Kingdom is promised to those who are converted and become like *children* (Mt 18:3). He is in fact very close to the doctrine of John 3:5. One must be born again to a new life in order to enter.

The condition for entry put forward by Mark is different (v. 15). The Kingdom is offered to men and must be welcomed with the freshness and simplicity of a child who neither reasons nor calculates, but gives himself altogether without hesitation. Mark's attitude is psychological, whereas Matthew's is ontological.

Christ's reception of children then cannot be regarded as a recommendation of infantilism, or another vain search for primeval innocence. What he is recommending is the adult attitude which acknowledges limitations and accepts dependence upon God with interdependence between men. It is an attitude which gives due place to reason, but employs all the person, the heart included, in the quest for faith. The child, who acts with all his being, is in the final analysis more human and more integral than the thinker who becomes entangled in arguments and worry about motives.

EIGHTH SUNDAY

A. THE WORD

**I. Isaiah
49:14-15
1st reading
1st cycle**
The future depicted by Second-Isaiah for his contemporaries, in order to console them in exile, had to be depicted in symbolic terms, so as not to attract notice from the oppressor. Thus the image of a child, repudiated by its mother, who recovers love and happiness was quite safe. What pagan, ignorant of Scripture, could discern here the promise of a new covenant?

a) For a Jew, however, the image was particularly rich. Previously Hosea had likened Israel's infidelity to that of an adulterous spouse (Ho 2:14-15), but already for him the punishment could only be passing and had the purpose of bringing back the unfaithful one (Ho 2:16-25). Thus God's love is faithful and is its own justification. It is an uncalculating love extended to someone unworthy of it, simply for love's sake.

After centuries Second-Isaiah takes up again this image. God is faithful in *love* and pardons his spouse or his child (Is 47:1-3; 50:1; 51:17—52:2; 54:1-5; 49:17-22). Life can regain once more the climate of love and fruitfulness, and the covenant can be restored.

b) Second Isaiah's theology and his *monotheist* faith give this theme of the recovered wife or child a particularly new orientation. When a husband repudiated his wife he could not take her back again. All she could do was to go to those who had seduced her. Likewise rupture between parents and children was irretrievable; the maledictions pronounced in these cases being indelible. But because God was unique, his spouse could not go to other suitors, nor his child to another mother. If life were to continue, he would have to pardon both. In this pardon he was once more manifesting his superiority over Gentile gods.

II. Hosea	Hosea lived in the northern kingdom in the

II. **Hosea**
2:16-17,
21-22
1st reading
2nd cycle

Hosea lived in the northern kingdom in the 8th century, at a time when world politics were tending to obliterate smaller kingdoms. His role is to show the presence of God in the midst of these human political upheavals.

His basic insight is that the disappearance of the northern kingdom is linked to the Canaanization and decadence of its religion. Baalism is having a disintegrating influence on the people's minds and vitality. Only by a return to firm monotheism, can they regain stability and their proper role in the world.

a) Today's passage is concerned with the theme of return to the pristine monotheist fidelity. By prolonging it a little (to verse 25) one can discern three distinct oracles, each introduced by the phrase "on that day."

The first is an invective against Baal. His very name will become so shameful that people will hesitate to use it (chiefly, doubtless, in the formation of proper names). Men will be delivered, that is to say, from tutelage to a *God of nature* and will hold free dialogue with the God of liberty, mold history with him, and thus take their proper place in the turbulent stream of events.

b) This free encounter between God and a humanity delivered from Baalism will result in a *new covenant*. Here we have the theme of the second oracle (vv. 20-22). The first result of this covenant will be the realization of peace (symbolized by the taming of savage animals; cf. Is 2:4; 11:6-8; 65:25; Ze 9:10; Ez 34:25). The covenant will take the form of a "betrothal" where the spouses exchange gifts. The husband (God) brings justice and right, fidelity and mercy, pledges that the covenant will be maintained. The wife (Israel) brings knowledge of God, humanity's readiness to live in communion with God.

c) The third oracle contemplates the content of the covenant (vv. 23-25). It is compared with the continuous mutual response between persons. We note that the response takes place between natural elements: from heaven to earth, from earth to wheat, from wheat to Israel, etc. This is a way of affirming that the personal covenant between God and man will have a *cosmic dimension,* achieving harmony in the elements and placing them at the service of men, something that the cult of Baal had not succeeded in doing.

In using the name of the person, Israel, to describe the country of Israel, the author reminds us that this plain was both the richest granary in the Promised Land, and the place of battle where the royal house had played its final card before succumbing to slavery about 733. Thus it is at the very scene of failure that the covenant will come to fruition. God himself will "fecundate" his spouse in a dialogue of love.

In our day, what corresponds to Baal is man's mastery over nature. This can be just as alienating as pretechnological man's fear before nature. We can see this at work for instance in the one-dimensional communist societies. Hosea is a prophet for the 20th century in that he insists that human mastery of nature is the result not of human lust for domination and conquest but of free and gratuitous encounter with the divine, which is unpredictable and not to be manipulated.

III. Sirach For Ben Sirach speech has the same impor-
   27:5-8 tance as Matthew 7:16; 15:18 or James 3.
   1st reading
   3rd cycle The *Word* reveals the bottom of the heart and
       betrays it even when people try to conceal it
(vv. 4-6). The mark of the sage is to be able so to master his

language that he becomes known only to the wise, and to allow the other to speak sufficiently long so that his heart can be judged (v. 7).

Our passage is just a brief echo of a teaching to which Sirach attaches great importance. He knows all the sins of the tongue; the quarrels it provokes (Si 8:1-19; 28:8-12), the hasty oaths (Si 23:7-15), the lies and gossip (Si 20-24-26; 19:4-12), and above all else the duplicity (Si 5:14—6:1; 28:13-16).

Speech then belongs to a man's innermost core. It reveals his force and vitality, his spirit and his purpose. If speech be allowed to issue without engaging the core of the person, this is not only sin but a serious dichotomy and disequilibrium. Our modern culture, so much influenced by publicity and propaganda, alienates speech. It detaches it from its human roots and makes it such a pawn in a chaotic game that language loses its quality of communication. Language does not now join persons together. Masses of people are gathered together in an immense tower of Babel, who fancy they are using the same vocabulary and speaking the same language. Not alone is the heart revealed by the word now. The very heart of a civilization in decay is revealed.

IV. 1 Corinthians
4:1-5
2nd reading
1st cycle

When they were converted, the Corinthian Christians received the doctrine of the Lord, but they also became attached to the particular mentality of certain preachers. The Good News is always liable to be linked with personal preoccupations and concepts. This results in different choices by the faithful, even when it stops short of parties, cabals and factions. The universalism of the message may be jeopardized. Having devoted a long discussion to the matter, Saint Paul, in our passage, is reaching his conclusion.

First of all, he points out that preachers are no more than the "agents" of the gospel; they are "stewards" who have no right to alter the matter they are treating. They must be "faithful servants. This theme of *service* to the mysteries of God is highly important in the first Christian theology of the priesthood. It forms the inspiration for many of the Lord's sayings about the apostles' role after his departure. They will have to administer the blessings of the Father and be the guardians of his family while he is absent (Mt 24:45-51; 25:14-30; 20:24-28).

Secondly, Paul goes on to mention the account the apostle will have to render at the judgment. Here he takes the same viewpoint as the parable of the stewards (Mt 24:45-51). The test of all the steward's "service" will be, not the sympathy he wins or the success he encounters, but essentially the appreciation he receives from the head of the household on his return.

V. 2 Corinthians   Saint Paul continues the apologia for his min-
3:17—4:2   istry. His principal point is the contrast he
2nd reading   makes between the two covenants and their
2nd cycle   respective ministers (2 Co 3:11-16), and his
                    insistence on the lordship of Christ, the pivotal
figure in the change from one covenant to the other (2 Co 3:17-18).

a) The ministers of the old covenant are far from possessing the confidence and hardihood of those of the new. They are under the veil of Moses, because they have only an obscure knowledge of the Word they proclaim, and because the people they address have hardened hearts.

Conversion to Christ is the only way of dispelling this veil (v. 16). Only he who has fulfilled the Old Testament and revealed the end of the law can free the heart and the intelligence of their blindness (v. 17).

b) The basic difference then between the covenants is that between the pilgrimage and the goal. If it seems a chasm and a contrast, this is not due to the essence of the covenants but to the attitude adopted by the Jews. Conversion alone makes it clear that the difference is merely a distinction.

The Lord in verse 17 indicates God (as in Ex 34:34 which is always in the background of our passage), not Christ. Paul's idea is clear. Like Moses, he is demanding that the Jews be converted to the Lord Yahweh, but he knows that in reality the conversion will be to the *Spirit* promised by Jeremiah 31:31. In fact the Lord Yahweh of Exodus 34:34 is one with the Spirit of the new covenant. And just as Yahweh transfigured the face of Moses, the Spirit will illumine those that turn to him.

c) In verse 18 we have a few difficulties. The basic idea is simple. In the Old Testament the illumination of Moses by the Lord was the privilege of a single person and it was passing. Now it is the privilege of all Christians. However, neither under the new or old covenant can man see God directly (Gn 32:30; Dt 4:33; 5:24-26; Is 6:5). He sees him indirectly "as in a mirror." The new then is not superior to the old by reason of a direct vision of God. The superiority lies in the fact that, indirect as it is, the vision is now available in a permanent fashion to everyone.

The mirror by means of which the Christian reaches a knowledge of God and is gradually transformed, is Christ himself. In him the glory of the Lord God can be contemplated.

d) Having analyzed the two covenants, Paul returns to the qualities of the Christian minister. He emphasizes above all the *confidence* (v. 1) which characterizes the minister of the light, by contrast with the shame and silence of the ministry of Moses, who had to veil his face as a precaution against saying everything (v. 2). Paul realizes, of course, that this confidence does not guarantee him complete success; a great many of his hearers refuse to believe in his gospel. To this objection his answer is that he is neither more nor less privileged than Moses. The veil is not something interposed by the message or the minister; it is the blindness in the hearers' hearts (v. 3).

VI. 1 Corinthians This passage brings to a conclusion the
15:54-58 apostles' long disquisition on the manner of
2nd reading bodily resurrection. There is special considera-
3rd cycle tion of the manner of transformation in the
case of those who will be still living at this
moment (vv. 51-53), and there is a doxology to chapter 15 as a
whole (vv. 54-57).

The problem in the earlier verses is still Jewish in nature. If
the *resurrection of the body* is a necessary preliminary stage in
the restoration of the Kingdom, what is to be the case of those
still living at this time? Must they die before being raised up?
Paul answers, no. Ressurrection is a means, not an end in itself.
The thing that counts really is sharing the glorious, incorruptible
life of the Lord. In that bodily resurrection is merely a stage,
those living will evidently be dispensed from it. The transformation they will experience will be one whereby their physical
body, hitherto moved by the soul, will become "pneumatic,"
henceforth moved by the Spirit (1 Co 15:44).

Another Jewish aspect of the piece is the reference to resurrection ceremonial, particularly to the final trumpet (already mentioned in 1 Th 4:13-18). The trumpet is the special instrument for
convoking the tribes of Israel to great festive assemblies (cf. Nb
29:1-6; Lv 23:23-25) and the instrument for acclaiming the expected messianic king (Nb 23:21; 1 K 1:34-40). The actual image
of course need not necessarily be insisted on. Its deep meaning is
clear. The resurrection of the body is a collective phenomenon,
the first stage in the great assembly, the sign of the new people.

In this specific Jewish context however, Paul puts forward a
teaching that is specifically Christian. The resurrection expected
by the Jews was at bottom a sort of recovery of the physical body,
that would share a kingdom which was in itself material. The
paschal mystery has enabled Paul to transcend this view. The
resurrection will be more than recovery in this sense; it will be
transformation, and the attainment by our body of the state of

Christ's glorified body. So that the Christian idea differs from the rabbinic. Paul's concept is the result of the Christian concept of "being with Christ." The resurrection being more than the resuscitation of a dead body, access to a new spiritual corporeity, it is naturally a transformation for the living as well as the dead. They will both "be with Christ" in whatever state the Parousia finds them.

The concluding doxology could very well be the hymn on the lips of the risen ones after their victory over death and sin. It is the hymn of all humanity at last attaining the promised state.

We should take care not to get lost in the maze of questions concerning the manner of bodily resurrection. At the beginning of chapter 15 Paul has clearly stated the fact of our resurrection in union with Christ. He has also stated that the mystery, like that of Christ's own resurrection transcends human understanding. No one can speak of resurrection except those who have arisen. Saint Paul, pressured by the Corinthians' questions, does try one or other explanation occasionally, but these are really in the order of hypothesis and do not touch the root of the problem. Or they do so only insofar as they stress the solidarity between Christ and men, and the continuity between "being with Jesus" and "resurrection."

VII. Matthew
6:24-34
Gospel
1st cycle

This lesson in detachment could well form the conclusion to the parable of the foolish rich man who gathered stores into his granaries that death was to filch from him (Lk 12:16-20). Luke in fact does follow that parable with a somewhat similar text, where birds are mentioned who do not "gather in granaries." In Luke then, and probably in the original context, there was an antithesis between the "uneasiness" of the rich man and the "detachment" of the birds.

Matthew, however, joins with these counsels about detachment a sentence about the impossibility of serving two masters: God and Mammon. There is of course a difference between "serving Mammon" and being concerned about what one will eat. The latter can be a very sensible procedure, far from slavery to Mammon. Matthew was doubtless anxious to stress the importance of the sermon on the mount by adding several other counsels to it, in not quite satisfactory order. By placing one of these sayings where he does, he makes it appear more harsh and intransigent than Jesus meant it to be.

Accordingly the teaching of the piece is double. On the one hand it stresses the impossibility of serving two masters at once (v. 24). On the other it presents the Christian attitude towards unease (vv. 25-33). In the first case Jesus is addressing the rich (see the context in which Luke places the sentence 16:1-9, 13-15). In the second he is speaking to the poor, who are in danger of being disturbed by their distress and of losing their freedom of spirit. The message of the gospel, however, is single. Whether we be rich or poor, our lives are oriented towards the Kingdom. This basic direction cannot be jeopardized by other preoccupations.

a) The service of God cannot *be shared* Dt 6:13; 10:20; 11:13). The option of faith* demands an interior attitude of freedom where everything else is concerned, especially anything that could attach us to the world (cf. Qo 5:9-16; 1 Tm 6:10).

b) If God watches with solicitude over creatures so frail as the birds and the flowers which are insignificant, what care will he not exhibit for creatures with the dignity of men who collaborate in his work. Jesus releases people from their uneasiness (but he does not recommend them to be as thoughtless as the birds) in order that they can give themselves more wholly to the quest for the Kingdom (vv. 31-33). At this point he introduces the term "Father," showing that their natural uneasiness ought to be allayed by their filial state. For the benefit of those whose unease can only be allayed by material sharing in the Kingdom, Matthew

* See the doctrinal theme: *option of faith,* p. 341.

adds to Jesus' saying "and its justice" (as previously in Mt 5:6, 10). He wants to point out that the full palliative for unease can only be attained by observance of this new justice, that is being defined in the beatitudes and the sermon on the mount.

c) This passage is one of the first to be concerned with the *fatherhood of God*. We should examine the meaning given by Jesus and Matthew to this concept. In the Old Testament and Judaism it had never occupied more than a very secondary place (cf. Ex 4:22-23; Is 63:16; Mt 1:31; Jr 4:22; Is 45:10, etc.). At least we only find it to describe the personal, ethical relations between God and his chosen people, never in the philosophical relation between creator and creature. Those Old Testament texts which do speak of fatherhood will not consider God in his aspects of power and authority, but of love and solicitude (Ho 11:1; Dt 1:31; Jr 3:19-22; 31:9-20; Pss 67/68:6; 102/103). It is a theme almost exclusively confined to prayers.

Matthew's treatment belongs to this context. He only speaks of divine fatherhood in sentiments of ethical import (the bond with Christian perfection; Mt 6:1-6, 16-18), or in prayers (Mt 6:9; 7:7-11; 6:14-15).

The counsel in fact seems to belong to a totally different context, where there is question of the solicitude of the creator for the creature, as in Matthew 5:45. Confining ourselves to the framework of Jewish thought however, the concept is not philosophic, but seen in terms of salvation history. The Jews had made creation the symbol of their election, and were always to use nature in celebrating the happiness that would be theirs according to God's promise (Ps 102/103).

Accordingly, though one cannot altogether disregard the idea of pholosophic paternity (v. 34) in this passage, it must be admitted that the idea of election is predominant in verse 26. Man is said to be superior to the birds because he is dedicated to the service of God, just as in verse 30 the phrase "people of little faith" indicates the disciples in their personal relationship with Christ (as in Mt 8:26; 14:31; 16:8; 17:20). Likewise, in verse 32, the attitude concerning uneasiness is in contrast with the Gentile attitude. So that, here, the concept of God's fatherhood is to be seen against the background of the particular covenant in which God communicates his love to "his own."

VIII. Mark At this stage Jesus is just at the beginning of
    2:18-22 his career as rabbi. Yet already his regimen for
    Gospel his disciples is a source of scandal for the
    2nd cycle crowds; it has nothing in common with the
    discipline of other rabbis. The disciples of
the Baptist and those of the Pharisees observe certain days of fast, but those of Jesus seem to dispense themselves (v. 18). The question at issue is the independence displayed by Jesus and his disciples where traditional observances are concerned. They are always unworried about the Sabbath (the episode immediately following our passage: Mk 2:23-27), or the ablution rubrics (Mk 7:1-23). Jesus justifies this by an affirmation about the presence of the spouse (vv. 19-20), and by two short parables.

a) Fast in the Old Testament, and in Judaism generally, was connected with the wait for the Messiah's coming. To abstain from food and wine, characteristic traits of the nazirite state (Lk 22:14-20), indicated dissatisfaction with the present time and impatience for the coming consolation of Israel. John the Baptist in particular had made this a basic principle of his message (Lk 1:15). Thus when Jesus and his disciples dispensed themselves from legal and voluntary fast, they gave the impression of being disinterested in the advent of the Messiah, or messianic hope. Jesus' reply clarifies this. The reason is that they have nothing to wait for. The *messianic times* actually have arrived. His disciples need not prepare by ascetic practices for the coming of someone in whose intimacy they are actually living. The intimacy of course will be interrupted by their Master's passion and death. In that hour they will fast (v. 20: cf. Lk 22:18), until the time when the spouse is restored in the resurrection and the definitive kingdom.

b) The parables of the cloth and the wine-skin are another response to the astonishment of John's disciples and the Pharisees. Jesus, as inaugurator of the messianic times, realizes that what he is bringing has nothing in common with the standards hitherto followed by men (cf. Lk 16:16 or the miracle of Cana in Jn 2:10). The two similitudes are not making value judgments about the old being better than the new (true of wine), or the new better than the old (true of cloth). They do not make a contrast but affirm an *incompatibility*. The new and the old cannot be associated without running the risk of destroying both one and the other. The repatched cloth will be a failure, just as the old wine-skin will be irretrievably ruined . . . and also the new wine. The moral is clear: one has to choose, rejecting compromises where everything is lost.*

c) The parables were probably given by Jesus as simple proverbs. The synoptics however, by placing them immediately after his affirmation of the messianic times because of the presence of the spouse, give them the dimension of allegory. In fact both mantle and wine were classic symbols for the messianic times (cf. Lk 15:22; Nb 15:23; Pr 9:1-5). Old mantles and old wine-bottles; all that was old has passed away and salvation is manifested in *newness.* Thus an early teaching of Jesus concerning incompatibility becomes the ecclesial teaching concerning the radical newness of the age that has dawned.

IX. Luke	Our passage here is taken from an ensemble
6:39-45	that is quite important doctrinally, but of
Gospel	rather mixed redaction. In Luke 6:36-49 we
3rd cycle	have a sort of moral catecheism which was put
	together for Gentile converts from sayings by

Jesus which are united by key-words (measure, in v. 38; eye, in vv. 39 concerning the blind and 41-42 concerning the splinter and

* See the doctrinal theme: *option of faith,* p. 341.

the plank), where the overly Jewish context of the original has been somewhat softened.

What we have in today's reading combines quite disparate elements: the similitude of the splinter and the plank (vv. 41-42) which illustrates the obligation of "not judging" proclaimed in vv. 36-38; then two distinct sayings which are associated through the key-word "tree" (vv. 43-44); and finally a saying about the good and the bad (v. 45), suggested by the use of these words in verse 43.

The result is a somewhat mixed text. It has the merit at least of indicating the methods used by oral tradition in preserving the Lord's sayings.

a) Verses 43-44 certainly give us the central message. We find them in the same form in Matthew (7:16-18 and 12:33-35). He applies them to false prophets, whereas Luke refers them to the disciples themselves. Moral life is indicated by its *fruits* (cf. Jm 3:12; Lk 13:6-9; 23:27-31; Is 5:1-7; Ez 19:10-14). The origin of the idea is the sapiental tradition, where the just man is frequently compared to a tree which gives wholesome fruit when other trees are barren (Ps 1; 91/92:13-14; Ct 2:1-3; Si 24:12-27). The just man brings forth good fruit because he is irrigated by divine waters. In the eschatological era the fruits will be particularly abundant (Ez 47-1-12). The Christian, a branch of the tree of life which is Jesus (Jn 15:1-18), bears the fruits of the Spirit (Ga 5:5-26; 6:17-16), whereas the tree of Judaism is becoming barren (Mt 3:8-10; 21:18-19).

b) In Matthew the fruits of the new ethic are still described in Jewish terms: justice and perfection (Mt 5:20-38). For Luke on the other hand these fruits are in terms of *charity* above all. Thus we can see why the similitude of the splinter and the plank is linked with that of fruits. Christian ethic will bear its best fruit in mutual pardon and the refusal to be the other's judge. It will manifest at its deepest level the divine life which irrigates the tree.

B. DOCTRINE

The Theme of the Option of Faith

When Jesus proclaims the Good News of the Kingdom, he multiplies paradoxes. In the Gospel of today's first cycle we have this: "Do not ask, what shall we eat, or what shall we drink, or wherewith shall we be clothed. After all this do the Gentiles seek. Your Father in heaven knows that you have need of all these things. Seek you first the Kingdom of God and its justice, and all this will be added unto you" (Mt 6:31-33; cf. further Mk 2:18-22, second Gospel today). In general Christians realize that they have to make a definite choice, if they are to be faithful to the evangelic precepts. But they are troubled about the meaning of such a text as this. They find in it "exaggerations" that it would be dangerous to interpret literally.

It is an opportunity for us to clarify the real nature of the Christian option. Do not these evangelic paradoxes challenge the Christian to transcend his natural inclinations? Is he not being summoned to look further and deeper? If his choice must be to seek the Kingdom of God and its justice, does that not require a degree of interiority which only a rash man would attempt to define precisely? In the following pages we shall put forward a few reflections in attempted explanation.

Option of faith and observance of law in Israel

Adherents of all traditional religions attached great importance to special ritual procedures which provided avenues of communication with the sacral world. Side by side with these, the law governing daily existence would impose ethical obligations arising from custom, or, at a later stage, some system of wisdom. Observance on both of these levels would help a man to feel integrated into some cosmic harmony where things and beings were justly disposed. Failure to observe would be abandonment of the road to happiness and voluntary self destruction.

In Israel, however, the option of faith brought about an extraordinary interiorization. The acceptance of the unforeseeable event as the focus of Yahweh's liberating interventions made Jewish man constantly dubious about the security which ritual or legal observance could provide. The salvation of which he was in quest henceforward depended on the prior initiative of God. No effort on his own part could constrain God to intervene in his favor. And yet Yahweh does not save man without man's cooperation. He makes a covenant with Israel, and expects from man the loyalty of faith. It was attempts to probe the nature of this fidelity that gradually led Israel to greater depths of interiorization and renunciation. The process however, as we shall see, would not be completed until the intervention of Jesus.

In this development observance of the Law came to assume tremendous importance, but there were actually two conceptions of this sort of observance, varying according to awareness of the link between the Law and the Covenant. Historically, the two were intimately related; the Law only made sense in the order of Faith. This was particularly clear when the people were called upon to observe in the insecurity of the desert. In this Mosaic concept of observance, the reason for fulfilling the precepts was that man would be led to ever greater openness. His poverty before the interventions of God would become more and more radical. The Law was something living, constant "rereadings" of which would provide deeper and deeper insight. In the other conception, which was indeed more common in that it corresponded to man's natural inclination, observance of the Law became fixed and stereotyped, the multiple applications of the various precepts being worked out in scribal tradition. From that, it was a short step to regarding legal observance as the fidelity required by the Covenant. The next step was obvious and inevitable, the one in which sinful man would seek by one means or another to merit his own salvation.

This, and the ambiguity that was always possible even among the better Jews concerning legal observance, shows that Israel was unable to complete the process of interiorization demanded by the option of faith. Had it done so, Israel would have been altogether absorbed in the religion of waiting. Jewish man would have come to understand that fidelity of this calibre, which molds a man's active response to the divine initiative, is itself a gift of God to be awaited in the future.

The option of faith fully clarified in Jesus

With the coming of the Messiah all ambiguity concerning the Law is finally removed. Going beyond the traditions which had obscured its original meaning, Jesus affirmed that the essence of the Mosaic Law is its intimate link with the order of faith. Brought to fulfillment in himself, the Law can be summed up in the single commandment of love. This is the option of faith. With full lucidity, a man is challenged to relinquish the security offered by fulfilling precepts, and accept encounter with God in the unpredictable event. Absolute stripping of the self is required. This obedience to God in the event, even in the event of death, brings one along the road where one cannot see ahead. At each stage there must be deepening, purification, interiorization. And at the end of the road there is nothing left but poverty and acceptance.

The option becomes particularly clear, when, with Jesus and in him, the religion of waiting yields to the religion of fulfillment. All the dimensions manifest themselves. The option is no longer just the attitude of the man who awaits the liberating intervention of God. It is the attitude of the adoptive child, who, in Jesus Christ, has found access to the Father. The total self-renunciation required by faith is the basic step in fulfillment of the human vocation; the stripping off of the creature, delivery from the chains of pride, so that the gift of adoptive sonship can take shape within one's being. This gift is altogether bound up with the Incarnation of the Word, and when Jesus asks us to follow him, he is putting the option of faith in its clearest light.

The implications of the Christian faith

From its very beginnings, the Church has not ceased to deepen insight about this option. The primitive community preserved

Jesus' teaching concerning it with meticulous care, because this was of the essence. If frequently the teaching seemed to be paradoxical, the reason was that an option which ran so counter to a man's natural inclination had to be clarified. The baptized person, true, acquires by grace the capacity for the option, but the full option is shaped only in the existential living of a pilgrimage that will not end until death.

To begin with, it is not one option among others. Of itself it offers no security other than God. No moral performance is considered adequate qualification. When a man opts for the faith, he does not see a clear road before him. All remains to be discovered gradually in the pattern of events, in the dull texture of everyday living. The deepest thing in human existence is faith, but it does not obtrude itself. It is never spectacular, but essentially discreet. What we *can* identify in Jesus' teachings is emphasis on this discretion, simultaneously with emphasis on the all-embracing nature of its demands.

Nor is the option of faith a choice made once for all. The exercise of charity, which is its expression, is always forcing the believer to review his commitment. There are no limits to the interiorization which will be required; constantly, there are new levels to be explored. The believer will be challenged to yet another conversion. He reaches the nearest cross-roads, only to discover that the road still leads on.

If the option is lived in full fidelity, it will place all human responsibilities in their proper perspective. The believer will come to see the terrestrial mission of the creature for what it really is. Far from leading him to recession, it will inspire him to muster all his energies for the enterprise of civilization. Once this is motivated by love, it is indissolubly associated with the building of the Kingdom. This is an aspect that has only been sufficiently recognized by the Church after long centuries of maturation. And it is an insight of which it would be difficult to overestimate the importance in the present pattern of Church-world relationships.

Option for the kingdom and missionary witness

We must ask ourselves in what sense the exclusive option of faith proves basic in missionary witness. The desire to succeed, very legitimate in itself, often tends to tarnish the quality of missionary witness and reduce it to the level of proselytism or annexation.

Whenever missionary witness is inspired by a living faith, it is a witness to universalism. The Christian missionary who confronts his non-Christian brethren does not do so as a possessor of all truth, as if he had investigated everything and discovered once for all a formulation for truth. His baptism does not dispense him from the duty of being a searcher for God. On the contrary it draws him away from immediate securities and launches him on a spiritual adventure, the successful issue of which, he knows, will depend on his living link with Christ in the Church. He must be open to the spiritual pilgrimage of those he evangelizes, ready to share it though it is not his. He must be able to discern there the action of the Spirit, ready to see like light on the horizon the ineffable mystery of Christ about to take new root. By constant renewal of his own option for the Kingdom, he will realize that the witness in this new environment of his faith will produce that lucidity and interiorization that leads to conversions.

This sort of missionary witness reflects the essence of the evangelic law. It inspires the missionary himself to a more intense obedience to God in the event. It manifests the double love, in Christ, of God and men. It urges towards communion with the other, while maintaining full respect for otherness, individual or collective. The missionary becomes a figure of love, and love is the area where the divine summons to salvation finds fulfillment.

The option of faith and the eucharistic celebration

In this gradual deepening of faith the eucharistic celebration has an essential role. This is not accomplished automatically. If the Mass is merely an occasion for Christians to experience togetherness in a warm and reassuring brotherhood, it is not fulfilling its purpose.

Every eucharistic celebration should be a challenge for those assembled to deeper faith. It should detach them from illusory securities, and plunge them ever deeper into the sometimes disconcerting profundities. This applies to the liturgy of the Word as well as that of the Bread. The whole purpose of the proclamation of the Word is that the faithful should be able to view the event, with all its weight of unpredictability and death, lucidly. They should experience a constant urge towards conversion and acceptance. As for the Bread, which is destined for all, it should open consciences more and more to the universal horizons of love. The genuine Christian thanksgiving involves us in the gigantic stream of divine life, which is destined one day in Christ to absorb all humanity.

EIGHTH WEEK

I. Sirach
17:19-27
1st reading
1st cycle
Monday

This brief summons to penance does not have any difficulties in interpretation.

Ben Sirach is convinced about the extent of sin's dominion over all humanity. He sees it as a dominion which extends even to the just. The child often pays for his father (Si 3:11; 41:7; 23:23-25), and the fault of the wicked is likely always to involve somehow the just (Si 39:29; 40:10). There is only one solution. One must trust in God's mercy (v. 29), and attainment of such openness requires conversion from any self-sufficiency (vv. 25-26).

II. 1 Peter
1:3-9
1st reading
2nd cycle
Monday

The author of this letter seems to have been inspired by a primitive Christian hymn. It must have had three strophes, concerned, in order, with praise of the Father, the author of the new creation (paraphrased in vv. 3-5); of the Son, the object of our love even in trial (paraphrased in vv. 6-9); and of the Spirit as manifested in the prophets (paraphrased in vv. 10-12, not in our reading). We have another paraphrase of this hymn in Titus 3:4-8. The strophes are united by the common themes of Exodus, the resurrection of Christ, and Christian baptism.

The first portion of the letter probably gives us the ceremonial of a paschal liturgy. Exegetes have found in it all the elements, according to 1 Corinthians 14:26-27, of a celebration: canticle, teaching, revelation, etc. The passage today paraphrases the inaugural canticle, a sort of prayer of blessing.

We shall comment first on the hymn itself, insofar as it can be reconstructed, then on the paraphrase which the letter gives us.

a) The hymn can possibly be reconstructed as follows:

Blessed be God the Father of our Lord Jesus Christ
According to his great mercy, he has regenerated us
By the resurrection of Jesus Christ from among the dead
For a living hope,
For an incorruptible heritage conserved in heaven
For a salvation to be manifested in the final times.

The principal subject of this "blessing" is our *regeneration* (cf. Tt 3:5; Jn 3:3-5; Jm 1:17-18). What is contemplated apparently is the transformation wrought in every man by a Word of God, which is not only proclaimed from outside, but graven in his heart (Jr 31:31-34; Dt 30:11-14). This Word of God in us (cf. Lk 8:11-15) is the commandment of love (1 Jn 3:9-10). Only this can regenerate humanity and provide the eternal, incorruptible heritage to which humanity aspires.

The sign of this rebirth, and its cause, is Christ's resurrection. This shows that humanity can be restored because, in Christ, it is already glorified. The Word of love sown in us can lead us to rebirth because Christ's love for his father and his brothers enabled him to triumph over death.

b) Regeneration through the Word brings humanity to an *eschatological state* which the author describes as hope. This is not the virtue of hope, but the object of hope, as in Romans 8:24. In primitive Christian language the object of hope is none other than divine glory (Rm 5:2; 1 P 4:13-14; Col 1:27). Hope is "living," because the glory will resuscitate our mortal bodies (Ph 3:21; Rm 6:4; 8:18-23; 1 Co 15:40-45). It is an incorruptible heritage, far superior to the land promised to the people of the covenant (Ex 32:13). Christ has already won it by his resurrection (Ga 3:16), and those who are regenerated with him will inherit it in their turn (Ga 3:26-29). Finally the hope is "salvation," in the sense that it enables men to escape eternal decay, just as it has now rescued them from sin.

c) The author's paraphrases of the hymn concentrates on the value of *faith under trial*. Peter describes in glowing terms the happiness for which men are destined in Jesus Christ in order to strengthen their faith which is being tested by persecution. Persecution is likened to the fire that tries gold in order to reveal its brilliance. There may be sacrificial imagery here. Trial is to faith what fire is to the sacrificial victim (cf. Ml 3:2-3). It makes believers a spiritual offering, a royal priesthood for the praise of God. And there is also an eschatological symbolism. Fire sifts the essential from the inessential, the nugget from its shell, and thus prepares the "revelation of Jesus Christ" among a humanity that has at last been purified (1 Co 3:13).

Christian hope is no longer that of the Jews. The coming of the Son of man did not take place as the Jews had anticipated it; the Judge of the nations appearing on the clouds and avenging his elect. The new world of which the Son is laying the foundations is not born in a single flash; it comes at the end of a slow ripening of the Word of love in human hearts. This gradual growth was seen in the person of Jesus, leading him to his victory over death. It is a similar growth in each Christian, throughout all the vicissitudes of trial, that will assure him the glorious and incorruptible heritage. To humanity is guaranteed total regeneration.

III. Mark 10:17-27 Gospel Monday This particular text had considerable manipulations before redaction but they are easy to reconstruct. Only in the definitive redaction were the two elements which go to make it up combined. The first was originally a vocation narrative (vv. 17-22), without reference, or reference that was no more than incidental, to the wealth of the candidate (v. 22).

The second was limited to verses 24b, 25 (without any mention of "a rich man"), 26 and 27. It concerned, in general terms, entry to the Kingdom without reference to riches. Jesus and his disciples, contemplating the incredulity of the crowds, are asking themselves how many of the chosen people will be saved. Jesus remits the matter to God "to whom nothing is impossible." This is a reference to Genesis 18:14, consequently to the promise made to Abraham, and an affirmation that God can very well raise up a new people (Mt 3:9; cf. Rm 11:11-32).

At this early stage probably Jesus and the disciples, who were experiencing the first formal rejections on the part of the Jews, were disturbed about the outcome of the messianic mission (cf. Mt 22:14). The later redactional stage, which is already evident in Mark, makes both items lessons concerning poverty, according to the outlook of the primitive community. Verses 23 and 24, which are really just superfluous doublets of 24b and 26, are added. Jesus is made to say exactly what he said in 24b, with now a reference to riches. The disturbance of the disciples in verse 26, when they fear that few will be saved, is understandable. It is not so however in verse 24, when they hear that the rich will have much difficulty in entering the Kingdom. They themselves were poor (cf. v. 28), and Jesus' audience generally was made up of simple folk. Why then the "astonishment"?

It is easy to see what happened. The primitive community read the items thus, because they wanted to influence members who were overly attached to the goods of this world (cf. Ac 4:36-5:14). They had made material poverty practically an exclusive condition for entry to the Kingdom (Lk 6:20-24). Unlike Matthew and Luke, Mark has not succeeded in obliterating the traces of the rehandling and consequently enables us to reconstruct it.

Two separate emphases are intermingled in the text: the primitive theme of Jewish incredulity, illustrated by the young man's refusal, and the later theme of the difficulty of entering the Kingdom with riches.

a) Jesus completed his ministry as an itinerant rabbi without achieving the hoped for success. The chosen people were rejecting their Messiah and his death was becoming a probability. Evidently the Kingdom of God was not about to be invaded by large crowds (v. 24).

In Matthew and Luke Jesus' reaction to this situation is fairly strong. He curses this people of hardened heart, and predicts for them a fate like Sodom (Mt 11:20-24). Mark is different. He is more anxious to take account of Jesus' interior psychological development. Jesus and the disciples certainly did not contemplate the failure of the mission without consternation. They are "exceedingly astonished" (v. 26; cf. the reference, peculiar to Mark, in v. 21 to the love in vain of Jesus). Verse 27 however gives us Jesus' *surrender* to God's decision. God alone saves. And if it has not been impossible for him to raise up a people from the sterile loins of Abraham, he will not find it difficult to build his Kingdom from an apparently unsuccessful mission. The servant is merely a witness of God's plan, not necessarily its executor. God reserves for himself the ultimate measures in constructing the Kingdom. He is the only one who knows (cf. Mk 13:32).

b) Jesus cannot however refrain from pointing out the reasons for the people's *incredulity*. In this connection the episode of the young man is particularly revealing.

To begin with, he poses the one important question: what must one do to be saved (v. 17)? But he puts it badly by addressing Jesus as "good master," one among many (v. 17). He is merely looking for the opinion of a school among other schools. Because there are other, different views, he is reserving in advance the right to choose between them, or not to choose at all. Jesus immediately rejects this approach by reminding him of the existence of the one good God (v. 28). He implies that his answer will not be a school opinion, but a divine command, demanding action rather than endless discussion.

He reminds his questioner of the essentials of the law (v. 19). The young man then raises a new question, not with a view to proper acceptance, but rather to prolong the discussion and thus delay the moment of acceptance (same attitude in Lk 10:29).

At this point the young man's good legalist, pharisaic conscience blocks him. He is proud of fulfilling all his obligations and believes he obeys all the law (v. 20). What more does he need to be saved?

At once Jesus rebuffs the legalism, which is merely another pretext for not believing. He gives a precise command: "follow me" (v. 21). Now, the questioner shows that his earlier questions were but subterfuges. Faced with the challenge of believing, he admits that he has not the capacity. He withdraws precisely at the moment when he is called upon to transcend ethical discussion and legalism, and encounter and follow the person of Jesus.

Believing and being saved, in the long run, mean attachment to the person of Jesus.

c) The retouches made by the primitive community add a new obstacle to salvation. Not alone are ethical discussions and pharisaic legalism obstacles to entry to the Kingdom; wealth is too (vv. 22, 23 and the word rich in v. 25). The first Christians, at Jerusalem above all, sometimes confused the Kingdom with the social class of poor. The assembly envisaged by Christ, however, made no distinction on a social, cultural or national level. Matthew will modify this exclusion by speaking of the "poor in spirit" (Mt 5:3) and suppressing the malediction on the rich that we find in Luke 6:24.

It would be simply another brand of legalism to maintain that the rich must become materially poor to share the Kingdom. Just as it would be illusory to affirm that the poor are blessed because they are destined one day to enter a regime of well-being.

True poverty for the rich man does not consist in "having nothing." It consists in being identified with the poor, especially those who cannot organize, defend, or free themselves. Such involvement is particularly necessary for those Christians who freely relinquish material goods and take a vow of poverty.

To follow the way of poverty in our day requires that we should analyze the causes for human misery. We should take the question of class very seriously, and determine means to better the lot of every man. It is only then that our poverty will become genuinely evangelic.

IV. Sirach	Ben Sirach is sometimes a zealot for the liturgy
35:1-12	(cf. Si 50) and sometimes a faithful observer
1st reading	of the law. Today's passage illustrates both
1st cycle	tendencies.
Tuesday	

The combination gives us one of the most explicit Old Testament texts on the doctrine of *spiritual sacrifice*. Instead of offerings we must have obedience; instead of sacrifices, charity (vv. 1-2); instead of expiation, conversion (v. 3).

God progressively led his people from the bloody sacrifices of the beginnings to the sacrifice of spiritual oblation inaugurated by Christ. We can distinguish several stages in the development.

There is first the "quantitative" stage, when the Jews offered holocausts of the pagan kind, tithing and first fruits of their goods (Lv 2; Dt 26:1-11). This was really a sacrifice of riches. A man's wealth and abundance was manifested even in his sacrifice, thus assuring him greater importance (and religious status) (2 Ch 7:1-17).

However, such sacrifices were carried out without really involving the offerer. The Jewish peasant would bring his victim, which the priest would immolate according to the rubrics. Only the victim was involved, and he was unaware. We are still far from the ideal sacrifice where priest and victim are the same.

Prophetic reaction to these sacrifices, which in the long run ignored both spiritual and moral attitudes, was violent but unavailing (Am 5:21-27; Jr 7:1-14; Is 1:11-17; Ho 6:5-6). Not until the exile did any concept of spiritual sacrifice take shape.

In the expiation sacrifice, which became common at this time (Nb 29:7-11), the quantitative aspect began to yield in importance to sentiments of humility and poverty. The most thorough step towards spiritualization begins to be felt in the psalms above all (Pss 39/40:7-10; 50/51:18-19; 49/50; Jl 1:13-14; Dn 3:37-43). Gradually the awareness dawned that the essential in sacrifice is personal attitude. The sacrifice of the future would be that of the suffering Servant (Is 53:1-10).

Into this tradition Jesus fitted. The content of his sacrifice was his obedience and his poverty (He 2:17-18; Rm 5:19; He 10:5-7; Mt 27:38-60; Lk 18:9-14). He was the suffering Servant *par excellence* (Jn 13:1-15; Lk 22:20; 23:37; Mt 26:3-5).

The sacrifice of the Christian must follow the pattern set by Christ: a life of obedience and love, which derives priestly value from its association with Christ (Rm 12:1-2; He 9:14).

V. 1 Peter
1:10-16
1st reading
2nd cycle
Tuesday

The authenticity of the first letter of Peter has been much discussed. Many passages are drawn from primitive hymns that were probably used at baptism or Easter liturgy. The first part of the letter seems indeed to be a sort of "formulary" for the Easter celebration. The important question is whether such considerations allow us to maintain Petrine authorship and a date around 64 AD. Many commentators think, yes. In any case the letter is the oldest synthesis we have concerning the baptismal, Christian life. Thanks to the resurrection of Christ, the Christian is regenerated. This means a new relationship with his brothers, a life of pilgrimage on earth, important priestly responsibilities before God for all humanity, and a theological, Christological attitude towards suffering throughout all the banal circumstances of life.

Today's passage is somewhat disparate. Verses 10-12 belong to the conclusion of the introduction. Verses 13-16 belong to the first portion of the letter strictly speaking, where the author is reminding Christians of the holiness of their life.

a) The first two verses, the conclusion of the doxology, give us essential points in the theology of *salvation-history*. The author mentions the chronological aspect of this (in former times . . . today), the centrality of Christ; and he places in perspective the roles of the prophets and evangelists.

Before going on to describe Christian life, he alludes to salvation history after the manner of the first Christian preachers (cf. the discourses of Peter in the Acts). This was a demonstration that the prophets, being serious, reflective men, had interpreted events and the laws of the universe as a basis for their hope that all would come to have meaning one day in Christ (v. 11).

Because of this quest, the term of which they could not see, the prophets were authentic servants of salvation-history (v. 12). They inaugurated a service that is now fulfilled by the preachers of the gospel (here described as "angels," envoys, as in Lk 7:24; 9:52; Mt 24:31; Ga 4:14). They too scrutinize events with the same attention, and in the same Spirit, as their predecessors, in order to see salvation at work.

b) The second part of our passage (vv. 13-16) could well be the outline for a homily on Exodus 12, which was a reading for the feast of the Pasch in Jewish as well as Christian liturgy.

It is recommended that the prescriptions of the Jewish ritual be transposed to the spiritual plane. The girt loins (v. 13; cf. Ex 12:11; Jb 38:3; 40:7; Ep 6:14) become the "girt minds," a recommendation that our attention be alert, as we keep vigil before events in order to interpret them properly. The night in vigil, so that the event can be seen with lucidity and openness of heart, becomes for the Christian, sobriety.

Thus is the Christian life a *paschal life*. What the Jews lived through for a single night, becomes now the permanent attitude of the Christian. Born again thanks to the obedience of Jesus, he is veritably a "child of obedience." This obedience is his new nature. No longer can he give way to the "lusts" of the desert (v. 14; cf. 1 Co 10:6).

c) Because his life is paschal, it takes place around a spiritual Sinai, where he can hear the law of *holiness* propounded by God (vv. 15-16), and adhere to it more faithfully than his Jewish ancestors (Lv 11:44-45; 20:7-8). As the author sees it, this holiness suggests, as in the Old Testament, the notion of transcendence. The Christian's behavior in the world is indeed "altogether other," because of the interpretation he gives to his action and to events. They are gifts of God and occasions for communion with God.

Detached from the typology of its context, the moral this passage gives us is the historic dimension of the Christian life. The Jews were in the desert for a time and had one night in the year when they recalled it. Christians are at all times in the desert and at all times celebrating Pasch. The moral obedience of the Jews at Sinai becomes an ontological state for Christians. Obedience from now on signifies sonship and access to God's holiness. So rich is the Christian's life that he does not have to recall the past. At each moment he is living his sonship with such intensity that he can dispense with particular feasts. It is always feast, and always Pasch, insofar at least as he learns like the prophets to interpret events. Their lucid view brought them the true meaning of the sojourn in the desert, and an understanding of the drama of obedience and the paschal ritual.

VI. Mark
10:28-31
Gospel
Tuesday

This narrative follows the account of the rich young man, and the considerations put forward by Christ and the apostles about the danger of riches (Mk 10:17-27). The present episode was easily associated with it. Peter draws Jesus' attention to the case of the disciples who have abandoned everything to follow him (v. 28). Jesus replies with a solemn promise to all those who renounce riches or family (vv. 29-30) to follow him. Verse 31 is an authentic *logion,* but the synoptics who no longer know its original context, place it where they can (Lk 13:30; Mt 19:30; 20:16).

Mark's description (v. 30) of the hundred-fold promise is somewhat more extended than the others. Houses and fields, brothers and sisters and persecution are somewhat curiously juxtaposed.

The text, in Matthew's version above all, is still considerably colored by the Jewish notion of *retribution*. The disciples' gesture in following Jesus must have its recompense. Jesus' description of it is not confined to the eschatological future; it will be to some extent in the present life.

Mark on the other hand is very conscious of how materially a terrestrial recompense might be interpreted. Thus he proceeds to modify it by reference to persecutions, something much closer to what Jesus generally promised his followers (cf. Mk 10:38; 8:34-38). The house, the brothers and sisters, promised in this life, are furthermore a spiritual blessing. The disciple who has impoverished and isolated himself to follow Jesus will find communities of brothers and sisters (cf. Mk 3:34-35), and welcoming houses, in greater number than those of his own family, even in persecution. What Jesus is promising is a life of communion that will be a hundred times better than what they knew before. Persecutions will not prevent this; the fraternal communion offered by Jesus is the sign of his cross.

Seen thus, Jesus' reply is in harmony with what we always have from him. The disciple will become part of a people who bear witness to the love of the cross.

Some systems of spirituality could find the recompense for the disciples here below an embarrassment. Nevertheless what we have is a sensible realism, and a completely Christian viewpoint.

The disciples are utterly disconcerted. Success has not crowned the effort of preaching. The sacrifices they made, separation from family and married life, will have no recompense.

We might expect Jesus to allay their anxieties by a promise of eternal life in heaven. That he does indeed; eternal life comes at the end of the promise. But it is preceded by a considerable number of terrestrial blessings.

These are constituted by the joy and freedom offered for instance in human relations to the person who sacrifices sexuality for celibacy. They are also constituted by the use of material goods that is offered the person who becomes poor for the sake of others. He finds himself sustained by those very people to whom he has given all. Happiness of this nature is always accompanied by persecution and challenge, by failure and frustration. It is at the deepest level of one's being, and remains immune to all challenges. This is the level of the self where a man communes with God and his fellow man.

Some concept of deep happiness, however terrestrial, is a necessary preliminary to the concept of eternal life. Heaven cannot be regarded as a consolation for those who have been unsuccessful here below. Nor should it be used to convince those who feel dubious about the meaning of a life of celibacy or poverty.

The celibate whose choice of life fails to provide the happiness and liberty of multiple human relations (brothers, sisters, mothers . . .) is losing a basic earthly happiness which is the pledge of eternal life. Heaven will not recompense such a person. Likewise, the one who chooses voluntary poverty, but does not find through this renunciation the happiness and liberty of love given and received, is losing the one sure pledge of eternal happiness. The one who endures persecution too, if failure reduces everything to nothing for him, cannot enter life eternal. In the fidelity he shows, he must experience even here below some morsel of spiritual happiness.

Heaven is not a recompense for earthly failure. Our failure should leave us with enough taste for happiness to blossom one day into eternal happiness. It is through the terrestrial that this "hundred-fold" reward is shaped.

VII. Sirach
36:1, 5-6,
10-17
1st reading
1st cycle
Wednesday

This psalm seems to be the prayer of a Jew who is deeply influenced by the Bible, but also by stoicism. One of the most striking qualities in the prayer indeed is that its better sentiments have their source in pagan thought.

The whole impression is that Ben Sirach wants to reconcile his Jewish faith in a unique God with the stoic idea of world-unity. It is the first time we have a Jew praying in such terms for world unity (vv. 1, 17), asking that the unity of the people (vv. 10-13) yield to the hope for a larger unity. This is to be realized not by Israel's victory over the nations, but by a common confession of the same unique God (v. 4), a God who is "master of the world" (v. 1: a title unique in the Bible but common in stoicism).

Ben Sirach was writing at a time when the quest for unity was intense. He believed in unity and shared the hope of many Greek philosophers that it could be achieved not by force of arms, but by ideas. He goes further than the Greeks in making it depend on a common faith in the unique God. Events were destined to falsify the hope. Soon the East would be bloodied by armies, and Israel engulfed in the worst sort of nationalism.

Our century is also seeking unity. Many value it above force, but military might continues to hold sway. Many hope that unity will come through association of minds and cultures, but always nationalism raises its head once again, blocking genuine dialogue and constructive encounter. Men want unity, but do not want to transcend themselves. The prayer of Ben Sirach continues to be utopian.

VIII. 1 Peter   Portion at least of the first letter of Peter seems
1:18-25   to be a sort of formulary for the celebration of
1st reading   the Christian Pasch, or more accurately, an
2nd cycle   outline for a homily on Exodus 12:21-28. The
Wednesday homily would be in three parts: the first giving
                     a Christian spiritual interpretation of the Exo-
dus text (1 P 1:13-21); the second celebrating the newness of the
paschal life (1 P 1:22-2:2); the third analyzing the present life of
the Church and Christians in the light of the paschal mystery (1
P 2:3-10).

a) In verse 9 we have the central idea of the passage. The
Christians constitute the *new Israel,* because they have the charter which consecrated the ancient people (Ex 19:5-6, read by
1 Peter in the light of Is 43:20-21). All the titles reserved for
Israel are now applicable to the Church: a chosen race, because
selected from among the nations (Ex 19:5; Dt 7:6; 14:2); a
royal priesthood (cf. Ex 19:6) capable of offering, instead of the
Sinai immolations (Ex 24:5-8) the spiritual sacrifice of the new
covenant (cf. 1 P 2:5; Rev 1:6); a holy people, because separated
from the world, no longer by an exterior rite but by the Holy
Spirit (1 P 2:1-2); a people acquired by God, not alone by Yahweh's marvelous intervention as in Exodus, but by the blood of his
Son (Ac 20:28; v. 19); in sum, the people of God, gathering in
not only the twelve tribes, but all the nations hitherto plunged in
darkness (1 P 2:10; cf. Is 9:1).

b) To justify this transference of titles, the author uses the
biblical theme of the *rock* (1 P 2:4-8). The old covenant was
accomplished round the rock of Sinai, which the people could not
approach under pain of death (Ex 19:23). The new is sealed
around the "new rock," a living "stone" which is the Risen Christ,
a rock that, unlike that of Sinai, may be approached (1 P 2:4).

Thus the new people are assembled round a person who has
manifested himself in death and resurrection ("rejected . . . but
chosen" 1 P 2:4), and discloses his personality to all. They con-

stitute a spiritual temple, because what they offer is personal attitudes, no longer rites (1 P 2:5; cf. Rm 12:1; He 13:16). Their link with Christ is not secured by ablution but by faith and involvement (1 P 2:6-8).

For this reason, in 1 P 2:1-2, we are reminded that the spiritual sacrifice of Christians is of the moral order. It depends on constant conversion throughout the continuous pilgrimage of a lifetime. The spiritual milk referred to in these verses in none other than the Word of God. It is taught at the moment of baptismal conversion, but is continued unceasingly in order to ensure the growth and renewal of the faithful (vv. 22-27).

The summaries in the Acts (Ac 6:1-7; 9:26-31; 14:20-26), and above all Ac 2:42-47, shows us a Christian community that is still very linked with Judaism. The disciples certainly believed themselves to be the true Israel, but could not the same be said of the Pharisees, the Zealots, the Essenes, and the Sadducees?

This text gives us a very different perspective. These Christians believe themselves to be not only the true Israel, but the new Israel. It is precisely the personal, experiential knowledge of the Risen Lord (the "rock" of the new people) that leads a group who were at the beginning no more than a Jewish sect to become a new people. It was not of grave moment that the Jerusalem community preserved the Jewish institutions over long. Sooner or later their faith in the "rock" was bound to bring these institutions to an end.

And so, in 1 Peter, the Church has come to recognize herself as the new, eschatological people. She is the fulfillment of all the potentialities of the old.

What the Sinai-event was to Israel, Christ's death and resurrection were for the Church, the nucleus of the new people and the royal priesthood. The great difference lay in the fact that a person and his sacrifice, a "living being" and his love, were now substituted for the tables of the law. Humanity was being offered a new type of covenant, based on a new heart. Men could become involved in the will of the Father, and constitute a new spiritual temple for the offering of the only cult agreeable to God.

We might ask why the Church was so concerned to present herself in terms of ancient Jewish notions, holy people, priestly assembly, etc.

One reason, it appears, was because these notions preclude any over-clericalization. All the faithful make up the people of God, and the people of God is a unity. Whatever be the ministry we exercise in the Church, the thing of basic importance is that we be simple believers capable of offering the spiritual sacrifice. The people of God concept really excludes any individualistic interpretation of the encounter with the Risen Lord. The Church is not just an association of people who happen to believe in the same way. Antecedent to the belief of anyone, is the will of God to set up a people round the new "Rock."

Furthermore, these concrete Jewish notions preclude any idealization of the Church. It is of course an entity set up by God, but it is composed of actual human beings. Without men there would be no Church. Naturally then it is subject to the limitations of its terrestrial constitution and of sinfulness. Constantly it must be undergoing reform and purification.

The eucharistic celebration is a harmonious expression of all these notes. The people of God are assembled in the act of spiritual sacrifice, acting as a unity in response to God's summons. Their sacrifice is their faith in the Risen Christ, and their loyalty to the new law he inaugurated.

IX. Mark 10:32-45 *Gospel Wednesday*   Here we have Jesus' third prediction of his passion and death (cf. Mk 8:31-33 and Mk 9:30-32). As on the previous occasions this announcement meets with different reactions among the apostolic group. Some anticipate a special office in the coming Kingdom (vv. 35-40), but all are now aware that the journey to Jerusalem concerns them all equally. It brings nearer the cup that must be drunk (v. 39), or the service that must be rendered to the brethren (v. 43).

a) It is conceivable that Jesus did not actually describe his *passion* with all the details, and in the terms, that Mark and the other evangelists employ (vv. 33-34). We can detect in the predictions the influence of the primitive community's redaction, which had by now the quality of a *Credo*. Mark gives the longest enumeration of the cruelties Jesus must undergo. Likewise, he is the only one to stress Jesus' attitude of hurrying towards the hour of his death. He actually walks alone in front of the group, the apostles being dismayed at the future that is looming (v. 32).

We notice in the three predictions a *crescendo* that mounts to paroxysm. In the first two, Jesus still confines himself to "instructing" his disciples about the fate the Son of man must undergo. In the third it is no longer the rabbi who is speaking. It is a dedicated man who knows where his duty lies and is resolutely launched on the road that will lead him to the death reserved for prophets and trouble-makers.

In the first prediction the apostles do not want to understand and do everything to oppose such a future. In the second they still do not understand. In the third they understand so well that they are stupefied. Where the other evangelists only give one or other of these psychological details *en passant*, Mark is more sensitive to them and gives all, even adding certain notes himself.

b) In the dialogue with the sons of Zebedee, Jesus presents his passion in terms of two themes, which Mark is the only one to combine: *the cup and the baptism*. Both are very revealing where Jesus' understanding of his role is concerned. In the Old Testament the cup indicates God's judgment on sinners (Ho 5:10; Na 1:6; So 3:8; Jr 6:11; 7:20; 42:18; 44:6; Is 51:15-22). It is a cup that must be drunk to the dregs (Jr 25:28; Ez 23:31-34). It has a sacrificial value (Nb 4:14; 7:23; 19:25; Ze 9:15). Jesus expects then to undergo the judgment of sinners in a sacrificial way. Isolated, rejected by the sinful world, nevertheless he wants to die for it. This sacrificial death will break the shackles forged about men by unbelief, which keeps them from seeing the will of God.

The baptism image conveys the same teaching (cf. Lk 12:49-50). What we have is a symbol of God's judgment, proclaimed by the prophets, whereby the world will be "submerged." Fire, water and wind will overwhelm it and thus prepare the new heaven and the new earth. Thus Jesus is substituting himself for the universe, drawing upon himself this purifying judgment which ushers in the new age.

Drinking this cup and being baptized with this baptism are, however, roles reserved to a single person, the suffering Servant, the Redeemer. The disciples can never join him in this unique, incommunicable task. That is why the question posed in verse 38 grammatically expects the answer no. They are not suffering servants and saviors in the sense that he is.

Except in a secondary sense. They will drink the cup of martyrdom and be baptized in suffering. By foretelling this, Jesus is not determining the precise manner of martyrdom for John and James. The legend which has James drink a poisoned cup and John baptized in boiling oil is very late.

Jesus' words concerning suffering also suggest the sacramental economy. Through the sacraments the Christian is associated with his passion. He dies in the waters of baptism and lives the fruits of the resurrection in the Eucharist. Thus the disciples are being allotted a share in his life, through the sacraments and martyrdom.

c) The sons of Zebedee's request for *thrones* beside Jesus in his glory (v. 37) is more comprehensible in Matthew's context. This (Mt 19:28) places it after Jesus' affirmation that the disciples will sit on thrones judging the tribes of Israel, as assessors of the sovereign judge (Mt 25:31).

At this stage in the public life, the apostles were aware that he would be much more than a nationalist Messiah. He was the Son of Man himself, to whom God would entrust the judgment and condemnation of the Gentiles (Dn 7:9-27). Daniel's oracle (7:9-

10) describes the Son of Man as surrounded by a tribunal on thrones. The apostles thought they would constitute this tribunal, something that is confirmed by the request of James and John. They realized that Jesus would be delivered over to the Gentiles (v. 33, the only time the Gentiles are mentioned in the passion predictions), but their hope is that the judgment given by the Son of Man will punish the Gentiles for their crime. They will participate in this divine revenge.

We can imagine how painful such calculations were for Jesus. He begins by saying that access to the thrones of judgment comes through suffering, by drinking a chalice and being overwhelmed by trials (vv. 38-39). He then adds that in any case it is for God alone to fix the hour of judgment and the composition of the tribunal (v. 40). The functions to be exercised in the final times depend on divine choice only, and will be stamped by the paschal mystery.

(d) What he has just said to the sons of Zebedee he then repeats in general terms to the other ten, taking up the theme of *service* (vv. 41-45). This is also revealing with regard to his consciousness of his own role. He is Messiah and Son of Man, but also the suffering Servant immolated for the multitude (v. 45; cf. Is 53:11-12). Aware of his mission as leader and of his approaching death which will impede that mission, he puts his trust in God and discerns that he will only be fully leader when he has discharged the function of Yahweh's servant.

He wants his apostles to develop the same psychological insight. If he has discovered his role as suffering Servant, they too should discover the meaning of service (vv. 43-44).

One passage then considers Jesus' passion and resurrection as they affect the Christian life itself. "It must be" that the chalice be drunk in order to sit on the thrones. One must be baptized in trial in order to judge the earth, serve in order to be leader. Suffering is basic in the disciple's life. This will be not only the accidental suffering, physical or moral, which is part of the human state; but the suffering of rejection and abandonment which brought Jesus to the cross.

In our secularized and atheistic world, the isolation that the Christian must endure is a taste perhaps of that rejection. As we celebrate the Eucharist we can feel that we are carrying the cross with Jesus.

X. Sirach
42:15-25
1st reading
1st cycle
Thursday

Here we have Ben Sirach's meditation on the work of God's wisdom in creation.

His viewpoint is that of an epoch when people believed that *creation* was completed before man entered the scene, completed so perfectly that man's main function was one of admiration and thanksgiving.

A modern man's view would be different. We are more conscious of the human role, and of man's own creative power. We think more of a God who reveals himself as man moves forward, and discovers his power over creation.

XI. 1 Peter
2:2-5, 9-12
1st reading
2nd cycle
Thursday

Peter continues with his preaching. From the description of baptismal holiness, he goes on to define the spiritual cult to which Christians are admitted. We must remember that the letter is addressed to Christians who are dispersed (1 P 1:1) in Gentile territory, doubtless as a result of one persecution or another (Ac 22:19-20). They dream of returning to Jerusalem. They still think that it is only in the temple, erected on the "rock" of Sion, that the sacrifice pleasing to God is offered, and that the definitive reassembly of the nations will take place. The author shows them that it is no longer necessary for them to be centered on the material Jerusalem. In their own assembly, in themselves, they have something much better than they can find in Sion. For his proof, he uses ideas that were already common at Qumran.

a) His first image concerns the status of the newly baptized. They are like new-born *infants,* and ought, with the infants' instinct, to turn to the milk of the Word in order to grow to the adult state (vv. 2-3). Traditionally milk represented all that was good (Ex 3:8; 13:5; Ct 4:11), especially the paradisal and eschatological banquet (Jl 4:18; Is 55:1; 60:16). In verse 4, Psalm 33/34:9 is quoted, to convince Christians that their hunger for the eschatological Word will certainly be assuaged. The growth of the baptized to adulthood is assured (cf. Jn 6:35).

b) For them, becoming adult means abandoning all reference to the terrestrial Jerusalem and all ancient structures.

To those who are still too enslaved to the law, too anxious to approach the rock of Sion on which the temple is built, he asserts that they will be adult to the extent that they are ready to approach a more fundamental *rock*: Christ himself (cf. He 12:22). He gives Christ the messianic titles of stone and rock (Mt 32:4; 2 S 23:3; Is 26:4; 30:29), which he modifies at once by speaking of a living rock (v. 4). Here he joins the current we find in the fourth gospel: the bread of life, the living way (He 10:20), living water (Jn 4:10-14), etc. In other words the rock on which the Christian economy is based is no longer a "thing" but a person. Mediation between God and man will no longer be accomplished by natural or sacral elements but by the man-God, particularly by the man-God in his death (the stone rejected).

c) The passage from the religion of the rock to that of the living rock means inevitably that the faithful, passive in the first religion, becoming living in the second ("living stones": v. 5). Since the attitude of the living rock, Christ, made him the new temple (Jn 2:19), a new focus of general reassembly (Mt 23:37-39), every man that lives in the same attitude can also become a living stone, contributing to the building of the *spiritual temple* (v. 5; cf. 1 Co 3:9-12; 14:4; He 11:10). It is no longer necessary to reenter Jerusalem and offer sacrifices in its temple. Whoever adopts the attitude of Christ constitutes the new temple, or contributes to its building.

d) Better still, made a living stone by the attitudes of its members, every Christian assembly shares a holy *priesthood* (vv. 5 and 9). There is no reason to regret not having the priestly caste of Aaron's descendants. The Christian people themselves, united to their Lord, exercise fully the priestly prerogatives (Rm 12:1; 15:16; Jm 1:27; Ac 10:4; He 13:15-16; Ph 4:18; Ep 5:2).

To define this priesthood of the holy people, Peter uses a cento of biblical texts that was compiled doubtless at Qumran. "Chosen race" (Is 43:20) is a title that was already used by Jesus for the disciples (Lk 18:7; Jn 13:18; 15:16). "Royal priesthood" is from Exodus 19:6. It is the title given Israel by Yahweh after the sealing of the covenant. The people thus become a "clergy" among nations; they are the means the nations use, knowingly or otherwise, to pray to God and receive his directions (2 M 2:17; Is 61:6). The Christian assembly accordingly is fitted to present itself before God as the priest of all humanity, and obtain from God, for all humanity, proofs of its salvation.

The next title "holy nation" is also from Exodus 19:6, and applies to the people in its function of cultic worship. Likewise the expression "people acquired" (Ex 19:5); but the "acquisition" of the people was totally renewed by the blood of Christ. It was the price paid (Tt 2:14) for the acquisition of a new people as absolute property.

These priestly titles of the ancient people now pass to the Christians. Verse 10 demonstrates this by the use of a quotation from Hosea 2:25 (or 1:6-9): the love of God is capable of incorporating in his people whomsoever he wishes.

e) Peter's correspondents are dispersed and want to set themselves up again as an established people. He tries to dissuade them in this. They are *nomads* and strangers and should remain so in this world. They should not try to regroup themselves at any price, or become just another socio-political entity in addition to existing ones.

Not by stability or institutionalism does the Church best fulfill her priestly mission and mediation for humanity. The people of God can be truly priestly even when nomad. It is the attitude, not the panoply, that counts.

XII. Mark 10:46-52 *Gospel Thursday*   The cure of the blind man of Jericho is recounted by Mark with some details unknown to the other synoptics. In the first place he mentions only one blind man and he names him (v. 46), where Matthew speaks of two blind men and Luke of one. It seems very likely that Mark has exact information which the others did not consider it necessary to transmit. The blind man's cry to Jesus is fairly different in the three versions: "Lord, Son of David" in Matthew 20:30; "Son of David, Jesus" in Mark 10:47; and "Jesus, Son of David" in Luke 18:28. It would seem that these reflect different formulas of piety and worship in the different communities. Mark's has the best chance of being exact. Verses 49-50 are peculiar to Mark, and set the tone for his whole version, which makes the narrative a sort of catechumenal ritual.

Initiation to faith begins with a manifestation of Jesus in the texture of a man's life. Christ must "pass by" (Mt 20:30). It is a mysterious manifestation. The blind man, who symbolizes the man on the road to faith, does not see Jesus. He senses the presence of the Lord in events (v. 47a), expressing already the beginnings of faith by trusting himself to God's salvific initiative (v. 47b). Such openness to faith is immediately queried by the world which surrounds the initiate (v. 48a), and it requires all his courage to persevere in his approach (v. 48b).

Now he becomes an object of attention for people who reveal

to him God's call, encourage him, and invite him to be converted ("get up" or be resuscitated, and "cast aside his cloak" or strip off the old man: vv. 49 and 50).

Then begins the final dialogue between God and man: "What do you wish" (v. 51). This is the definitive encounter, couched in the form of question and answer, the better to show the complete liberty of two parties to a contract.

Finally, vision is granted the blind man, the vision of faith (vv. 51-52); and he immediately "follows" Christ "on the way."

The blind man is the perfect witness of passage from the flesh to the Spirit, from egoism to mission. There are five stages: the turning towards God under the urge of personal conscience in spite of the obstacles of the world; the turning towards Christ at his call and the hearing of his word; the offering of self to the Master by conversion and stripping off the old man; communion with Christ in the vision of faith; finally, following Christ throughout the world as a sign of the Kingdom.

XIII. Sirach
44:1, 9-13
1st reading
1st cycle
Friday

This is an extract from the eulogy of the Patriarchs. The author makes his purpose clear in verse 1. He wants to gather in a prestigious gallery the celebrated figures of the past (Ben Sirach probably wrote "pious men," but his grandson, already Hellenized, substitutes "illustrious men"). What he is using then is a stoic procedure, which he makes a literary genre long before Cornelius Nepos, Plutarch and other pagan writers.

His purpose however is apologetic too. At a time when his compatriots were being subjected to Greek influence, he thought it essential that they should learn to value the qualities of their own ancestors.

His grandson, in translating "pious" by "illustrious," also has an apologetic purpose, but not quite that of his grandfather. He is not so much concerned with sustaining the faith of his own people, as with demonstrating to the Gentile world that the Israelite culture vies with the best.

Verse 9, in Ben Sirach's own version, referred to the numerous pagan heroes who disappeared without leaving a trace and were rapidly forgotten. This is evidence of the emptiness and vanity of the pagan quest. His grandson thought the verse, like the preceding ones, referred to Jewish heroes. Consequently he touches up the phraseology.

Verses 10-13 begin the eulogy of the Jewish heroes strictly speaking, and their survival in memory. One cannot but be astonished by the frailty of hope among "pious men" of this epoch. They were sustained only by the tenuous certitude that they would survive in men's memory after death, something pagans might do as well. If one's idea of glory be confined to the memory one hopes to leave, it is a dubious consolation. Ben Sirach, however, had actually written, in verse 10, "of whom the memory will not perish." That at least had the merit of being open to interpretation as a certain immortality. His grandson suppressed the phrase, doubtless to avoid offending pagans who did not believe in the resurrection. He mentions only "virtues that are not forgotten."

XIV. 1 Peter
4:7-13
1st reading
2nd cycle
Friday

This letter is addressed to the newly baptized. The author has reminded them of their membership in a new people and a new priesthood (1 P 2:4). He has shown them how their baptism has transformed them into the likeness of Christ (1 P 3:18-4:7). It remains for them to bear witness to this transformation in everyday life.

The witness will be that of *charity* above all (v. 8). It is manifested as the author sees it in two particular ways. The first is mutual welcome, that hospitality so dear to the oriental spirit, which finds in Christ a new meaning. He enables us to triumph over the barriers that divide men from one another. The second is the manner of celebration of the Eucharist. All charisms should accommodate themselves to the good of one's neighbor, so that the assembly will be unique, a sign of the universal reassembly which God is accomplishing among men (vv. 10-11; cf. 1 Co 12).

In eucharistic celebrations of our time, for the most part provision is certainly made that charity will not be jeopardized in this domain. There is little likelihood of charisms clashing or causing trouble, when they are practically reduced to silence. Unless there is mutual welcome and common intermixing at the Eucharist, average Christians are not likely to set up encounter and dialogue that will extend to social, cultural and political life. Yet, for all that, the laity do have proper charisms: experience of ordinary life and the ability to translate this into rite and thanksgiving. Women have a charism, because they are open to welcome and interiority. . . . Yet we have long ago silenced their gift.

Doubtless by a return to domestic liturgies we shall recover some of the exchange and collaboration we have lost. Interpersonal action will be more possible where each member is known to all, and respected for what he is.

XV. **Mark**
11:11-26
Gospel
Friday

The story of the barren fig-tree is one of the most difficult to understand. Some regard it as a historical incident that took place at a different time of the year; others as a simple parable that was made fact by oral tradition; others still as a real incident that took place around the time of Pasch, but with an altogether symbolic meaning. In any case the commentary given by the evangelist in verses 20-25 is couched in terms, and presents a view, so different to verses 12-14, that it is scarcely possible to see it as other than a production of the primi-

tive community. It was doubtless based on an authentic teaching
of Jesus that belongs to a totally different context.

a) It is usual to place the events of Mark's eleventh chapter
in Autumn, at the feast of Tabernacles. At this feast Yahweh and
his King were enthroned again. Consequently it would be a
natural time for Jesus to make his messianic entry to Jerusalem
(Mk 11:1-11). The branches torn from the trees to accompany
his cortege are far too reminiscent to autumn ritual to place the
event at any other time (2 M 10:7; Ne 8:14-16). Likewise, the
temple was purified once a year, just before this autumn feast.
Jesus, in carrying out this purification (Mk 11:15-19) after his
own fashion, is opposing the formalist rites of expiation. His gesture is without meaning unless it takes place in the context of the
autumn festival.

It thus becomes evident why the fig-tree episode should be
placed in September, when the trees give their fruit.

Accepting such a reconstruction, Jesus' gesture takes on considerable meaning. At the very moment when the people are
gathering the fruits of the earth, he reveals their *barrenness*. The
fig-tree was a symbol of the fruitfulness of the Promised Land
(Nb 13:23; Dt 8:8; 1 K 5:5), but Israel has not produced the
fruit that God expected. Accordingly, in conformity with the
prophecies of Hosea 2:13; Isaiah 34:4; Jeremiah 5:17; 8:13 and
Joel 1:2-12, Jesus is condemning the fig-tree Israel. By his gesture
he affirms that the judgment has come, and that there will be no
more respite for conversion (contrary to Lk 13:6-9).

b) If this hypothesis is correct, we should have to suppose that
the pieces describing Jesus' attitude during the feast of Tabernacles were placed in a paschal context by the Christian community. The Pasch now supplanted the ancient festival of the
New Year. This meant that the fig-tree episode changed meaning, because the tree cannot bear fruit at Pasch (v. 13b, the remark is peculiar to Mark, and was doubtless added by him). The
theme of Israel's sterility yields to that of the *passion*. In fact the

image of Jesus collecting nonexistent figs just before his death is a singular fulfillment of the prophecy of Micah 7:1-6 (according to the Hebrew text). The prophet is isolated among a people who want his death. Faced with judges who are paid to condemn him, he compares himself to a harvester without grape or fig in the full vintage season.

c) The early Christians, however, fairly soon lost sight of both interpretations; and were forced, in order to explain Jesus' extraordinary gesture of condemnation, to make the episode, maladroitly indeed, an example of the efficacy of *prayer*. They added some sayings of Jesus on this topic (vv. 21-25). He is insisting on the two conditions essential for prayer: confidence in God and his love (vv. 23-24), and pardon first of all for one's adversaries (v. 25). Needless to say, this is not relevant to the fig-tree episode.

d) Jewish tradition has preserved the memory of continuous conflicts between merchants of the temple (controlled by Herod) and merchants of Mount Olivet (controlled by the Sanhedrin). It is not impossible that Jesus intervened in this conflict, but its real character is unknown to us. His motive may have been similar to that of the Zealots, the protagonists of *zeal* for the law (Jn 2:17). Many texts do in fact attribute violent language to Jesus (Mk 9:42-44; 8:34-35; Mt 5:17-19, 31-32; Mk 10:10-12; Lk 16:16; 12:49-53), which leads us to suppose that some violence, verbal at least, characterized his ministry. It was not that of a sect as violent as the Zealots however, but at most that of a sympathizer.

e) Among the primitive communities such an image quickly yielded to the more exact ones of the suffering Servant and the Son of Man. Mark gives a new orientation to the episode of expelling the vendors, partly by the context in which he places it, partly by his Old Testament quotations. The context is that of the controversies between Jesus and the authorities of the people (Mk 11:27-12:37), more especially the condemnation of these authorities as represented by the barren fig-tree. Oddly enough he places the temple episode right in the middle of the fig-tree one. The fig-tree really stands for the high priests (temple-episode), the murderous vineyard workers (Mk 12:1-12), the Herodians (Mk 12:13-17), the Sadducees (Mk 12:18-27), and the Scribes (Mk 12:28-40). The whole ensemble, which begins in the temple with the expulsion of the vendors, ends also in the temple with the widow's mite (Mk 12:41-44). Its central point is the discussion about the authority of Jesus (Mk 12:27-33). Behind the episode of the vendors in other words, we have the mystery of the person of Jesus.

f) In citing a text so *universalist* as Isaiah 56:7, Mark is echoing the primitive Christian attitude to the temple. When these Jerusalem Christians continued to celebrate feasts in the temple, the reason was doubtless that they still hoped for a purification and universalization of cult. They were awaiting the feast foreseen in Zecchariah 14:16-21, and found in the expulsion of the vendors a new reason for hope.

Jesus, however, died without achieving this, and the Christians had to abandon the temple under pressure of persecution. It was then that they came to realize that they themselves were the temple. Through love and purity of intention they would be open to all nations, thanks to the death of him who gave his blood "for the multitude."

XVI. Sirach
51:12-20
1st reading
1st cycle
Saturday

Ben Sirach concludes his book with an alphabetic poem (Si 51:13-30), where he describes his purpose in the work. Palestine had passed under the power of the Seleucids, which meant an invasion of the country by Greek culture. It charmed the intellectuals and disconcerted the simple. The Siracid was concerned to maintain Jewish religious tradition against this new influx, and returned to his native sapiental sources. He found that Wisdom comes from God not men

(Si 24:1-22). It guarantees its disciples the happiness sought by Greek philosophers.

At this time when Israel is under the influence of Greek humanism and seeks God in human science and philosophy, Ben Sirach's reaction becomes meaningful. The *search for God* cannot be accomplished by intellectual effort; it demands moral conversion and a concrete way of life. Wisdom is not a catalogue of proofs, but a gift of God offered, in communion of life, to those who are sufficiently open, through renunciation, to receive it.

XVII. Jude   Jude is probably not the apostle of the same
    17:20-25   name (Lk 6:13-16) but a brother of the Lord
    1st reading and James (Mt 13:55). He succeeded his older
    2nd cycle   brother as leader of the Jerusalem community.
    Saturday   His letter contains only a few verses, but it is
particularly violent against heretics (gnostics doubtless, who compounded their doctrinal errors with faults of impurity). Even its conclusion, from which today's reading is taken, reveals the author's intense feeling against these heretics.

According to usual primitive Christian practice, the conclusion is a trinitarian hymn (cf. vv. 20 and 25), of which a portion at least may have been inspired by a doxology from the primitive liturgy (v. 25).

Mention of the Trinity leads the author to another triad: *the theological virtues.* He mentions faith first (v. 20), a topic to be expected in a letter concerning heresy; then charity (v. 21), which is based on the mercy of God, and all the more necessary because it enables the community to "guard themselves" against heresy. Finally, *hope,* though not mentioned explicitly, is implicit in the confidence with which the Christian is recommended to await his presentation to the Lord. Hope is necessary, because the Christian cannot presume to happiness, unless he gets the grace from God to be preserved from fall and be without reproach before God (v. 24). The hope of being presented to the Lord in a recognition of God's determining initiative in our salvation.

XVIII. Mark
11:27-33
Gospel
Saturday

The leaders of the people, who have failed to discern the mystery of Jesus' personality, dare for the first time to ask him what authority covers his activity. Doubtless the temple incident (Mk 11:15-19) is the occasion for this inquiry, but at issue also probably are Jesus' general pretensions as Messiah, Son of Man, suffering Servant and Assembler of mankind.

Jesus, cleverer than his challengers, leads them back to their own disputes (as in Mk 12:13-17). His reply, however, does throw some light on the *authority* from which he has his mandate. His line of argument hints to his audience how poorly qualified they are to scrutinize his personality and the authority of his mission, since they failed to do this in the case of the Baptist. It amounts to an affirmation that he, like the prophet John, holds his mandate from God. But what is the use of telling people to whom God is imperceptible how he reveals himself?

Jesus' authority can never be the object of an inquiry or investigation. From the human point of view there are many ways of understanding him and forming an idea of his message. Many questions can be posed to him, but none of them will ever be conclusive. It is not by questioning, investigating and quibbling that one reaches any person, *a fortiori* Jesus. One must encounter, accept, love. It is by communing with Jesus that one knows who he is.

TABLE OF READINGS